THE QUEST FOR MILLENNIAL HOPE

THE QUEST FOR
MILLENNIAL
HOPE

RICHARD WILSON

Historicist with a Futurist Focus,
Postmillennial Apology on the
Book of Revelation – Chapter 12 to 22

XULON PRESS

Xulon Press
2301 Lucien Way #415
Maitland, FL 32751
407.339.4217
www.xulonpress.com

© 2020 by Richard Wilson
Edit: Christine Elam

All rights reserved solely by the author. The author guarantees all contents are original and do not infringe upon the legal rights of any other person or work. No part of this book may be reproduced in any form without the permission of the author. The views expressed in this book are not necessarily those of the publisher.

Unless otherwise indicated, Scripture quotations taken from the New King James Version (NKJV). Copyright © 1982 by Thomas Nelson, Inc. Used by permission. All rights reserved.

Printed in the United States of America

Paperback ISBN-13: 9780994195807
Ebook ISBN-13: 9781631297410

DEDICATED TO:

Ann, my loving wife
Our children with their spouses who honour their parents:
Andrew and Ellen Wilson
Mark and Katie Wilson
Scott and Stacy Wilson
Danny and Joanna Hindle

Behold, I am coming as a thief.
Blessed is he who watches and keeps his garments,
lest he walk naked and they see his shame.
(Revelation 16:15)

PERSONAL PROFILE

Richard is married to Ann. He was ordained into the pastoral ministry of Word and Sacrament in 1980 by the Presbyterian Church of Victoria, Bendigo Presbytery and served with the Rochester Presbyterian Church in the north-west region of Victoria, Australia.

Ten years earlier, soon after his conversion in Sydney under the ministry of the Anglican Church, Richard felt a call to the ministry of the Gospel and served with Operation Mobilisation on the Gospel ship MV Logos as an engineer. Later he served on travelling evangelistic teams in India with the Indian Indigenous Assemblies Movement, commonly known as the Bakht Singh Assemblies. It was there Richard cut his teeth as a preacher in open-air meetings in Indian cities and villages.

Richard returned to Australia and married Ann. Richard started theological training first at Ridley College, Parkville, Melbourne and then became a candidate for the Presbyterian ministry through the Presbyterian Theological Hall (College), Melbourne. Ann gained the meritorious award of PHT (Putting Hubby Through). By this time, Richard's reformed and Presbyterian convictions were well-formed, largely through reading Reformed theologians and Puritan literature produced by the Banner of Truth Trust.

His passion for mission and church-based evangelism saw him commencing new church-planting ministries in Canberra and Brisbane. His other passion is for Christian education and he was instrumental in establishing Covenant College in Tuggeranong, Canberra, serving as the Pastoral Headmaster for eighteen months through the establishment phase of the school. He then took a two-year appointment in the Hunter-Barrington Congregation of the Presbyterian Church of Eastern Australia.

After receiving a call from Brisbane to start a church-planting work along Free Church lines, Richard and Ann, with their growing family Andrew, Mark, Scott and Joanna, pastored this small congregation for some seven years and also taught at Southside Christian College, Westside Christian College, and Brisbane Boys' College. These were truly happy years, although they were extremely busy.

Once all the children were happily married, having been soundly converted, Richard and Ann reached something of a crossroads in the ministry of the Gospel. At this time, our Lord opened up a new ministry that would take them both back to India. In 2004-8, Richard used the generous long Christmas holidays enjoyed while teaching at Brisbane Boys' College to establish a pioneering Reformed and Presbyterian church mission support agency called the Indian Reformed Fellowship—Australia (IRFA). Richard was set apart by the Presbyterian Church of Australia as the Pastoral Coordinator of IRFA in 2008. He resigned as a secondary teacher at Brisbane Boys' College, and he now regularly visits India on a full-time basis at the invitation of Presbyterian and Reformed churches on the Indian subcontinent to contribute to and support these churches in their ministry.

FOREWARD

THE BIBLE, God's glorious, complete Word, sets out for us the Being, Word and Work of the Triune God in Creation, Providence and Redemption. It is the narrative of His work from the moment He said 'Let there be light' and there was light, through the centuries when He displayed His Fatherly care over the created order despite the sin of man; it outlines His plan of Salvation, culminating in the life, birth, death, resurrection and ascension of His only-begotten Son; it promises the culmination of all things and the return of the Lord Jesus Christ in the Father's good time to judge the living and the dead and to restore the created order to be as God intended it to be.

In this book, Richard Wilson guides us through the variety of major interpretations of those things which are revealed in the Book of Revelation, highlighting what is called the Historicist Postmillennial view. He does this with the skill of the accomplished teacher that he is and a sensitive understanding of other points of view while sustaining a convincing argument for the Postmillennial view.

I warmly commend this book to the earnest enquirer after God's truth. Some will be more firmly grounded in their understanding of this important subject, while some may be drawn to it and find a more satisfying interpretation of the End Times. And in the good purposes of our Sovereign God, may all be helped in their quest to 'glorify God and enjoy Him forever.'

– *Bob Thomas, Editor, New Life Christian Newspaper*

PREFACE

You could be forgiven, as you thumb through these pages, for taking a cursory glance at its content and saying to yourself, "Yes, yet another doomsday treatment of the book of Revelation." Indeed, these pages look squarely at those malignant institutional figures of *the harlot*, *the beast* that has *the number 666* (13:18) and *Babylon the great* (17:5-6), along with *the false prophet*, constantly doing battle with those who *kept the commandments of God and have the testimony of Jesus Christ* (12:17). This war well describes world and church history during the last two millennia that could be described as *the Great Tribulation* (7:14).

This description is helpful for us to understand the background to the days in which we live in our twenty-first century. Even though the kingdom of God has advanced relentlessly and has grown through these turbulent years of spiritual warfare, human conflict, and natural disaster, we will realise there has been no sustained Christian age of millennial proportions in world history. We are, in fact, living in a pre-Christian era, not a post-Christian world. Indeed, these days, in the providence of God, are marching forward to a world crisis of global proportions that has its precedent in the universal flood in the days of Noah. This is not spelling out "doom" for planet earth and the saints of Christ, but is actually an Exodus reminiscent of Israel's Exodus from the land of Egypt in the days of Moses. This global Exodus that is initiated by the *seven last plagues* of Revelation chapter 16 is, indeed, the event known as *that great day of God Almighty* (16:14).

Even though this *great day* concludes with *a great earthquake, such a mighty and great earthquake as had not occurred since men were on the earth* (16:18), and the human loss will be of immense proportions, there will be a great deliverance and restoration. A genuine Christian era of peace in millennial proportions will dawn in which *The kingdoms of the world have become the kingdoms of our Lord and of His Christ, and he shall reign forever and ever* (11:15)*!* At the most basic level of scriptural teaching, this will be in fulfilment of that original "Covenant of Creation" made with Adam and spoken of by the prophets such as is found in Isaiah 65:18-25 and Psalm 72.

Even though this "Covenant of Creation" was broken by man, God did not break this Covenant, and man's sin and failure did not frustrate God's purposes or faithfulness in keeping His original Covenant in the earthly paradise of Eden. Although in this "paradise restored" sin still exists, the redeemed establish godly order and righteousness as *the salt of the earth* and *the light of the world* (Matt 5:13-14). The kingdom of God is finally consummated and God's dominion establishes true liberty.

This book is not a commentary on the book of Revelation (there are many excellent commentaries on the Revelation), though it is a careful verse by verse and chapter by chapter study of chapters 12 to 22 of the text of the Apocalypse. These pages are a historicist postmillennial apology and explanation for the Biblical "Quest for Millennial Hope."

TABLE OF CONTENTS

Dedicated to: v
Personal Profile vii
Foreward ix
Preface xi
Chapter 1 - Interpretive Principles Used 1
  "Scriptura Scripturae interpres" 1
  Generalist interpretation versus particular interpretation 7
Chapter 2 - In Heaven, So On Earth 22
Chapter 3 - "The Glorious Testimony Of The Lamb And His Church" 26
  Understanding the Signs of our Times 26
  The foundation of the "Covenant of Creation" 27
    The dividing factor in all the affairs of man 27
    Understanding Biblical prophesy 29
    How then should we understand? 30
  Great Tribulation 31
    The problem of evil 33
    Prophetic mileposts that mark out the history of God's kingdom ... 35
    The events of the "last days" of the Old Testament dispensation 36
    Events that push forward the purposes of the kingdom of God 37
    Having the perspective of the last Day in everything of the present . 38
    God has His order in these events that we should not lose sight 39
    First the 'mystery of lawlessness' 39
    The restraining of "mystery of lawlessness" 42
  The **man of sin** is then revealed that takes place just before **that Day** .. 43
Chapter 4 - The Woman, The Body Of Christ In The Wilderness 45
  The "great sign appeared in heaven," the "woman" 46

  The woman giving birth continually in great labour and pain but in hope........ 48
Now, the battle line is drawn with **another sign**
  [that] appears in heaven.................49
  Stalemate became checkmate.................51
  The kingdom of God comes................ 53
The time cue of "one thousand two hundred and sixty days"......... 55
  War broke out in heaven between the archangel Michael and the dragon......... 59
  The dragon was cast to the earth................ 65
The Church in the Wilderness – Her Tried and True Testimony........67
  Born on eagles' wings................ 70
  The sheer weight of moral degradation................71
  The dragon was enraged with the woman making war with her offspring................ 73

Chapter 5 - The Rise And Rise Of The Beast – Revelation 13.. 76
Likely candidates in modern evangelical eschatology................77
The beast is not a single person but a socio-political institutional power. 78
  The symbiotic relationship between Satan and man............... 79
  The cosmology of the beast................81
  The crumbling foundations of the beast................ 83
  The beast's revival................ 84
The identity of **the beast**................85
  Conception of the Holy Roman Empire................ 88
  The conception of the harlot................ 90
  The rising of the beast................ 93
  The beast's coming of age at the Synod of Whitby in A.D. 666...... 96
  The Beast Coming Up Out of the Earth–Post-1332............... 104
The wilderness years of the Church were now coming to an end...... 106
  Revival of the body of Christ................ 106
  Reformation of the body of Christ................ 109
The harlot church with her beast performs great signs............... 112
  The revival given to the beast................ 114
  The economics of the beast................ 118
Here is wisdom................ 123

Chapter 6 - The Victory Of The Kingdom Of God – Revelation 14 129

TABLE OF CONTENTS

    The Glorious Universal Exodus from the House of Bondage and its Dispossession 129
        The global place of this Exodus 130
        This glorious Exodus is found in one Biblical word, 'sanctification' . 130
        The means of sanctification has a destination of truth 133
        The Lamb and the "hundred and forty-four thousand" 138
        The true worship of the 'hundred and forty-four thousand' as one in Spirit and Truth 143
        An exodus by transformation to reformation according to the truth of God's Word 148
    The powerful and persistent preaching of the seven angels 150
        The ministry of the Word is incarnated in the Church, the whole body of Christ 158
        First and foremost is evangelistic preaching 159
        Preaching that calls for holiness 161
        Preaching warnings against religious unfaithfulness 164
        Preaching comfort to the faithful saints 166
        Evangelical preaching that announces the limits of God's sovereign mercy 168
        The preacher in the Days of Vengeance and the Reaping of the Grapes of Wrath 171

Chapter 7 - That Great Day Of God Almighty 176
    Prelude In Heaven–Revelation 15 179
    A Sign In Heaven 179

Chapter 8 - Seven Angels Pour Out The Seven Bowls 188
    The Great Crisis Of World History 188
        Now "the Battle of the Great Day of God Almighty" (16:14) 188
        The focus of this great wrath of God 189
        Served over a relatively short period 190
        A comprehensive victory of the kingdom of God on earth 190
        The scale of what is described has yet to be fulfilled 196
        Separate events that have distinct purposes to fulfil 198
    Seven Bowls Of God's Wrath – Revelation 16 199
        First Bowl on the Earth: Sore on the Beast's worshipers (16:2) 200
        Second Bowl on the Sea: Blood and Death (16:3) 202
        Third Bowl on the Rivers and Springs: The Waters Turn to Blood (16:4-7) 204
        Fourth Bowl on the Sun: Men are Scorched (16: 8-9) 206

  Fifth Bowl on the Beast's Throne: Darkness and Pain (16:10-11). . . 208
  Sixth Bowl on the River Euphrates: River Dries Up and the Armies of the
   East Marshalled (16:12-16) 209
  Seventh Bowl into the Air: the Earth Utterly Shaken (16:17-21). . . . 217
  The place for the powerful and persistent preaching of the Word
   of God 221
  Apostolic expectation of these events. 226

Chapter 9 - The Demise Of The Great Harlot—Revelation 17. 228

 The Revelation of the Mystery of the Great Harlot and her Beast. 231
  The catholicity of the great harlot. 231
  The kings of the earth committed fornication. 232
  The Kings of the Earth … Were Made Drunk with the Wine of Her
   Fornication. 235
  The inhabitants of the earth were made drunk with the wine of her for-
   nication. 236
 In the Spirit and in the Wilderness. 237
 The Kingdom of God and Its Advance 238
  "A Woman Sitting on a Scarlet Beast" 243
  The Woman that Possesses the Whole World 245
  Full of Abominations and the Filthiness of her Idolatrous
   Fornication. 247
  The Single, Sinister, Spirit with the Catholic Sign 248
  Disclosure of The Mystery of The Woman 250
  Gog and Magog, To Gather the Nations Together to Battle at the End of
   the Millennium 253
  The Lamb and His Saints 259
 Brief Retrospective and Reminder! 260

Chapter 10 - The Fall Of Babylon The Great—Revelation 18 . 264

 Some Special Considerations 264
 Babylon the Great Is Fallen, Is Fallen! 267
 The World Laments for Great City Babylon 272
 God's Final Vengeance upon Babylon the Great 278

Chapter 11 - A Great Multitude In Heaven Rejoices—
Revelation 19 282

 Some Special Considerations 282
 Unanimous Chorus of Alleluia! in Heaven and Earth 284
 The Church's Renewed Hope Has Come. 289

TABLE OF CONTENTS

The Battle Of The Great Day Of God Almighty. 292
    Heaven Opened Revealing the Conquering Christ Seated upon a White Horse. 292
    "He had a Name written that no one knew except Himself" 295
    "He was clothed with a robe dipped in blood, and His Name is called The Word of God.". 296
    Vengeance is Mine, I will repay 298
    The King of kings and Lord of lords 298
    "It is Done!" 299
    Mobilisation In Battle Formation in the Place Called, in Hebrew, Armageddon 299
    Captured 304

Chapter 12 - An Overview Of Millennialism. 306
    Premillennialism 307
    Amillennialism 316
    Preterism 319
    Postmillennialism. 322
        The wars against the kingdom of God 323
        Being citizens of the kingdom of God 324
        Covenant of Creation 325
        Protestant Reformation and the Renaissance 327
        The Secular Humanist and Babylon the Great 330
        Christ's Kingdom Consummated – The Millennium 333
        What will the millennium look like? 345

Chapter 13 - The Millennium—Revelation 20 353
    Common ground of 'historicism' 353
    Prophetic history is for our assurance because our Lord has said, ...if it were not so, I would have told you (John 14:1). 354
        Amillennial recapitulation 355
        Premillennial futurism 357
        Dispensational Speculative millennialism. 358
        Preterist realised millennialism 359
        Historicist postmillennialism 359
    Textual comment:. 361
    The intervention of a powerful angelic being and not the "Angel of the Lord." 361

The spiritual identity that lies behind the institutional enemies of the church and the kingdom of God is bound and disposed of during the millennial period. 361
The saints' weapons of warfare are never carnal but spiritual (Eph. 6: 10-20) 363
This world has remained "Antichrist" with its institutions at centre-stage. 364
The kingdom of God and its millennium 365
The millennium and the "paradise theme" 366
The expression "a new heaven and a new earth" after the millennium . 367
Christ's decree in His providence, the Kingdom of God and the millennium. 368
The thrones in heaven, as Christ so the ascended saints. 370
Spiritual cosmology and its earthly effects 375
The saints in heaven and on earth reign together with Christ within the Kingdom of God. 377
The dead without Christ remain in the place of the dead until after the millennium. 379
The First and Second resurrection 380

Chapter 14 - Satan's Release For A Little While – Revelation 20 385
Gog and Magog 385
The thousand years have finished. 386
Satan's sinister final work and the appearance of the Antichrist. 389
The final battle of Gog "the Antichrist" against the saints and the beloved city 392
Satan is now finally assigned to perdition 395

Chapter 15 - The Final Judgement – Revelation 20 398
The Last Day 398
The great white throne appears 400
The Second Advent 400
The resurrection. 401
The second or "general resurrection" and the "rapture" 404
The Book of Life is opened 404
The scales of justice are absolute. 405
All the dead outside Christ are raised with an immortal body. 406
Judgment is executed in "the second death." 407

Our names and the "Book of Life" 407

Chapter 16 - All Things New—Revelation 21 409
New heavens and a new earth 409
Passing away of the 'first heaven and the first earth' 410
The passing away and resurrection of the heavens and the earth 415
New Jerusalem, coming down out of heaven from God 416
Truly, Holy Matrimony 418
"It is done!" 419
Our Fiancé's encouragements as we wait 420

Chapter 17 - The New Jerusalem – Revelation 21 423
Heresies abound! 423
New Jerusalem is gathering in readiness for the marriage of the Lamb. 424
The grand entry of the bride, the Lamb's wife 426
The Bride of Christ...having the glory of God 427
The perfect Wife! 428
No temple! 431
The New Jerusalem in the past 433

Chapter 18 - The Tree Of Life—Revelation 22 435
The Very Life of God Himself directly sustains His New Jerusalem 435
Christ the Tree of Life in time and eternity, on earth and in heaven 436
The Kingdom of God eternal 438
Saints see God's face personally, sealed, sanctified and secured 438

Chapter 19 - A Final Exultation – Matter Of Urgency 440
Introductory Notes 440
When did predictive canonical prophesy cease? 440
"The soon prophecies" 442
The SOON Cues in Prophetic Passages of Scripture 446
Notes on the text 460
"These words are faithful and true." 460
This prophecy is the final word – Christ is alive and active now. ... 461
John's sin 462
The time is at hand 463
By their works you shall know them 463
No Time To Speculate 464
Jesus says, "My reward...is given to everyone according to his work" and quickly! 464

The things which are impossible with man are possible with God. (Luke 18:27) *466*
The authenticity of these revelations *468*
Freely offered *468*
Solemn Warning. 469
The Continual Note Of Urgency 473
Bibliography **479**

CHAPTER 1
INTERPRETIVE PRINCIPLES USED

"Scriptura Scripturae interpres"

Louis Berkoff's excellent treatment of "Principles of Biblical Interpretation"[1] reaffirms the Reformation mantra *"Scriptura Scripturae interpres."* The English translation from Latin is

---

[1] Berkoff, L., *Principles of Biblical Interpretation*, Baker Book House, Grand Rapids, 1977, pp 11-13, 26.

This book holds to the reformed position of Biblical interpretation which affirms the verbal and plenary inspiration of Scripture in the original autographs. Not only the meaning of the Word of God, but every word of Scripture was God-breathed, and therefore the Scriptures are the sole and final infallible authority of God in the church. All of Scripture was consistent and self-interpretive, yielding its own interpretation. The Reformers' position is perfectly evident from the statement that the church does not determine what the Scriptures teach. The essential character of their exegesis resulted from two fundamental principles: (1) "Scripture is the interpreter of Scripture;" and (2) "all understanding and exposition of Scripture is to be in conformity with 'the analogy of faith' being the uniform teaching of Scripture." This, of course, is a circular argument and would not be consistent if it was not in the consistency of the character of God who is Himself the only autonomous, self-disclosing and ultimate foundation of truth. In other words, God is in the revelation loop. If we move away from this ultimate foundation then there can be no reality, reason and order.

"Scripture is the interpreter of Scripture." This statement has been attributed to Augustine of Hippo (354-430 AD), but was also found in the other early church fathers. The historical development of the church's doctrinal understanding of theological themes based on Scripture is, in most cases, where we will commence our understanding of the Word of God. We learn from our fathers' understanding of Scripture so that we might stand on their shoulders and look into Biblical horizons of knowledge and understanding to seek greater light in God's revelation in the Scriptures.

During the mediaeval period, the authority of the church assumed the proportions of a colossus. The authority of ecclesiastical tradition chained the Scriptures to the church's will. The Scriptures themselves had become locked up in the Vulgate, the only "authorised" translation of the Bible. Although the Vulgate was an excellent translation into the academic language of Latin, it was far from the reach of the common people. Therefore, Biblical scholarship was controlled in its interpretation of Scripture by the scholastic authorities of the church and to the unanimous consent of the church fathers. These scholastic authorities increasingly imposed upon Scripture their interpretations from outside Scripture rather than allowing Scripture to speak for itself. The external apparatus that became regulative in interpreting Scripture—such as preconceived complicated allegorical interpretation—in the end confounded the meaning of the Scriptures and made them incomprehensible, or bent Scripture so it was interpreted in a manner that contradicted other parts of Scripture. The church's doctrine evolved increasingly into man-centred and ecclesiastically-orientated interpretation of Scripture, and in the end Scripture was appealed to in a fragmented manner to justify such doctrine. Such an approach was not easy to challenge when the Scriptures could not be understood by the congregation of God's common people.

Martin Luther protested by translating the Bible into the German vernacular; he defended the right of private judgement (Jer. 31:33-34); established "the necessity of taking the context and historical circumstances into account; demanded faith and spiritual insight in the interpreter; and designed to find Christ everywhere in Scripture."[2] Philip Melanchthon, Luther's right hand and his superior in learning, maintained that "Scriptures must be understood grammatically before they can be understood theologically; and the Scriptures have got one certain and simple sense."[3] John Calvin, who was regarded as the greatest exegete of the Reformation, concurred with Luther and Melanchthon, but was much more rigorous and consistent. Calvin firmly believed in the typical significance of much that is found in the Old Testament, but did not share in Luther's assertion that Christ should be found everywhere in Scripture. Moreover, he reduced the number of Psalms that could be recognised as Messianic. In the mediaeval allegorical method of interpretation, Calvin saw a contrivance of Satan to obscure the sense of Scripture. He insisted that the prophets should be interpreted in the light of historical circumstances, thus pioneering "Biblical theology" where the Biblical themes such as worship, covenant, and kingdom emerged throughout the history of revelation. Calvin regarded the expositor's "chief excellency" should be "lucid brevity" and declared that "The first business of an interpreter [is] that its author say what he does say, instead of attributing to him what we think he ought to say."[4]

Louis Berkoff develops principles of interpretation around three general heads: grammatical, historical, and theological

---

[2] ibid, p. 26

[3] Ibid, p. 26

[4] Ibid, p. 27

interpretation. We fully concur with these sound principles, but we won't make a summary of these principles here. However, these principles will become evident as we deal with relevant texts of various portions of Scripture with particular focus on the book of Revelation.

The linguistic and grammatical rules of the texts should be taken as the foundation of any discussion and it is, as it were, the field within which we work. Among evangelicals, there will be rare disagreement on this point, once the text is understood. However, it requires considerable skill and wisdom to exercise the rules of interpretation so we come to a clear understanding about just what the text is saying and drawing the meaning of the text into a doctrinal development and establishing the storyline that is relevant and true. Extracting the linguistic and grammatical meaning is known as exegesis. Conversely, we need to avoid the reverse process of "eisegesis" where we import our own meaning into the text. We must allow the text to speak for itself in its context.

Then, from the standpoint of "historical theology," we learn from the theological discussion in the past, and as we approach the Scriptures we will develop a doctrinal model that we will be tested against Scripture as greater light is given. When we do this, we are adopting a scientific methodology to understand the truth of our understanding. A scientist will be required to adopt a hypothesis that models his scientific understanding. Then he must test that model against gathering evidence that either proves or disproves his model. In the context of the theology of eschatology, most of us have moved into certain millennial models of understanding that others have devised before us. The present writer has moved from the hypothesis of premillennial dispensationalism to historic premillennialism to amillennialism, and is now making a case for historicist and futuristic postmillennialism. These doctrinal constructions and others have been discussed under the heading "An Overview of Millennialism," which is best read before our discussion on Revelation 20 that deals with Biblical teaching on the millennium.

Probably the most important rule of interpretation is the context of the text whose meaning we are seeking to understand. The etymology or meaning of words may be helpful but not definitive because Biblical words may carry a different meaning than the one they carry when used in the wider world. The context in which words are found should carry greater weight than the etymology of a word, or an expression, as it is used in a cultural context outside Scripture. After establishing the linguistic context of particular texts of Scripture, we must determine the relationship between these texts and other passages in Scripture where similar or related teaching emerges. As we examine the context of the immediate position of the text, we will see wider contexts of other Scriptures that can be found in different books and even different historical contexts and Testaments. Although the Scriptures were penned under the inspiration of the Holy Spirit by various prophets and Apostles, the entire Scripture is first and foremost God-breathed. There is a single Author, God Himself. Therefore, a study of the Scriptures results in a deepening revelation of God, which in turn leads to an understanding of the themes that create a doctrinal context within the unitary corpus of Scripture itself.

Since the Reformation, systematic theology has helped to contextualise doctrine. This is equally true of the discipline known as Biblical theology, which considers the history of revelation and its canonical centres (or Biblical themes) that emerge at creation and find their maturity and fulfilment in the New Testament Scriptures, the capstone being the book of the Revelation. These canonical themes form the centre of the Scriptures. In Reformed circles, the unilateral sovereign promise of God has been at the centre of covenant theology, Biblical worship, and the kingdom of God theology. Biblical theology has emphasised the dynamic unitary development of the Scriptures and their completion with the cessation of Biblical revelation.

As we study the Biblical theology inherent within Scripture, we will find that individual texts and passages have significance when they are placed within their historical and Biblical context. This can revolutionise the way we look at the Scriptures.

If we apply these principles to Premillennial Dispensationalism, which was the predominant eschatological view among evangelicals in the twentieth century, we see its disregard for Biblical covenant theology results in many contradictions that shake the foundations upon which it stands. In this book, we will consider some of these contradictions.

Premillennial Dispensationalism is an elaborate and complicated scheme of interpreting the Scriptures that has increasingly carried the church into an unorthodox position because of its tendency to disregard historic confessional standards of the church, such as the Westminster Confession of Faith and the Belgic Confession. Extreme forms of Premillennial Dispensationalism did violence to the Gospel and proposed different Gospel administrations in different historical periods of Biblical history. They compound their errors with highly speculative interpretations of Biblical prophecies that predict a pessimistic future that is fundamentally unbiblical. The absence of a unitary, well-articulated Biblical theology leaves particular portions of Scripture with no context within the history of revelation. The result has been to fragment the Scriptures and detrimentally redefine terminology.[5]

---

[5] This will be further discussed under the head "An Overview of Millennialism."

Generalist interpretation versus particular interpretation

William Hendriksen's commentary on the book of Revelation, *More Than Conquerors*, was a steadying hand against the kinds of eschatology that had strayed far from the orthodox confessional testimony entrenched within the Protestant and reformed confessions. Hendriksen issued a clarion call to return to the Reformed faith as the sectarian spirit was fed with this highly speculative premillennial dispensational eschatology. There was a need for a soberer eschatology that wasn't radically restructuring orthodox theology. Hendriksen's book has become a standard work used extensively by preachers of the word of God and has helped to turn the tide against premillennialism, particularly its dispensational variety, at least in Reformed circles.

Generalist approaches to the interpretation of prophecy—and the book of Revelation in particular—tend to spiritualise Scriptural texts that lend themselves to a plainer interpretation. Such an approach may be appropriate at times, but it is too easy to miss the inconvenient truth. The plain teaching of Scripture can be offensive and against the grain of human nature. If we are not careful, such clear teaching can lose its cutting-edge because we have interpreted the passage according to the canons of reasonableness rather than allowing the truth to yield its message.

The particularist approach takes the plain and evident teaching of the text and links it with other teachings of Scripture that further explains the text. This approach gives greater weight to such teaching, and the truth becomes evident as it stands with the rest of Scripture. Such interpretations can be startling and unexpected as they may not enjoy a majority position. It may also be unnerving because such teaching runs counter to the prevailing culture within the world and even the church. The difficulty with such an approach is that devilish interpretations that go beyond the teaching of Scripture have gained currency, so that they major on minors that skew other related teachings of Scripture and extremes become emphasised.

All who wish to find the truth of prophecy will dig deeply into the Scriptures and will formulate a system of understanding that should emerge from Scripture itself. We cannot avoid such systematisation, because doctrine is necessary to provide a framework for understanding. Such a framework is essential to fit the parts into the structure of doctrine, but when the components do not fit, then the structure needs to be adjusted to accommodate this. Fanaticism develops when we force the components into a structure that is unable to yield to their doctrinal framework. We then force teaching to fit and we fail to let the model of doctrinal structure yield its truth. Truth may be found not in the volume of material but in its weight, because the weight of a single text could outweigh a larger body of teaching found elsewhere. This of course may present difficulties. Truth is like a diamond. Many elements in Scripture make up the diamond of truth. The skills of a master diamond cutter and polisher are employed to cut the gem so that both its beauty and toughness are exposed. Diamonds have different uses; some find their place in the crown jewels, while others are used in cutting machines to cleave hard materials. As the elements of truth are brought together into a diamond of truth, as it were, we can construct a doctrinal statement that has its particular purpose in the overall structure of the Christian faith. It will be necessary to model such statements, as we have traditionally, for the millennial question. We will need to test these doctrinal models against the various elements of truth found in Scripture. But when these truths conflict with our model, we should adjust our model rather than cut the diamond of truth to fit that model. If we were to cut the diamond of truth further, then its lustre, beauty and cutting-edge would be lost. It is possible to so generalise the specifics of the prophetic material scattered throughout Scripture that the prophetic message is lost, and the cutting-edge of the truth no longer has the desired effect.

The generalist interpretation of amillennialism has on balance correctly interpreted many passages relating to prophecy in that a more spiritualised interpretation can only be possible. However, in many areas of prophetic interpretation, this generalist approach has glossed over some of the plainer prophetic texts. Although the orthodox doctrines of Scripture are firmly in place, various texts that can be interpreted on a plainer or more literal basis are moulded into the amillennial doctrinal framework to escape from the inconvenient truth.

For example, concerning the teaching of the kingdom of God, the amillennialist emphasises the words of the Lord Jesus Christ to Pontius Pilate, *My kingdom is not of this world. If my kingdom were of this world, my servants would fight, so that I should not be delivered to the Jews; but now my kingdom is not from here* (Jn. 18:36). The amillennialist interprets the kingdom of God as a growing entity in heaven alone where Christ is in His ascendant position as "King of kings and Lord of lords." Such teaching holds that, strictly speaking, there will be no millennium on earth because there is no kingdom of God on earth. Certainly the kingdom of God is among believers and their presence might be construed as a kingdom presence on earth, but never in a dominant or ruling position.

Amillennialists baulk at the belief that the kingdom of God, *on earth as it is in heaven* (Matt. 6:10), as a robust rule of Christ from heaven with His saints in heaven and on earth[6] (Isa. 9:6-7; Matt. 13:33; 19:28; Lk 18:28-29; 22:29-30; Eph. 2:6) will, in the fullness of time, be consummated with a sustained peace in millennial proportions (Rev. 20:4-6; Isa. 2:5-21; 11:1-9; 12:5; 65:17-25). Only after the millennium will Christ return in His final glory on that Last Day (Acts 17:31; 2 Corinthians 5:10; Romans 2:16; Matthew 12:36).

The kingdom of God was announced by Christ the King during His first advent, demonstrated in the resurrection of Christ (Rom. 1:4), established at His ascension and enthronement at the right hand of the Father, proclaimed through the preaching of the Gospel both in Word and Spirit, and advances throughout the Gospel age. The growth of the kingdom of God is continuous and relentless throughout the Gospel age.

The kingdom of God begins with the destruction of the Babylonian, Medo-Persian and Roman Empires of the Old Testament. The kingdom of God, as a *stone that was cut without hands*, was cast from heaven to shatter the old-world order, and then grew into *a great mountain that fills the whole earth* (Dan. 2:35). Christ's kingdom, beginning like *a mustard seed*, becomes the greatest tree in the garden of all the earth (Matt. 13:31-32). *For the earth shall be full of the knowledge of the Lord as the waters cover the sea* (Isa. 11:9). It may be likened to a grain of *leaven* that is placed in the dough of this world that *leavens the whole lump* (Matt. 13: 33).

More specifically, amillennialists like William Hendriksen equate the judgements of the *seals and trumpets* in chapters 6 to

---

[6] The imperfect church that is redeemed by the blood of the Lamb and in the world throughout all generations of the Gospel era, described in the book of Revelation as the seven churches, gain the victory (Revelation 2:1–3:22).

9 of Revelation with *the seven bowls of the wrath of God on the earth* in chapter 16. Despite interesting similarities between the two movements of God's providence upon the earth, the two events should be seen as distinct and separate, otherwise they would be contradictory. This is illustrated in the instruments of God which administer these judgements. The Seals and Trumpets are administered by *the four living creatures* (4:8; 5:14), which is the regular providential mediator throughout history as described for us in Ezekiel chapters 1 and 10. They are revealed in the book of Revelation as the supervising agencies that God uses to exercise His general providence across the universe, including the seals and trumpets, and with specific reference to the earth. It is significant that these *four living creatures* hand over to *the seven angels seven golden bowls full of the wrath of God who lives forever and ever* (15:7). Whatever our interpretation of these figures, in God's administration of His providence they are significantly different personalities within the angelic hosts with significantly different responsibilities. This in itself would indicate that the sequence of events under the Seals and Trumpets is different from the sequence of events in the pouring out of *the seven bowls of God's wrath*. Even though these sequences of events may intersect at some point in history, they cannot be parallel to each other in some sort of interdependent provinces of God. The effect of the opening of the seven seals and the blowing of the seven trumpets is characterised by limitation, where the judgment refrains of *one third* is employed during these events. The effect of the seven plagues is total and universal. This in itself indicates that these sequences cannot be parallel but occur in a continuum, describing an event in history.

The amillennial device of recapitulation[7] is sensible and should be applied to chapters 2 and 3 concerning the messages that Christ delivers to His Church. It can also apply to chapters 6 to 9 concerning the ministry of the Word through the Church to the world in the Seals and Trumpets. To a lesser degree, it can be applied to chapters 12 and 13 concerning the rise of the beastly antichrist. However, even applying the recapitulation principle, there is a historic forward movement that begins with the growth of the kingdom of God. By the end of chapter 13, we find ourselves at the mighty historic climax, not in the midst of a recapitulation, and at the beginning of chapter 15 we reach a point in history that is described as *that great day of God Almighty* (16:14). These so-called recapitulations of history are set in parallel, but by the time we get to chapter 15 we come to a maturing of history and the Providence of God, to a settled prophetic milepost and an entirely new orchestral

---

[7] Recapitulation is a literary device that structures the book of Revelation around parallel themes that run, not consecutively, but concurrently, covering the same ground from different perspectives. William Hendriksen, in his book *More Than Conquerors* (IVP, 1973, p 21), posits seven parallels to give the full prophetic picture of the message of Revelation as follows:

1. 'Christ in the midst of the seven golden lampstands' (1–3).
2. The book of the seven seals (4–7).
3. The seven trumpets of judgement (8–11).
4. The woman and the Man-child persecuted by the dragon and his helpers (the beast and the harlot) (12–14).
5. The seven bowls of wrath (15, 16).
6. The fall of the great harlot and of the beast (17–19).
7. The judgement upon the Dragon (Satan) followed by the new heaven and earth, new Jerusalem (20–22).

These parallel events are recapitulations in terms of the time-span of the Gospel age, from the first coming of Christ to the last day at the second coming of Christ. So, the message of the book of Revelation, though set in the context of this history, does not make judgements about specific times for these events. Rather, they are seen as occurring cyclically throughout the history of the Gospel age.

theme in history. The sequence in the book of Revelation is now moving forward from the Great Tribulation of the Seals and the Trumpets and the satanic hegemony of the institutionalised religious system of the harlot and her beast that caused havoc within the Church, the body of Christ, where her blood *...cried with a loud voice saying, "How long, O Lord, holy and true, until you judge and avenge our blood on those who dwell on the earth?"* (6:10).

Specific signs such as the drying up of the Euphrates river (16:12) are spiritualised by amillennial theologians; however, the fact that it could be a sign of a prophetic event in history is never investigated. If Noah of old had heard the message that God was going to send a global flood to kill every living creature on the face of the earth but could not bring himself to believe the plain words that he heard, he would never have prepared the ark for the salvation of his family or the deliverance of every *'kind'* of animal on earth. If he had taken a spiritualised interpretation of these prophecies, he would have missed the boat altogether. If we fail to see the specifics and spiritualise prophecy, we are in danger of misrepresenting God's Word even though we are sailing a safe ship of orthodoxy through the perilous seas of prophetic theology. If we miss the meaning of scriptural prophecy, we will be unable to read accurately the prophetic mileposts that have been graciously given to us for our edification.

Likewise, if Moses could not bring himself to believe the plain words about the plagues that would descend suddenly upon Egypt[8] then the eerie darkness of the Angel of Death visiting Egypt on every firstborn in the land would not have been perceived prophetically and the Israelites would not have killed the Passover lamb that preserved their families. They would have joined the

---

[8] The water becoming blood, so the Egyptians etc...

Egyptians in their hardheartedness on that one fateful night that took the lives of all the firstborn of both animal and human families in Egypt. Such would have been the case, not because they were unreasonable or because they were not orthodox in the fundamentals of the faith, but because they failed to see the specific and plain meaning of the word of God concerning these prophetic warnings. The prophet Moses did not say that these kinds of things would somehow fall upon the Egyptians in some general sense of the word if they remained hardhearted and refused to let the people of Israel go, but he was specific and said that these plagues of Egypt would supernaturally and successively happen as a sign to the Egyptians that the living and true God was the sovereign God of heaven and earth, and that His people Israel were His people by Covenant and adoption.

Perhaps the drying up of the Euphrates River (16:12) is nothing more than a pictorial way of saying that the influence of the enemies of God historically in the Mohamedan Turkish nations will dry up. Theologians may well follow the accepted norm in the interpretation of this passage and therefore avoid being designated as radical doomsday theologians. However, if the drying up of the Euphrates River is literal and it is set as a sign of a dramatic physical judgment of God unleashed upon the world in unprecedented magnitude in the likeness of the flood in Noah's day, or the plagues of Egypt in Moses' day, then we will be unprepared for such an event that may come upon us like "a thief in the night."

But how do we ascertain whether we should adopt the more generalist interpretation or the more particularistic understanding of these texts from God's Word? If we are going to look at a more particularistic understanding of these pieces of prophecy, we should find agreement as they stand in Scripture, observing the context in which they are made. Let them stand in their place and speak to us rather than trying to make them fit some theological system that might be neat and reasonable but may miss the point.

William Hendriksen assumes that the battle of Armageddon is described in Revelation 16:12-16. Hendriksen then describes the titanic spiritual battle that is arrayed against the saints, and describes this battle of Armageddon as figurative of the spiritual war that we are called upon to wage. There are a great marshalling and much posturing of armies but there is no war mentioned in this passage. What is mentioned is that a great gathering is marshalled in battle formation in *the place called in Hebrew, Armageddon* (16: 16), which is described as a gathering *to do battle for that great day of God Almighty*. God Almighty, through His providence, intervenes with *a great earthquake, such a mighty and great earthquake as has not occurred since men were on the earth (16:18)*. When reading *that great day of God Almighty*, the amillennialist immediately thinks of the very last day with the second coming of Christ. The context of this *great day of God Almighty* is significant because it appears at the end of *the Seals and Trumpets* and the description of the relentless Great Tribulation that was inflicted by the institutional enemies of the children of God–the *harlot, beast and Babylon the great* along with the *false prophet*. Therefore, this marshalling of military forces at a place called *Armageddon* and its association with *the great day of God Almighty*, which is signified by the drying up of the Euphrates River, is a prophetic milepost at a point in history. This cannot be a description of the spiritual battles and the physical wars during the days of the Great Tribulation described under the Seals and Trumpets, because there is no description of an actual war or spiritual battle that engages the spiritual enemy of the powers of darkness, the saints of Christ.

If the natural flow in the book of Revelation is allowed to progress as it is written, without being subjected to a scissors-and-paste job, then this *great day of God Almighty* comes before the description of the millennium in chapter 20 and not after the millennium. This description of *the great day of God Almighty* is the defining moment where God intervenes providentially and brings His people out of the turmoil of battle into the sustained peace of the millennium itself. The providential intervention of God is here described as *a great earthquake, such a mighty and great earthquake as had not occurred since men were on the earth* (Rev. 16:18). The whole sequence of events described as *the seven bowls of the wrath of God on the earth that are poured out* by *seven angels* (16:1) should be understood as a single historical prophetic event that takes a relatively short period, which is well illustrated in the plagues of Egypt at the time of Moses. The succeeding chapters—chapters 17, 18 and 19—are divine commentaries on this decisive moment described in chapter 16—the *Seven Last Plagues* of the seven bowls of God's wrath (Rev. 15:1; 21:9).

The judgements that were associated with the Seals and Trumpets (Rev. 6-9) are God's providential use of natural disasters and instruments of wrath within the natural order as a result of the ministry of the Word of God being preached by the citizens of the kingdom of God. These judgements are *the wrath of God revealed from heaven against all ungodliness and unrighteousness of men who suppress the truth in unrighteousness* (Rom. 1:18). The judgements that are issued under the Seals and Trumpets are of a different order of magnitude and character from the judgements issued under the Seven Last Plagues, which bear the characteristics of the plagues of Egypt in the days of Moses.

The judgments issued under the sound of the trumpets are described as characteristic of a recurring theme in the style of a recapitulation of events. Under the first trumpet (8:7), *hail and fire followed, mingled with blood, and they were thrown to the earth.*

These acts of wrath are characterised by having a boundary of limitations. Each of the acts of wrath significantly devastates the environment such that *a third of the trees were burned up, and all green grass was burned up.* This is an environmental disaster and is a sign to the people. In the second trumpet (Rev. 8:8-9), *something like a great mountain burning with fire was thrown into the sea*, which depicts volcanic and geological activity. This becomes noticed by the people in the world as 'an act of God' revealing the wrath of God from heaven. This brings ecological devastation to the oceans and the marine environment. But characteristically there are boundaries of limitations and *a third of the sea became blood. And a third of the living creatures in the sea died, and a third of the ships were destroyed.* Historically speaking, these kinds of disasters re-occur: earthquakes break forth, volcanoes erupt, tsunamis leave their devastation and the pollution from such natural disasters or acts of God are far-reaching, even regional but not universal.

Under the third trumpet (8:10-11) *a great star fell from heaven, burning like a torch, and fell on a third of the rivers and on the springs of water*. Whatever this torch from heaven is, its target is the lifeblood of the land upon which man lives. Without a constant source of water, human habitation is not viable. In this act of God's wrath, the pollution of *wormwood*, the very water supplies to cities, towns and rural communities become so polluted that *many men die from the water because it was made bitter* or polluted. Again, this may be a recurring theme in history and is undoubtedly a current issue in our modern world.

Under *the fourth trumpet*, as *the angel* or the preacher sounds the crown rights of Christ's kingdom, heavenly and celestial events take place (8:12-13). *And a third of the sun was struck, a third of the moon, and a third of the stars, so that a third of them were darkened. A third of the day did not shine, and likewise the night.*

Perhaps at this point apocalyptic language is employed as a literary device indicating times of cataclysmic events such as the conquest of Israel and Judea by Assyria and later by the Babylonian king Nebuchadnezzar. Rational language gives way to apocalyptic language to describe such a cataclysmic event in the same way that Isaiah the prophet describes such an event:

For the stars of heaven and their constellations,
Will not give their light;
The sun will be darkened in its going forth,
And the moon will not cause its light to shine (Isaiah 13:10).

This introduces a succession of three great *Woes! that were sounded by a flying angel in the midst of heaven*, which we take to be the spiritual world. That becomes the subject of the last three trumpets, but we move from the natural world of disaster into the spiritual world.

With the fifth angel sounding his trumpet (9:1-12), we are brought into the caverns of the spiritual world where the Apostle John witnesses *a star fallen* (past tense) *from heaven to the earth* (9:1). When the Lord Jesus was reviewing the missionary work of the 'seventy' that He had commissioned to make known the coming of the kingdom of God in all of Israel he said, *I saw Satan fall like lightning from heaven* (Luke 10:18). Satan was a most beautiful angel that fell and was consigned to earth in a bodiless form and is known as *the prince of the power of the air* (Eph. 2:2). *To him was given the key to the bottomless pit* (9:1). This is to say that He had gained the authority to exercise power over all the fallen angels, and of course He usurped the power of lawlessness over the human races that fell with Adam in the Garden of Eden and who are separated from God in the condition of death because of their sin. Spiritual powers of darkness became Satan's brutal autocratic rule of torture, misery and endless devastation. Under this trumpet, Satan *opened the bottomless pit, and smoke arose out of the pit like the smoke of a great furnace. So the sun and the air were darkened because of the smoke of the pit. Then out of the smoke locusts came upon the earth. And to them was gave power, as the scorpions of the earth have power* (Rev. 9:2-3). In response to the ever-increasing growth of the kingdom of God throughout the Gospel age and the shrinking of Satan's hegemony on earth, Satan unleashes every sinister spiritual power of demons and their devilish designs. Truly *we do not wrestle against flesh and blood, but against principalities, against powers, against the rulers of the darkness of this age, against spiritual hosts of wickedness in the heavenly places* (Eph. 6:12). Again, this is not a single event but the state-of-play during the entire Gospel age. In this trumpet, Satan is exercising power to release the demons from the bottomless pit, but the events of the *seven last plagues* of chapters 16, 17, 18 and 19 of Revelation are concluded when a strong angel from heaven *having the key to the bottomless pit...laid hold of the dragon, the serpent of old, who is the devil and Satan, and bound him for a thousand years; and he cast him into the bottomless pit and shut him up and set a seal on him so that he should deceive the nations no more...* (Rev. 20:1-3) The great tribulation prevails, now for some 2000 years, though the kingdom of God irresistibly grows throughout the Gospel age. Christ's kingdom is consummated with the events of 'the great day of God Almighty' who providentially intervenes and peace breaks out throughout all the nations. As the seventh angel sounds his trumpet *there were loud voices in heaven, saying, "The kingdoms of this world have become the kingdoms of our Lord and of His Christ, and He shall reign forever and ever!"* (11:15).

There is an inherent contradiction within the amillennial position that the events of 'seals and trumpets' are, historically speaking, running in parallel with the *seven last plagues*. With the releasing of locusts from the bottomless pit that *had as king over them the angel the fallen star from heaven to the earth* (9:1) *of the bottomless pit whose name in Hebrew is Abaddon, but in Greek he has the name of Apollyon* (9:11), Satan is doing war in the spiritual world and this manifests itself through physical war. This period is characterised by tribulation—even great tribulation——as the three *woes* (8:13) occur. The very reverse process is taking place when we see the bottomless pit revealed again after the 'great tribulation' at *the great day of God Almighty* where Satan is cast into the bottomless pit for a thousand years at the beginning of the millennial peace. These are separate historical movements—the *great tribulation* and *the great day of God Almighty*.

If we take these prophetic pictures of *the great tribulation* and the great day of God Almighty in sequence rather than in parallel, then many things fit together logically and paint a clear picture of the flow of history. In Revelation 9:13-21, the sixth angel sounds his trumpet to *Release the four angels who are bound at the great river Euphrates* and these angels *prepared for the hour and day and month and year, were released to kill a third of mankind* (9:15). Again, war breaks out and there is the impending intervention. This can be taken literally because this is the only time it ever happens and it is yet to happen. Here, during the *seven last plagues*, one of seven angels is pouring out the plagues handed to them by *the four living creatures*. These *four living creatures* have been supervising the general providence of God throughout all the ages, but they now give this task of pouring out the *seven last plagues* to these seven angelic beings. There are two administrators of these historical prophetic events, which distinguishes the events to follow as a sequence rather than some kind of parallelism. Here there are three unclean spirits, not angels, which come out of the dragon's mouth and out of the mouth of the false prophet. These are signs which authenticate these prophecies when they are fulfilled. It may also be noted that in the "seals and trumpets" there are no particular landmark signs but they are set as characteristic events that may reoccur in the corridors of history, but here in these events of *the great day of God Almighty* there are signs for the believer to recognise the fulfilment when it arrives.

CHAPTER 2

IN HEAVEN, SO ON EARTH

In the book of Revelation and other parts of Scripture the reality of existence extends far beyond the logic of modern science. Modern science sees the extent of real existence as a "mono-cameral system" and cannot see beyond the finite "chamber" of the physical creation. Atheistic science calls all other notions of existence 'myth', because such existence cannot be understood through the five senses of sight, hearing, taste, smell, or touch, or through any scientific instruments of observation.

When we use the word "cameral" (Latin *camera*, chamber), we are invoking an ancient word which is commonly used to refer to our Westminster parliamentary and legal system of government. The two houses of parliament, the House of Representatives and the Senate, are known as a bicameral parliamentary system. The two houses are under the governance of one but they function separately with respect to the other. All authority is vested in "the Crown" but is delegated to the various levels of governance proportionately with their own sphere of responsibility and their own authority.

Scripture teaches a tri-cameral order of existence. There is the physical "chamber" (in the book of Revelation this was the universe that the Apostle John could know through the physical senses,

Rev. 1:9), and the spiritual "chamber" (John saw this by special revelation in the Spirit, understanding this revelation through the immaterial senses of the spirit, Rev. 1:10-20). These chambers of existence are governed by one autonomous self-existent God who is uncreated and transcendent, existing in His own Holy order, or chamber (1:8). The physical and spiritual chambers of existence are governed by the One whose authority is delegated to each proportionately, having their own authority, function and kind of existence. These in turn delegate appropriate authority to every level and part within each "camera," or order of existence.

The greater reality is the spiritual over the physical because the physical is dependent upon the spiritual. The finite is that physical creation that generates and regenerates but is never self-existent. The existence of life is dependent on sources in the transcendent (John 1:1-5). The immanence of life and the transcendent power of the self-existent God is the overriding law of existence in the physical or finite world, which we may call God's providence (Dan. 4: 34-35, Ps. 135:6, Acts 17:25-28). As there is a beginning, by definition there is an end to the finite universe (Gen. 1, 2 Pet. 3:10-12).

The presence of the spiritual is an extension of space by the power of the ultimate order of existence in the person of God. The existence of God's power and providence brings about the nature of all that exists. The material of the spiritual is incomprehensible to the finite or the physical material because it is of another order of existence. The substance of angels is of their own kind. The material substance of the resurrected soul and body is of its particular kind. The oneness of the substance of God Himself, with the diversity of the three Persons of the Triune God, is the self-existent, eternal order of glory itself.

The kingdom of God is in the order of the spirit but has a territory that is universal and its material is spiritual and has a power that overrides competing *principalities…powers…and rulers…in the heavenly places* (Eph. 6: 12).

The *New Jerusalem* is, by definition, of the same material substance as the Second Person of God (Rev. 21:2-3; 9-27). The *new heavens and a new earth* is of the spiritual material of the kingdom of God but of yet another order of existence that is distinct from the heaven of God Himself or the heaven of the angels (Isa. 65:17; 66:22; 2 Pet. 3:13). This distinct place is a place that Christ Himself *prepares* (John 14:2-3) in complete sameness to that dwelling place of the Triune God. This is the eternal habitation of the New Jerusalem, with Christ and His Bride, the true Church triumphant and glorified, that are One (21:2).

The existence of place in the spiritual is related to but is not the same as the dimensions of finite matter. The dimensions of the physical universe are different only in order, not in proportion. So, it follows for the existence of matter and time that the material of the spiritual resurrected body of the Lord Jesus in His post-resurrection appearances took the form of a physical body and was recognisable and was not confined to physical limits (John 20:6-10). The material of the spiritual is different in order from, but in proportion bears the likeness of, the physical material (1 Cor. 15:42-44). The substance of the spiritual has the bearing of the finite but is not constrained by the laws of existence found in the physical universe. It is subject only to the laws of righteousness, holiness and goodness.

The finite nature of existence generates (is self-perpetuating) and regenerates (reproduces or renews) because of life and is due to the immanence of God in His providence. (Acts 17:28, Col. 1:17)

The eternal process or movement is of a distinct order of existence to time. Eternal motion is of the absolute, but time passes away.

This so-called tri-cameral universe finds its absolute unity of the various parts of existence in the self-existent, uncreated and autonomous Being, in the Person of God Almighty who in His providence sustains all things and gives life to all things according to His sole authority and His unction or power.

Such is the geography of the Biblical view of the tri-cameral understanding of existence. If we are to understand the book of Revelation as it is written, we will need to maintain this broader view of the reality of existence. Otherwise the concrete reality of existence will be little more than intangible feelings of religious mythology that only serve the purpose of giving colour and form to our deep historical expressions of religious language and imagination.

CHAPTER 3

"THE GLORIOUS TESTIMONY OF THE LAMB AND HIS CHURCH"

UNDERSTANDING THE SIGNS OF OUR TIMES

The completion of the apostolic age at the time of the destruction of the Jerusalem Temple in A.D. 70 heralded the closing of the canon of Scripture. The book of Revelation was given as a timeless guide to the Church, which was suffering and testifying for the sake of that Name which is above every name, Jesus Christ, Lord of heaven and earth. We propose in the following pages to give Scriptural guidance to interpret and understand our times according to Christ's providential rule on earth, both in His Church and His kingdom, from His heavenly throne at the right hand of the Father by the power of God the Holy Spirit. This wise understanding of the signs of our times is intensely practical and should never lead to pure speculation. It should always lead to a deepening love for God and a strengthening of that common faith that exists amongst the saints. Our shared faith should refurbish genuine spiritual hope amid an otherwise confusing landscape of personalities and principalities that appear to ravage and displace the absolute authority and power of God.

The Foundation of the "Covenant of Creation"

Contrary to the teaching of modern atheistic science, the fundamental reason why the finite world continues to exist is that God determined from the beginning that He would honour His "Covenant" at creation (Jer. 31:35 ff; 33:20, 21, 25, 26). This "Covenant of Creation" installed mankind as God's vice-regent over the entire creation. When God created the heavens and the earth by calling all things into existence out of nothing by the power of His Word, the single law of God was for man to govern all things according to the Creator's will, for *in Him we live and move and have our being* (Acts 17:27). Despite the willful violation of this Covenant by man which could have spelt the end of the entire created finite universe, God determined to complete what had begun at creation, as God's purposes are not frustrated by the rebellion of man. He therefore introduced an enabling Covenant that would restore man as God's vice-regent over creation. This was achieved in a gracious covenant, that could be described as the "Covenant of Redemption," by the work of God's appointed Redeemer that would be both God and man.

The Dividing Factor in All the Affairs of Man

This Gospel of redemption is the dividing factor in all the affairs of man throughout history. As the Lord Jesus Christ puts it, *I came to send fire on the earth, and how I wish it were already kindled! But I have a baptism to be baptised with, and how distressed I am till it is accomplished!* (He is referring to the baptism of Christ's redemptive death.) *Do you suppose that I came to give peace on earth? I tell you, not at all, but rather division. For from now on five in one house will be divided: three against two, and two against three. Father will be divided against son and son against father, mother against daughter and daughter against mother, mother-in-law against her daughter-in-law and daughter-in-law against her mother-in-law* (Luke 12:49-53).

When "the fall" (Gen. 3:6-7) took place in the Garden of Eden, it created the potential for a one-world order to exist. Under the usurper's authority, Satan would have an extended autonomy of the *principalities...powers...the rulers of the darkness of this age, against spiritual hosts of wickedness in the heavenly places* (Eph. 6:12). Hegemony in both the spiritual world and the material universe, co-existing in a state of stalemate against God, was then the grand design of the fallen angelic beings.

> God pronounced judgment against Satan with the words:
> *I will put enmity*
> *Between you and the woman,*
> *And between your seed and her seed;*
> *He shall bruise your head,*
> *And you shall bruise his heel* (Gen. 3:15).

Thus, He instituted a new eternal covenant, the "Covenant of Redemption," by the intervention of His predestinating decree that would lead to the redemption of God's people and the restoration of "all."

The essential ingredient in this 'Covenant of Redemption' is the *He*. The Apostle Paul, reflecting upon the further revelation of this Covenant to our forefather Abraham (Gen. 22:18), spoke of the singular *Seed* (Gal. 3:16-17). This was referring to Christ, who was born of woman, lived under the law, and was attested as being *the Son of God with power according to the spirit of holiness, by the resurrection from the dead* (Rom. 1:4). So according to theologians describing this relationship in what is known as "Federal Theology," a new representative Head of the living has been now established as *the last Adam*, and that Head is Christ (1 Cor. 15:45). The identifying principle of this new humanity is faith in the Covenant of Redemption, which was thoroughly and perfectly accomplished through the redemptive and meritorious work of Jesus Christ, *...the Lamb of God that takes away the sin of the world* (Jn. 1:29).

As the Apostle Paul puts it, *For if by one man's offence many died, much more the grace of God and the gift by the grace of the one Man, Jesus Christ, abounded to many. And the gift is not like that which came through the one who sinned. For the judgement which came from one offence resulted in condemnation, but the free gift which came from many offences resulted in justification. For if by the one man's offence death reigned through the one, much more those who receive abundance of grace and of the gift of righteousness will reign in life through the One, Jesus Christ.* (Rom. 5:15-17)

UNDERSTANDING BIBLICAL PROPHESY

From this basic foundation of Scriptural truth, it should be possible for us to understand the signs of our times, particularly if we are reflecting upon that abiding prophecy that is disclosed to us in the book of Revelation, and in the many portions of prophecy throughout Scripture. Such things should be discernible to the children of God, who are spiritually-minded people. The Lord Jesus, reflecting upon His own generation, made this accusation concerning them: *... when you see a cloud rising out of the west, immediately you say, a shower is coming; and so it is. And when you see the south wind blow, you say, there will be hot weather; and there is. Hypocrites! You can discern the face of the sky and of the earth, but how is it that you do not discern this time?* (Luke 12:54-56) They had been blessed as God's Covenant people, granted the oracles of God in the Old Testament Scriptures, and had standing in their midst the very Temple of God that represented the Gospel that granted them so great a salvation, and yet they had not discerned the times. Predicting the weather in those days may not have been an exact science, and even today precise predictions of the weather may not be achieved. Jesus seems to indicate that the average farmer can make reasonable predictions that will enable him to manage his crops. In fact, most farmers can read the weather with sufficient accuracy to make the right decisions under a range of circumstances. Yet when it comes to spiritual discernment and understanding of Scripture, things are actually clearer, when looking at the signs of our time, if we rightly apply those principles to our regular life and times. The point is that as we are living by faith in the God of the Scriptures, we ought to be wise and understanding of the circumstances in which we find ourselves and we should not be shaken by events, or by irrational people that seem to be possessed of a malignant spirit that casts a dark shadow over all that is good. War, famine, earthquakes, flood, pestilence and the Wormwood of pollution and disease can shake the very foundations of our faith in the living and true God. Evil men and women seem to lay hold of the power that even shakes the foundations of the Church of God, and *the Gates of Hell* seem to prevail over the household of God.

How then should we understand?

Getting our minds and hearts above these circumstances is extremely important if we hope to conduct a faithful walk as disciples of Christ, even in *the valley of the shadow of death* so that we *fear no evil* (Ps. 23:4). How then should we understand so that our love is restored as the pristine first love of the days of our conversion, our personal faith and walk with God is made more ardent, and we "do not lose heart" but make our confidence and hope ever surer? Eschatology—or the study of prophecy—is not something to avoid as we tell ourselves that these things are too difficult and "it will all pan out in the end." If we wish to live the Christian life the best way we can, we must take due cognisance of the issues and the circumstances that face the Christian church and Christ's Kingdom. We may feel as though we are in a small lifeboat, cast away with no resources in a terrifying storm or in a dead calm at the mercy of an empty ocean. If we have lost our bearings and our ability to proceed, we may die prematurely and give up, becoming cold in our love for God, directionless in our faith toward Christ, and abandoned to the circumstances of our day without hope. However, if we give attention to these things, our worldview being governed by the instrument of truth, the Word of God, our spiritual navigation will be made surer. If we rightly apply the doctrine and truth of a Biblical worldview to situations and events in our lives, we will gain a certain spiritual bearing that will help us to embrace our day and time with confidence and liveliness of faith, fixing our eyes upon *the author and the finisher of our faith* (Heb. 12:2), so that our *love may abound still more and more in knowledge and all discernment* (Phil. 1:9).

GREAT TRIBULATION

In chapters 4 to 14 of the book of Revelation, earthly reality is disclosed to us from a heavenly perspective. These chapters describe world events in such a way as to make it possible to discern and make sense of the times in which we live. These chapters describe a Great Tribulation (7:14) that has spanned some two millennia of human history, from the days of the Apostles to our own. The breathtaking events that are described in these chapters of Revelation may also be discerned in a cursory understanding of world history that should be comprehended from the perspective of a lively faith in the Lord Jesus Christ.

We will not be like those that have read of or experienced the battlefields and killing fields of the last century, which caused terrible carnage and human loss of "apocalyptic" proportions. Such people, having recourse to the statistics, declare, "I cannot believe in God any longer. How can God allow such terrible atrocity?" The war dead from both Axis and Allied troops in the First World War (1914-18) reached 15 million, and civilian deaths reached 12.5 million. The loss of life during the Second World War (1939-45) was even higher, with 66 million dead, including those who perished in the Jewish Holocaust. The death toll exceeds 20 million under the Soviet Union during Stalin's regime from 1924 to 1953, let alone the death toll of 9 million during the Cultural Revolution from 1917 to 1922. The loss of human life from 1949 to 1975 under Mao Zedong's regime in the Peoples' Republic of China was due to genocide, famine and plague against his own people and led to more than 40 million deaths.[9]

God is the Sustainer of all things, including those that perpetrate crimes against humanity and everything good, that sustains human social family order and stable and free government. If we attribute such terrible losses to Him, we may well fail to believe correctly and blame God for creating the world, or even our own lives, and for the terrible consequences of evil. To be sure, God is *the God of good and evil* (Genesis 2:4), but to describe God as evil is a step too far. If God is not sovereign then the question arises, "Who is?" At the most fundamental level, we are living in a universe, not a poliverse, that has room for only One autonomous, self-existent, personal Being, in whom *all things consist*, that One being God Himself (Col. 1:17). God is not evil, but God so uses evil so that His providential rule and predestinating purposes, that are righteous, good and perfect, are maintained. In the

---

[9] These figures are conservative as there are many calculations that would even drive these figures far higher. http://necrometrics.com/20c5m.htm#Mao

doctrine of "contingencies of second causes"[10], God grants man limited autonomy to exercise his vice-recency freely and responsibly as a personal gift of God, according to the original "Covenant of Creation." Man may well use such liberty for evil purposes to exercise power and authority that belongs to God with horrible consequences that lead to such misery. The origin of sin is not with God but with man. The ravages of sin are man's responsibility and he will one day have to give an account for his stewardship before God the Almighty.

THE PROBLEM OF EVIL

God is at war against the armies of those that seized power and authority in the dominion of darkness, in the estate of sin and death. God's truth has been disclosed in the revelation of the Scriptures, and God has established the "Covenant of Redemption," which was accomplished by the Son of God, the Lord Jesus Christ, at the triumph of redemption on the cross of Calvary, where the ransom price was paid for the sin of the world.

The old order amongst God's people in the days of Israel has been thoroughly reformed and the reality of distant things has now become personal and real, being of the heart and the spirit. It is the gift of grace by God the Holy Spirit who has begun calling those whom God appoints from the darkness of death into the marvellous light of eternal life in Christ. The spiritual Church of the body of Christ is organically united to the risen Christ who has ascended on high *above all principality and power and might and dominion and every name that is named, not only in this age but also in that which is to come...* (Eph. 1:20-21). Thus, the *King of kings and Lord of Lords* establishes the kingdom of God, which

---

[10] Westminster Confession of Faith, Free Presbyterian Publication, Glasgow G3 6LE, 1985, V:ii

at first is *like a mustard seed* but becomes the largest tree in the garden of this world, *so that the birds of the air come and nest in its branches* (Matt. 13:32). Or, as the prophecy of Daniel states, the kingdom of God is like *a stone that was cut out of the mountain without hands* that strikes the old-world order before the coming of Christ, and that stone grows and *becomes a great mountain and fills the whole earth* (Dan. 2:45; 35). Because of Christ's rule and intervention throughout history according to the purposes of God, the statute of limitations in the kingdom of God, as well as God's general providence, prevents things from becoming as bad as they could be. Indeed, the more surprising thing to comprehend is not 'the problem of evil' but the presence of grace and mercy. The existence of the love of God among men can be comprehended only in the Gospel of Jesus Christ. In hell, the place of perdition, which will be the end of all this evil and sin, there will be no statute of limitations and it will be as bad as it could be (2 Pet. 3:7; Rev. 17:8,11). However, the purposes of God are fully played out on the basis of the two foundational Covenants of Scripture, namely the "Covenant of Creation" to do with that single inclusive decree of the foreknowledge of God, and the "Covenant of Redemption" that is played out through the redemptive exclusive decree of the predestinating purpose of God through the elect in Christ. Although evil is sustained and even ordained in the purposes of God, we know from Scripture that in the fullness of time, *...all things work together for good to those who love God, to those who are called according to His purpose. For whom he foreknew, he also predestined to be conformed to the image of His Son, that he might be the firstborn among many brethren. Moreover, whom He predestined, these He also called; whom He called, these He also justified, and whom He justified these He also glorified* (Rom. 8: 28-30).

The book of Revelation is the capstone of the entire scriptural revelation of the truth of God that explains the events of history in the new situation so that the future is set in its perspective. It is said of believers throughout the ages, *For Your [God's] sake we are killed all day long; we are accounted as sheep for the slaughter* (Rom. 8:36). Yet Christian faith is strengthened so that we do not faint; true love for God is revived, so we do not become hardened; and faithful hope is renewed, so that we do not lose heart.

Prophetic mileposts that mark out the history of God's kingdom

Our Lord Jesus warns against speculation in matters of prophecy by saying, *But of that day and hour no one knows, not even the angels of heaven, but My Father only* (Matt. 24:36). However, Jesus goes on to strengthen the faith of His disciples, as He teaches them concerning the destruction of the Jerusalem Temple that they were observing from their vantage point on the Mount of Olives. They were to be like Noah of old who was warned concerning the universal flood, and who by faith built the Ark that was the necessary work of faith that saved him and his family, along with every kind of animal that lived on the face of the earth. Noah came to this knowledge by the clear revelation of God, acted upon that knowledge, and prepared for the coming judgement of God that would consume the entire world. Even though he did not know *the day or hour*, he worked according to faith in God, and this work of faith would be completed according to the sovereign purposes of God, not one day too early or one hour too late. Noah knew that he was woven into the glorious purposes of God as God's vice-regent in God's plan, and so he walked by faith, loving God with all his heart, not losing hope in this present world or for heaven itself.

The intricacies of the book of Revelation can be somewhat overwhelming and may seem complicated and difficult to understand. Therefore, it helps greatly to be able to find and set prophetic markers that are clearly stated in Scripture with particular reference to the book of Revelation.

Yet before the book of Revelation was given through the Apostle John, the Apostle Paul, when writing to the Thessalonian church concerning God's kind intention for the future era beyond the Apostolic Age, establishes a future prophetic agenda. Paul encourages the believers at Thessalonica, who were being heavily persecuted for their faith, saying, *...all your persecution and tribulations that you endure, ...is manifest evidence of the righteous judgement of God that you may be counted worthy of the kingdom of God, for which you also suffer; since it is a righteous thing with God to repay with tribulation those who trouble you and to give you who are troubled rest with us* (2 Thess. 1:4-7a). That is to say that God will bring vengeance upon those that are troubling the church with persecution and tribulation, but in the meantime the Thessalonians are to be patient in faith and endure these hardships because God's purpose is being fulfilled according to the providence of God.

THE EVENTS OF THE "LAST DAYS" OF THE OLD TESTAMENT DISPENSATION

The complete and final destruction of the Jerusalem Temple and the casting off of *the natural branch* of Israel (Rom. 11) was the big event of which all the Apostles were fully aware from the teachings of our Lord Jesus in the Mount Olivet Discourse (Matt. 23-25; Mark 13; Luke 17:20-27; 21:5-38). This was yet to be fulfilled, and would conclude the Apostolic Age.[11] This event, described also by

---

[11] The discussion relating to the interpretation of the prophecies of the Lord Jesus on the Mount of Olives concerning the destruction of Jerusalem will be taken up in many places in this present discourse. However, the fullest discussion will be found in these notes that address Revelation 22 under the heading of "the soon prophecies of Jesus." The position of this writer is that

the Apostle Paul, would establish a kind of rest from the Jewish persecution that was racking the church. *The Lord Jesus is revealed from heaven with his mighty angels, in flaming fire taking vengeance on those who do not know God, and on those who do not obey the Gospel of our Lord Jesus Christ* (2 Thess. 1:7b-8). For the Apostles and the Apostolic Church, the great defining moment of the day would be this single event of the destruction of Jerusalem with her Temple. This would mark the passing of *the last days* of the Old Testament into the consummated era of the Church.

Events that push forward the purposes of the kingdom of God

In every epoch of church history, there will be great and amazing works of God that push forward the purposes of the kingdom of God. These events will be accompanied by great persecution and tribulation within the household of God, and she will be greatly purified in her testimony. The vengeance of God will also be poured out on the unbelieving world like a flaming fire restraining its evil

---

these prophecies of Jesus are referring to events surrounding the destruction of the Temple of Jerusalem and the sacking of the city exclusively.

In apocalyptic language of Matthew 24:29-31 *After the tribulation...The sun will be darkened and the moon will not give its light; the stars will fall from heaven, and the powers of the heavens will be shaken....The son of man will appear in heaven...Coming on the clouds of heaven with power and great glory....* This is a reference to the dramatic appearance of the Lord Jesus Christ in the heavens at the destruction of the Jerusalem temple in A.D. 70 and is actually recorded by the Jewish historian Josephus but should not be taken as a reference to the Second Advent of Christ. This is reinforced by a further reference affirmed by our Lord Jesus after these things when He says, *Assuredly, I say to you, this generation will by no means pass away till all these things take place. Heaven and earth will parcel way, but my words will by no means pass away.* (Matt. 24:34-35) In other words, all these things shall take place within the present generation of the apostles listening to Jesus whilst observing the Temple from their vantage point on the Mount of Olives.

for the sake of the preservation and maintenance of God's goodness and mercy in all things.

HAVING THE PERSPECTIVE OF THE LAST DAY IN EVERYTHING OF THE PRESENT

All this has a far-distant event reference point that goes beyond any present generation to the end of history itself known as *that Day*. This last and final Day is dramatically described by the Apostle Paul in his first letter to the Thessalonians thus: *For the Lord himself will descend from heaven with a shout, with the voice of an archangel, and with the trumpet of God. And the dead in Christ will rise first. Then we who are alive and remain shall be caught up together with them in the clouds to meet the Lord in the air. And thus we shall always be with the Lord.* (1 Thess. 4:16-17) On that Last Day at the great and final Judgement, everything will have to give an account, when all human flesh from Adam to the last human being ever born will be raised with an incorruptible and indestructible resurrected body. All people will be divided, the sheep from the goats, to be assigned with Christ or sent to perdition in a Christless eternity. *These shall be punished with everlasting destruction from the presence of the Lord and from the glory of His power when He comes, in that Day to be glorified in his saints and to be admired among all those who believe because our testimony among you was believed* (2 Thess. 1:9-10).

Our present situation and the particular work of God in the kingdom of God in our time of service, begins a series of events that move toward the ultimate end of history. These events will culminate in that final event of history, the Second Advent of Christ. The annals of history play out according to God's providence in the intervening events of the advancing and growing kingdom of God in history. We can understand these providences of God because we have the revelation of Biblical truth. Wisdom provides a Biblical commentary of these events so that we are left with hope in and praise to the God of heaven and earth. The imperative for the Church throughout the ages is that we are called upon as members of the universal body of Christ and citizens of the kingdom of God to hold fast under the rule of Christ the King, to suffer and endure persecution *for righteousness sake (so that ours) is the kingdom of heaven [God]* (Matt. 5:10). We do this always for the greater glory of God, which in earthly terms will be made manifest on the Last Day. To be sure, generation will follow generation accomplishing the purposes of the kingdom of God at every stage. This will not be easily won but will be a titanic wrestle with every sinister force arrayed against the Anointed One, our Lord Jesus Christ and his body the true Church (Ps. 2). But the victory is certain, not only on the Last Day but also through the various epochs of history; indeed, victory is certain in the life of every individual life who has been redeemed and knows the salvation of God.

GOD HAS HIS ORDER IN THESE EVENTS THAT WE SHOULD NOT LOSE SIGHT

The Apostle Paul reminds the believers in Thessalonica that they should *not be easily shaken in mind or troubled, neither by spirit or by word or by letter, as if from us as though the Day of Christ had come* (2 Thess. 2: 3). Yes, even though we do not know the timing of the coming of Christ on the Last Day, we do know that there are certain preconditions.

FIRST THE 'MYSTERY OF LAWLESSNESS'

First there is that malignant figure that the Apostle Paul refers to as being, *the man of sin...the son of perdition, who opposes and exalts himself above all that is called God all of that is worshipped, so that he sits as God in the temple of God showing himself that he is God* (2 Thess. 2:3-4). Associated with the rise of the man of sin will also be a final falling away (that) comes first, before the last Day. This event, and seemingly the whole world relating to *the man of sin*, is described by the Apostle Paul as *the mystery of lawlessness which is already at work...*(2 Thess. 2:7) The final manifestation or "revealing of the man of sin" is related to the great apostasy from the Church that was so greatly blessed during the millennium. From the added perspective of Revelation chapter 20, we can see from the Apostle Paul that *the falling away comes first* before that great Day of Christ's Second Advent (2 Thess. 2:3). However, in the same spirit as *the man of sin* who will be *revealed*, as described by the Apostle Paul, *the mystery of lawlessness which is already at work,* rises and rises, taking centre stage throughout the long history of the Church during the Great Tribulation. The fate of this malignant spirit of Satan is described as follows: He is finally, *...bound for a thousand years and he cast him into the bottomless pit, and shut him up and set a seal on him, so that he should not deceive the nations anymore till the thousand years were finished*. (Rev. 20:2-3)

There was no doubt much unrecorded but well-understood discussion and teaching on this subject between the Apostle Paul and the Thessalonian Church. No doubt apostolic teaching was somewhat eclipsed by the Revelation to the Apostle John, which was given some considerable time after this teaching to the Thessalonians. This personality of *the man of sin* in the form of *the mystery of lawlessness that is already at work* figures everywhere in the book of Revelation and it is probably that teaching that was also understood to some lesser degree in the teaching of the Apostle Paul, particularly to the Thessalonians.

The point is that the history of *the man of sin* as revealed in the book of Revelation is yet to be played out through the corridors of history to that event known as *the falling away that comes first* (2 Thess. 2:3). That event is described at the end of the millennium in Revelation chapter 20 verses 4 to 6, and then comes the falling away in verses 7 to 10. It is only then that the Last Day comes, as described in the following verses 11 to 15.

There is a single spirit lying behind *the man of sin*. According to the Apostle Paul, the *lawless one is according to the working of Satan, with all power, signs, and lying wonders* (2 Thess. 2:9). He is described by the Apostle John in his letters as *the Antichrist*, but he goes on to say, *even now many antichrists have come* (1 John 2:18). It seems that there is a certain character described by the Apostle John as follows: *They went out from us, but they were not of us*, referring to apostate Christians. These people with this Antichrist spirit pose as Christians but are not of Christ. Using the language of Christians and behaving like Christians, they are counterfeits who seek by worldly means to undermine the place of the Christian testimony as the outward legitimate Church. These churches are known in Scripture as *synagogue[s] of Satan* (Rev. 2:9; 3:9), but they politically organise in such a way as to heavily persecute true Christians inside the church, leaving the true church in the wilderness as they take the place of the true testimony of Christ. The true Christians can see that this work of Satan is not to destroy the church of God but to control it, and that this counterfeit church would be cloaked in the garments of true religion and *outwardly appear as sheep but inwardly are ravenous wolves* (Matt. 7:17). Emerging from this *synagogue of Satan* arises *the beast* (Rev. 13). Following the great schism that occurred at the Synod of the Whitby in 664, this political personage described in Revelation is revealed as being *the beast*, and his harlot the Popish priest of Rome who takes the place of God in the church and is truly anti (in the place of) Christ. The history of this usurper, fully described in chapters 12 to 13 of Revelation, has been a terrible and bloody one. In the sinister spirit of *the man of sin*, described by the Apostle Paul to the Thessalonians (2 Thess. 2:3) as yet to be revealed, the harlot comes riding her *beast*, who in the fullness of time becomes Babylon the Great and appears to possess the entire world.

THE RESTRAINING OF "MYSTERY OF LAWLESSNESS"

This *mystery of lawlessness that is already at work* is *restrained*. He is restrained for the purposes of the kingdom of God as it advances relentlessly from one generation to the next and the Gospel advances into all nations. The book of Revelation chapters 5 to 11 describes four horses and riders with seven trumpets that loose seven seals of the sacred Covenant. This is a mighty work of God in all the earth that not only advances the kingdom of God and sets the Gospel loose but also restrains *the mystery of lawlessness*. There are advancing cycles that "recapitulate"[12] throughout history as the Gospel goes out according to the Great Commission of Christ the King. But in a rear-guard retreat strategy of Satan through *the Great Tribulation* (Rev. 7:14) of heavy persecution of the saints and the spilling of their blood, warfare is waged. Christ our King not only reserves His final judgement on the Last Day but *…the wrath of God is revealed from heaven against all ungodliness and unrighteousness of men, who suppress the truth in unrighteousness* (Rom. 1:18). He does this by metering out these judgements

---

[12] William Hendriksen, *More Than Conquerors*, IVP 1967. Hendriksen best describes the literary concept of "recapitulation" to describe the cycles of history having characteristic re-occurrences in the providence of God from one generation to another. He sees seven kinds of recapitulations around which the book of Revelation is constructed. The present writer is satisfied with Hendriksen's concept of recapitulation in chapters 1 to 3 concerning Christ's word to the seven churches, and in chapters 4 to 11 concerning the Gospel going out into the world in the Seven Seals and the Seven Trumpets. However, in chapters 12 to 14 that describes the *great tribulation* (Rev. 7:14) imposed upon the church by the rise and rise of *the beast* and its *harlot*, there is a heavy linear direction revealed in the historical the *mystery of lawlessness*. By the time we come to chapter 15 to 19, there is a crisis in history described and we have argued that this section is not recapitulation but a description of *the battle of the great day of God Almighty* (Rev. 16:14).

so that the vengeance of God is enacted for the sake of the saints. In the natural order of creation through the instrumentality of *the four living creatures* (Revelation 4:6; 6:1, 3, 5-6), God providentially unleashes the powers of nature against the spiritually inspired *mystery of lawlessness* to restrain sin and evil. However, this is done in a measured and limited way, in proportions of thirds. In this way, the greater mystery for this world to witness is God's love and mercy.

This *mystery of lawlessness* will begin to over-stretch itself so that, in the fullness of time, a great crisis in history occurs. This is described as *the battle of the great day of God Almighty* (Rev. 16:14) and is described in chapters 16 to 19 of Revelation. This will lead to the eventual *laying hold of the dragon that serpent of old, who is the devil and Satan, and [who] is bound for a thousand years; and he cast him into the bottomless pit, and shut him up, and set a seal on him, so that he should deceive the nations no more...* (Rev. 20:1-3). The kingdom of God is consummated, as expressed in the original "covenant of creation" and secured by the "covenant of redemption." The whole earth will then yield its bloom for a sustained and continuous period in millennial proportions. It will be as it is written: the kingdom of God will come *on earth as it is in heaven*. Thus, the great prophecies such as Isaiah 65:17-25 will know their fulfilment.

The *MAN OF SIN* is then revealed that takes place just before *THAT DAY*

After the millennial reign, there is a shockingly violent but short season of Satanic rebellion after he is released from the bottomless pit. *The man of sin* will be revealed as *the Antichrist* (1 Jn. 2:18). There will be a great *falling away* which is spoken of by the Apostle Paul, and it is this *falling away* that is the pretext for the *last Day* where our Lord Jesus Christ returns to the earth in the Second Advent.

CHAPTER 4

THE WOMAN, THE BODY OF CHRIST IN THE WILDERNESS - HER TRIED AND TRUE TESTIMONY - REVELATION 12

There is an extensive description in Revelation chapters 10 and 11 of the powerful and persistent proclamation of the Gospel throughout the ages. The opening of the 'seven seals' of the exclusive "Covenant of Redemption," which is based on the election of God in Christ, enables the inclusive "Covenant of Creation," founded upon God's creation, to find its consummation and fulfilment. The "seven trumpets" of Revelation chapters 8 and 9 proclaim the Word of God, which is the Gospel of redemption. They also proclaim the kingdom of God in which salvation is wrought through the powerful and persistent preaching of the word of God and the prayers of the saints. God in His foreknowledge has accomplished His kind intentions embodied in the "Covenant of Creation" that incorporates every area of life, so that *He [Christ] is the head of the body, the church, who is the beginning, the firstborn from the dead, that in all things He [Christ] may have the pre-eminence* (Col. 1:18). This has been effected through the "Covenant of Redemption," which is God's predestined plan of salvation. The Gospel of Christ is demonstrated in the body of Christ, the very

Church of God, throughout all the ages. We have also seen that in the "seventh seal," seven trumpets were sounded, and at the seventh trumpet *...there were loud voices in heaven, saying, The kingdoms of this world have become the kingdoms of our Lord and of his Christ, and he shall reign forever and ever!* (11:15). This fulfilment of the kingdom of God in all the earth has its particular point of realisation in millennial proportions during the rule of Christ with his saints on earth, as it is in heaven. The kingdom of God began with the ascension of Christ the King forty days after His redemptive sacrifice and resurrection. The kingdom begins like a little stone which, made without hands and cast from heaven, strikes the nations with significant effect. The little stone of the kingdom of God grows gradually throughout all the ages to become like a mountain that fills the whole earth. The institutional enemies of the Gospel and the kingdom of Christ are embodied in the harlot, her beast and Babylon the great, along with the false prophet, described in chapters 12 to 14. The force of the dark spirit of Satan himself rules through these institutions, posing as Christ, and is thus the Antichrist. He consistently takes centre stage and leaves the true Church in a place of wilderness, where world powers and authorities are governed by these institutional enemies of God and His Anointed (Ps. 2; 110). We will see that these institutional enemies of Christ will be utterly crushed and that there will be a global rule of Christ in the consummated kingdom of God, where the peace of the Gospel of the Lord Jesus Christ with His kingdom will be sustained in millennial proportions, as described in the seventh trumpet of the seventh seal (11:15-19).

THE "GREAT SIGN APPEARED IN HEAVEN," THE "WOMAN"

Let us consider Revelation 12:1 and 2. The word *now'*, indicates that this *great sign (that) appeared in heaven* to the Apostle John is a present and continuous reality established in heavenly places with earthly effects. The identity of this *woman clothed with the sun, with the moon under her feet, and on her head a garland of twelve stars* could be confusing. We may jump to the idea that this woman is the figure of the Virgin Mary and the glorious event of the incarnation of Christ. However, these verses do not refer to the virgin Mary. It is said of this woman that, *then being with child, she cried out in labour and in pain to give birth.* Mary, of course, bore the Son of God in the same pain of childbirth that all women experience. However, the childbirth in chapter 12 is a long and sustained labour that continues throughout the season of the Gospel and sees the full delivery of both the 'Covenant of Redemption' and the full number of the elect children of God. The Gospels nowhere state that the young Mary *cries out in pain to give birth* at the incarnation of our Lord Jesus Christ.

The description given here seems to suggest that this is a long and sustained anguish of pain. It could be said that this birthing process is sustained by the true Church of God, who is born from above, and who is, in turn, instrumental in birthing the children of God throughout the ages. In great labour and persecution, she raises her family of God in all respects to the glory of her Husband, Christ the King and Head of the Church which is the very body of Christ. There is only one body of Christ, which is regenerated from above, but birthed through the body of Christ, the eternally Begotten of the Father. That body of Christ will be complete only when the last elect child of God is called into the Church, the living resurrected body of Christ, through the ministry of the preaching and teaching of the Gospel. The Bride of Christ has the commission to disciple *every nation to observe all things* that her Husband has commanded (Matt. 28:19-20).

THE WOMAN GIVING BIRTH CONTINUALLY IN GREAT LABOUR AND PAIN BUT IN HOPE

How will the true Church of God testify to this most extraordinary commission of birthing the body of Christ at every point of history and in its eschatological fulfilment of glorification on the Last Day? The Church of God will bear the birthing process of the mysterious begetting of the body of Christ through evangelisation with *the water* of the Word and power of the Holy *Spirit* (Jn. 3:5-6). Thus, in the begetting of the child of the one body of Christ in tribulation and persecution, *she cried out in labour and in pain to give birth*. The Church of Jesus Christ endures to the end because she is sustained by the Spirit of Christ, her betrothed Husband, the Lamb of God that redeemed her by His very own blood and gave her the eternal life of his resurrection. This Gospel ministry of the Church is described here as a bearing ministry. The body of Christ has as her *Good Shepherd* the Lord Jesus Christ, but *the sheep of His pasture* are the ones that bear her lambs. So, the saying is true, The Shepherd does not bear sheep but it is the sheep that bear sheep, and therefore it is His Church that has been commissioned to bear the fruit of her womb. The mother Church has her children.

This sign of *a woman* that appears in heaven cannot refer to the Lord Jesus Christ. Such a description of being *clothed with the sun, with the moon under her feet, and on her head a garland of twelve stars* never describes Christ in like terms anywhere in Scripture. However, the church is described thus. Christ, the creator of heaven and earth, cannot be clothed in His own creation for He is the one autonomous and self-sufficient original Being who is never describes in terms of *giving birth* (12:2). The Church as *the light of the world* and *the salt of the earth* (Matt. 5:13-16) is a radiant testimony of the light of God in all the earth. As Christ said, *I am the light of the world. He who follows Me shall not walk in darkness, but have the light of life* (John 8:12). The Church is not merely a reflection of Christ but she has *the light of life*, bearing the resurrection life as the very garment that clothes her. So, it is entirely fitting that the Church is described in figurative terms as being *clothed with the sun*, the greatest light in all the earth. She is also described as having *the moon under her feet*. The true Church, the redeemed of the Lord, is now a restored vice-regent of God in the kingdom of God. Like her master, of whom it is said *Heaven is My [Lord's] throne and earth is My [Lord's] footstool*, (Isa. 66:1), the Church exercises the dominion of Christ, as it were, and *the moon is under her feet*. Her *head is a garland of twelve stars*, being the raw testimony in the history of the covenanted people of God that will be the abiding heritage of God, the twelve tribes of Israel. The godly history of Israel is the heritage of the Church. She is never perfect but bears the abiding testimony of God because of God's faithfulness to Israel, and He will be faithful to the new Israel of God, the very Church of Jesus Christ.

NOW, THE BATTLE LINE IS DRAWN WITH *ANOTHER SIGN [THAT] APPEARS IN HEAVEN*

Now, in verses 3-4, the battle line is drawn with *another sign [that] appears in heaven*. The exact opposite now appears in heavenly places but with devastating earthly consequences. *Behold, a great fiery red dragon…* is a serpentine figure of old that is already under the judgement of God, and *is cursed more than all cattle, more than every beast of the field; who is to go on his belly and he shall eat dust all the days of his life* (Gen. 3: 14). In the mythology of the east, this serpentine figure is *a great fiery red dragon* that has feet, but in Biblical western culture, *the serpent of old* is without feet and is symbolic of the devil or Satan, that spiritual personality that was a glorious angel that rebelled in heavenly places. This sinister serpentine figure that is ingrained within every culture is one, and is, in fact, what the Apostle Paul describes in his letter to the

Ephesians, as *the Prince of the power of the air, the spirit that now works in the sons of disobedience*, (Eph. 2:2) and as *...the rulers of the darkness of this age... spiritual hosts of wickedness in the heavenly places* (Eph. 6:12). The Apostle John also sees that this sinister personality has *seven heads and ten horns, and seven diadems on his head*, which is a description of *the beast* in chapter 13 *that rises up out of the sea* (13:1). This will be discussed when we reach that portion of Scripture, but we are given the identity of that *beast* as being *the great fiery red dragon* that lies behind all the spiritual powers of the wickedness of Antichrist (1 John 2:18-22). In contrast to the vision of *the woman*, which is a description of the Church that regenerates and begets, this spirit of Antichrist has no begetting ability but is, as his name *Antichrist* suggests, a usurper who takes what is not his.

In the cosmology of the New Testament era with the coming of Christ to establish His redemptive work, as promised in the Old Testament, Jesus said to His disciples during His ministry, *I saw Satan fall like lightning from heaven* (Luke 10:18). *His tail drew a third of the stars of heaven and threw them to the earth*, which is describing a heavenly rebellion amongst the angels that yielded to *the father of lies*, the devil, that is also called Satan, and described here as *the dragon*. This seduction in heavenly places occurred before the foundation of the world, because this same personality seduces Eve through the serpent in the Garden of Eden. He said, *You will not surely die. For God knows that in the day that you eat [of the tree of knowledge and good and evil] of it your eyes will be open, and you will be like God, knowing good and evil* (Gen. 3: 4 – 5).

However, our text says that it is Satan that casts the fallen angels from heaven to colonise earth, and that Satan, who is *the prince of the power of the air* (Eph. 2: 2), rules his kingdom of darkness in place of God. It seems that a third of the angels, which are now described as "demons," were implanted in the spiritual chamber (being spiritual beings) on planet earth. The earth is the special creation of God which He intended should be inhabited by the special creation of man, created in the image of God, in both the spiritual and material sense. Of course, once the fall of man was accomplished through the seduction of Satan, then he had planet earth under control because the conduit between the spiritual and material is complete.

STALEMATE BECAME CHECKMATE

There was now a state of stalemate between Satan and God because the existence of the physical creation was in covenant with God, and God could not and would not break His promise given in truth. God intervened with a new decree that would redeem both creation itself and His people from the prison of death created by the sin that violated the covenant with God. He did this by setting an inimical division *Between you [Satan] and the woman, and between your [Satan's] seed [of succeeding generations in human reproduction] and her Seed; He [singular Christ] shall bruise your [Satan] head, and you [Satan] shall bruise His [Christ] heel [at the cross of Calvary]* (Gen. 3:15). So, in the fullness of time, the Lord Jesus Christ would have His victory, and the "Covenant of Creation" would be preserved according to truth, as the "Covenant of Redemption" intervened according to the predestinating will of God.

So, when Jesus ...*saw Satan fall like lightning from heaven* (Luke 10:18), Satan is being expelled from heaven itself, which he sought to occupy both during the Old Testament period, before the accomplishments of Christ's redemptive work in His flesh, and to some degree during the New Testament period, as the kingdom of God was yet to find its zenith. Chapter 12 discloses a titanic contest and ...*the dragon stood before the woman who was ready to give birth, to devour her Child as soon as it was born.* This contest begins, of course, with "the incarnation" of the Son of man, *the firstborn among many brethren* (Rom. 8:29), at His most vulnerable as a baby in the care of His mother, the very mortal Mary, and her guardian and betrothed, Joseph (Matthew 1:18-25). By direct revelation, Joseph was warned to depart from Bethlehem to *flee to Egypt and stay there until I bring you word; for Herod will seek the young Child to destroy Him* (Matt. 2:13). Herod, knowing that he had been outfoxed by the wise men from the east, tried to destroy the Child by putting ...*to death all the male children who were in Bethlehem and in all its districts, from two years old and under according to the time which he had determined from the wise men* (Matt. 2:16).

In verse 5, the singular *He* of Genesis 3:15 now enters from eternity into time, through the conception of the Holy Spirit in Mary's womb (Matt. 1:18), with a material human body. This is the incarnation of Christ, who is fully man and fully God. This *He*, born of woman, lived under the law, was attested of God by miracles as being the Son of God, was declared by God the Father to be ...*My beloved Son in whom I am well pleased* (Matt. 3:17), and was declared by John the Baptist to be *the Lamb of God who takes away the sin of the world* (John 1:29; 35). Jesus ...*was in all points tempted as we are, yet without sin* (Heb. 4:15). He suffered under Pontius Pilate, was crucified, dead and buried, being thus *bruised on the heel,* but on the third day He rose from the dead and gained the decisive victory by *bruising* Satan and his cohort fatally *on the head*, because God could not be held by death (Acts 2:23-24).

Even though *the great, fiery red dragon* stood before the simple, lowly-positioned woman in the person of Mary, the weakness of God is always more wise and powerful than the dark dominion of man and the sinister spirit that lies behind fallen man. Mary, the woman, *bore a male Child [that he might be the Firstborn among many brethren] who was to rule all nations with a rod of iron* (Rom. 8:29). This Child was born to rule the nations, and He would do so through the kingdom of God that would commence in a small way with the first advent of Christ, but which will encompass all the nations in fulfilment of such passages as Psalm 2:7-9:

> *I will declare the decree:*
> *The LORD has said to Me,*
> *"You are My Son,*
> *Today I have begotten You.*
> *Ask of Me, and I will give You*
> *The nations for Your inheritance,*
> *And the ends of the earth for Your possession.*
> *You shall break them with a rod of iron;*
> *You shall dash them to pieces like a potter's vessel."*

THE KINGDOM OF GOD COMES

Having fulfilled the terms of the "Covenant of Redemption" in His sacrifice as the Lamb of God, Jesus rose again so that He ascended on high to be seated at the right hand of the Father, establishing and extending the kingdom of God throughout all the ages of remaining history to the last Day. Thus, Mary's *child was caught up to God and his throne* (cf Luke 24:50-53), which was to the advantage of the second-born, the disciples of Jesus, for he said, *"If I do not go away the Helper will not come to you; but if I depart I will send Him to you. And when He has come, He will convict the world of sin, and of righteousness, and judgement... However, when He, the Spirit of truth, has come, He will guide you into all truth; for He will not speak on His own authority, but whatever He hears He will speak; and He will tell you things to come"* (Jn. 16:7-9; 13). The Lord Jesus Christ upon his ascended throne is not exercising His authority in absentia, but in the power of God the Holy Spirit, the Spirit of Truth. The Spirit of Christ is performing the work of Christ through His Church, the Bride of Christ that is bearing the child of the body of Christ throughout the generations of the Gospel age. As the kingdom of God is being extended from one generation to the next, so the territory of Satan is being lost as Christ is redeeming the full number of His elect, and all the earth will know the restoration of His power over all things that was usurped by the devil (cf. Rom. 8:19 – 21).

Let us consider verse 6. With the passing of the Apostolic Age at the destruction of Jerusalem and her Temple in A.D. 70, the complete Canon of Scripture was granted to the Church. The Apostolic Church advanced into the entire known world, both in the Jewish world and the Gentile nations, and even to the barbarian tribal nations. She planted the Church, described in our text as the woman regenerating and bearing her child. However, *the woman fled into the wilderness* as a diaspora was forced upon the Church by the persecution and tribulation that accompanied the work of fulfilling her commission. This was to the advantage of the Gospel, but those who persecuted the Church took centre place through political machinations in the church as *Antichrist*, in the political affairs of the nations, and the visible church. As the Apostle John says in his letters, *They went about from us, but they were not of us,* becoming "apostates" (1 John 2:19) and turning the politics of civil governance against the true Church.

The Church lives by faith in her Saviour, the Anointed One who rules the nations through the kingdom of God. The prophet Elijah of old pronounced the judgement of God on Israel, saying, *As the Lord God of Israel lives, before whom I stand, there will be no dew or rain these years except at my word* (1 Kings 17:1). God prepared a place for Elijah at *the Brook Cherith which flows into the*

Jordan where he drank the water that God provided, and the Lord commanded the ravens to feed him [Elijah] there. So, the history of the true Church militant is packed full to overflowing. There are libraries of biography that testify to the faithfulness of the living and true God in preserving the woman that bears her Child.

This wilderness place is found in all parts of the earth that have been under the blessing of God but have not thus far known the powers of the kingdom of God. But with the coming of the Gospel, God has prepared these wilderness places for the Church to be established so that the kingdom of God might grow into these places where the Church is planted.

THE TIME CUE OF "ONE THOUSAND TWO HUNDRED AND SIXTY DAYS"

Now there is a time cue that appears several times in these chapters: *one thousand two hundred and sixty days*. In chapter 11 verse 2, the converted Gentiles *tread the holy city underfoot for forty-two months*. When calculated in today's time, this is one thousand two hundred and sixty days. Power is given to the *two witnesses* to *prophesy one thousand two hundred and sixty days, clothed in sackcloth*. These are godly figures. Then in chapter 13 verse 5, the very opposite kind of figure appears. The same amount of time is given for this figure, who is in direct opposition to God. He is called a *beast rising out of the sea…(13:1) the dragon who gave authority to the beast; and they worshipped the beast, saying, "Who is like the beast? Who is able to make war with him?" …He was given authority to continue for forty-two months* (13:4-5). If we translate months into days, we will have *one thousand two hundred and sixty days*. If we now look at our text and try and apply a literal meaning to these numbers, we will make little sense of them. The important thing is that the marker in our text is found in verse 5 where ...*her [Mary's] child was caught up to God and His throne*, which can be interpreted only in terms of Christ's Ascension forty days after His resurrection. *One thousand two hundred and sixty days* calculates to 3.75 years, which has no significance in relation to that many days after Christ's Ascension.[13]

---

[13] Kenneth L Gentry, *He Shall Have Dominion, A Postmillennial Eschatology*, Apologetics Group Media, Draper, Virginia, 1997, p158ff. This is an extensive study of what is known as Preterism. 'The term Preterism derives from the Latin *Preteritus*, which means "go by, past." The Preterist sees certain prophetic passages as being already fulfilled. There is extensive discussion among American theologians that would teach that the Olivet Discourses of our Lord concerning the destruction of the Jerusalem Temple in A.D. 70 are entirely fulfilled. We discuss this kind of Preterism when I take up 'the soon' passages of this book in dealing with chapter 22 of Revelation. This is understood among American theologians as the 'partial Preterist' position. I have argued for a partial Preterist position in that it answers many questions in terms of 'the soon passages' that are found in the Gospels.

However, Gentry argues for a more extensive Preterist position but avoids what is known as a full 'hyper-Preterist' position among American theologians. He argues for the inclusion of almost all the book of Revelation as being fulfilled at the time of the destruction of the Jerusalem Temple in A.D. 70. But he does not include in this chapters 20-22, which would include the final resurrection on the last Day.

I would suggest that such a position is in fact a reconstructed hyper-Preterist position because nowhere in the book of Revelation is recorded the destruction of the Temple of Jerusalem except maybe a prophecy in chapter 1 verse 7 that could be a reference to the Olivet Discourse in Matthew 24: 30. Gentry makes an excellent case for the dating of the book of Revelation and places it just before A.D. 70. It is the persuasion of this writer that the book of Revelation is a word of prophecy throughout the Christian age of the Gospel and it is pertinent for every generation and every Christian that has ever lived during this age. If the book of Revelation is Preterist then it is history and not prophecy. It is merely written for the church living at best a few years and who lived through the horrors of the destruction of Jerusalem and its Temple in A.D. 70.

These passages that are before us cannot refer to a Preterist option because the context of this begins with Christ's ascension (v5) and 1260 days which is equal to 3.75 years is of no particular significance. If we try and force this

However, we can use an old method of interpreting these figures using day-year calculations, as the reformed theologians of the Protestant Reformation did. If we do this, with the benefit of hindsight, we have a long and extended period that would point in retrospect to significant events in history. If we employ this method, we see that *one thousand two hundred and sixty* years from the Ascension of Christ would bring us to a pre-Reformation point in history. In our Lord's Mount Olivet Discourse, recorded in all the Synoptic Gospels, He refers to His own mysterious appearance in the sky in *the clouds of heaven with power and great glory* (Matt. 24:30) in A.D. 70. This is also recorded by the Jewish historian Josephus. If we calculate *one thousand two hundred and sixty* years from this event, it would mean that the Church's wilderness existence would draw significantly to around A.D. 1293 or 1330, which is the date that the Lord sent a great plague called the 'Black Death' that wiped out half the population of Europe and western Asia. It would be safe to say that such a devastating physical judgement on the world indicates that there was a significant spiritual condition that required correction. In chapter 11, where the same time cue is used, we have two dramatic witnesses who boldly *prophesy one thousand two hundred and sixty days*. These are years, which we take as being "a vignette" or "a parabolic picture" of the powerful Gospel testimony of the Hebrew and Gentile Church of the Lord Jesus Christ. *These two olive trees and the two lampstands standing before the God of the earth* (11:3) powerfully and persistently preach and prophesy with great spiritual power and *devour their enemies, and if anyone wants to harm them he must be*

---

figure to 3 1/2 years before the destruction of Jerusalem in A.D. 70 and say that Christians fled to the safety of a prepared place outside Jerusalem, and if we are appealing to the historian Josephus, there is no such reference to interpret these days accordingly. It is trying to find far too much in the Jewish historian to fit this into a Preterist prophetic model. The time of the ascension to A.D. 70 is more like 35 to 38 years.

killed in this manner (11:5), not by the prophet or the Church, but providentially through the acts of God in natural disaster or war. In the old tradition of Elijah, God Himself providentially provides power to the prophets' testimony of the living and true God in the Scriptures. God uses the natural elements in drought, floods and plagues (11:6) to display *the wrath of God upon all ungodliness and unrighteousness of men who suppress the truth in unrighteousness* (Rom. 1:18).

In the spirit of Satan, *the beast that ascends out of the bottomless pit will make war* against these typical witnesses in a counter-attack against their testimony (11:7). The powerful and faithful testimony of God's witnesses throughout history has resulted in martyrdom, and *their bodies will lie in the street of the great city*. This is a reference to Jerusalem, over whom our Lord laments when He says she, *kills the prophets and crucifies them* (Matt. 23:30-36). This is the city *which spiritually is called Sodom and Egypt, where also our Lord was crucified* (11:8). Typically, the physical bodies of God's martyrs [witnesses] are desecrated, and the people of the world rejoice *because the preachers of truth and righteousness* are silenced and the people's conscience is no longer troubled. In the sovereignty of God Himself, He revives His testimony, resurrects His witnesses, and Biblically reforms His church.

In chapter 13 we also find the *one thousand two hundred and sixty* time cue applied where the Apostle John saw *a beast rising out of the sea* (13:1). The counter-attack of the *beast* is also sustained through the generations of the Gospel age, and in God's infinite wisdom *it was granted to him [the beast] to make war with the saints and to overcome them* (13: 7). This seems to be the state-of-play particularly during the Mediaeval period. If we examine Church history throughout the Gospel age, there is a kind of wilderness experience that the Church is going through described by the Apostle John in chapter 7 of Revelation as the *Great Tribulation* (7:14). The consequences of preaching the Gospel are always persecution and tribulation for the faithful witnesses of Christ the King.

We have argued that the great tribulation is not confined to seven years or a 3.5-year period before the second coming of Christ and a rapture before a millennium, but is in fact the state of play throughout the Gospel age. However, this will come to an end with ...*an angel coming down from heaven, having the key to the bottomless pit and a chain in his hand. He laid hold of the dragon, that serpent of old, who is the Devil and Satan, and bound him for a thousand years; and he cast him into the bottomless pit, and shut him up, and set a seal on him, so that he should deceive the nations no more till the thousand years were finished* (20:1-3). So, the church should not lose her nerve when she sees the institutional bodies of Antichrist, *the beast* – who may even bear the name of "church"—overcome the saints (13:7). The loving-kindness and patient faith of the saints is always purified in these great tests when they are overwhelmed by opposition to the true Church of the Lord Jesus Christ. It may seem interminable, and we may be overwhelmed for an extended period, but in the fullness of time, our sovereign King and Head of the Church will give strength and power and will always sustain His witness.

WAR BROKE OUT IN HEAVEN BETWEEN THE ARCHANGEL MICHAEL AND THE DRAGON

Verses 7-8 say, *And war broke out in heaven...* This is a war in the unseen spiritual realms of heaven occupied by the spirits of angels and the demonic powers of darkness (Eph. 6:12). The conjunction *And* indicates that this particular war existed in that period that is nominated by *one thousand two hundred and sixty* days. We have established that this is the period that we call pre-Reformation history. This period is often called the "Dark Ages" or the

"Mediaeval Age." We know that whatever happens in heaven has its effects on earth, and if there was a war that broke out in heaven, then there was a period of darkness on earth in spiritual terms. This would explain this period of history during which the earthly institutionalised *'beast'* described in chapter 13 of Revelation opened his *mouth in blasphemy against God, to blaspheme His name, His tabernacle and those who dwell in heaven* (13:6). This continued for these *forty-two months* (13:5), which translates into *one thousand two hundred and sixty day (years)*.

This war in heavenly places was a contest between the heavenly hosts of light and darkness. There was no human involvement in this war. Indeed, we are given the personalities that are at war. *Michael and his angels fought with the dragon; and the dragon and his angels fought.* The mysterious dimension of the spiritual world that exists separate to the material universe, and yet is interlocked with it, is difficult for us to comprehend. The truth of this spiritual dimension is set in our consciousness and explained according to truth in the Scriptures. I suspect that there are things too magnificent and too glorious for us to know, and that there are probably deep, dark mysteries of Sheol and hell that we would be wise not to know about. The dark arts of sorcery and demonology are everywhere seen in pagan cultures and wherever the spirit of God's grace establishes the kingdom of God, these dark and sinister worlds are exposed in truly horrible realities.

The scriptures consistently reveal the archangel Michael as being of great assistance to the saints at various points in history. For example, the prophet Daniel was in the state of mourning for three full weeks in the spirit of prayer, and after that time his eyes were opened to a mysterious figure coming toward him. There is no doubt that this was a theophany of Christ in his pre-incarnate existence. He said to Daniel *"...do not fear, Daniel, for from the first day that you set your heart to understand, and to humble yourself before your God, your words were heard; and I have come because of your words. But the prince of the kingdom of Persia withstood me twenty-one days; and behold, Michael, one of the chief princes, came to help me for I had been left alone there with the kings of Persia. Now I have come to make you understand what will happen to your people in the latter days, for the vision refers to many days yet to come"* (Dan. 10:12-14). As the Apostle Paul says ...*We do not wrestle against flesh and blood, but against principalities, against powers, against the rulers of the darkness of this age, against spiritual hosts of wickedness in the heavenly places* (Eph. 6:12). The spiritual world is a world of personalities that are vying for power, and in the days of the Old Testament personality Daniel, these powers were waiting for liberation so that even the pre-incarnate Christ was delayed in His coming in answer to the prayers of Daniel the prophet. The cosmology of the New Testament has dramatically changed with the completed work of the Lord Jesus Christ in redemption and the sending forth of God the Holy Spirit, who applies the redemption of Christ in the salvation of God's people and extends the kingdom of God progressively throughout history.

The archangel Michael also took an active role in protecting the body of Moses from desecration by the devil when Moses passed away in the wilderness. Michael was God's advocate against the devil so that he could not make *reviling accusation,* against Moses, but Michael said, *The Lord rebuke you!* (Jude 9) It seems extraordinary that this malignant personality, the devil, who seduced one-third (12:4) of the angels of heaven into rebellion against God, would have any place in heaven at all. In the trial of Job, we find Satan the accuser, when there was ...*a day* [presumably the day set by God for worship] *when the sons of God* [those that are in Christ through the grace of salvation] *came to present themselves before the Lord, and Satan also came along with them* (Job 1:6). The whole book of Job is predicated on this accusation of Satan, and establishes Job as being *blameless and upright, and one who feared God and shunned evil* (Job 1:1). Job's getting of wisdom that puts God first in everything was vindicated and established beyond any reasonable doubt, but why was Satan allowed to raise such questions against the children of God? Why, when Satan rebelled against God, was he not banished immediately, as man was from the Garden of Eden? The answer, of course, is in the infinite wisdom of God. But there is a reality in the universe of the spiritual and material, the spiritual of infinite proportions, and the material of finite matter. The planet earth is in a Covenant with God that is impossible for God to break. God Himself unilaterally established the "Covenant of Creation" (Gen. 1-3). God purposes to work out the redemption of His covenants in the process of time, and time is in the hands of God.

This particular war that broke out in heaven, and that was sustained nominally for *one thousand two hundred and sixty days* (years), saw the prevailing hand of Michael and his angels over the dragon and his angels, because the satanic spirit of darkness did not prevail between these spiritual Titans. Hence, a certain peace broke out on earth because these 'foul fiends' were being defeated. However, the most important thing to see in this text is not in the words *...nor was a place found for them in heaven any longer* (12:8). It seems that the very cosmology of heaven is forever changed at the end of this war of *one thousand two hundred and sixty days* (years). Satan is further banished from heaven and confined to earth and that place described as *the bottomless pit*, (11:7) as there was *no place found* for these foul fiends *in heaven any longer*.

Verse 9 tells us *...that great dragon was cast out, the serpent of old, called the devil and Satan...* This was not some strategic victory for Michael the archangel and his angels, but was an everlasting cosmic victory in which the great dragon, the devil and Satan, was banished forever out of heaven. This was not merely a strategic advantage but was a complete victory and a cleansing of Satan from a place in the spiritual world called heaven so that he no longer accompanies the angels of light or the sons of God. Yes, Satan is still *the prince of the power of the air*, but he has no place in the domain of light or heaven. Satan with his demons continues to *deceive the whole world* as *the prince of the power of the air*, but his accusations and deceiving practices are confined to earth, as it says, *...he was cast to the earth, and his angels [demons] were cast with him*. The dominion of Satan is further shrunk and his world is becoming more dungeon-like as the kingdom of God advances.

In **verse 10**, this significant victory is lauded in heaven with *...a loud voice saying in heaven, "Now salvation, and strength, and the kingdom of our God, and the power of His Christ have come, for the accuser of the brethren, who accused them before our God day and night, has been cast down."* The heavenly host *says* this without singing, because angelic beings do not sing in Scripture. Observing the events of history as the kingdom of God extends, they see what our finite mortality does not normally see: that heaven is now cleansed of the devil and demons. This is accomplished somewhere in New Testament history, and from our perspective significantly before the outbreak of revival in the Protestant Reformation.

Satan is described as *...the accuser of the brethren, who accused them before our God day and night*. It seems that the frailties of the brethren who sin often brought them into condemnation by their accuser Satan because they fell short of the standard of God's word. This does not mean perfection, as none are perfect except God, but is a falling short of the standards of Biblical faith which is the mark of saving faith in God. The accusations, though made against the brethren, were in fact against God Himself, which gave an advantage in terms of truth to Satan. This constant barking of *the dog that returns to his own vomit* at the heels of the living and true God concerning the brethren whom Christ died for was patiently taken into account, but God the Holy Spirit and Christ the Intercessor at the right hand of God constantly bring the prayers for the saints before the Father, pleading the cause of the brethren (Rom. 8:26-27).

So Satan the accuser of the brethren has no audience in heaven but *has been cast down* and the strategic position that Satan once exploited is held by him no longer. Even though accusations from the pit are made against the saints, he cannot do it from heaven any longer as he *has been cast down*.

In **verses 11-12**, the *loud voice…in heaven* continues by *saying, "And they overcame him by the blood of the Lamb and by the word of their testimony and they did not love their lives to the death."* The accusations of the devil are increasingly and consistently answered by the growing ability of the true Church to grow in the knowledge and grace of the Gospel as the church learns the full breadth of the great salvation that they have in Christ. The Church wrestled with the doctrine of the Trinity, for example, and became settled in their orthodox Biblical understanding that, "There are three persons in the Godhead; the Father, the Son, and the Holy Spirit; and these three are one God, the same in substance, equal in power and glory."[14] As the church grew in the knowledge of their faith and more consistently defined *the faith once delivered unto the saints*, the Church was able to walk in a more orderly and precise Biblical fashion. In this way, they overcame their accuser by the Gospel

---

[14] Westminster Shorter Catechism, Q/A 6

alone, which is *by the blood of the lamb* and by living consistently in this glorious testimony of Christ's redemptive work. Throughout the history of the Church, the challenges of Satan and the heresies that could be levelled against the Church were understood and her testimony refined. Any good book on Historical Theology[15] will outline the growing theological awareness of the Church throughout all the ages. In this regard, it would seem that there was a landmark point in history at the end of *one thousand two hundred and sixty days* (years) that was to herald in a new phase of the progressive growth in the kingdom of God that would open with the fourteenth and fifteenth-century Protestant Reformation. However, throughout the Gospel age—and particularly during this period of *one thousand two hundred and sixty days* (years)—*they did not love their lives to the death* (12:11). Martyrdom was a particular feature in the early history of the church under Emperor Nero and Domitian, but "the blood of the martyrs was the seed of the Church" and they were sustained through these dreadful atrocities that were committed against the body of Christ. The persecution was largely from outside the Church up until the days of the Roman Emperor Constantine, during his reign, it became politically acceptable to be a Christian, and this caused the planting of the seeds of the institutionalised *Antichrist* type of *beast* as the Christian *harlot* began to ride her political *beast*. By the time of the seventh century, when this *beast* that bears the mark 666 had risen *out of the sea* (13:1) of paganism, (13:18) the Church itself had become the persecutor of the Church that was *in the wilderness* (12:6).

THE DRAGON WAS CAST TO THE EARTH

The "Church triumphant" that gathers in heaven with the Lord Jesus Christ rejoices greatly because *the dragon was cast to the*

---

[15] William Cunningham, *Historical Theology*, A Review Of The Principle Doctrinally Discussions, In The Christian Church Since, The Apostolic Age, Banner Of Truth Trust, 1960, Vols I and II.

earth, and his angels were cast out with him (12:9), which gives them great cause to rejoice. However, the heavenly voice goes on to say, *"Woe to the inhabitants of the earth and the sea! For the devil has come down to you, having great wrath, because he knows that he has a short time."* Satan's focus is now exclusively upon *the earth* and his fury will be unabated against *the woman* who is the 'Church Militant', namely the true Church in the wilderness. If the severe tribulation of the saints occurred in that era of *one thousand two hundred and sixty days* (years), then a greater tribulation will now arise, particularly for *the woman*, with what the Apostle Paul calls *the mystery of lawlessness* (2 Thess. 2:7) that is already at work. All inhabitants of planet earth are affected, as the nations will be deceived by his dark arts, so the constant and active providence of God will impose *restraint* (2 Thess. 2:7). This *restraint* will come in the form of natural disaster, economic hardship and war.

For the devil has come down to you, having great wrath, because he knows that he has a short time. From our end of history, we may view this "short time" as a long time, but even in that long time, the devil's chain is being shortened as the kingdom of God advances. We have advanced the thesis that in general terms the existing tenure of Satan has been some four millennia, from the fall of man (and some would suggest a lot longer) to the coming of the Redeemer, Jesus Christ. We are sitting at the end of two millennia since the First Advent of Christ, and the text that we are studying sets itself at *one thousand two hundred and sixty days* (years) at least after Christ's Ascension. During these two millennia, ethnic Israel in her unbelief has been without a king. Hosea the prophet predicts that *after two days He* [the Lord of Israel] *will revive us* [Israel] (Hosea 6:2). The Apostle Peter asserts *that with the Lord, one day is as a thousand years, and a thousand years as one day* (2 Pet. 3: 8), which means that this prophecy is speaking of two millennia in which the ethnic Israel spoken of by the Apostle Paul in Romans 11:12 has been without a King. Hosea, however, does not leave us there because he goes on to say, *After two days He will revive us; on the third day He will raise us up that we may live in His sight* (Hosea 6:3). It would seem that there is a third day yet to come that would represent a third millennium, because the Apostle Paul in Romans 11:15 says, *For if there being cast away is the reconciling of the world, what will their acceptance be but life from the dead?* This third millennium is a time when Satan will be banished entirely, because *...the dragon, the serpent of old who is the Devil* was bound *for a thousand years; and He cast him into the bottomless pit, and shut him up, and set a seal on him, so that he should deceive the nations no more till the thousand years were finished* (20:2-3). It is in this millennium that we expect to see that the saints or *priests of God and of Christ, ... shall reign with him a thousand years* (20:6). So, in terms of Satan's longevity of dominion, he is looking down the barrel of oblivion from where we stand in history, and even at the end of 1260 years, he has only something like 700 years. If we calculate the time from the beginning of the history of man, during which Satan has ruled with brutality across the nations, as being 6,000 years, then for him, 700 years is a very *short time*.

THE CHURCH IN THE WILDERNESS – HER TRIED AND TRUE TESTIMONY

Verse 13: *Now when the dragon saw that he had been cast to the earth, he persecuted the woman who gave birth to the male Child.* The vehemence of Satan's persecution will be more concentrated upon the Church as she regenerates the body of Christ with the whole number of the elect of God, from local to national Churches, and from one generation to the next, until the end of the Gospel age at the second coming of Christ the King. The true Church of God consists of the children of Abraham throughout all the ages and will be numbered as the sand of the seashore or as the stars of heaven.

But in terms of the number on earth at any one time, there is a significant disparity in numbers between the children of this world and the children of God. Never in history in any nation has there been a majority of truly born-again disciples of Christ. The powerful witness of these born-again Christians has always been more powerful and more influential than their numbers would suggest. In my own nation of Australia, it would probably be optimistic to say that 1% of the population were genuine born-again Christians. The figure is probably closer to 0.1%, and perhaps even fewer. We are living in what could be described as a country that has known great Christian blessing and would be regarded as a Christian nation when compared with say, India. However, the Christian influence at a national level has been systematically minimised so that any Biblical witness is silenced and driven into the wilderness. This has been achieved, not through direct persecution of Christians or blood in the streets or the torture chamber of Inquisition as it was in the pre-Reformation, Reformation and Counter-Reformation years, but by a systematic dismantling of Christian institutions and Biblical law in the affairs of society and state.

The Christian testimony in Australia has been systematically dismantled by European migration from Roman Catholic countries so that today Australia is dominated by Roman Catholicism. The Protestant churches in the mainline denominations within one generation saw the Bible ripped out of the heart of these churches by German higher critical liberalism and Darwinian atheism. By the 1960s, there was hardly a single mainline Protestant church of any colour that had not completely capitulated to theological liberalism. In the 1970s, the Church witnessed the rise and rise of the Charismatic and Pentecostal phenomena of pragmatic existential worship that mocked Biblical Christianity and shook the traditional Church that had already lost the Bible. They therefore had no incentive to maintain any Biblical traditions, and eliminate church from the Church.

In the secular state, the laws and government were surrendered to secular humanist principles of man-centred socialist statecraft. The social proprieties of society have witnessed an extraordinary deterioration from Biblical standards of behaviour. Marriage and family laws, especially those concerning divorce, were the first to be undermined, and the family has become nothing more than a social convenience that can be jettisoned when it becomes an inconvenience. With the communication revolution and the internet, pornography became so easily accessible that it was almost impossible to regulate any form of media. The media became a self-regulated propaganda machine against Christianity.

Abortion laws have been so liberalised that we now have abortion on demand, and in some states abortion may be performed up until birth. Society has been turned on its head through "the women's liberation movement" that was triggered by the indiscriminate use of contraception, which has led to declining birth rates. This in turn has led to multiculturalism, the effect of which has been to obliterate any Christian body politic and the successful undermining of Protestant Christianity. The two-income family has become a financial necessity to meet escalating living costs and to cater to covetous lifestyles.

In the area of law, the honoured tradition of "law that is above the law"—i.e., regulation by Biblical norms—was undermined at the High Court level. Public opinion has replaced the objective nature of the law as revealed in the Scriptures, which was the basis of the law as adopted by the Magna Carta principle of "Lex Rex" (the law is king). The socialist body politic which says, "We know what is best for you!" is now the king.

BORN ON EAGLES' WINGS

In **verse 14** we read, *But the woman was given two wings of a great eagle, that she might fly into the wilderness to her place...* The woman, being the true Church of the Lord Jesus Christ, is mobile and always on the move as pilgrims and strangers in the land. She has been *given wings of a great eagle*, even as the children of Israel were when they were redeemed from Egypt, the house of bondage. With an outstretched hand God delivered them, who witnessed great miracles in the plagues of Egypt. He carried them through the Red Sea that parted in front of them; He protected them by the pillar of fire that was their rear-guard and guided them by a pillar of cloud. It was said concerning the children of Israel, *You have seen what I did to the Egyptians, and how I bore you on eagles' wings and brought you to Myself* (Exo. 19:4). Jn. 3:7-8 says this of all those that are born-again of the Spirit: as *...the wind blows were it wishes, and you hear the sound of it, but cannot tell where it comes from and where it goes, so is everyone who is born of the Spirit.* The people of Israel were led into the wilderness, where God provided manna from heaven for food, and established a Rock that provided water for drinking. Their clothes did not wear out. The cloud governed them and protected them from the severe heat in the wilderness, and the pillar of fire kept them warm in the below-freezing cold at night. They were thus fully provided for, and they bore great testimony to the all-sufficient God that had redeemed His people from the house of bondage.

Furthermore, they were delivered in battle. Even though they were outgunned and extremely vulnerable with their women and children, they were delivered militarily and saved miraculously so that the nations dared not harm this people of the living and true God of Israel. This has always been the experience of the true Church of God as she lives by faith in her Saviour and Lord, which is still her wilderness place for life and witness.

We are then given another curious time cue with the words, ... *where she is nourished for a time and times and half a time from the presence of the serpent*. If we may pick up where we left off at the previous time cue of "one thousand two hundred and sixty days" (years) and look at the prophecy of Hosea, we see that this Gospel age could be seen in terms of three millennia. The first two millennia see Israel without a King. This could also the period that occurs until *the times of the Gentiles are fulfilled* (Luke 21:24). The last millennium, which from our perspective is yet to come, begins with the Lord raising Israel again, so that there will be *life from the dead* (Rom. 11:15). This may be described as the days of the Jews, where Israel will be restored into the kingdom of God. This time cue of *time and times and half a time* is speaking about the same period of time, except using different words. It would fit in as follows: a *time* is a thousand years, *times* is a second thousand years, and *half a time* is half the two thousand years, which gives us the third millennium, which is the full millennial reign of Christ and His saints. If we regard chapter 12 as a vignette of the Gospel history of the Church pictured as the woman bearing her Child, then we have in perspective the whole Gospel age between the First and the Second Advents of Christ. The safety of the church is secure, spiritually if not physically. The serpent shall not touch the soul of the redeemed throughout the Gospel age. As the Lord Jesus says, *...I gave them eternal life, and they shall never perish; neither shall anyone snatch them out My hand...no one is able to snatch them out of My Father's hand* (John 10:28-29).

THE SHEER WEIGHT OF MORAL DEGRADATION

In **verse 15** we read, *So the serpent spewed water out of his mouth like a flood after the woman...* to overwhelm the Church, and so *the enemy comes in like a flood* (Isa. 59:19). Very often, it is not false teaching or heresy that is designed to split or fragmented the Church, but the sheer weight of moral degradation, such as pertained in the days of Lot (Gen. 19:1-11), who was overwhelmed by Sodom's homosexual depravity. The testimony of God's servants becomes overwhelmed by a torrent of moral degradation spewed out by Satan. This was the case with the faithful testimony of righteous Lot, who was oppressed by the filthy conduct of the wicked. 2 Peter 2:7-8 says of him, *for the righteous man, dwelling among them, tormented his righteous soul from day to day by seeing and hearing their lawless deeds*. The devil's purpose is to overwhelm the Church, so *that he might cause her to be carried away by the flood* of moral degradation. In our day, in western developed countries, heresy abounds, but the sheer weight of moral degradation is overwhelming and consuming.

However, verse 16 tells us that, at times like this, the natural processes of the created order self-correct such indecency and moral degeneration, as it were. We are told, *...the earth opened its mouth and swallowed up the flood which the dragon had spewed out of his mouth*. If a society drinks in the full implications of their sin and evil, that society will self-destruct. If the government of China implements a one-child policy and aborts every child that does not conform to government regulation, then parents choose to have a male child. As a result, whole towns and villages have no female children growing into the community, and those communities are deprived of the prospect of marriage. In a similar vein, if the creational ordinance of marriage is denigrated and de facto marriages are legitimised, then the security of family life for children is also denigrated, and the social implications are self-destructive. To go against the created order in moral terms is, in the end, self-destructive, and society itself degenerates. As the saying goes, "What goes around comes around," and eventually a corrupt society necessarily has to self-correct to some degree if it is going to survive.

THE DRAGON WAS ENRAGED WITH THE WOMAN MAKING WAR WITH HER OFFSPRING

Verse 17 Even the fall in creation itself testifies against Satan and the devil, which only further enrages the dragon with his insane obsession against *the woman* that continually regenerates and bears the body of Christ through the ministry of the Gospel. This war against the woman is relentless and continues throughout the Gospel age, while the complete body of Christ is testifying in each generation of the Church of Jesus Christ. Those that are regenerated are adopted as children of God, being justified by faith, live by faith and repent of their sin. They are then without any condemnation in Christ Jesus. They walk, not according to the flesh, but according to the Spirit, and by works of faith they progressively put to death their sin and live according to righteousness, so that they *keep the commandments of God and the testimony of Jesus Christ.*

Strategically, it is hard work for *the dragon* to make his enraged persecution against *the woman* who is the Church because she knows the strength of matured and tested faith and she will not be easily broken. So, the tendency is to not focus on the matured faith of the generation passing but to concentrate on *the offspring*, i.e., the future generation. The offspring are untested and easily rattled by heresy and the moral degradation in the world. Covenant children of Christian parents become the focus of the devil and his wiles. So, any Christian family and their attending Churches and schools will know that it is the practice of the devil *to make war with the rest of her offspring*. Satan's strategy is to single out the *little lambs* of God's flock, *the sheep of his pasture,* the very *offspring* of *the woman* for his special treatment.

The devil's strategy is to break the covenantal arrangements that God has provided within Christian families. God promises that the provisions that He has made in the 'Covenant of redemption' are not only for an individual bond between believers in the Lord Jesus Christ; this covenant is also a family Covenant, sealed in covenantal baptism that includes every member of the family, including the children and even adopted children that were *once far off* (Acts 2:38-39).

The devil arranges secular society—and sadly the Christian Church—to separate our Covenant children into schools that are dedicated to secular humanism, where those in authority attempt to stand in loco parentis, undermining the authority of the real parents, and before long we have walked into the devil's trap. Christian family values are surreptitiously undermined, godly discipline is ignored, parents become overwhelmed in trying to correct undisciplined behaviour at home, and any inconsistency at home is easily exploited in the mind of the child. If this still does not steal the hearts of our Covenant children, their peer groups will. Families begin to wake up to the fact that their teenage children are living in a completely different world and have given their hearts to a "love match" that has been dictated by the culture outside the Christian faith rather than governed by the counter-culture of the Christian faith.

If churches fail to disciple whole families, teaching them to honour the headship of husbands and preparing those husbands to teach their families in family worship and Christian instruction, then those Churches are sowing the seeds of destruction in the very families that attend. Children must be included across the full range of spiritual activities in family, Church, school and society. They must be taught to be appropriately engaged, practically and diligently, in all the covenantal graces set out in Scripture. Children should be given proper instruction, not only to make a "profession of faith," but also to be able to reproduce Covenant family life in their own marriages and to be priests of the living God in the world. We have more than adequate means of grace, and if we fail to use them, we do so at our peril. Any laxity that the devil can exploit, he will.

CHAPTER 5

THE RISE AND RISE OF THE BEAST - REVELATION 13.

We are challenged by the Apostle John at the end of this chapter, *Here is wisdom. Let him who has understanding calculate the number of the beast, for it is the number of a man: his number is 666* (13:18). Most of us will be confronted with, and to varying degrees influenced by, the popular evangelical culture in connection with this beast of the Apocalypse. Modern evangelicalism believes that we are living in the very last times of the last days, and if the surveys[16] on Christian belief are to be believed,

---

[16] *Newsweek*, November edition 1999, found as a result of a poll conducted in the United States that, "19% of Americans, and nearly half of all those who accept Biblical prophecy, believe that the Antichrist is on the earth now." The film media such as Hollywood has cashed in and crafted their own brand of eschatology that largely reflects Dispensational Premillennial eschatology. Films in this genre include *The Omen III: The Final Conflict* by 20th Century Fox, *End of Days* by Universal Studios and *The Prophecy* by Dimension Films as well as such productions as the X- Files by 20th Century Fox that states "...that the book of Revelation describes the end of the fiscal world in a battle between heaven and hell, good against evil and many of us believe that the time is upon us." Also, Tim La Haye's book, *Left Behind*, became a New York Times bestseller in 1999. The beast is depicted as a diabolical world dictator who establishes a New One World Order that controls society in absolute terms. The mark of this man is 666 which is imprinted with a credit card identity on the right-hand or a universal barcode imprinted on the forehead of every citizen or a retina scan that identifies the citizens of the beast. In the

there is consensus that the Antichrist, who is *the beast*, the very personification and incarnation of the man of evil, stands in the midst of us now, ready to be revealed, and a certain type of elite Christian stands poised to be 'raptured'.

We used to smile when we saw a sticker on the dashboard of the car warning the passengers that if they were not born-again Christians, they may suddenly find the driver raptured out of the vehicle and if so, the reader might find themselves in a severe accident. The call was that the passenger should not be "left behind," but become a born again Christian by praying the prayer inscribed below. This should be done immediately because you do *not know the time or the hour of the coming of Christ* when He raptures born-again Christians into the air with Christ (1 Thess. 4:17).

LIKELY CANDIDATES IN MODERN EVANGELICAL ESCHATOLOGY

Just who is this evil-incarnate reprobate, the great persecutor of God's people described as *...the man of sin...*(2 Thess. 2:3)*... the Antichrist...*(1 John 2:18)*...that Antichrist (who) is coming by which we know that it is the last hour...?* (1 John 2:18). Some of the candidates that have been put forward are certainly gruesome characters and could fit the bill. The hideously cruel and psychopathic Emperor Nero of Rome before the fall of Jerusalem in A.D. 70 was the prime candidate.[17] At the time of the Crusades, it was

---

computer age a computer chip is implanted that knows more about yourself than you do; upon which information Citizen X can trade.

[17] David Chilton, *Days of Vengeance, An Exposition of the Book of Revelation*, Dominion Press, Texas 1987, p 351, makes this comment: "It is significant that 'all the earliest Christian writers on the Apocalypse, from Irenaeus down to Victorinus of Pettau and Commodian in the fourth, and Andreas in the fifth, and St. Beatus in the eighth century, connect Nero, or some Roman emperor,

Mohammed. Then at the time of the Reformation, it was Pope Leo X or Pope Pius V with their seat at the *seven heads* that equalled the *seven mountain* city of Rome (13:1, 17:9). Napoleon Bonaparte was also a candidate as he was the first of three destroyers of Europe. Nostradamus called him an antichrist as he was born in Ajaccio, Corsica, and the cube root of 666 is a number that, if applied as mapping coordinates, is the location of the birthplace of Napoleon. At the time of the First World War, it was the German Kaiser, Wilhelm II, and at the time of the Second World War it was Adolf Hitler, the architect of the Third Reich, and Mussolini, the Italian military dictator whose seat was Rome. In popular American evangelicalism, Henry Kissinger, the head of Central Intelligence of America, was the *man of lawlessness*, the beast of Revelation. At one time it was thought that the president of "the evil empire" of the Soviet Union, Gorbachev with his birthmark on his forehead, that red Russian "bear from North," must surely be "the one." The conservative American President Ronald Reagan was another candidate, with six letters in each of his three names (Ronald Wilson Reagan, 666), and even Bill Gates is the suspected Antichrist, being the computer microchip man.

THE BEAST IS NOT A SINGLE PERSON BUT A SOCIO-POLITICAL INSTITUTIONAL POWER

The first thing that should be said about *the beast* of chapter 13 of Revelation is that this beast is not a single person but a figure in history, or more accurately an institutional movement of power

---

with the Apocalyptic Beast'. There should be no reasonable doubt about this identification. St. John was writing to first-century Christians, warning them of things that were "shortly" to take place. They were engaged in the most crucial battle of history, against the Dragon and the evil Empire which he possessed. The purpose of the Revelation was to comfort the Church with the assurance that God was in control, so that even the awesome might of the Dragon and the Beast would not stand before the armies of Jesus Christ."

and authority in history. It is what the Apostle Paul discloses to the Thessalonian Christians, before these apocalyptic visions to the Apostle John, as being *the mystery of lawlessness [that] is already at work* (2 Thess. 2:7). This institutional power will go through several manifestations and appear with different features. He will, as it were, arise *out of the sea* and will appear *like a leopard, his feet...like the feet of a bear, and his mouth like the mouth of a lion* (13:1-2). Later on he will arise *out of the land'* and will appear *like a lamb* with *two horns* (13:11). Both these figures are of the same beast-like stature and are therefore one. There is one spirit that gives authority and power to these beasts, the sinister spirit of *the dragon,* spoken of in chapter 12, that sets him against *the woman*, (12:4) and, in that great cosmic war in heavenly places, against the archangel Michael (12:7).

The beast appears *out of the sea* and *out of the earth* as a material institutional force but not an incarnate *man of lawlessness* (2 Thess. 2:3). It is an institution of political power and authority establishing the affairs of nations and national institutions that sets the will of fallen man and base spirits of lawlessness against the law of God.

THE SYMBIOTIC RELATIONSHIP BETWEEN SATAN AND MAN

This dragon or serpentine spirit of lawlessness comprises shared power with fallen man and Satan. Satan has spiritual power, being by nature of the spiritual, but with no legitimate authority outside himself. Man has legitimate authority, even as fallen man, for although diminished because of moral failure, he never lost his authority because the "Covenant of Creation" fundamentally binds God. Man therefore remains God's vice-regent of all the earth, but has lost power because of his spiritual loss in death.

So, in the temptations of our Lord Jesus Christ, for example, Satan seeks to do deals with the son of God. *If you are the Son of God, command that these stones become bread* (Matt. 4: 3). So, Satan is suggesting, "You need bread desperately now. Your solution is to use Your authority as a man, and even better as the Son of God in man's flesh, deriving authority from God as God's vice-regent, to feed Yourself to Your own satisfaction." Of course, any power to change stones into bread that is not from God is from Satan. To yield at this point would be accepting Satan's deal. "Take matters into Your own hands and be satisfied." Instead, Jesus replied, "The law of God says, *It is written, 'Man shall not live by bread alone, but by every word that proceeds from the mouth of God'*" (Matt. 4:4). Jesus's power and authority come from His Father. Jesus said in another place, *My food is to do the will of Him who sent me, and to finish His work* (John 4:34).

The other two temptations of Satan against the Lord Jesus are of the same character, but the scope is increased from the personal need for food, to achieving significance in the eyes of the children of God in the nation of Israel. Satan wanted Jesus to cast Himself from the pinnacle of the Temple so that the children of God would witness the body of Jesus being held up by the hands of the angels. Satan gained his limited hegemony, being *the prince of the power of the air* (Eph. 2:2) and certain limited authority over creation through the fall, as man is controlled by the spiritual powers of darkness. In this temptation, Satan proposes a deal that amounts to an enduring covenant with Jesus (being fully God), that the man Jesus be offered this lost ground back (to the Lord Jesus) that would otherwise require redemption. Jesus the man would join the ranks of man having dominion of all the earth according to the 'Covenant of Creation' granted by God, but under the spiritual power of Satan. But *the kingdoms of the world and their glory* (Matt. 4: 8) would be restored to their rightful king.

This was a real temptation with a real deal and rationally worth contemplation, as it was in the Garden of Eden when Adam was tempted indirectly through his wife Eve. This *mystery of lawlessness* is about shared power and authority. God does not and cannot share such authority. In the end, all authority has its source in God alone. There is only one God and one autonomous Being and there is only one universe. God is the only One that is worthy of worship. Jesus did not yield but said, *Away with you Satan! For it is written, "You shall worship the Lord your God, and Him only you shall serve"* (Matt. 4:10). Again, the answer against such a temptation is explicit obedience to the word of God, which is the authority of God in which we trust. The lawless insinuations of Satan can only be met with the law of God, the truth.

Satan is an eternal nocturnal spiritual being that needs a conduit for his power, so that he obtains real and legitimate authority between the spiritual and material. Man craves significance and well-being. Satan seeks to trade so that he can conquer and have dominion over what is God's. Fallen man seeks the advantage of lost ground in his spiritual banishment and limited material autonomy. This crossover from the lawless power of Satan and the legitimate authority of fallen man as God's vice-regent of all the earth gained a socio-political institution that is described here as *the beast*.

THE COSMOLOGY OF THE BEAST

This is a spiritual kingdom of darkness that has a material effect on the exploitation of all creation. The dark satanic powers have dominion on earth only through the vice-regency of fallen man. Man is the vice-regent of God only while he is alive in the physical body, for it is only as he is in the body that he can exercise stewardship of all things under the "Covenant of Creation." Once the eternal soul of man passes from this material existence into the eternal abyss, then the vice-regency of man ceases. Due to man's mortality, Satan requires a kind of tradition of exploitation that always existed from the days of Adam and Eve, continuing through the genealogies of the *daughters of men* in Cain's line. Cain himself *built a city* and attempted to vest an eternal interest in it by naming that city *after his son's name Enoch*, (Gen. 4:17). These daughters of men were great herdsmen, (Gen. 4:20) makers of music, (Gen. 4:21) outstanding craftsmen in bronze and iron (Gen. 4:22), being self-made men. So, one generation invested forward in the next generation, which built the dynasties of man that engineered the socio-political institution which we could call *the beast*. However, the coherent spirit of this beastly socio-political institution was the devil, the great dragon.

Beyond Noah's flood, man sought to *make a name for himself* (Gen. 11:4) and *the sons of men* built a city with a tower called Babel in its midst that reached into heaven, to God-proof themselves against the absolute sovereignty of God. God confounded their single language and they started to speak with many tongues. This prompted the great diaspora into all the ends of the earth (Gen. 11:4), and the dynasties of man civilised and coalesced into the great empires of ancient history.

These ancient empires were not only socio-political entities; they were also given coherence by their systems of belief that were the direct conduit to their father Satan and the demonic world. These practices of worship provided a kind of galvanised continuity from one generation to the next, being their religious foundation. What a man believes is the most powerful instrument in what he does. Man's religion is the matrix of his conscience, the culture of his life, and establishes his significance and place in society. If that is not properly settled, even in a man-centred way, then there cannot be faith, even if it is in himself. He must be able to justify himself when his conscience is accused. Satan is a master in inventing religion.

THE CRUMBLING FOUNDATIONS OF THE BEAST

The ancient empires were subject to a decline in the civilising effect that was possible through their exploitation of the "Covenant of Creation." During these days, this movement downwards was a corruption, an enveloping death, which led to a kind of travail across the society of man and creation itself. Creation was winding down because the power of lawlessness was exploiting the corrupt stewardship of God's law in creation. Nonetheless, God *restrains* (2 Thess. 2:7) this *bondage and corruption* (Rom. 8:21) by using the natural order of events and general care of creation in His "common grace," even using natural disaster and war in this process of God's providential governance. In the Old Testament, the 'Covenant of Redemption' instilled the *earnest expectation*, as stated by the Apostle Paul: *For we know that the whole creation groans and labours with birth pangs together until now…Even we ourselves groan within ourselves, earnestly waiting for the adoption, the redemption of our body* (Rom. 8:22-23).

However, the "Covenant of Redemption" has been consummated in our Lord Jesus Christ's work to fulfil the requirements of this redemptive Covenant. The kingdom of God is in direct opposition to the beast of the *mystery of lawlessness*, *For the earnest expectation of the creation eagerly waits for the revealing of the sons of God. For the creation was subjected to futility, not willingly, but because of Him who subjected it in hope; because the creation itself also will be delivered from the bondage of corruption into the glorious liberty of the children of God* (Rom. 8:19-21). Starting at the point of the "Covenant of Redemption," which had been consummated in the Lord Jesus Christ, the power of God's light now dispels the power of darkness under the brutal reign of Satan. The redeemed children of God become redeemed vice-regents that progressively sanctify themselves, and the world with which they have to do. The spiritual kingdom of God through the instrumentality of the redeemed vice-regents have a material effect in God's world, and the resources of God's world are now held in trust and the stewardship of this trust is for the glory of God. The redeemed children of God are citizens of the kingdom of God, and His kingdom arises out of small beginnings and grows into *a great mountain* that will, in the fullness of time, *fill the whole earth* (Dan. 2:35).

THE BEAST'S REVIVAL

The socio-political institution of *the beast* refocuses on this backdrop of a radically changed cosmology. There is a sense in which the beast receives new life because there is more to exploit. This *mystery of lawlessness* still has his unredeemed vice-regents who are still linked to the "Covenant of Creation." As the knowledge of the Lord is released—as the redeemed of the Lord receive a kind of inspiration of wisdom–the resources of the earth inevitably are utilised according to God's law both in general revelation (the truth that exists in all creation) and special revelation (the truth verbally stated that becomes a key to all knowledge). When this knowledge is used, it can be used according to the stewardship of God's wisdom that will bring *glorious liberty* (Rom. 8:21) in like kind that is already enjoyed by every redeemed child of God. Such knowledge can also be used for the purpose of *the beast*. He uses the advances in knowledge to build his own Babylonian empire that is not always bad, but never gives glory to God. *The beast* is about managing the lawless socio-political institutional power that is directly set against the law of God.

So, the history of *the beast* as recorded in chapter 13 of Revelation is set against this theological backdrop and history of God's providence.

THE IDENTITY OF *THE BEAST*

Let us consider verses 1-3 of Revelation 13. We have seen that this *beast* is not an individual but a socio-political institution that gathers to itself people into a socio-political identity that is rooted in a geographical area and identified as a cultural and linguistic entity under national and imperial political authority. However, ... *the dragon gave him [the beast] his power, his throne, and great authority*. There are only two kinds of people on planet earth: the *daughters of man* and the *sons of God*. This is evident only in an individual's faith. He either serves Satan his father, or serves the living and true God in the Lord Jesus Christ.

The Apostle John *stood on the sand of the sea...* within his penal settlement on the Isle of Patmos (1:9) and he saw a fresh vision of *a beast rising up out of the sea...* This beast is identified as the one whom God gave *authority over every tribe, tongue, and nation* (13:7). The text continues: *All who dwell on the earth will worship him, whose names have not been written in the Book of Life of the Lamb slain from the foundation of the earth* (13:8). This suggests that this socio-political institution is global and arises out of the nations and empires of the world. It is, as it were, rising out of the sea of the cacophony of paganism, the vast ocean of the peoples of this world. This rising of the beast is an event that can be tracked from the *last days* of the Old Testament, concluding with the Apostolic Age and marked by the destruction of the Temple in A.D. 70. It is, as it were, a new beginning. Satan's house has to be reshaped and his strategy has to take on new dimensions with his institutional socio-political *beast* that will be antichrist (1 John 2:18) and in direct opposition to what was discussed in chapter 12, to the woman bearing her Child, the Church being the Body of Christ.

The beast has *seven heads*[18] and refers to this *mystery of law-*

---

[18] Kenneth L Gentry, *The Beast of Revelation*, American Vision, Powder Springs, Georgia, 2002. Gentry makes the case for the Preterist interpretation of the book of Revelation where the entire message of Revelation, except for the general resurrection in chapter 20 and onwards, is entirely fulfilled before the close of prophecy that is symbolised in the destruction of the Temple and Jerusalem in A.D. 70. Driven by that interpretive perspective, the beast of chapter 13 is an individual, namely Caesar Nero A.D. 54-68., who was a brutal emperor living in Rome, the seven-mountain city that was seated on the seven heads of Rome in Revelation 17:7, 9. An identification is then made according to Revelation 17 of the seven Imperial Roman Emperors using the text ... *the beast that was, and is not, and yet is* (17:8). This text is combined with chapter 13:1 and the seven heads are interpreted as the seven Imperial Roman Emperors. There are five of the beast *that was*; Julius 49-44 BC, Augustus 31 BC-A.D. 14, Tiberius A.D. 14-37, Gaius A.D. 41-54 and Claudius A.D. 41-54. Then, from the Apostle John's perspective on the Isle of Patmos, comes *the one that is not*. As he stands on the seashore looking across the sea to Rome, a beast arises *out of the sea* which is the tyrant who claims to be deity, Nero A.D. 54-68, who would commit suicide on June 8, A.D. 68. The one that *yet is* was Galba A.D. 68-69 who ruled for only 6 months. This interpretation has many difficulties. Firstly, to equate the beast of chapter 13 with the woman and the beast of chapter 17:7-18 is a big assumption. Certainly, the same spirit is with both, being the spirit of the dragon. But we would assert that the beast of chapter 13 is what the Apostle Paul describes as *the mystery of lawlessness (which) is already at work* (2 Thess. 2:7). However, the beast of chapter 17 describes the prospective coming of ...*the man of sin (who) is revealed, the son of perdition*... (2 Thess. 2:3). This is *the Antichrist* (1 John 2:18) that is to be revealed after the millennium and just before the Second Advent of Christ. Secondly, John in his letters describes ...*many antichrists... [that]... went out from us, but they were not of us; for if they had been of us, they would have continued with us; but they went out that they might be made manifest...* (1 John 2:18-19). Nero was certainly an evil man of monumental proportions. However, he never belonged to the Christian Church nor was he part of any Christian community, so this disqualifies him from being Antichrist, for Antichrist took the place of Christ in the Church. Thirdly, in chapter 17:11, the beast is identified as being ...*the one that was, and is not ...himself also the eighth, and is of the seven, and is going to perdition*. Gentry's candidate in the words *and is not*, being the Roman Emperor Nero, sits at the sixth position not the seventh which is to come, which is also the eighth. On this account, even if we were to take the sequence of emperors as being the beast, Nero is not in step with this latter description and cannot be the beast spoken of in this portion of Scripture. Also, from the Apostle John's perspective, Nero who *was,*

lessness in antiquity, the ancient empires of man. These are more symbolic or representative rather than a comprehensive description of the dynasties and streams of civilisation from the days of the Tower of Babel to the coming of Christ. The *seven heads* are the Egyptian dynasty under the Pharaohs, and the Assyrian Empire; then the prophet Daniel speaks of four empires arising out of the streams of man-centred civilisation. The first was the Babylonian Empire that finally conquered Israel, during which Daniel found himself in the deportation of Israel to Babylon. The second was also witnessed by Daniel in his older age. This was the Medo-Persian Empire, being *the ram that has two horns* from Daniel 8:20, in which Cyrus was God's instrument in returning the Jewish exiles to Jerusalem and reintroducing Biblical worship by having the Temple rebuilt and Jerusalem re-fortified. Daniel spoke of another Greco-Macedonian Empire and predicted the rise of Alexander the Great, who conquered the world (Dan. 8:5, 21). This was also an end to Old Testament prophecy in the year 397 BC. The fourth empire that Daniel predicted was the Roman Empire, having *feet of iron and clay*, which is where our Lord Jesus Christ with the Apostolic Fathers ministered in the *latter time* (Dan. 8:19) or the *last days*.

Daniel spoke of the coming of the kingdom of God in Daniel 2:34-35 as being like *a stone that was cut out without hands, which struck the image* of the ancient empires *on its feet of iron and clay*, being the Roman Empire, and broke them in pieces. The

---

and is not is still very much an *is* in this cryptic clue. Fourthly, if the Antichrist is the Emperor Galba that reigned for only 6 months, he would have to have *no kingdom* to conform to the prophecy described in chapter 17 of Revelation. It says that *...the ten horns which you saw are ten kings who have received no kingdom as yet...* (17:12). These ten horns that are ten kings are spoken of in Ezekiel 38-39 in association with the battle of Gog and Magog that takes place after the millennium (20:7-10). For our explanation from a historicist postmillennial view, refer to the notes on chapter 17.

little *stone of the kingdom of God that struck the image became a great mountain and fills the whole earth*. These are six heads of the seven-headed beast.

The Apostle John in verse 2 draws our attention to a further description of this sixth beast that emerges out of the ancient world powers but points to the emergence of the seventh as *...a leopard, (whose) feet were like the feet of a bear, and his mouth like the mouth of the lion*. This beast was originally identified by the prophet Daniel in his vision of four beasts of Daniel chapter 7. From Daniel's perspective, these four beasts are of John's *seven heads*, but Daniel talks of just four. In Daniel's context, these empires were the Babylonian, Medo-Persian, Greek, and Roman. The last of these empires is described in very Romanesque terms as like *the leopard* of John's vision, which is further described as having feet like a bear and a mouth like a lion. However, Daniel speaks of the *mortal wound* and being *healed* in Revelation 13:3 using other words to describe the same thing. *There was another horn, a little one, coming up among them, before whom three of the first horns were plucked out by the roots. And there, in this horn, were eyes like the eyes of a man, and a mouth speaking blasphemous words* (Daniel 7:8). This Antichrist power is revived and is transformed into an ecclesiastical, socio-political institution having a new persona that fits a new era for deadly warfare against the saints of the Anointed One. Our purpose is not to fully expound Daniel's vision but to see that we are looking at the same beast and that the visions agree.

CONCEPTION OF THE HOLY ROMAN EMPIRE

The Apostle John in verse 3 of our text describes the seventh head. With the fall of Imperial Rome, there was the rise of the Roman-Byzantine Empire around its capital Constantinople. At the same time, another political-religious power, of an ecclesiastical kind, was being shaped. As the prophet Daniel indicates, this was ... *different from all the other beasts that were before it* (Dan. 7:7) and rides this beast. In fallen Rome, the seven-mountain city, the Holy Roman Empire was emerging with her preposterous Antichrist claim of apostolic succession from the Apostle Peter, being the Papal throne in Rome and *the harlot* of Revelation (17:3-4). The Apostle John said *I saw one of his heads, [being one of the seven heads], as if it had been mortally wounded, and his deadly wound was healed. And the entire world marvelled and followed the beast.*

The Roman Empire gave the Church a lot of advantages for the advancement of the Gospel and the extension of the kingdom of God, in that the entire Roman Empire gave access to the nations of the empire, indeed to the entire world. Christian preachers followed reasonably secure trade routes that gave them access to nations that otherwise would have been closed. Greek was a common language across the Roman Empire. However, Daniel the prophet saw that the Roman Empire, being the last of the old-world empires, would fall as the Gospel of Jesus Christ was preached across the nations of the entire world, and that the kingdom of God would take root. Simultaneously, the lawless socio-political institutions of the old world would come crashing down under the inherent weakness that was in the Roman Empire, being its Pagan religions. The beast would be Satan's answer to the kingdom of God. Imperial Rome fell in A.D. 476.

Caesar Constantine saw the potential collapse of the Roman Empire and moved its centre from Rome to Constantinople, which became "Christianised" and became the centre of learning and commerce from east to west. This lasted for a thousand years until it was sacked by the Mohammedans. The Byzantine Empire was focused on Europe that became influential in terms of culture, *having ten horns and on his horns ten crowns* (13:1). These ten horns that were wearing ten crowns were ten kingdoms that the Roman Empire subdued and Christianised. It should be underscored that the crowns are not on the seven heads, but the ten horns are on one head [Rome] and the ten crowns are on the ten horns. This indicates that there is a kind of imperial identity, which will be the Holy Roman Empire, being the seventh head, of this beast, who was *mortally wounded and his deadly wound was healed* (13:3). These ten nation-states were England (Britannia of Imperial Rome), France (Gaul of Imperial Rome), Germany (Saxony of Imperial Rome), Switzerland (Scandinavia of Imperial Rome), Portugal, Spain (Spain of Imperial Rome), Italy (the seat of Imperial Rome), Austria (eastern Saxony of Imperial Rome), central Europe (Greece and Macedonia of Imperial Rome) and Eastern Europe (Bohemia of Imperial Rome).

The true Church being *the salt of the earth* and *the light of the world* is secreted in this Christianised Babylonian socio-political institution the beast. Though they are kept small in number, *and "...for your sake we are killed all day long; we are accounted as sheep for the slaughter"* (Rom. 8:36), they are not to take up arms in revenge in the name of the Church for, *"Vengeance is mine, I will repay," says the Lord* (Rom. 12:19). Instead they are to be like Gideon's army, without the weapons of this world's warfare, but with the Lord on their side. The beast reorientates the advances of the kingdom against the law of God by exploiting the gains in Christian knowledge. He uses the raw power of the lawless underworld with the authentic authority of unconverted citizen vice-regents.

THE CONCEPTION OF THE HARLOT

As in the old-world empires, the cultural mortar of its society is its religion. Without this culture of religion, the citizens of the Babylonian beast have no inner sense of well-being and significance.

Also, the succeeding generations could not be secured through the mystery of religious observance. Unlike the animals, man must believe, and must worship a holy other. There also needs to be an essential cohesive moral order to maintain sound practice and personal and social discipline that will construct the humanist edifice. As it was, at the time of Babel, the city was built but its cohesion in the conscience of the Babylonian citizens was the religion, which was the seat of its culture. It built *a tower whose top is in the heavens* (Gen. 11:4), which was probably a temple-like structure. Yes, it was a man-made structure but it was based on a system of belief that gave them faith and hope with a system of behaviour among their fellow citizens, without which man cannot live. A religion was required in the beast, but it had to be credible in this new age of the kingdom of God, where the Gospel of Jesus Christ was thundering forth. This new religion of the beast would be Christianity in inoculated form; it gave just enough Christianity, but it would immunise against the real thing.

Heavy persecution was hurled against the Church that was in the wilderness (12:13-14), initially from the Jews before the destruction of Jerusalem and its Temple in A.D. 70. The destruction of Jerusalem gave some relief to the Church from persecution from the Jews. Then, for some 250 years, the brutal persecution from Imperial Rome was relentless. The saying was coined, "The blood of the martyrs is the seed of the Church," and by God's supernatural sustaining grace, the Church grew throughout the Roman world and beyond. Under Imperial Rome, from "the profligate and tyrant" Nero to Diocletian, when some of the heaviest and the most general persecution took place, *the gates of hell did not prevail* (Matt. 16:18). The Lord continued to build His Church and the kingdom of God was extended. Emperor Constantine was converted in AD 313 and Imperial Rome looked to the Church to provide religious cohesion.

It was at this point in history that the Church faced another great challenge. It was now socially acceptable to be a Christian. The challenges came from within the Church and were directed at the very faith of the Church where the false teachers came into the Church *dressed in sheep's clothing but inwardly were ravenous wolves* seeking to devour the flock of Jesus Christ. Heresies abounded but God raised great orthodox fathers of the faith, from Polycarp to Augustine of Hippo, and there was a separation within the professing Church. Some followed the various heresies of the day, whom the Apostle John describes thus: *They went out from us, but they were not of us; for if they had been of us, they would have continued with us; but they went out that they might be made manifest, that none of them were of us* (1 Jn. 2:19). These were in time the *many antichrists that have come* (1 Jn. 2:18). Such apostates did not go back into paganism for they *...were once enlightened, and have tasted the heavenly gift,...having become partakers of the Holy Spirit, and having tasted the good word of God and the powers of the age to come...and put him [Christ] to open shame* (Heb. 6:4-6). These were ashamed to participate in the discredited beggarly elements of paganism. Instead they formed a church that was Antichrist, the synagogue of Satan that was in the place of the true Church of God. They had learnt through observing the challenges of heresy over these years how they could come very close, without being a true disciple of Jesus Christ and incurring all that persecution. *These people draw near to Me with their mouth, And honour Me with their lips, But their heart is far from Me* (Matt. 15:8).

The mother Church would authenticate their faith. They would receive grace through the priestcraft of a sacramental system without the thunderings of the word of God that would have disturbed their conscience and ignited faith through a regenerated heart. In this way, orthodoxy can be endorsed but never obeyed. We can become masters and sovereign agents in this world, because the Church will look after us and grant us high positions after being educated in the best schools. Politically, this Church is on top of things and it is thoroughly organised so that true Biblical "narrowness" of law-abiding righteousness that gives no favour to man is expunged from our lives. Give me my last rites at death and let me die with the assurance of the Church. At least in this life I will have my portion. Anyway, who can be certain about things we have not seen? This sacerdotal Gospel that shifts its focus to the Church and away from the Lord Jesus Christ and what he has done in fulfilling the "Covenant of Redemption" is being inoculated with Christianity, so that you are immune to the real thing. This is the religion of the beast.

THE RISING OF THE BEAST

As spiritual authority evolved through a process of gradualism, Churches all over the Roman world deferred to Roman power because of its superior organisation and its ability to adjudicate to resolve disputes in the Church. The Roman Church had a reputation of orthodoxy, and when compared to other sources of authority, the kudos of having your case deliberated upon in Rome was most persuasive in the wilderness. The physical edifice gave great visual authentication to being the true Church. This church became an efficient hierarchy that served the common good. As its authority increased, so did its impatience with those who would criticise such authority. In the fullness of time, it turned into a persecuting institution of those who were of *the woman giving birth in the wilderness* (12:13-14). As in the days when the Lord Jesus was among us in the flesh, the socio-political religious institution of Judaism, the religious elite of the Pharisees and Sadducees enjoying the acclaim of Israel, became the Antichrist and even put the King of the Jews to death. This is what is described later on in the book of Revelation as *the harlot that rides the beast* (17:3).

The *blasphemous name on his forehead* is as stated in chapter 17 of Revelation, *Mystery, Babylon the great, the mother of harlots and the abomination of the earth*. This *mystery of lawlessness* is a man-centred Babylonian socio-political institution that is given authority by the harlot church, the church that claims to have direct apostolic succession from the Apostle Peter that excludes and is intolerant of all others that name Christ, and which inoculates her people with a sacerdotal gospel that requires human intermediaries to receive grace. This is a preposterous travesty of the truth. It is only the Roman Catholic Church with its succession of Popes throughout its history that could consistently fulfil this description.

We now turn to verses 3b-4. By the time the metamorphosis of the beast was complete, Imperial Rome had fallen and indiscriminate persecution of the visible Church was now moderated by the existence of the ecclesiastical religiopolitical Papal system that only gradually gained authority and could not be ecclesiastically autocratic until beyond A.D. 666. The ecclesiastical mission of the ten nations of European Imperial Rome was to build secure city-states with impressive city cathedrals and parish churches, thus slowly developing a Church-centred sacerdotal Gospel with an army of priests and nuns that served in hospitals, orphanages, schools and universities.

The socio-political civil powers developed the economy in commercial enterprises and trade between nations. The monarchs built city-states and established secure defences from a common purse for the mutual good of society that was vested in the state, which was a hierarchical body politic of king to citizen. Landowners could farm within the shadow of security in the fortified city and the artisan could work with effect and productivity, the scholar could teach the next generation, the scientists could discover new things so that society was regenerating and civilisation was advancing.

The ecclesiastical religiopolitical institution of the beast provided a catholicity across the nations so that the hearts of citizens throughout the nations were pastorally supervised through one Church, one faith and one baptism, which was marked sacramentally *on their right hand or on their foreheads* (13:16). The kings, being the ruler of the realm, entered into a strategic balance with other kings of the Holy Roman Empire, so that the defence of the realm could be secure and trade with other kingdoms could be undertaken with secure trade routes. The religious ecclesiastical beast was a kind of 'league of nations' where nations could build measured and increasing trust with other nations and prosperity could increase across the nations. Civilisation was dependent upon the getting of knowledge and wisdom that could be utilised so that *man could make a name for himself.* The exploitation of the new dynamic of the kingdom of God was essential for the Babylonian beast to rise and rise.

This new Babylonian beginning affected the common life of every citizen, and the old autocratic pagan empire structure was supplanted by the lively dynamic of a growing civilisation. This was not utopia but it was progress. *And the entire world marvelled and followed the beast.* What the devil could not secure from Christ, the son of God, during the forty days of temptation (Matt. 4:1-11), he did with the Babylonian beast. *All these things I will give to you if you will fall down and worship me,* the devil said to the ten kingdoms of Europe. So the ecclesiastical beast was secreted throughout the Holy Roman Empire, and *...they worshipped the dragon, who gave authority to the beast: and they worshipped the beast, saying, "Who is like the beast? Who is able to make war with him?"* However, the citizens of the kingdom of God, redeemed by the blood of the Lamb according to the "Covenant of Redemption," did not yield to such temptation but preferred instead to know the exile of wilderness wanderings as pilgrims and strangers in a world that was not worthy of them.

THE BEAST'S COMING OF AGE AT THE SYNOD OF WHITBY IN A.D. 666

Verses 5-6 tell us that the beast then came of age and reached his majority where the harlot that was riding the beast (17:3) reached a formal blasphemous point in history. A schism took place in the visible Church that would separate the harlot from *the woman* spoken of in chapter 12, which is a picture of the true Church as opposed to the harlot ...*whose mouth speaks great things and blasphemies*. The great things that this beastly harlot speaks are the orthodox doublespeak of Roman Catholic doctrine. It had learnt what was orthodox when compared to those holding to doctrinal error. She endorses the Ecumenical Creeds of the Apostles' Creed of Nicaea in A.D. 325, Nicene Creed of Constantinople in A.D. 381, and Athanasian Creed, and the Twenty-Eight Canons of Chalcedon in Constantinople A.D. 451. However, all the time she is developing a sacerdotal Gospel that is mediated by a priestly clergy through a developing sacramental system that is increasingly becoming the focus of the Christian Gospel rather than free grace in the Lord Jesus Christ. So, the Church is replacing the Saviour, which is Jesus Christ, who is *the only name given among men, by which we must be saved*, (Acts 4: 12) with a Church that will be the ark of salvation. This Church is in the place of Christ, Anti[in the place of]christ rather than Christ being the focus of our faith.

Coupled with this substitutionary Church was a substitution of the Gospel to replace the substitutionary atonement of Christ. There was a major controversy between the great Church father Augustine of Hippo and an Irish monk called Pelagius who lived in Rome. Pelagius emphasised man in salvation and taught that God gave every man the possibility of living a sinless life.

According to Pelagius, this possibility is God's gift, as a man does not have it of himself. But man does have a will to live such a life, and this will, is, part of man's being. For this is the way he was created. Thus, man has the power to lead a sinless life, which he also possesses. The reason man sins, according to this theology, is that he has an evil example to follow. Hence sin is not a human condition from which man must be set free, as it consists of separate sinful actions. Man by nature is good, and when he is born he has a clean slate. If he does sin, he does it because of weakness because he has yielded to frequent sinful examples. The pathway to a sinless life is given to us by God who has disclosed His law, and He has sent Christ to be our example. Baptism, as do the other sacraments, puts our shortcomings and failures behind us so that we are again free to do the good that God commands us to do.

Augustine of Hippo found this to be blasphemy because such doctrine contradicted both the teaching of Scripture and his own religious experience. Augustine reaffirmed the scriptural teaching that man was totally depraved and that that depravity was inherited from our first parents, Adam and Eve. Transgressions of the law are caused by the fall of man and his inability in "the bondage of the will." All men, without exception, are born with this sinful nature. It is only by God's sovereign grace that a man may be regenerated and begin to live by faith in the Lord Jesus Christ. This discloses his election *before the foundation of the world* (Eph. 1:5) for it is only through Jesus, *...the way, the truth, and the life. [For] no one comes to the Father except through* (Jn. 14:6) the *Lamb slain from the foundation of the world* (13:8). This justifies man by God's declaration of righteousness on the basis of Christ having fulfilled the 'Covenant of Redemption'. It is only then that man is given the power to deal with sin by dying to it and living by the righteousness of God alone, which is a free gift as *...it is God who works in you both to will and to do for His good pleasure* (Phil. 2:13). This grace of God is irresistible to those that are predestined to eternal life, but as a matter of consequence such grace is not given to the non-elect or the reprobate.

Augustine's teaching on sin and grace was endorsed at a Synod held in Carthage in 416 A.D. and this decision was confirmed by Pope Innocent I. A second Council, held two years later and endorsed by the then Pope Zosimus, reaffirmed the Church's orthodoxy in Augustine of Hippo. However, a century later in 529 A.D., at a Synod held in Orange, Gaul, where general acceptance of Augustine's Biblical teaching was stated, predestination to eternal death and the sovereign nature of God's grace was sidelined. A certain propensity to good works was proposed of which Augustine would not have approved. So, this semi-Pelagian position became the Roman Catholic position. The will of God in salvation was supplanted by the will of man.

With the beast's doctrine of the Church as the "ark of salvation" and with the substitutionary atonement being replaced with the Gospel of the free will of man, the platform was now set for the beast to enter his-her majority. The true wilderness Church had been sustained in the Roman colony of Britannia and the Gospel had taken root under Patrick of Ireland, the venerable Bede of Jarrow, and the Iona community in Scotland, and an ever-increasing number were converted from paganism. Gregory I, known as the Great, "who stands out as one of the chief architects of the papal system which has influenced so greatly the history of the world"[19] between 541-604 A.D., sent missionaries to Britain from Rome. A wedge was developing between the Evangelicals represented in the Iona Community established by teaching monks from Ireland in

---

[19] Renwick AM and Harman AM, *The Story of the Church*, 2nd and enlarged edition, IVP, Leicester, 1993, p64.

563 A.D.[20] and the politically astute Roman Church. "From around 600 A.D. onwards, only the Bishop of Rome was called Pope, which means 'Holy Father.' The first papal mission to Britain in 600 A.D., and following Austin of Rome, was then stoutly resisted by the Culdee or [Evangelical] British Celtic Christians [represented at Iona]. Only after the 664 Synod of Whitby, from about 666 A.D. onwards, did most of Europe and some of England (but not Ireland, Scotland and Wales) became increasingly Romanised. Thus during the days of the Italian Pope Vitalian (664-679 A.D.), the Romish papal power or 'horn' became strong or 'stout' and long sat and ruled in the Temple of God, while claiming to be [God's] spokesman. However, that spokesman was in fact [the?] Antichrist."[21] Martin Luther observes from his perspective during the Reformation that this beast that "arises out of the sea" would have the beastly manifestation until 666 years later, when the 1332 A.D. (666+666=1332) Black Plague occurred in judgement against this beast, where more than half of Europe and Asia was put to death. It was then only 32 years later that John Wycliffe of Oxford was raised as the morning star of the Protestant Reformation, and John Hus of Prague was burnt to death at the stake for his Evangelical Faith. In Hus's words, Hus is "a goose that is roasted today." As Hus roasted at the stake, he prophesied that "a swan" would arise in a hundred years.[22] Martin Luther was converted exactly one

---

[20] http://en.wikipedia.org/wiki/Iona_Abbey "In 563, Columba came to Iona from Ireland with twelve companions, and founded a monastery which grew to be an influential centre for the spread of Christianity among the Picts and Scots."

[21] Nigel Lee, *Notes Distributed on Teaching on the Downfall of the Papacy gleaned from Martin Luther and John Calvin*.

[22] *Foxe's Book of the Martyrs*, Chapter 8: "When the fagots were piled up to his very neck, the duke of Bavaria was so officious as to desire him to abjure. 'No,' (said Hus;) 'I never preached any doctrine of an evil tendency; and what I taught with my lips I now seal with my blood.' He then said to the executioner,

hundred years later and was "the swan" of the Reformation that thundered out at its official starting date when Luther posted his ninety-five theses on the church door at Wittenberg on All Saints day 1517 A.D.

As history moves forward, we noted in the previous chapter 12 that there was *a war [that] broke out in heaven: Michael and his angels fought with the dragon; and the dragon and his angels fought but they did not prevail, nor was a place found for them in heaven any longer. So the great dragon was cast out...* (12:7-8) We saw that this war in heaven in the spiritual world of *principalities and powers and might and dominion...*(Eph. 1:21) was waged for some *one thousand two hundred and sixty days* (years), and if we commence these years from the end of the apostolic age, being the end of the Old Testament dispensation from A.D. 70, then we establish a date at A.D. 1330, which is the year that the black plague struck Europe and western Asia. Satan is cast out of heaven to planet earth, then while he was able to roam heaven and reign on earth through the beast it says that *he [Satan] was given authority to continue for forty-two months* in a fairly unfettered manner (13:5). Of course, *forty-two months* agrees with *one thousand two hundred and sixty day*-year. This means that the disclosure about the woman, (being the Church of Jesus Christ, giving birth continually through the generations to the body of Christ, who is *in the wilderness*) and *the beast* (that is Antichrist because he takes the place of Christ of the true Church, *to blaspheme His name, His tabernacle and of those who dwell in heaven...to make war with the saints*) are set in parallel to each other to give a full revelation of both of these figures in history.

'You are now going to burn a goose, (Hus signifying goose in the Bohemian language:) but in a century you will have a swan which you can neither roast nor boil.' If he were prophetic, he must have meant Martin Luther, who shone about a hundred years after, and who had a swan for his arms."

Verses 7-9 reveal that even though the kingdom of God was relentlessly advancing and taking the ground of Satan, increasingly the power of the beast was *granted to him [Satan] to make war with the saints and to overcome them*. This is to say that the beast strategically realigns himself within a Christian persona by taking centre stage in matters of religion, becoming the representative head of the Church, the Pope of Rome, who is the "Holy Father" and the "priest" as the only "mediator of God" in the Church, and "the Vicar of Christ," seizing the very *tabernacle* (13:6) of God. Satan also became the possessor of *every tribe, tongue, and nation* by seizing the knowledge of God that was released through the advancement of the kingdom of God, and that would bring the great civilisation into the world that was in darkness after the fall of man. Through a Babylonian style of civil society, politically controlled by unredeemed vice-regents of the nations that were beguiled by the superstition of the sacerdotal Gospel of the Roman Church, this beast was given universal authority over every tribe, tongue, and nation.

During this period of history, there was also a universal Christianisation of these nation-states, which universally worshipped this man-made Christian religion. This religion inoculated the people's conscience with enough Christianity to make them feel safe in their self-assurance and the insurance that the Church gave them. There was a universal adherence across these nations that gave homage to this sacerdotal religion. As the Apostle John saw this vision being disclosed, he saw that, *all who dwel[t] on the earth [will] worship[ed] him, whose names have not been written in the Book of Life of the Lamb slain from the foundation of the world*. Conversely, God preserves His own in the wilderness Church, and even though their bodies are being sacrificed as a testimony to Christ, these martyrs for the faith maintained a healthy and secure soul. Satan was not able to steal the work of Christ that had been purchased by the Lamb of God, being the very Son of

God with whom the Father is well-pleased. However, Satan is a master tactician and he *overcomes* the Church and he does take holy ground and possesses the holy temple, the very tabernacle of God's assembly in earthly terms but never in heavenly terms.

We will now consider **verse 10**. In reality, of course, Satan is fighting a rear-guard action in the retreat from his absolute authority on earth from the days of the fall until the coming of Christ in His First Advent. The kingdom of God that begins with Christ's First Advent and His ascension to the right hand of the Father is marching forward invincibly to a sure victory. Satan's battle plan is one of guerrilla warfare in that he is dependent upon the resources of his enemy, the kingdom of God. He must have its products without serving the purposes of God. The purposes of Satan in his beast and his harlot can find effective counter-attack force against the anointed one and His Church only by using the advances of the kingdom of God against these powers of light. Satan is always brokering a deal of granting mankind significance and temporal well-being for captivity and dutiful subservience. If you cannot broker such deals, then the action of last resort is to bring to bear the torture chamber of the Inquisition, which was instigated by what was called the Holy Order. The terror of public execution was regularly used in communities that did not comply with the religious standards of the Antichrist Roman Church. This had an enormously sobering effect on people jumping out of the Roman Ark of salvation into the wilderness of the evangelical Church. To protest was to become a Protestant, and to become a Protestant was often to lead the life of a fugitive and exile. If whole nations were falling away from the Holy Roman Empire, then war was instigated against those nations. The Roman Catholic Church had a mercenary army that was superior to most armies and was often used to brutal effect. The Catholic kings and princes were brought into the extremely sophisticated world of politics and were called upon to subdue nations, and there was always a payoff for the loyal subjects.

The spiritual law of retribution is pronounced on this kind of beastly politics and religion. *He who leads into captivity shall go into captivity; he who kills with the sword must be killed with a sword* (13:10). The Apostle Paul says, *Beloved, do not avenge yourselves, but rather give place to wrath; for it is written, "Vengeance is mine, I will repay", says the Lord. Therefore, "If your enemy is hungry, feed him; if he is thirsty, give him a drink; for in so doing you will heap up coals of fire on his head"* (Rom. 12:19-20). As the saints of God, we are not to resort to such politics of man and man-made solutions which in the end is against God. There is a godly politics that exalts righteousness and God's law and the days will come when, *The kingdoms of the world have become the kingdoms of our Lord and of His Christ, and He shall reign forever and ever!* (11:15). There may be a time when Christians will take up arms against another nation in a "just war" that is defending the boundaries of the nation (Acts 20:26), or against an evil tyrant when national sovereignty is threatened, or in the protection of a man's realm as a matter of defence. Those who enter into an unholy "league of nations," where man's trust is in man and not in God, *shall go into captivity* and shall *be killed with the sword*. However, the saints are to be patient in suffering, wise in action, and constantly looking to the Lord for deliverance, *For here is the patience of the faith of the saints*.

THE BEAST COMING UP OUT OF THE EARTH—POST-1332

Verses 11-12 continue John's vision. *Then I saw another beast coming up out of the earth, and he had two horns like a lamb and spoke like a dragon…* This beast is of the same stuff as the *beast rising up out of the sea* that Christianised the ten nation-states of Europe through Constantinople. But now the *beast coming up out* *of the land* has been culturally and politically Christianised with his coming of age in the year 666 A.D. In a mediaeval fashion, a top-to-bottom rule of society gave great power to the rulers of these sovereign states. A Machiavellian style of government was often self-interested and controlled the knowledge of the Lord by educating only the elite of society and granting a burdensome, subsistence type of living to the ordinary person. Although the Bible was freely translated into vernacular languages up until 500 or 600 A.D., the Church hierarchy increasingly chained the Bible to the scholars of the day or had it confined to the Latin Vulgate as being the Authorised Version of the Word of God. This severely curtailed the advancement of a Christian Biblically-oriented counter-culture, and successfully imposed a Babylonish captivity over the Church. The previous beast of the older world order could not maintain its socio-political hegemony if the knowledge of the Lord were now to be released into the world. The beast's strategy was to have a new persona to maintain its strategic control at the centre stage of world politics and religious credibility. This persona was to appear as a substitute, in place of Christ the *Lamb slain from the foundation of the world* (13:8), which would be his ultimate blasphemy. The two horns of this lamb would be two distinct powers, Church and state, but moving forward into the future together. In the mediaeval period of history, there was no real distinction between Church and state. But now there would be a sphere of sovereignty of the Church and a certain dominion given to the state. The State would handle the nasty things in politics, often at the instigation of the Church. Now the mystique of the sacerdotal Gospel, peddled by the priesthood, became the moral guardian in the conscience of society. This beast was now a Christianised Babylonian Holy Roman Empire that would build his significance in a most impressive edifice of buildings, a physical superstructure that the world has never known before with monasteries, universities, schools, cathedrals and parish Churches, hospitals and orphanages. Literally, this beast arises out of the earth. The persona of the Church possessed the image of a lamb. However, this lamb spoke like a dragon. *And he exercised all the authority of the first beast in his presence, and causes the earth and those who dwell in it to worship the first beast* (13:11-12). The other side of this coin is the state, which possesses the power of the sword. But the power of this beast is always at the behest of the dragon and his religious *harlot*, which will be used as a fearful persecuting tool against the evangelical Church.

Now the *forty-two months*, being *one thousand two hundred and sixty days* (years) is completed. The cosmic war in spiritual places was being waged by the archangel *Michael and his angels with the dragon; and the dragon and his angels fought, but they did not prevail, nor was a place found for them in heaven any longer* (13:7-8). The dragon in the form of the beast had made *war with the saints …to overcome them* (13:7). As God promised the patriarch Abraham of old, so he promises to all the children of Abraham that come to faith in the God of Abraham, the Lord Jesus Christ, *I will bless those who bless you, And I will curse him who curses you; And in you all the families of the earth shall be blessed* (Gen. 12:3). As a matter of spiritual principle, the Apostle Paul says, that God *restrains* the beast and brings vengeance against him who has stretched out his hand against His Anointed with the very saints of Jesus Christ. So, in the fullness of time, in the year 1330 A.D., God sent the horrific Black Plague that swept across the civilised world, killing most of the ungodly inhabitants and wiping out nearly half the population of Europe and western Asia.

THE WILDERNESS YEARS OF THE CHURCH WERE NOW COMING TO AN END

The wilderness years of the Church were now coming to an end and there was to be a certain "crossing of the Jordan into the

Promised Land" by the people of God. The time had arrived where the Church would begin to possess the land that was once the stronghold of the serpent. This struggle would not be easily won but *Blessed are the meek, for they shall inherit the earth* (Matt. 5:5). The dragon has *no place in heaven* any longer and he was *cast to the earth* (12:8-9). Now the battle for the earth must begin.

God provided great leaders some 30 years after the Black Plague starting with John Wycliffe at Oxford 1328-84. He would become like a Joshua of old as the people of Israel crossed the Jordan from the wilderness after 40 years to possess the Promised Land. He was the morning star of the Reformation to come. He attacked the belief structure of the beast by calling into question the beast's Gospel, the sacerdotal system of the harlot, and the semi-Pelagian doctrine of the "free will" of man, which was against the sovereign grace of the Bible. The Bible had been locked up in monasteries and also in the Latin translation of the Vulgate. Wycliffe set about translating the Vulgate into the language of the people. He trained poor preachers who disseminated the Word of God to every corner, and to the *highways and byways* of the people. An awakening was dawning that would begin a great era of light.

REVIVAL OF THE BODY OF CHRIST

A German Augustinian monk, Martin Luther was awakened by his study of Paul's letter to the Romans and found that there was a *righteousness apart from the law* in the Lord Jesus Christ, being the redemptive Lamb slain for our sin. Luther learned that, by believing upon Him, a man is justified by this faith in Christ alone, and this faith was a free gift of God's grace alone. The Word of God was therefore the supreme authority of the Church, and any human being, including the Pope, was subject to the Word of God in the Scriptures. Luther protested against the corrupt practice of issuing papal indulgences. Those who donated money for the building of St Peter's Basilica in Rome were issued with certificates. These certificates, known as "indulgences," promised that the purchaser would release a dead loved one's soul from a place called "Purgatory," being an intermediate place of discipline that a sinner inhabited before entering heaven, when perfection was achieved. Martin Luther protested against this practice on 31 October 1517 by posting 95 Thesis upon the Wittenberg Church Door some two years after his conversion. The formal title of the 95 Thesis was "Dispute on the Power and Efficacy of Indulgences." The printing press had not long been invented. Printers took a copy of the 95 Thesis and published it abroad. This had an enormous effect upon the conscience of many people who were in the grip of the Babylonian captivity of the harlot church. Luther translated the Bible into the German language, and before long the Bible had been translated into many languages all over Europe. This sparked a genuine spiritual revival, and thousands of people were converted to the Biblical Gospel of grace alone through faith in the Lord Jesus Christ alone.

The humanist scholar Desiderius Erasmus of Rotterdam had done good work in bringing together the Greek manuscripts of the New Testament. This gave the reformers better documentary material with which to translate the Bible into the vernacular languages. However, Erasmus did not have the heart for thorough Reformation and wrote a book called the *On the Freedom of the Will* that supported and sought to justify the Roman Catholic doctrine of semi-Pelagianism. Luther wrote one of the most significant books that have ever been written against Erasmus, called *On the Bondage of the Will*, that presented the Protestant doctrine of the extent to which we have been saved in the Biblical Gospel of Jesus Christ. Luther comprehensively answered the semi-Pelagian view of Erasmus, and showed that, rather than man in the original Adam being merely ignorant, wounded or sick with sin, man is, in fact, dead in his sins and trespasses. Erasmus was affirming that man is not 'totally depraved' but is ignorant in some cases and sick in others, but not dead. For Luther, the only solution was a Gospel of resurrection, but Erasmus set out a more complex, man-cooperative solution of proper teaching and sacramental medicine and, of course, resurrection. Luther retorts that it is by the powerful and persistent preaching of God's Word that the Holy Spirit calls the sinner to the resurrection of regeneration that gives life by faith and repentance. In this, man is justified and the righteousness he receives from Christ is the righteousness of God, credited to his account, fully justifying the sinner.

Luther preached with a clarion call the Gospel that ignited a true revival of Biblical proportions, but it was left to others to bring about a Biblical Reformation of doctrine and practice that was essential in matters of both Church and state. One Roman Catholic source, which is hard to trace, put it this way: *It cannot be denied that Calvin was the greatest man of the Protestant rebellion. But for him, Luther's movement would probably have died out with him and his associates. Calvin organised it, gave it form and consistency, and his spirit has sustained it to this day. If Luther preceded him, it is still by this name "Calvin" rather than Luther's that the rebellion should be called; and the only form of Protestantism that still shows any sign of life is unquestionably Calvinism.*[23]

Reformation of the body of Christ

John Calvin of Geneva brought Reformation that forged ahead with a new era in the progress of the kingdom of God with its Gospel of eternal life. Calvin's deep spiritual character is reflected across some of the most significant and influential theological

---

[23] William Wileman, *John Calvin, His Life, His Teaching, and His Influence*, Gospel Mission Press, 1981. This quote is from *The Tablet*. It is from the issue of January 25, 1877

writing that has ever been produced in the history of the Church. This scholarship provided a strong and valid apologetic against the beast of Rome. His work was first and foremost Biblical, and a comprehensive theological system developed throughout the succeeding generations of the Christian Church. Calvin's system of theology was unitary, beginning at the doctrine of God who is sovereign in all things and decrees in His foreknowledge all creation, and providentially cares for every detail in that creation. Calvin draws out the Biblical teaching that God entered into Covenant with man as God's vice-regent in the stewardship of all His creation in a "Covenant of Creation." With the fall of man, God in His Grace established an enabling Covenant that would redeem God's vice-regents based on God's election as a predestinating decree that could be described as a "Covenant of Redemption." As man is awakened and comes alive through the regeneration, being effectually called out of death into the resurrection life in Christ, he is redeemed for good works. Having been justified, he is now sanctified and enabled to live as a redeemed vice-regent in God's world. In this way, the priesthood of all believers is emphasised and becomes the powerhouse of Reformation in all the nations.

The Protestant Reformation was built around distinctive Biblical theology that drew directly from Biblical revelation in the context of Covenant theology, true worship, and the theology of the kingdom of God. Calvin also drew heavily on historical theology that learnt from the past testimony of the true Church, and systematic theology that codified the truth of the Bible. Calvin published a standard work called *The Institutes of the Christian Religion* that was one of the most widely-read Reformed works of theology ever written. It was influential in formulating the confessional standards of the Protestant Churches. In continental Europe, these were the Three Forms of Unity (the Belgic Confession), the Heidelberg Catechism, and the Five Points of Calvinism. The Westminster

Standards were used in Britain. Throughout the ministry of Calvin, he also published commentaries on each book of the Bible that would assist ministers of the Gospel in preaching and teaching. In addition, the extensive correspondence of Calvin is legendary and shows the heart of a pastor as he interacts with the Church and national leaders across all the nations.

The distinctive Biblical truth that arose out of the Reformed Churches is the sovereign doctrines of grace in what became known as the Five Points of Calvinism. Covenant theology gave coherence to Biblical revelation, and expressed in covenantal sacramental theology the doctrines of baptism and the Lord's Supper. The Biblical theology of the kingdom of God that gave a comprehensive world and life view across all departments of knowledge both secular and sacred, was being developed. The distinctively Reformed view on Biblically regulated worship, known as "the regulative principle of worship," required worship to be conducted both in family units and in corporate worship, and to be practised as commanded in God's Word; worship that is not commanded in God's word is regarded as idolatry. Furthermore, the ministry of the Gospel and Church government should have Biblical checks and balances. In other words, the discipline of the body of Christ is the exclusive role of the offices of the Church, the offices are clearly defined: the pastor is the minister of the "word and sacrament," ruling elders are the pastoral overseers of the Church, and deacons are the pastoral carers of temporal affairs in the Church. The power of the sword was never given to the Church. The state is given the power of the sword by God, and is required to maintain law and order in the realm, secure the defence of its borders, and conduct international relationships with other nation-states. Church and state relationship was to be separate but intersecting in what was called the "Establishment Principle," where the Church proclaimed Biblical truth to the state and the state endorsed the true Church of God, where Christ was the King and Head of the Church, and this was demonstrated through practical obedience of the Church to the Scriptures. Church and state were to be ruled by the law of God, the law of liberty, and all men were subject to this law, whether king or pastor.

This Reformation was a remarkable spiritual revival that began to disciple whole nations. The conversion of literally millions of people was experienced, and the sanctifying effect of the sanctified Church took the Crown Rights of Christ into every department of society. There was a great outpouring of *the knowledge of the Lord*, not only in matters of religion but also across the creation itself. The "general revelation" of God that is locked in every particle of creation was also discovered, as *the keys of the kingdom*, being the Gospel of the word of God, unlocked the great mysteries of creation through economics, the sciences, technology and the arts. There was an irrepressible Renaissance because of the Reformation of Biblical truth that gave promise to a new era of civilisation and development. The kingdom of God was on the march and about to grow in unprecedented proportions.

The rest of chapter 13 of Revelation is the story of how the beast was to counteract the advances of the Reformation with its own Renaissance. If the beast had ignored the challenge of this revival, his socio-political and religious institution of Roman Catholicism would have become an insignificant force in the world today and would be a sect of little consequence. Brilliantly and strategically, the beast rises to counteract *the power of God that brings salvation* (Rom. 1:16) and the kingdom of God that relentlessly possesses the ground of *Antichrist* (1 John 2:18), the *mystery of lawlessness* (2 Thess. 2:7).

THE HARLOT CHURCH WITH HER BEAST PERFORMS GREAT SIGNS

Verses 13-14 tell us that *He performs great signs, so that he even makes fire come down from heaven on the earth in the sight of man. And he deceives those who dwell on the earth by those signs which he was granted to do in the sight of the beast, telling those who dwell on the earth to make an image to the beast who was wounded by the sword and lived*. The supernatural dimension in Roman Catholicism is kept alive by the spiritual power that lies behind this beast, the spiritual power of *the dragon who gives authority to the beast* (13:4). The magicians of Egypt in the days of Moses were able to copy the signs of Moses. Satan can counterfeit the miracles of God through his spiritual powers of darkness and deceive many (Exod. 7:8-13) The thing he cannot do is to produce the righteousness of God, regenerate the heart of man, or sanctify the life of the believer in every spiritual grace that comes from Jesus our Lord. Satan can indeed heal the sick, raise the dead to life, cause people to speak in tongues, slay people in the spirit, give strength to those that are crippled and ...*even make fire come down from heaven on the earth in the sight of man*. In the Roman Catholic veneration of the saints, an elite group of people that achieve remarkable levels of human goodness become members of the sainthood if there are certain rules for sainthood fulfilled. One of those rules is that a prospective candidate must be able to perform a miraculous sign that confirms such a status within the Roman Church. There is a long succession of exceptional people who have apparently demonstrated miraculous signs, and the Pope of Rome canonises such persons as saints who are worthy to be venerated and prayed to.

One of these saints is St. Ignatius of Loyola (1491-1556), who was contemporary to and yet spiritually the exact opposite of the godly reformer Martin Luther and his contribution to the Reformation. Ignatius of Loyola was a Spanish soldier who had a religious experience with 'the Madonna' and became a fanatical Roman Catholic. For a short time, Loyola adopted the life of a hermit and had a miraculous series of visions that seemed to authenticate his calling as a knight of the Roman Catholic Church. He instituted a pilgrimage to the Holy Land on a path of self-denial and sacrifice. His religious plan of religious exercises towards spiritual enlightenment and obedience was the foundation of the religious order that would follow. Absolute loyalty to the Church and the Pope was the Creed of Loyola. So, by 1534, he had gathered six key companions, all of whom he met as fellow students at the University—Francis Xavier, Alfonso Salmeron, Diego Laynez, and Nicholas Bobadilla, all Spanish; Peter Faber, a Frenchman; and Simão Rodrigues of Portugal. Later he was joined by Saint Francis Borgia (a member of the House of Borgia who was the principal aide of Emperor Charles V), and other nobles. "On the morning of the 15th of August, 1534, in the crypt of the Church of Our Lady of the Martyrs, at Montmartre, Loyola and his six companions, of whom only one was a priest, met and took upon themselves the solemn vows of their lifelong work." "Ignatius of Loyola was the main creator and initial Superior General of the Society of Jesus, a religious organisation of the Catholic Church whose members, known as Jesuits, served the Pope as missionaries."[24] This became the Gestapo-like inner circle of the Holy Roman Empire. With brutal political exactness and the very best intelligence under the Machiavellian dictum, "The end justifies the means," the Jesuits to this day are "a brood of vipers" (Matt. 3:7) in the belly of the *harlot* and her beast (17:3).

---

[24] http://en.wikipedia.org/wiki/Ignatius_of_Loyola

THE REVIVAL GIVEN TO THE BEAST

In **verse 15**, we are told that *he was granted power to give breath to the image of the beast, that the image of the beast should both speak and cause as many as would not worship the image of the beast to be killed.*

Between the years 1545–63 the Roman Catholic Council of Trent convened to discuss the topic, "Protestantism, Counter-Reformation." At the beginning, the Council struggled to find continuity because of the various wars and political upheavals that Europe was going through in these early days of the Reformation. However, as the Council proceeded, mainly under the leadership of the Jesuits, the Council of Trent countered Protestant doctrine as they formulated "seventeen dogmatic decrees," covering all aspects of the Catholic religion. These decrees were stated directly against the Biblical Reformed and Protestant faith. Probably the most sinister aspect of the Council of Trent as it arose at its conclusion in 1563 is that the Roman Catholic Church sanctioned the Jesuit Order that would turn out to be one of the most brutal instruments in the beast's arsenal against the Protestant Churches.

In France during the years 1555 to 1562, a most remarkable spiritual revival took place in the French Reformed Churches that had grown from just one fully supporting organised Church in 1555 to something like just under 2000 Churches that represented some 3 million people in France, who were attending these Churches under terrible persecution. The Scottish reformer John Knox said concerning Geneva and the French reformed Churches at this time that it was "The most excellent school of Christ since apostolic times." This represented something like 10% of the population of France. Then, by 1572, the Jesuits had infiltrated the political structure of France and incited the French Catholic population against the Protestants, and without warning on the day of

St Bartholomew, they massacred something like 70,000 French Huguenot Protestants in one night. Over the next several years, the French Protestants were slaughtered. Most of the French Reformed Christians were killed, and the borders of France were even sealed to prevent them from escaping into other lands. Some did escape to the Netherlands, and their descendants subsequently settled in South Africa. This was a devastating blow to Protestantism, and the discouragement was overwhelming in most cases. It has been calculated that during the period of the Reformation and Counter-Reformation, a period of about 200 years, something like 68 million Protestants were killed in the European region by Inquisition, war, ethnic cleansing and massacre. If modern calculations in the science of demographics were applied to this period of history, the figure would be even higher.[25] If we doubt these figures, and we

---

[25] David A. Plaisted, *Estimates of the Number Killed by the Papacy in the Middle Ages*, 2006 -http://webwitness.org.au/estimates.html This extensive and well-documented paper is a thorough treatment of this question of the very bloodthirsty nature of the Papacy, tracing the subject through respected historians that lived closer to these atrocities who had access to material that is buried by modern popularized works of revisionist historians that don't want to believe the awful facts of history. Plaisted then verifies these figures by a very thorough treatment using statistical analysis of the demographics throughout the Middle Ages that also include the Reformation years and the counter-Reformation and beyond. These figures not only verify the extraordinary numbers that were persecuted unto death by the Papacy but would indicate that the death toll is in fact a lot worse than the respected historians of former times have indicated by their own computations from available documentary records of the day. It is probably an impossible task to gather every record ever written that would establish the exact figure. Even if we could, it would not change the terrible conclusion that the Papacy as it welds together its alliances with nation states that there is no other institution anywhere in history and throughout history that can equal the atrocities of the great harlot Church. The blood-lust and the sinister lust for power has no parallel in history. Under modern figures such as Joseph Stalin, Adolf Hitler, Mao Zedong or Pol Pot, although the rates of genocide may be higher than what the Papacy perpetrated, the sheer numbers throughout history that can be placed at the feet of the Papacy and the brutality under the Inquisition really has no parallel in history.

might, the fact is that Europe to this day is overwhelmingly Roman Catholic. Only the Netherlands, some parts of Germany, and maybe some parts of the Scandinavian mountains, along with Britain, are the exceptions to this rule. The Jesuits were aggressive missionaries, and they set up missionary work in China, Japan, India, South America and, to a limited extent, in North America with the specific purpose of preventing Protestantism from getting a foothold in the far-flung New World.

This being the dark work of religious fanaticism and raw political power, the other major strategy in the Roman Catholic arsenal was matchless education at the parish level, in regional situations and universities that provide the highest standard of education. This strategy also provided venues for the expanding parish Church into every suburban city situation, town, village and hamlet. They would take all the advances in the Renaissance and turn these institutions into man-centred places of educational excellence. They exploited the disclosures of *the knowledge of the Lord* so that civilisation and progress would be served in Babylon the great. The Babylonian beast takes its form beyond the socialist French Revolution (1789-1799) and the atheistic secular humanism, into the Communist Experiment (1918-1991), and then into the socialist, secular, humanist socio-political beast of Babylon the great with its monetary policy, using free enterprise, as its milk cow, to fund the Secular City's massive tax system, and to feed its socialist appetite. In this way, the "image of the beast" (13:15) was given new life and remains at the centre stage of religion and politics throughout the succeeding centuries to our own day.

However, chapter 17 of Revelation indicates that toward the end of the dominion of the harlot and her beast described for us in chapter 13, hatred will develop between the "harlot" and the beast. From the days of the Reformation, there has been a practical division between the ecclesiastical harlot and the socio-political beast. As the conscience of the beast became more and more atheistic, in socialist-statism, particularly in the twentieth century, a certain parting of the ways has taken place. In left-wing socialist politics where there remains a democratic vote, it could be relied upon that Roman Catholics would characteristically vote for the Labour or Democratic parties. It was also very common that political representatives who were adherents of left-wing socialist politics arose out of the Roman Catholic Church and Roman Catholic school system. With secular atheistic state education becoming universally available, there is a comprehensive philosophical and political secular humanist position driven forward in such state institutions that presents the socio-political dictums of the beast. Increasingly, the *harlot* represented in the Roman Catholic Church has become less and less relevant to this socialist agenda. Of course, if the socialist left-wing political situations have to have religion, then it will be Roman Catholicism. Certainly, Biblical and evangelical Protestantism is hated with great intensity, and in countries where the democratic facilities of "checks and balances" have been overturned, these atheistic statist governments have heavily persecuted the Biblical and evangelical Protestant Church. This is seen in places like China, North Korea, Russia and the ex-Soviet States, South America, the nation-states of central and north Africa, and the far-eastern Asian region. It has been said that there are more martyrs and people killed because of their Christian profession and association with the Christian Church in the twentieth and twenty-first centuries than have ever fallen in past generations to the harlot's political devices and the beast's purges of the body of Christ.

So it is written in Revelation chapter 17:16, *And the ten horns which you saw on the beast, these will hate the harlot, make her desolate and naked, eat her flesh and burn her with fire.* The *harlot* Church in our own day is taking a severe body blow with the current allegation of "child abuse" in her religious institutions. The abuses in these institutions are legendary, particularly against the nuns by the priests and the widespread practice of infanticide of babies born to nuns. Child abuse was also widespread, and it is legally easy to prove such criminal behaviour. Very few are presenting to become priests and nuns as a result of the public infamy against the Roman Catholic Church, and there is a real crisis facing the Church. For example, in Australia there is no place to train nuns, and if anybody wishes to become a nun, they are sent to the Philippines for training. The disreputable position of the Church has caused great alienation between its *harlot* Church and its socio-political inspired beast.

THE ECONOMICS OF THE BEAST

Verses 16-17 tell us, *He causes all, both small and great, rich and poor, free and slave, to receive a mark on their right hand or on their foreheads, and that no one may buy or sell except one who has the mark or the name of the beast, or the number of his name.*

If we interpret the beast as being an individual and not a "religious socio-political entity throughout history," then we may be tempted to think of *the mark of the beast* as being a literal writing of 666 on the forehead. This may well be codified in a modern form, such as a barcode or a microchip that has been surgically inserted below the skin on the *right hand* or the *forehead*. It has been suggested that such an instrument would be a total global security system, and every single word, thought and action of "Citizen X" would be monitored by a "Big Brother" type of organic computer system. We may modify such a suggestion as having a credit card in your *right hand* that has all your security details in a "smart chip," and without such a credit card you will not be able to trade in the world that is totally under the dominion of the beast. We have argued that the beast is an earthly religious socio-political historical movement that is spiritually inspired by *the dragon* (13:4).

Therefore, any explanation of *the mark of the beast* would require a mark that is continuous and historically identifiable of in all those that *worshipped the beast* (13:4) throughout the generations.

For those that serve the beast with religious devotion, *...whose names have not been written in the Book of Life of the Lamb slain from the foundation of the world* (13:8), then there is a certain preferential treatment. We have stated earlier that the Holy Roman Empire was a kind of "League of Nations" that had economic and strategic benefits for the nations that belonged to it. The politics between nations was a coherent politics around the Christianisation of nations that were either in the Holy Roman Empire or disloyal to that empire. For instance, when the Reformation came to the Church, the leaders of nations maintained political solidarity with the Roman Catholic Church, whereas the people of these nations were being converted to Biblical and Protestant doctrine. These national kings and national leaders knew what side their bread was buttered, and that to be outside the "league of nations" politically and economically would incur certain inhibitions in terms of trade and even war. The mortar of the Holy Roman Empire was its religious adherence to the "harlot Church" and the great majority of their populations were adherents to the visible and virtually all-powerful universal religious institution that was at the very heart and culture of the people. It was politically expedient for the monarchies to throw in their lot with the priests, who controlled the hearts of the people and therefore the commerce of the body politic. The Protestant Church appeared to be rebellious and seditious, particularly if the radicals on the revolutionary side of politics among the Anabaptists were seen as part of the Reformation.[26] Martin

---

[26] This element had two distinct streams from mediaeval life, the one social and the other religious—the revolts of peasants and artisans, and the successions of "the Brethren." The social and economic suppression of the mediaeval period of history was at times extremely brutal and many of these communities were

Luther's contribution in this area is often overlooked but it is a crucial aspect of the Reformation to establish the difference between Reformation and revolution. The Reformation had to become more inclusive of those bent on revolution so that Reformation could take place among those who were shedding their blood in the cause of Christ. The most successful attempt to achieve this was in France under the influence of John Calvin's Geneva, where the French Reformed Churches saw such revival of true Biblical religion that the Waldensians and other Anabaptists were wholeheartedly included within the French Reformed Churches among the Huguenots. This was never entirely worked out during the Reformation, and even to our own day these separations still exist.

---

a political tinderbox ready to explode into revolution. The Reformation gave voice to these oppressed communities that fermented within this political climate. Martin Luther had to write a strong letter to the German Nobility to put down this seditious rebellion in Germany. (Its title being: *Against the Murderous, Thieving Hordes of Peasants*), if he had not, the whole political situation would have descended into anarchy. So, the German Peasants' War (1524-1526) broke out and the German nobility did their work with brutal effect, which is something that Luther carried to his grave with deep regret and even depression. Terrible bloodshed was exacted against the so-called Anabaptist elements in the society. They probably shared the greatest burden of martyrdom of any segment of the Reformation as a movement. Later on, in the German city of Munster in an 18-month period in 1534-1535 radical Anabaptists took over the city and established what they described as the New Jerusalem with strong pre-millennial expectation. These 'free spirits' were extreme and had little affinity with sober, Biblical Reformation. There was a religious individualism that ran rampant. Their final authority was the individual's conscience—the "inward word" which Church, tradition, and even the Bible (for some) had no right to judge. Notwithstanding these extremes, Anabaptists in the Netherlands, in Britain and what was left of the Waldensians in northern Italy and France made a worthy contribution to the Reformation as they grasped the tenets of reformed theology that moderated their revolutionary origins.

The commercial and economic system revolved around whether a nation and the citizens of nations were part and parcel of the religious socio-political entity of the Holy Roman Empire. This was the political system of the dragon that enforced his dominion across the beast. To be a member of the Holy Roman Empire, you were required to take baptism from the priest who exercised his apostolic function by succession from the Apostle Peter, the only means of grace being through the Pope of Rome in the Church Catholic. The first sacrament of the seven would directly regenerate the child's soul by the operation of the priest, which would secure the salvation and eternal security of each individual. This universal sign was essential for membership in the Holy Roman Empire. This baptism, being on your forehead, symbolically imposed the mark of the beast. In Imperial Rome, every soldier would raise his right hand in what was called the "Sacramentum." In the "Sacramentum," a Roman soldier swore a life or death oath of allegiance to the Emperor. In the Roman Catholic Church, the word 'Sacramentum' is borrowed and the seven sacraments that are applied within the Church of Rome constitute the sacramental system of faith. When a child, having been baptised, comes of age, he or she swears an oath of allegiance in the 'Sacramentum' of 'confirmation' where the priestly bishop confers, by the laying on of hands, the Holy Spirit for service within the Holy Roman Empire. These marks conferred by the Roman Catholic Church are the fundamental *signs and seals* of membership and their union with the Church, the body of Christ. This, of course, is the language of the Bible, but its content is twisted to establish a sacerdotal man-centred religion that has all the language of Biblical fidelity. But here in the book of Revelation they are actually, ...*a mark on their right hand and their foreheads* ...that numbers them as being citizens of the beast. This has been so throughout the history of the beast from 666 A.D. to our present day.

There is a comprehensive inclusiveness that enters into the day-to-day lives of every citizen within this political system and dominion of *the dragon*. There is an economic interdependence such that, unless you are a bona fides citizen, it will be extremely difficult for you to trade in the local market place, be employed across the many institutions of Rome, and even get a job in a local business if you are not of the Catholic religion. The relationship between Catholic and Protestant throughout the history of Western civilisation has been a deep divide in every community and nation to varying degrees. Even in so-called Protestant nations, this divide has been bitter. The demarcation between Catholic and Protestant communities is literally a social, political and even commercial divide that affects every individual *both small and great, rich and poor, free and slave*, as it were.

This was so throughout the various eras of history, certainly in the days of mediaeval Europe and in the days of the Reformation and Counter-Reformation. As Church and state separated and the humanist enlightenment began to more formally develop the secular humanist city-state, *Babylon the great* developed a conglomerate monetary system. This Babylonian system has developed an advanced scientific and technological society with an exacting unified "one world economy" that has socially and politically engineered "the global village" to God-proof humanity against the absolute sovereignty of God. Every need and duty of the Babylonian citizen, from the cradle to the grave, is subsumed under the authority of this beast. It is nearly impossible to exist outside such a monetary system in the international context or at a personal level. We may not need the marks of baptism and confirmation to participate in this Babylonian economy, but it will be required that you sell your soul to gain a place in this world. The words of Jesus are so poignant at this point where He says, *For what will it profit a man if he gains the whole world, and loses his soul? Or what will a man give in exchange for his soul?* (Mk. 8:36-37) The only alternative to this Babylonian system is the Gospel of the Lord Jesus Christ and following Him as we *deny [ourselves] and take up His cross and follow [Jesus]. For whoever desires to save his life will lose it, but whoever loses his life for My sake and the Gospel's will save it* (Mk. 8:34-35).

As R.J. Rushdoony puts it so clearly, "Those who refused to participate in the worship of man, those who refused to surrender to man's complacent satisfaction with man and man's society, are increasingly branded as aliens. All who do not have the mark of the beast, or who do not surrender to the humanistic social order, are refused permission to buy and sell, that is, they are the objects of social, political, and economic ostracism. Every kind of subtle and direct pressure is employed to force the true believer into conformity with the City of Man and the creed of Cain."[27]

HERE IS WISDOM

As we come to verse 18, and as we return to the beginning of this chapter, the question is asked, *Here is wisdom. Let him who has understanding calculate the number of the beast, for it is the number of a man; his number is 666.* We have dealt with the historic religious socio-political earthly institution of the beast that the Apostle Paul refers to as *the mystery of lawlessness (which) is already at work* (2 Thess. 2:7). The Apostle John makes a distinction concerning Antichrist as being *many antichrists that have come* (1 Jn. 2:18). We have identified the beast as coming to his majority in the year A.D. 666 at the synod of Whitby when the Church formally declared the Pope of Rome to be the Holy Father. The

---

[27] R.J. Rushdoony, *Thy Kingdom Come, Studies in Daniel and Revelation*, Thoburn Press, 1978, pp 175-6.

sacerdotal system was generally accepted and the Pope of Rome was seen to be the priestly mediator that conveyed the grace of God in "the mass" between God and man. The Pope was described as the Vicar of Christ, being the priestly intermediary between God and the Church. The Pope of Rome became Antichrist in the sense that he took the place of God. We have only one Father, the very Father of the Lord Jesus Christ, only one High Priest, Jesus our Lamb, and only one Vicar of Christ, God the Holy Spirit, who proceeds from the Father and Son. For any human being to assume the Trinitarian place of God in the Church of God is blasphemy of the first order and therefore Antichrist.

It is not until we get to Revelation 17 that we are given a retrospective on the beast before the millennium and a perspective on the future mystery of the beast that arises out of *the bottomless pit* after being bound and sealed there for a thousand years ...*so that he should deceive the nations no more*. However, after the millennium is completed, the dragon is released for *a short time*, and it is there that *the man of sin (lawlessness)* is revealed, according to the Apostle Paul (2 Thess. 2:3, 8-9), and the Antichrist *is revealed*, according to the Apostle John (1 John 2:18). The Apostle John describes the historical manner in which *the man of sin – the Antichrist is revealed*. When John says, ...*they see the beast **that was**, and **is not**, and **yet is*** (17:8), he is describing the future return of the beast as a man. John observes the vision of *that Great Day of God Almighty* (16:14), which takes place at the great universal exodus that ushers in the millennium that is prompted by *the Seven Last Plagues* (15:1, 16:1-21). From this standpoint, **the beast that was** is the historic beast that has exercised dominion at the centre stage as a religious socio-political institution for the two thousand years to our own day. This beast is then destroyed in *the Seven Last Plagues,* as recorded in chapter 16, and in chapter 18 *Babylon the great* was destroyed.

In chapter 17, the continuing history of the beast is given. Chapter 19 describes how the two great enemies of the Church and the kingdom of God, i.e., *the beast* in the West, and *the false prophet*, (the Antichrist institution of Muhammadism and its Islamic socio-political institution that has concentrated in the East) grow alongside the beast, having very similar historical developments. During the next thousand years, the beast, with the false prophet, was killed and the dragon was cast into *the bottomless pit*, **and is not** (17:8). Then, after the years of the millennium are complete, the beast, driven by the spirit of the dragon, is said to be, **and yet is** (17:8). With the release of the dragon from the bottomless pit, he, for a short time, will cause a great spiritual *falling away* (2 Thess. 2:3), spoken of in chapter 20:7-10. This Satanic spiritual rebellion shall be crushed when ...*fire came down from God out of heaven and devoured them* (20:9) that follow *the Antichrist, the man of sin* and finally ...*the devil is cast into the lake of fire and brimstone where the beast and the false prophet are*...(20:10) and Satan will therefore be assigned to perdition.

Soon after these events, the Last Day comes with the Second Advent of Christ, and the general resurrection of the all the living and the dead and the Final Judgement takes place (20:11-15).

Once this context and the identity of *the man of sin* are established, it is hardly necessary to calculate 666. There is a vast array of theories that are put forward and each is consistent with a particular model of interpretation of the book of Revelation. But if we were to conclude what we have said, and draw together each detail into one, we would find that verse 18 is a summary of who this figure of the beast is, calculated into his number 666. We are told that this is *the number of a man*, or, more literally, *a human number*. Man was created on the sixth day of creation as God's vice-regent of all creation. Even beyond the fall into utter darkness, corruption and death, his vice-regency is maintained because God did not forsake that which he promised in the "Covenant of Creation." The spiritual figure of *the serpent*, a fallen angel in the heavenly hosts, became *the prince of the power of the air* (Eph. 2:2). He coveted the legitimate vice-regency of man and subverted God by transferring to man authority that was God's. He gave the spiritual power of darkness to the image of God in man so that humanity, under the dominion of their father Satan, is Antichrist. Through the generations of man's earthly dominion, there is a providence of Satan in the religious socio-political institution of the *mystery of lawlessness* (2 Thess. 2:7). This messianic Antichrist dominion of man, dare I say it, lasts for six millennia. From creation to the First Advent of Christ, there are four millennia according to Biblical chronology, and from Christ to "the Great Day of God Almighty" (16:14), through the generations of the Great Tribulation, two millennia. In the years of the millennium, being the seventh millennium, a millennium of peace and sabbatical rest is sustained when the beast *is not* (17:8). Then we have 6, which is the number of man created having God's vice-regency under the "Covenant of Creation." Then we have six millennia of the dominion of Satan exercised through unredeemed man that is the Babylonian City of Man, being the Antichrist beast. Now the final 6 of man-centred dominion is found in the revelation of *the man of sin* after the millennium and after *the falling away*, in the time cue, of the *yet is*.

Then *Satan will be released from his prison and will go out and deceive the nations which are in the four corners of the earth* (20:7-8) and the final drama of this man-centred messianic figure will be manifest in what the Apostle John says in chapter 20 of Revelation, and what the prophet Ezekiel says in his prophecy in chapters 38 to 39, *when Gog and Magog gather themselves together to battle, whose number is as the sand of the sea* (20:8). Gog (being the crowning messianic 6 of the number 666) becomes the messianic

Antichrist empowered by the pent-up spirit of a released Satan *from his prison* (20:7). Ezekiel names nine other nations: Magog, Rosh, Meshech, Tubal, Persia, Ethiopia, Libya, Gomer and Togarmah, but the horn will be in Gog (being the tenth) who gained all-out absolute power and authority (17:12). In a ten-nation military formation, Gog and Magog made a final assault on the anointed saints of God. *They went up on the breadth of the earth and surrounded the camp of the saints and the beloved city* (20:9), who were at the mercy of the cruel *man of sin*, the very *Antichrist*, to liquidate the testimony of God. The Church of the Lord Jesus Christ had been reduced to a relatively small number, even after the sustained peace of the millennium, which could have seen a vast majority converted and sustained in genuine Christian life but had *fallen away* (2 Thess. 2:3). This coming of ...*the lawless one is according to the working of Satan, with all power, signs, and lying wonders, and with all unrighteous deception among those who perish, because they did not receive the love of the truth, that they might be saved. And for this reason God will send them strong delusion, that they should believe the lie, that they all may be condemned who did not believe the truth but had no pleasure in unrighteousness* (2 Thess. 2:9-12). The Lord Jesus Christ seated at the right hand of the Father above all authority and power intervenes directly for His little flock, and ..*fire came down from God out of heaven and devoured them* (20:9) that were set against God.

R.J. Rushdoony sums it up well, "...the number 666 represents the essence of man's messianic pretensions as well as their futility: at its highest, it continually falls short of the divine totality and sovereignty. Neither 6 or 66, or 666 can ever become 7, or 77, or 777 in itself. Man is a creature and always remains a creature: his messianic dreams concerning himself cannot change the fact of his creaturehood or remove him from the divine judgement that faces his rebellion and sin. In [Revelation 13] verse 14, the faith of this beast, of this false Christianity, is clearly revealed: for all its moralism, it believes that basically that 'might is right' and exalts human creature because it exalts man. Self-exultation, self-justification, and the blind worship of power are behind all moralistic doctrines. Humanism progressively becomes a naked viciousness, and man is confirmed in his depravity. Moralism always reveals itself as basically immoralism."[28]

---

[28] Op. cit., p 176.

CHAPTER 6

THE VICTORY OF THE KINGDOM OF GOD - REVELATION 14

THE GLORIOUS UNIVERSAL EXODUS FROM THE HOUSE OF BONDAGE AND ITS DISPOSSESSION

There is a certain linear movement in chapters 12 to 14, and all within a single place. The single place is the *great tribulation* that has occupied the last two millennia to date. As the Apostle Paul says in the 8th of Romans and verse 18, *For I consider that the sufferings of this present time are not worthy to be compared with the glory which shall be revealed to us. For the earnest expectation of the creation eagerly waits for the revealing of the sons of God. For the creation was subjected to futility, not willingly, but because of Him who subjected it in hope;* (Rom. 8:18-20).

The exodus in the days of the prophet Moses was an illustrated prophecy of a more glorious Exodus that will reach into the millennium and heaven itself. This Exodus will gather a kind of *one hundred forty-four thousand who were redeemed from [all] the earth*...(14:3) throughout the generations of the *great tribulation* particularly, who were persecuted by *the dragon.* But *the woman who gave birth to the male Child* being the whole body of Christ

(12:13); *These are the ones who were not defiled with the [harlot] woman['s mark of the beast]* (13:14-18), *for they are virgins. These are the ones who followed the Lamb wherever He goes. These were redeemed from among men, being first-fruits to God and to the Lamb* (14:4).

THE GLOBAL PLACE OF THIS EXODUS

The global site of this Exodus may be for us the generation in which we live, or as an individual, our life-span, but in the scales of history the kingdom of God's Exodus has so far been two millennia. So, this Exodus is always near and soon, and is indeed something in which every believer is fully involved in their immediate world, but when seen through the corridors of history it is inclusive of every generation. It is not only a feature of the Church militant on earth but also the Church triumphant in heaven, where a New Jerusalem (21:9-7) is being gathered in Christ for eternity itself, in *the new heavens and a new earth* (21:1) throughout every generation. The Exodus of the kingdom of Heaven is to lead to an earthly redemption of the entire creation, ...*because the creation itself will be delivered from the bondage of corruption into the glorious liberty of the children of God*, (Rom. 8:20-21) where the saints are living ...*on earth as it is in heaven*, (Matt. 6:10) where they ...*lived and reigned with Christ for a thousand years*; (20:4) where ...*the kingdoms of this world have become the kingdom of our Lord and of His Christ, and He shall reign for ever and ever!* (11:15).

THIS GLORIOUS EXODUS IS FOUND IN ONE BIBLICAL WORD, 'SANCTIFICATION'

What will this look like to us as individuals, or to our family, or in our local Church life, or even in our workplace and the recreational world and our nation that moves forward in this glorious exodus? It will first of all be a spiritual dynamic that has a material effect in every part of our world. It is a refusal to participate in the delusory eschatological hope of *Babylon the great* that is looking for an ideal "green" world. This *Babylon* exploits everything that it can, so that the City of Man and its self-sufficient secular world (atheistic in behaviour but culturally religious in devotion) is a paradise made in the image of man. On the other hand, a positive expression of what it will look like when we are partakers in this glorious exodus is found in one Biblical word, "sanctification."

Undoubtedly the greatest liberty ever experienced by mankind is the grace of God unleashed in the finished work of Christ upon the cross. The forensic term, "justification," is pronounced upon everyone who believes in Christ the Redeemer, as an act of God's declaration of righteousness. So, the Apostle Paul can say, *There is therefore now no condemnation of those who are in Christ Jesus, who do not walk according to the flesh, but according to the Spirit* (Rom. 8:1). This has given us the liberty to serve God with mind, heart, soul and flesh. Justification releases us to serve but does not give us the power to serve. The Christian life is not seen in our justification, but it is in the dynamic of sanctification that the Christian life materialises—first of all spiritually in the individual and then secondly in every part of our lives, leaving nothing outside the purview of Christian living.

Sanctification is not moralism or some internal, private pietism that cloisters the Christian life in a separatist mindset that privately congratulates themselves for their spirituality and Christian zeal. Such a person may be found with the *Pharisee who stood and prayed thus with himself, "God, I thank you that I am not like other men – extortionists, unrighteous, adulterers, and even as this tax collector"* (Lk. 18:11), which in the end is self-indulgence. He may well sing to himself the old English nursery rhyme:

Little Jack Horner
Sat in the corner,
Eating a Christmas pie;
He put in his thumb,
And pulled out a plum,
And said 'What a good boy am I!

Such a concept of sanctification is the religion of the unfaithful *woman* riding the Babylonian beast of semi-plagiarism in the Roman Catholic Church and Arminianism in general evangelicalism. In Roman Catholicism, the elite classes within the clergy and holy orders bred religious fanaticism in just this way by retreating into asceticism and pietism and followed an image of Christianisation. In the end, they hated the truth and anybody that held to the truth as taught in the Word of God. Arminianism within general evangelicalism has behaved in the same way as Roman Catholicism but without the ecclesiastical pretence and theological framework. However, the same pietistic air and moralism that retreats into a spirituality that cloaks itself with deep religious tones of spurious humility and privately expresses itself in terms of thanking God, ... *that I am not like other men* (Lu. 18:11) is still everywhere evident, and their hatred of the doctrines of grace held by the Reformed confessions of faith is vehement.

The Apostle Paul was ...*bound to give thanks to God always for you* [the Church at Thessalonica] ...*Because God from the beginning chose you [them] for salvation through sanctification by the Spirit and belief in truth, to which he called you [them] by our [Apostolic] Gospel of our Lord Jesus Christ* (2 Thess. 2:13-14). Paul was able to say this because it could only have been God, who, by the power of this Gospel, had saved this particular people. Their sanctified lifestyle was a demonstration of their belief in the truth, being the whole body of doctrine found personified in the Christ of the Word of God and clearly applied across every part of their lives—not perfectly, but according to the truth. These Thessalonian Christians were, in fact, a new creature in Christ Jesus. They had been born from above, having heard the preaching of this Gospel that brought about clear spiritual resurrection from the dead. This was clearly evidenced in their new transformed lifestyle that was demonstrated in the manner of their life that gives glory to God in everything.

THE MEANS OF SANCTIFICATION HAS A DESTINATION OF TRUTH

The Westminster Shorter Catechism summarises the Biblical doctrine of sanctification by saying: "Sanctification is the work of God's free grace by which we are renewed throughout in the image of God, and are enabled more and more to die to sin and to live to righteousness."[29] As we *walk according to the Spirit and not according to the flesh* (Rom. 8:1) because *our eyes are fixed on the author and the finisher of our faith* (Heb. 12:2) there will be a work of God's grace that is freely and inexhaustibly available to us where there is a radical cleansing from sin and a renovation in righteousness. This radical cleansing from sin is a "dying to sin" that does not seek to discipline sin or to polish sin into a respectable persona, but a complete putting away or dying to sin. This does not happen instantly as this is God's work of grace, and the work will not be completed until our glorification. But sin is being dealt with, and in whatever area of the believer's life that God is dealing with in His providence, sin is mortified, for ...*whoever abides in Him does not sin* (1 Jn. 3:6). This is not perfectionism because if God were to reveal our complete sinfulness all at once, we would wither under the sheer weight of it. But God, according to our faith, mortifies our sins and renovates our lives piece by piece in His righteousness according to His perfect symmetry of truth in His grace and mercy.

---

[29] Westminster Shorter Catechism, question-and-answer 35.

The Apostle John says earlier, *If we say that we have not sinned, we make Him a liar, and His Word is not in us ... And if anyone sins, we have an Advocate with the Father, Jesus Christ the righteous. And He Himself is the propitiation for our sins, and not for ours only but also for the whole world* (1 Jn. 1:10-2:2). So, we are continually being saved by God's grace alone, and as God is dealing with us in terms of sin in our lives, there is a certain repentance that is effectual in that particular area, so that we truly mortify sin and we sin no longer in that area, having gained righteousness.

As *sin is lawlessness* (1 Jn. 3:4), so righteousness is a certain comprehensive lawfulness. We can only know what righteousness looks like when we see the righteousness of God in Christ who lived *under the law* (Gal. 4:4) *yet without sin* (Heb. 4:15). The righteousness of God is at least looking like the Ten Commandments of Moses, but typologically Moses and the people of Israel lived in a *weak and beggarly* age (Gal. 4:9) of "shadows" and "images" that looked forth to the truth of the "body" or reality that was yet to come. Therefore, Biblical righteousness is the righteousness of God that is outlined in terms of its description in the written Word of God with its law entirely intact. The image of righteousness is best seen in the revelation of the Lord Jesus Christ. Jesus said Himself, *I am the way, the truth, and the life. No one comes to the Father except through me* (Jn. 14:6).

If then we are to live to righteousness, the truth of God's word will be formed in our belief and performed in our life. Truth is not seen in our formulations of words. Truth may be articulated in our creeds and our understanding of the word of God, but it is seen in our sanctified living. The true powerhouse of the Christian life is in Biblical sanctification. If there is genuine Biblical sanctification, then we will know its presence in an individual, a family, a Church, our workplace and place of recreation, and even at a national level when the righteousness of God is formulated in day-to day-life in the progressive symmetry of truth. Truth is the wisdom and knowledge of God in relationship to the entire world in which we live. This rule of God across every area of life is the kingdom of God that gives glory to God so *...that in all things He might have the pre-eminence* (Col. 1:18). But the citizens of the kingdom of God are the redeemed vice-regents of all the earth, the very children of God, who are being sanctified in every respect for God's individual purpose for every man, woman and child who is covenanted before God and is God's priest in this world, bearing the counter-culture of this heavenly kingdom. The advancement of the kingdom of God is relentless and unstoppable and dispossesses Satan's ill-gotten possession, the beast and his brutal tyrannical rule of raw power that does not know the righteousness of God's law.

In this way the citizens of the kingdom of God are on the march in a global exodus. The kingdom of God should not be equated with the Church, but the Church has "the keys of the kingdom" in terms of true knowledge and wisdom that unlock the concealed treasures of the infallible general revelation of truth in creation itself. Since the coming and ascension of Christ our King and the kingdom of God, being the rule of Christ in every field of knowledge, there is no area that does not come under "the queen of the sciences," Theology.

The relentless and continuous growth of the kingdom of God is often sustained by extremely small numbers of those being converted by the Gospel of the Lord Jesus Christ. Every believer is individually and corporately being equipped for every good work of faith. These holy priests of God have a lasting influence that far outweighs their physical presence. Whether it is the humble calling of a labourer, a soldier, or a parent, or a Wilberforce pleading the cause against African slavery, these constitute a most effective force that dispossesses the beast's dominion.

This was brought home to me recently when I was travelling on an Indian railway with a highly politicised Hindutva[30] man. He came from a high caste Hindu background, and easily perceived my Christianity. He said that no greater force in India is more dangerous than Christianity! This somewhat startled me at the time because Indian paganism seems to saturate the Indian social and public life, and the religious culture of Hinduism is reasonably comprehensive in India. This highly-placed man feared Christianity more than anything else in the national life of India.

I said in general terms Christianity had done nothing but good in the national life of India as it had given India an education system that was the envy of every nation around it. Christianity has established a medical system that actually cares for the people across the community, and it has established social institutions such as orphanages, refuges of all kinds and relief agencies in times of disaster. Christianity was largely responsible for the Westminster parliamentary system of government that has granted great political stability to a nation of immense diversity and enabled it to remain

---

[30] http://en.wikipedia.org/wiki/Hindutva "Hinduness," a word coined by Vinayak Damodar Savarkar in his 1923 pamphlet entitled *Hindutva: Who is a Hindu?* is the set of movements advocating Hindu nationalism. Members of the movement are called *Hindutvavadi*s. According to a 1995 Supreme Court of India judgement the word Hindutva could be used to mean "the way of life of the Indian people and the Indian culture or ethos."

Elizabeth Kendall, *Religious Liberty Prayer Bulletin* | RLPB 158 | Wed 09 May 2012 states the following:

"Hindu nationalism–the idea that India should be a Hindu State–is the political construct of India's high caste Hindu powerbrokers who pursue political power for the purpose of perpetuating their own power and privilege."

intact as a definable nation and the largest democracy on earth. There have been a great many Christian believers and missionaries martyred by the Hindus and Moslems throughout the history of Christianity in India and yet never with reprisals or tit-for-tat type of revenge that does exist between the Hindus, Sikhs and Moslems. In addition, the Christian testimony in India faced almost insurmountable problems with theological liberalism and ecumenicalism that has caused a great crisis of faith in Indian Christianity as it has in global Christendom during the last hundred years. The evangelical testimony in India found it very difficult to make progress into India's religious framework culturally and Christianity was always regarded as a foreign white man's religion that had no home in India. This has changed to some degree since independence in 1947 but the evangelical testimony struggles on almost every front with corruption inside the missionary movement and Church life.

This Hindu man admitted that all these things might well be true about the Christian influence in India, but the Christian most effectively dispossessed the Indian identity as a Hindustan state. Even when Christianity is at its weakest, it is still a formidable force and the kingdom of God is extended even in these circumstances.

In 1793, the Calvinistic Baptist missionary William Carey inaugurated the Modern Missionary Movement from India that ushered in many outstanding missionaries from all over the world. The extraordinary achievements of these men and women never saw mass conversions among the Hindus. There was good and fruitful work among the tribal peoples in the far north-east of India in the states such as Mizoram, Nagaland, Meghalaya and Manipur, and these are regarded as Christian states today. Kerala in south India would also be regarded as heavily Christian. William Carey did an extraordinary job in translating the Bible into 23 Indian languages, standardising Sanskrit, and setting up schools and universities that today are regarded as world-class. Carey was also a leading scientist in biology and agriculture and he revolutionised Indian agricultural practices. The list of ground-breaking accomplishments Carey achieved is extraordinary and yet there is only one recorded convert from Hinduism to an abiding faith in Jesus Christ in the ministry of William Carey. He certainly opened the doors for many that did see more significant numbers of converts, but the ground was hard and unyielding during Carey's faithful ministry.

It could be said that India was never the same after Carey's work as a missionary to India. The departure of converts *who were redeemed from the earth* (14:3) has been relatively small out of Hinduism in the Indian subcontinent, but incredibly significant. Higher numbers joined the exodus from the Buddhist kingdom nations in the Himalayan mountain regions in Sikkim, Bhutan and Burma. Throughout the history of Muhammadanism, the exodus into the body of Christ has been minimal, and yet glorious testimonies of faith have been witnessed. Confucianism, reorganised by Chinese communism, is witnessing a great exodus in China in recent decades. Japanese Shintoism has been like brass. The exodus in Korea has been on a massive scale and yet under great persecution, the story of which is known only in heaven. Significant numbers have come out of pagan Africa, America, the Far East and Asia and the South Pacific island nation-states. There has been an exodus in Europe and the United Kingdom. The exodus out of Roman Catholicism has demonstrated extraordinary advances of the kingdom of God in all parts of the world, and the body of Christ has been drawn *from every nation, tribe, tongue, and people* (14:6).

THE LAMB AND THE "HUNDRED AND FORTY-FOUR THOUSAND"

Let us consider **verse 1**. Many have looked upon the very Jewish designation of the Lamb as the King of Israel on Mount

Zion as being the fulfilment of what was promised at the ascension of Christ after he pronounced the "great commission." In the Book of Acts, we see the five hundred (1 Cor. 15:6) *gazing toward heaven where two men stood by them in white apparel, who also said, men of Galilee why do you stand gazing up into heaven? This same Jesus who was taken up from you into heaven, will so come in like manner as you saw him go into heaven* (Acts 1:10-11). This is said to signify a pre-millennial Second Coming of Christ as the Lamb of God on Mount Zion, the geographic city of Jerusalem that has been preserved and to which the Jews returned 1948, and that the *hundred and forty-four thousand* are representative of a great number of Jewish believers that is gathered on this occasion. The other use of this signature number of *hundred and forty-four thousand* in the book of Revelation in chapter 7 verses 4-8 seems to put it in no doubt that these are of *all the tribes of the children of Israel (that) were sealed* (7:4). To reinforce this fact, we have all the historic tribes of Israel named and sealed; that makes this an exclusively Jewish statement.

The structural context of this chapter would work against adopting the interpretation that this is a second-coming passage, whether pre-millennial or postmillennial. What follows in this chapter is teaching about the powerful and persistent preaching of the Word of God. If we had arrived at a millennial peace, this kind of preaching would not be necessary, as in a pre-millennial interpretation of these chapters, the battle of the beast or the Antichrist has now been won and the Lord has intervened. If we hold to a post-millennial second coming in these verses, we have still got the turbulence of chapters 16, 17, 18 and 19 yet to be endured until we get to the millennial chapter 20. This is simply not a good fit in terms of the natural context and flow of the book of Revelation.

If this is a pre-millennial Second Coming of Christ to the city of Jerusalem, then it is not described here in the terms that it is described in other parts of Scripture. There is no actual description of the coming of Christ, neither are the events associated with the Second Coming of Christ described. Premillennial theologians would agree that 1 Thessalonians 4:15-17 is a clear description of the public coming of Christ at His second coming. We may differ as to where in prophetic history the second coming is placed, whether before the millennium or after the millennium, but at least some of the events associated with the coming of Christ should be evident.[31] For example, *...the Lord Himself will descend from heaven with a shout, with the voice of an archangel, and with the*

---

[31] Paul N Benware, *Understanding End Times Prophecy*, Moody Press, Chicago 1995; writes an excellent up-to-date summary of millennial beliefs of the Scripture from the point of view of Premillennialism and Dispensational Premillennialism. Paul Benware shows how premillennialism has concentrated so much of the teaching of Revelation into their interpretation of the Great Tribulation, being a seven-year period before the Second Coming of Christ before the millennium. I would submit that this is the reason why so much emphasis is placed upon chapter 13 of Revelation in terms of the revealing of the Beast, the Antichrist, which is not an historical, institutional, religious, socio-political anti-Christian beast that has menaced the Church throughout the Christian age. If the beast is an individual that arrives at the end of the so-called Church age, which is sensationalised and speculated about in Christian eschatological books and media, then chapter 14 would logically be a pre-millennial second coming of Christ that we are looking for. Because of this presupposition, there is a great desire to see chapter 14 of Revelation describe a pre-millennial return of Christ. Once you have established that the *hundred and forty-four thousand* are Jewish, and the Jews have remained largely outside the Gentile Gospel era, (it is painfully evident that very few Jews have been converted to the Gospel of the Lord Jesus Christ) there must have been a massive conversion (Rom. 11) for this *hundred and forty-four thousand* Jews to witness this return of their King whom they have been without for two millennia. We would maintain that Romans chapter 11 does speak of a comprehensive conversion of the Jews, but we believe this passage does not speak of such a conversion. Chapter 7 of Revelation may well speak of a comprehensive number of Jews that will be suddenly converted, and who will be included in the universal company of God's people that is described as a representative number of *one hundred and forty-four thousand* sealed ones.

trumpet of God. And the dead in Christ will rise first. Then we who are alive and remain shall be caught up together with them in the clouds to meet the Lord in the air (1 Thess. 4:16-17). We do have the Lamb of God in the presence of His people in a place called Mount Zion, which is, from our point of view, the abiding presence of the Lord Jesus Christ in His Church that is well described: *...the seven Churches [being] the seven lampstands which you saw are the seven Churches* (1:20, 2:1-3:22).

In this passage, we have a beautiful description of Christ the Lamb, our holy and righteous Redeemer, mercifully and graciously pastoring His flock. He infallibly stands alone in the framework of the doctrine of Scripture as the very body of Divinity of Mount Zion, the New Jerusalem that is *joined and knit together* (Eph. 4:16) in the truth of Christ, the King of heaven and earth. The Lamb pastorally speaks to the seven Churches of all generations and in every season of history and across all the earth that are described in this book. This great company of the Lamb on Mount Zion are never perfect, and mostly not ideal. But when they see Christ, they find repentance to sanctify themselves in the power of Christ's Word and Spirit. These, being the saints of God, are ideally suited for the purpose of Christ as a Church militant on earth that finds perfection in the Church triumphant in heaven with Christ who is seated at the right hand of the Father.

These saints of God are, without distinction, every believer in the Lord Jesus Christ, who is their Saviour, Redeemer and Lord. These are described as *one hundred and forty-four thousand, having His Father's Name written on their foreheads* (14:1). This signature number is used in Revelation chapter 7 of *all the tribes of the children of Israel (that) were sealed* (7:4). The twelve tribes of Israel are named as part of the signature number of the *one hundred and forty-four thousand* in a rather comprehensive way, but not exclusively, because this *great multitude* spoken of thus is actually from a throng *...that no one could number, of all nations, tribes, peoples, and tongues standing before the throne and before the Lamb, clothed with white robes, with palm branches in their hands, and crying out with a loud voice, saying, "Salvation belongs to our God who sits on the throne and to the Lamb!"* (7:4-10) This universal gathering of Christ's body known as Mount Zion the city of God is a *...redeemed people from among men being the firstfruits to God and to the Lamb* (14:4). They have a kind of signature that is more fully revealed in the image of the New Jerusalem in chapter 21 of Revelation, which describes *the bride, the Lamb's wife* (21:9) that is revealed as *...the great city, the holy Jerusalem descending out of heaven from God* (21:9-10). This city is measured with a kind of architectural signature in terms of proportion—the cube of 12,000 furlongs (16,560 miles). So, this New Jerusalem is an indescribably large facility, and yet this facility establishes an incomprehensible mathematical equation that further describes *the wall* of this living city of *the bride, the Lamb's wife* (21:9) as being *144 cubits, according to the measurement of a man, that is, of an angel* (21:17). Nigel Lee calculates the 144,000 as the whole number of the elect of God throughout every generation and encompassing the entire earth as equalling $(3 \times 4) \times (3 \times 4) \times 10^3$ saying, "They all represent the total of God's elect—everywhere, and down through the centuries, 144,000...where '3' represents the Trinity; where '4' represents all points of the compass; and where '10^3' represents the perfect number of fullness cubed (as it were). Such are all those who refuse to bear the mark of the anti-Christian beast."[32] They are symbolically sealed in ownership on their forehead as the spiritual reality of *...the Spirit of adoption by [whom] we cry out, Abba, Father. The Spirit Himself bears witness with our spirit that we are*

---

[32] Nigel Lee, *John's Revelation Unveiled*, Lamp Trimmers, The Historicism Research Foundation, El Paso, Texas, p 193.

children of God and if children, then heirs of God and joint-heirs with Christ...(Rom. 8:15-17).

So, the identity of this *hundred and forty-four thousand* is the whole number that makes up the *New Jerusalem*, being the elect of God that is being gathered throughout all generations *from every nation, tribe, tongue, and people*. This signatory number includes a comprehensive conversion of the Jewish people of Israel that will be gathered in throughout history, but particularly in an historic event spoken of in Romans chapter 11, *...until the fullness of the Gentiles has come in. And so* **all Israel will be saved**, *as it is written:*

> "*The Deliverer will come out of Zion,
> And He will turn away ungodliness from Jacob;
> For this is My covenant with them,
> When I take away their sin*"' (Rom. 11:25-36).

This conversion of the Jews will be dramatic and sudden at some point in history, and those that believe this believe that the time is close and that such a revival and glorious coming of Israel to her King will be as, *life from the dead* (Rom. 11:15). However, this conversion, as glorious as it will be, is not exclusive but inclusive with the whole Church of God, universal and eternal in the New Jerusalem, both Jews and Gentiles together, as *...one body and one spirit, just as you were called in one hope of your calling; one Lord, one faith, one baptism; one God and Father of all, who is above all, and through all, and in all* (Eph. 4:4-6).

THE TRUE WORSHIP OF THE 'HUNDRED AND FORTY-FOUR THOUSAND' AS ONE IN SPIRIT AND TRUTH

Verses 2-3 tell us *And I heard a voice from heaven...* This glorious voice that the Apostle John heard in this vision was the voice of his glorified brethren with whom the apostle awaits in hope to become numbered in heaven. They were making the *new song* of redemptive music and melody from their hearts of thanksgiving, presenting pure and acceptable worship witnessed before *the throne* of God and in the presence of *the four living creatures*. This could be sung only by the whole company of the *hundred and forty-four thousand*. This hallowed voice of the saints in heaven is the sound of music that runs over one with great refreshment, and yet is stated loudly and confidently in full assurance of their salvation. Chapter 15 of Revelation says, *They sing the song of Moses, the servant of God, and the song of the Lamb saying:*

> *"Great and marvellous are your works,*
> *Lord God Almighty! Just and true are your ways,*
> *O King of the saints! Who shall not fear you, O Lord, and glorify your name?*
> *For you alone are holy*
> *For all nations shall come and worship before you.*
> *For your judgements have been magnified"* (15:3-4).

This *song of Moses* that represents the Old Testament is also *the song of the Lamb* who is the fulfilment of the "Covenant of Redemption" and who enables the "Covenant of Creation" to also find redemption in that eternal Covenant that is *Yes and in Him Amen* (2 Cor. 1:20) in the Lord Jesus Christ. These are the Songs of Zion that are so aptly canonised in the Word of God, particularly in the book of Psalms, and are represented in the many songs of Scripture. These old words breathed by God Himself for the revelation of Himself and His purposes are sung with a new heart that is regenerated and a life that is redeemed by the blood of the Lamb. The *harp* that they used was the harp of their lips, singing a cappella, *...speaking to one another in psalms and hymns and spiritual songs, singing and making melody in [their] hearts to the*

Lord, giving thanks always for all things to God the Father in the name of our Lord Jesus Christ (Eph. 5:19-20). *No one could learn that song except the hundred and forty-four thousand'* because it was only they that *were redeemed from the earth* (14:3) by the Lord Jesus Christ in His redemptive sacrifice, which was applied to their hearts by God the Holy Spirit. This is heartfelt worship of a personal nature that renews and "transforms" their lives as *a living sacrifice holy and acceptable to God, which is your [their] reasonable service* (Rom. 12:1).

We have seen the identity of *the four living creatures* (4:6-9) that are spoken of in the prophet Ezekiel chapters 1 and 10. These spiritual beings are God's personal providence across every part of the physical creation of matter, space and time, and in *Him we live and move and have our being* (Acts 17:28). We see here that the rough-hewn, Biblically-regulated worship rendered by the saints throughout all the ages both in heaven and earth is met with approval by the Trinitarian God upon the throne of heaven. How do we know this? Worship is undoubtedly not true worship merely because the worshipper feels good and sincere while engaging in it. That was how Cain thought of his worship, but *God did not respect Cain and his offering* (Gen. 4:5). Why? It is God's appointment according to His word that we render worship in spirit and truth. This Biblically-regulated worship is rendered according to the righteousness of the law of God that is revealed in Moses, but which finds its spiritual and personal consummation in Christ (Jn. 4:21-24).

In **verses 4-5**, we learn that the sanctified, redeemed vice-regents, having a Godly focus in their faith, are the *hundred and forty-four thousand,* whose first duty is true worship of the true and living God. Their aim in everything they do is to "glorify God and to enjoy Him forever."[33] It is little wonder that those who ...*were redeemed from among man, being the firstfruits to God and to the Lamb* are called "saints" without exception. These holy "virgins" did "not defile" themselves with "the woman," the Babylonian beast of worldliness.

The temptation, when we are in such *a crooked perverse generation* (Phil. 2:15), is to cower under persecution and passively to suffer as we wait on God. Many in the Church are so waiting upon God for revival, as though this would propel them out of their misery. We should not stand by watching the world act while the Church passively suffers, waiting on God. It is at that point that a kind of anger against God develops in our heart, and we throw up our hands and say, "Where is the help of God?" We then move in and focus on ourselves and begin to cause ourselves harm in the condition called "Spiritual Depression." The influence of asceticism and pietism has been to withdraw the Christian from the world. But such waiting on God and such passive suffering are not marks of "holiness;" they can be described only as sin. The Church is not merely a victim in the world struggle, but it must be an active and aggressive army.

R.J. Rushdoony warns against this kind of "spiritual depression." "The reduction of the Kingdom of God to a spiritual realm [asceticism and pietism] is in effect a denial of the kingdom, whose claims are total. It surrenders the world to the enemy and retreats into defeat as though it were a victory. It is not surprising that alien creeds then take over." He then quotes from a liberal theologian, Reinhold Niebuhr, from Union Theological Seminary in the USA, who "observed early in his career how irrelevant the Church's role has become: 'The Church is like the Red Cross service in wartime.

---

[33] Westminster Shorter Catechism, Question-and-answer, Number 1.

It keeps life from degenerating into a consistent inhumanity, but it does not materially alter the fact of the struggle itself. The Red Cross neither wins the war nor abolishes it...' Each and every member of the body of Christ is a citizen of the Kingdom of God and therefore priests in the world. [All Christians] as part of this kingdom are to proclaim the whole counsel of God, to administer the sacraments, and to establish discipline within its framework. The Church must instruct its members conveying every aspect of the Christian's responsibility, in every sphere of law and life..." So, when Niebuhr compares the role of the pietistic Church to the Red Cross, such a conception of the Church visualises its role as that of the ***grand neutral*** on the human scene: this is a fearful perversion of the role of the Church and it labours under an illusion. The Church is in Christ's army, and there is no neutrality in this war between Christ and Satan. This warfare is in process in every sphere of life. The Church is the main contender, humanly speaking, on the world battle-field, and it cannot retire to the sidelines without conceding defeat and effecting its own execution. And this Christ will never permit His Church to do without inflicting fearful judgement upon her...

> The concept of neutrality is an invalid one in any sphere, and certainly never less appropriate than when held by the Church. The Church is not a political organisation, but it must instruct men in the fundamentals of Godly politics. It is not a welfare agency, but it must teach men the meaning of Godly charity. If the Church confines its teaching to spiritual matters, it must neglect most of Scripture, which speaks to man's condition in every area of life. Christian faith is either relevant to all of life or it is relevant to none of it: the claims of God are either total, or He is not God. To ask Christianity to stay in its own territory is to ask it to stay in all of

life. Religion as the Bible conceives of it declares it has no separate domain apart from the rest of life: it is the overall purpose and meaning of all life in its every sphere. Christianity is not an escapist religion.[34]

AN EXODUS BY TRANSFORMATION TO REFORMATION ACCORDING TO THE TRUTH OF GOD'S WORD

This war is waged, not with Kalashnikov submachine guns or the revolutionary politics of the mob, but in the statement of a Christ-like life that speaks the testimony of Christ not only in a sanctified holy lifestyle but also in measured timely words that testify to the truth in everything. The members of Christ are described as *virgins* who were not defiled, in the sense of 2 Corinthians 11:2, *I have betrothed you to one husband, that I may present you as a chaste virgin to Christ*. These saintly virgins are not defiled with 'the woman' but are acting as counter-cultural agents in this world and do not participate in the Babylonian beast; they are first and foremost disciples *who follow the Lamb*, who is the Lord Jesus Christ, *wherever He goes*. These "virgins" are in love with their Saviour and Redeemer and are governed by the Spirit of Christ, being the *Spirit of adoption by whom we [they] cry out, "Abba, Father"* (Rom. 8:15). For these disciples of Christ are the product of an eternal seed that was planted in their souls, (Matt. 13:1-23) the very word of God that has called them out of death into the resurrection life of Christ (1 Cor. 15:12-19) by the supernatural or spiritual work of preaching the Word of God (Rom. 10:14-21). "Thus the virginity of the true Church consists in its faithfulness to a God-centred faith as against the seductions of man-centred

---

[34] RJ Rushdoony, *Thy Kingdom Come, Studies in Daniel and Revelation*, Thoburn Press Virginia, 1978; pp 177-8.

theology, and the virginity of the kingdom is its resistance to the concept of a humanistic paradise apart from God."[35]

In this way *...in their mouth was found no deceit, for they are without fault before the throne of God* (14:5). These were not some elite spiritual group of people of ... *all the tribes of the children of Israel (that) were sealed* in perfection, but every believer throughout the generations of the kingdom of God, never perfect, but always sanctified and suited for this ministry of the word and the testimony of Jesus. As the Apostle Paul puts it, *...since we have this ministry, as we have received mercy, we do not lose heart. But we have renounced the hidden things of shame, not walking in craftiness or handling the word of God deceitfully, but by manifestation of the truth commending ourselves to every man's conscience in the sight of God...For we do not preach ourselves, but Christ Jesus the Lord, and ourselves your bondservants for Jesus' sake. For it is God who commanded light to shine out of darkness, who has shone into our hearts to give the light of the knowledge of the glory of God in the face of Jesus Christ* (2 Cor. 4:1-2, 5-6).

What follows in this chapter is all about the glorious ministry of the powerful and persistent preaching of God's Word that first of all transforms the heart in regeneration and then renovates with the same transforming Spirit the whole life in repentance or sanctification of the person and the entire world in which these "virgins" live. In this way, the kingdom of God is advanced as the rule of God is issued from heaven and is materialised as a spiritual kingdom on earth through the ministry of the Word of God. This is demonstrated in truth in the life and testimony of these redeemed saints that follow Jesus the Lamb according to radical faith in every

---

[35] R.J. Rushdoony, ibid., p179.

sphere of life, and as Christ's vice-regents bringing all things into subjection to the Lord Jesus Christ according to the Word of God.

THE POWERFUL AND PERSISTENT PREACHING OF THE SEVEN ANGELS

Verses 6-7: The *another angel* of verses 6-7 is part of a select group that fearlessly, powerfully and faithfully preach God's Word, being the media of God to bring about the 'new creation'. In the old creation, God spoke by the power of His Word and created all things out of nothing. So it is the ministry of these *seven* that proclaim the whole counsel of God that by Word and Spirit the will of God is established directly and supernaturally. As the entire creation is lost and dead under the weight of sin and corruption, so God redeems everything by *the Word that became flesh* who was the light and life of man by the power of the Word of God, and was *the light (that) shines in the darkness, and the darkness did not comprehend [overcome] it* (John 1:5).

These angels are of the same kind as the angels of the seven Churches of Revelation (2:1, 8, 12, 18; 3:1, 7, 14) where the Lord Jesus Christ pastorally addresses each of the seven Churches through its angel, its messenger that has been appointed by God, having been called, equipped and ordained, anointed by the Word and Spirit as the minister of Word and Sacrament. He is nothing less than the pastor of the local congregation.

There is a view that there are angels in the spiritual order of existence that are the patron angels of the Churches of God.[36] Of

---

[36] William Ramsay, *The Letters to the Seven Churches of Asia and Their Place in the Plan of the Apocalypse,* James Family Publications Co, Minneapolis, pp. 67-69. It is helpful at this point to quote R.J. Rushdoony concerning Platonism of Greek philosophy as opposed to Biblical thought as being typological,

never abstract, as it is Platonism. "Moreover, typology sees the reality often as manifests in history, not in an abstract and transcendental universe. Thus, typology in Scripture is of three kinds.

1. In one form, there is a threefold division: shadow – image – body. Thus, in Hebrews 10:1, the law of the Old Testament is defined as 'having a *shadow* of the good things to come, not the very image of the things,' which *image* appears with Christ; the *body* of the law is in the triune God. Similarly, in Hebrews 8:5, the Old Testament priesthood was a *shadow*, and Christ's 'more excellent ministry' in 'the true tabernacle' 'in the heavens' (8:1, 2, 6) is the *body*. Typology in this sense sees the *shadow* in the Old Testament, the *image* in the New, and the substance or *body* in God.

2. Again, there is type and anti-type, anti-type being that which a type prefigures. In this sense, the Old Testament *type* is a figure or parable of the reality which appears in the New Testament (Hebrews 9:8, 9).

3. The primary emphasis, however, can fall on the Old Testament fact. Thus, Melchizedek is the *model* or *reality*, Christ the *copy*, "after the order of Melchizedek" (Hebrews 6:20). However, this same image becomes altered when we read that Melchizedek was "made like unto the Son of God" (Hebrews 7:3), the Son became the *type*, and Melchizedek the *anti-type*.

Types, moreover, can *pre-figure* and *predict*. Thus, whereas reality is reserved to the realm of abstract universals by Platonism, Biblical faith, retaining always the priority of the ontological trinity by the sovereign and eternal decree, whereby the temporal order is predestined and subordinated to the eternal, nonetheless makes the temporal order a domain of reality by means of typology. *Reality is seen as a past, present, and future fact and is both temporal and eternal, whereas for Platonism reality is never temporal, having neither past, present, nor future, and, in its eternity, is both impersonal and abstract.* The great assurance of the believer that 'all things work together for good' (Rom. 8:28) is possible only in terms of the double fact that there is an eternal decree or absolute predestination, and that 'all things' have a reality, in that neither the time nor any eras in time are excluded from the present manifestation of, and integral relation to, reality. 'The angel of the Church of Ephesus' (for example) is thus not an abstract universal or 'a corresponding existence on another and higher plane but more pure in essence, more closely associated with the Divine nature than the individual Church on earth can be.' The 'angel' is the Church as shadow – image – body, as type and anti-type, as model a copy; it is a Church totally grasped 'in his right hand' (2:1), and yet not totally in Him. Reality is ascribed to its full position in Christ, and *reality* course, the angelic hosts do congregate among the Churches, particularly when the saints are at worship (1 Cor. 11:9-10), and they do assist the Churches (Matt. 4: 11). In heavenly places, they are called by our Lord to go to battle (2 Kings 6:17) and protect the members of the body of Christ at particularly dangerous times (Ps. 91:11). However, it would be endorsing Platonism to conceive of a spiritual "other" or the "ideal form" representing the physical as the material lesser. These pastors with their Churches are in the fullness of their life and reality, and are not some lesser extensions of a greater angelic reality. These pastors possess the genuine authority that exists in Christ directly and without the mediators as in the Old Testament, whose offices of Prophet, Priest and King are directly ascribed to the Church of Jesus Christ, the very body of Christ. These offices of Christ are expressed explicitly within the preacher as Christ's prophet and directly, though not specifically, as priest and king. Without going into this at length at this point, we would teach that the office of deacon is specifically expressed in Christ's office as priest and the office of king is specifically expressed in Christ's office of ruling elder of which the preacher and pastor is expressly and intricately part. So, in the three offices of Christ—Prophet, Priest and King—we have the three offices of the Church: the "pastor" is the preacher and teacher; the "deacon" is the steward of the Church and carer of the poor and needy; and the "ruling elders" govern the affairs of the Church. They have not only the complete authority of the Lord Jesus Christ, but also the grace and enabling to perform these tasks according to the power of God Himself.

---

is similarly ascribed to its present state of service and shortcomings. It is the Church whose past, present, future, and eternal states are closely interconnected, all possessing reality and yet shadowing and typifying one another. This is the Church in the fullness of its life and reality." Op. cit. pp 97-98.

These seven angels on "terra firma," though never perfect in person and ministry, for they bear the flesh of man that is redeemed and is being sanctified in readiness to be glorified, speak as one the infallible written Word of God. These are gifts of the ascended Christ as, *He Himself gave some to be Apostles, some prophets, some evangelists, and some pastors and teachers* (Eph. 4:11). The single infallible deposit of God's word thoroughly equips the *pastor and teacher* in every good work. It is, as it were, the "master builder's toolbox" for the preacher's lifelong service in the ministry of the Word and Sacrament as, *all Scripture is given by inspiration of God and is profitable for doctrine, for reproof, for correction, for instruction in righteousness, that the man of God may be complete, thoroughly equipped for every good work* (2 Tim. 3:16).

This ministry of the Word is carried out by the man of God, but lives in the Church, being the very body of Christ. There are many posing to be pastors in Christ's Church that are described as those *...who come to you in sheep's clothing, but inwardly they are ravenous wolves* (Matt. 7:15) and the Lord Jesus warns us against them. Such false teachers and pastors are either ordained without a call from God or self-appointed because of natural gifting and aspiration. They are seen because there are a false humility and a lack of Biblical fidelity to *the whole counsel of God*, and there is an absence of clear Biblical *narrowness* (Matt. 7:13-14) in their lifestyle and unguarded moments in their teaching. In their preaching and teaching, they pander to the felt needs of a congregation rather than the congregation's actual needs, and they will take the people as far as they want to go, rather than lead the people of God into radical Biblical faith. They will teach what may be well and good but fail to preach to the conscience. Their teaching is not faithful to sound doctrine. They will feed the goats but the sheep lay starving for want of the *bread of life*. In the end, such people stand opposed to the teaching of orthodox Biblical doctrine, which has stood the test of time as being "truth," and ...*will not endure sound doctrine but according to their own desires, because they have itching ears, they will heap up for themselves teachers and they will turn their ears away from the truth, and be turned aside to fables* (2 Tim. 4:3-4). Such people are involved in controversies with deeply spiritual, righteous and holy people even in their own congregations. The Apostle Paul, when passing through Miletus, pleads with the Ephesian elders to ... *take heed of yourselves and to the flock, among which the Holy Spirit has made you overseers [elders], to shepherd the Church of God which He purchased with His own blood. For I know this, that after my departure savage wolves will come in, not sparing the flock. Also from among yourselves men will rise up, speaking perverse things, to draw away the disciples after themselves. Therefore watch, and remember that for three years I did not cease to warn everyone night and day with tears* (Acts 20:28-31).

The pastor is first and foremost a man of God and therefore, as said earlier, called of God, equipped both in Word and Spirit, and anointed by Christ by virtue of Christ's office as prophet. This office is unique and there is no replication of the preacher in the natural world. Just because a man is a fine orator and can command the media of the day, this does not make him a preacher even if he is a person trained in the best theological colleges and has great skills in teaching the philosophies of this world and dazzles people with great ideas and eloquence. The supernatural or deeply spiritual element in the calling and appointing of the preacher that makes him God's man is fundamental to the work of preaching. The preacher is a man that fears God alone.

Eloquence may be a gift but it also can be a curse. They said concerning the Apostle Paul, *"For his letters,"* they say, *"are weighty and powerful, his bodily presence is weak, and his speech is contemptible"* (2 Cor. 10:10). Pastors may not be excellent orators, or good-looking, or well-dressed and refined in the manners of high society or have the acumen of politicians, but they are men of faith in Christ alone. Pastors are examples of deep Biblical righteousness of the highest moral and ethical standards, which is displayed not only in their public life but also in their family life.

He will contend for *the faith* at great personal cost and public condemnation, and will do anything it takes to pastor the flock of God. He is a man of prayer, interceding on behalf of all that touches his ministry. He is fundamentally a dying man so that Jesus may live within his pastorate and among his people. He knows that he cannot put any trust in the flesh for it is a weak *earthenware vessel*, but he also knows that in this weakness the power of the resurrection of Jesus is perfected. The pastor is pre-eminently a man who believes the Word of God so that he speaks it with sincerity and truth from his heart. He sees his calling as a preacher of the Word of God and his integrity in respect of that Word is more precious than life itself. It is a little wonder that the Apostle Paul says concerning the vital work of God through the preacher, …*as it is written:*

"How beautiful are the feet of those who preach the Gospel of peace,
Who bring glad tidings of good things!" (Rom. 10:15).

For preaching to be effective, it must always be accompanied by a certain kind of teaching. The foundations of truth are its facts that must be related to Christ who is the personification of the truth. This truth will lead to spiritual wisdom, which makes all things pre-eminent in Christ. Establishing sound doctrine that is both apostolic and thoroughly Biblical are the pillars of truth that give the Biblical testimony of the Scriptures its framework and structure. For example, if we believe in the doctrine of God's providence in all things, we will have the basis for interpreting history from a godly perspective. If we understand the doctrine of creation in the Scriptures, then the physical sciences of chemistry, physics and biology will have a certain perspective that will be consistent with Biblical theology. So, when the knowledge is found in the so-called secular fields of knowledge, it will be the theological foundations of doctrine that will give it its best reason and understanding. There is only one source of knowledge—God—but the key to physical and natural knowledge that is found in general revelation of creation is the Word of God uttered by the Lord Jesus Christ.

The exercise of preaching should never be conceived as merely pulpit ministry. It is not a Biblical approach to preaching when pastors entomb themselves in their studies, so that the only place that the world sees them is in the pulpit each week. It is to be noted that the Lord Jesus preached in every place and situation. There is not a recorded sermon in the book of Acts that was preached in the local synagogue. The Apostle Paul indeed used the synagogues for preaching, but the bulk of his instruction was done outside of the Church. He had a practice of evangelistic disputing with the Jews in their synagogues, often with small groups of people such as in Ephesus, of which the Bible says, *Now the men were about twelve in all. And he went into the synagogue and spoke boldly for three months, reasoning and persuading concerning the things of the kingdom of God. But when some were hardened and did not believe, but spoke evil of the Way before the multitude, he departed from them and withdrew the disciples, reasoning daily in the school of Tyrannus. And this he continued for two years, so that all who dwelt in Asia heard the word of the Lord Jesus, both Jews and Greeks* (Acts 19:7-10). Certainly, our Lord Jesus Christ attended and often taught in the local synagogue, and in His hometown of Nazareth He expounded the Scriptures of the prophecy Isaiah chapter 61 verses 1-3. But He also consistently taught His disciples daily and counselled those who came to him, such as Nicodemus (Jn. 3:1-21), and the Samaritan woman (John 4:7-26). These were all venues for preaching and teaching. The Apostle Paul told the Ephesian elders that he *...kept back nothing that was helpful, but proclaimed it to you, and taught you publicly and from house-to-house, testifying to Jews, and also the Greeks, repentance towards God and faith toward our Lord Jesus Christ* (Acts 20:20-21). So, his ministry was a comprehensive preaching and teaching ministry that included his public preaching at the regular worship services and across the community, both *publicly and from house-to-house*, unsettling the "status quo" with the counter-culture of Biblical faith to the degree that they said concerning the Apostle Paul that he was turning *the world upside down* (Acts 17:6). The two assistants of the Apostle Paul, Aquila and Priscilla, after hearing a very eloquent preacher in the person of Apollos from Alexandria, quietly counselled him to bring God's word to bear upon his life, and preached to him after taking him *...aside and explained to him the way of God more accurately* (Acts 18:25). So here in the context of counselling, teaching and preaching finds a venue. Also, one of the most effective means of preaching and teaching is through published material that has been influential not only in the generation of its publication but also through subsequent generations. The Apostle Paul knew the effectiveness of published material to communicate the Word of God in his preaching and teaching ministry, and so we have a representative deposit of these communications in the New Testament letters. The Church fathers wrote effectively to communicate the truth of the Word of God that was used by God the Holy Spirit to awaken successive generations to the truth of God's Word. For example, the works of Augustine of Hippo had the most profound effect upon the greatest of the reformers in the Reformation, John Calvin, who quotes Augustine more than he does any other of the Church fathers. The commentaries of Matthew Henry[37] were the closest companion of George Whitfield as he was converted and being prepared as God's servant to bring about the eighteenth-century revival in Britain and the United States.

THE MINISTRY OF THE WORD IS INCARNATED IN THE CHURCH, THE WHOLE BODY OF CHRIST

The preacher will prepare his congregation to be priests in their world so that by knowing the Gospel they are awakened to all knowledge and wisdom and will apply the truth of God's word to every area of life with a comprehensive Biblical worldview. As the Apostle Paul says to the Ephesians, the preacher and teacher from the local congregation is to equip ...*the saints for the work of ministry, for the edifying of the body of Christ, till we all come to the unity of the faith and of the knowledge of the son of God, to a perfect man, to the measure of the stature of the fullness of Christ* (Eph. 4:11-16).

The life of the body of Christ has an ecclesiastical structure in terms of authority and power which is found in each member, family and part of the Church. Each member of Christ's body is apportioned authority in proportion to their role and responsibility of service to carry out the role. So, for example, the husband is to rule his household and is the head of his wife, and he is to teach by "word and precept" the members of his household. According to the "Great Commission," he has been given authority to make known the Word of God in his world as priest of the Most High, proclaiming the "Crown Rights of Christ" according to the "Covenant of Creation". He is to be an example of righteousness and holiness, setting forth the love of Christ in his family, in his workplace and

---

[37] Arnold Dallimore, *George Whitfield, The Life and Times of the Great Evangelist of the 18th-Century Revival*, Banner of Truth, Edinburgh, Vol. 1, p 82.

in the local Church. Such authority is subject to the discipline of the Church, who has been given *the keys of the kingdom of heaven* (Matt. 16:18-19), and may be corrected by the wider Church. The wife likewise is subject to her husband and yet supports her husband in everything, assists in the teaching of her children, acts as a priest in establishing the stewardship of her household, and cares for each member of her household and extended family. She may assist her husband in the workplace and in their community. As an example of godliness, righteousness and holiness, she sets in order that which is disorderly. *Children are to obey their parents in the Lord* (Eph. 6:1), showing due respect to their father and mother. They are to receive their parents' instruction and to serve the Lord, taking hold of the benefits of the "Covenant of Redemption" in all truth. They are to take their role in the family as they are called upon to do so, caring for one another and assisting both father and mother as they are able.

FIRST AND FOREMOST IS EVANGELISTIC PREACHING

The point of entry into any preaching is evangelistic preaching. The Lord Jesus made this clear when he was preaching to Nicodemus who was a Pharisee, highly respected for his understanding of the law of God, and a ruler of the Jews. He came to Jesus at night, seeking the truth about Jesus (John 3:1-2). Jesus began his preaching to this very impressive man at the point of his real need. It was not more knowledge that would only "puff him up," but a new heart. Only then could he begin even to understand who Jesus was. He needed a regenerated heart that could only come from God, as it is only God who can give eternal life. And so, He spoke to him about the necessity of being born again. It was only as Nicodemus became a new creation in Christ that he could ever enter the kingdom of God. Anybody who is outside the kingdom of God could not be the redeemed vice-regent that he needed to become if he was going to give glory to God, which was his chief purpose and greatest joy. Without this first work, there can be no resurrection from the dead, no righteous service before God, and no godly significance in this world. (John 3:3-5) So Nicodemus was washed by the water of the Word of God through the preached word of Jesus; then it was the Spirit who was going to do the supernatural work of resurrecting Nicodemus out of the dead condition inherited from his first parent Adam, who had left his child Nicodemus in a condition of sin and death (Jn. 3:6-7). As he believed, with eternal life entering into his soul upon Jesus's preaching and teaching, he found the beckoning call of his Saviour to be his Redeemer and Lord. This probably did not happen as the Lord Jesus preached to Nicodemus that night, but there was evidence that a life of true faith and repentance had entered his soul (Jn. 3:9-21). In subsequent Scriptures, we are told that he took the side of Jesus when the elders were gathered to condemn Jesus (Jn. 7:45-52), and at the crucifixion of Christ, he was numbered with Joseph of Arimathea, who buried the body of Jesus in his own tomb (Jn. 19:32-39).

There are numerous examples of this kind of evangelistic focus in preaching where the preacher ...*(has) the everlasting Gospel to preach to those who dwell on the earth – to every nation, tribe, tongue, and people* (14:6). This kind of preaching has been commissioned to reach the ends of the earth, and none are to be excluded as we are commissioned to ...*preach the Gospel to every creature* (Mk. 16:15). But this Gospel is not something we sell or ask permission for the right to preach. The fear of God is in our souls because we have been commissioned by God who is the Creator and Redeemer of all things and the Judge of all things. Our message is not a message of negotiation but a message of mercy and a calling out of those that are already under the wrath of God and pending judgement. The voice of a preacher is *a loud voice* of heaven, *Fear God and give glory to Him, for the hour of His judgement has come...* (14:7). Today the Gospel call is that 'God loves you!' In more faithful days, when the fear of God moved preachers, the merciful call was, *Flee from the wrath the come* (Luke 3:7) and be saved, which is in keeping with this messenger (14:7). The only possible response to the hearing of this Gospel is to surrender to God's terms in the Lord Jesus Christ and put your faith in Christ your Redeemer, and as you walk in *the way* repent of all your sins and keep your eyes fixed upon *...the Author and the Finisher of our faith*, (Heb. 12:2) and *...worship Him who made heaven and earth, the sea and the springs of water* (14:7).

PREACHING THAT CALLS FOR HOLINESS

We shall consider verse 8. The constant need for preaching across the believer's entire life, both at a particular time of life and throughout his life, is imperative. The purpose of the Gospel is always radical discipleship throughout the life of every believer. Church-based evangelism is God's ordained way of reaching this world with the Gospel because it is the institution of the local church that is committed to the whole person for the whole of their life, discipling the congregation of God's people wherever they are occupied in the kingdom of God. The local Church is ecclesiastically set up to reflect all the offices of the Lord Jesus Christ as Prophet, Priest and King, and to establish Gospel discipline and Gospel life. The Church is first of all committed pastorally to the Christian family and then to the community of Christ, from the newborn child in baptism, through every phase of the believer's life, to their departure at their funeral, so that every believer can give glory to God and honour to His Name.

The *"Babylonian"* hope is of self-assurance and security in this world system, where if you work hard, pay your taxes, and contribute to your retirement plan, the good life becomes your right. In everything else, the secular humanist "city" state will look after you—in your education, in healthcare, in any natural disaster. It urges faith in science and technology because, "If we do not know now, we will know in the future, and maybe your cancer will be curable in your lifespan." This false hope urges one to be realistic and to have heaven on earth now where one can see it and feel it—so long as one does what society says. It encourages us to do as we like without the restraints of Biblical righteousness and morality. The "Babylonian" hope mocks Biblical righteousness that requires us to keep the Sabbath, observe our marriage vows even when it is difficult to do so, and not to murder the unborn child who proves inconvenient for your career or our station in life. Dwellers in Babylon exclaim, "They even tell us not to commit sodomy when we are biologically wired to follow the dictates of our lusts in terms of our homosexual tendencies, fornication, adultery and pornography. In all these things we are not hurting anybody, and so surely these things are all right. Even if the children of our broken marriage do get hurt, it is through no fault of my own because it is my partner that did it. What is wrong with being young and bullet-proof, having my life in front of me to live to the max? Why not try everything, be it at the rock concert or the "disco," and absorb every conceivable existential feeling? Being drunk and being on an illicit drug high is the experience of freedom and personal anarchy. Let me taste the toxic stimulated lifestyle that gives me the high, that I may indulge the experience of the sensual overload. All such restrictions are for religious fanatics, Christian fundamentalists, wowsers, legalists and puritanical killjoys."

The evangelical church in the Western world is busily trying to simulate the onslaught of this world system which has very clear eschatological hopes of establishing a coherent secular socio-political system that will unite all mankind of all nations into one world system known as Babylon the great. This is the vision of the Socialist Labour Movement across every nation that is a signatory to the United Nations and all allied organisations. This Secular

Humanism offers the promise of prosperity with an ever-improving standard of living across the nations of the world without God. It seeks global domination within a community of nations that are one economically and strategically. However, while culturally tolerant of all religion, it is implacably intolerant of historic Protestant Christianity, which it fears. This fear gives rise to great persecution of the Church worldwide. It is in this venue that the preacher cries out with all the authority of God Himself, *Babylon is fallen, is fallen, that great city, because she has made all nations drink of the wine of the wrath of her fornication* (14:8).

The nation of Germany was humiliated by its defeat in World War I, and during the years of the "Great Depression" Germany was forced to pay reparations to the Allies. This became the seed-bed for the nationalistic aspirations of a united National Socialistic Nazi dictatorship that would become the world Axis power and effect a millennium known as the "Third Reich." This would be achieved through military superiority initially, and then cultural superiority on a global basis. This became a power lust among the German people and they saw that it was in their grasp to become the "master race" in all the earth. The propaganda was relentless and the eschatological hope of an absolute millennial reign of man and the capture of any kind of kingdom of God was in their sights and a genuine possibility.

The Christian testimony was severely emasculated because of state control of the Church, but a very small testimony of Christ was preached into this situation through the lips of men like Dietrich Bonhoeffer, and it fulfilled the purposes of God in a situation that looked hopeless in the eyes of man. Bonhoeffer was executed April 9, 1945 only a month before the end of the Second World War, but he was faithful to the end. Such is the preacher's job to cry out,

Babylon is fallen, is fallen that great city, because she has made all nations drink of the wine of the wrath of her fornication (14:8).

PREACHING WARNINGS AGAINST RELIGIOUS UNFAITHFULNESS

Verses 9-12 show us that the most toxic form of error is religious error. There is nothing more powerful and more effective in the hands of the devil than false religion. It institutionalises heresy; it formalises faith as a cultural belief; and sanctions the lifestyle of their devotees as hard-bitten believers of the erroneous heresy. Religion is universal amongst mankind, as is the systematisation of religion, whether it is in the form of eastern religions or false versions of Christianity in their various heresies. These man-made religions are, in the end, the Babylonian *beast* and are the ultimate blasphemy against the living and true God that created the heavens and the earth and who rules over His work continually.

The *third angel*, being the pastor of the Churches of God, contends for the faith and defends it against such heresy. The preacher is called upon to uncover the idols (1 Thess. 1:9) that are in the hearts of those who trust in false religion so that those that follow them might be freed from the bondage of believing in that which does not save and cannot save. Such preaching hunts out religious error and establishes true religion according to the Scriptures. He *proclaims liberty to the captives and recovery of sight to the blind; to set at liberty those who are oppressed; to proclaim the acceptable year of the Lord* (Luke 4:18) with a loud and clear voice of Gospel truth.

The biggest threat posed by the citadels of false religion is the one that claims the place of true religion, Roman Catholicism. We have contended that the clearest picture of *the beast* is Roman Catholicism. Those who are seduced by the sacerdotal Gospel of Romanism and receive the sacraments as the marks of the Antichrist hear the voice of Biblical preaching and the testimony of Gospel examples of true Biblical faith, but they remain Gospel hardened. Then *...he himself shall also drink of the wine of the wrath of God, which is poured out full strength into the cup of His indignation. He shall be tormented with fire and brimstone in the presence of the holy angels and in the presence of the Lamb* (14:10). This torment may be reserved in life after death in the place of everlasting torment, but it may well come to these people in the vengeance of God in the form of bad days when the 'four horsemen' under the 'seven seals' of chapter 6 of Revelation inflict the vengeance of God in war, famine, oppression and natural disaster. *For the wrath of God is revealed from heaven against all ungodliness and unrighteousness of men, who suppress the truth in unrighteousness, because what may be known of God is manifest in them, for God has shown it to them* (Rom. 1:18-19).

A particular judgement is meted out upon those that belong to the beast. The most prominent representation of Antichrist has been by far the worst persecutor of the true children of God. Because of their shameful treatment of the anointed of God, the very "apple of God's eye," they may incur the very worst torment on earth, but definitely for eternity, as it is stated here: *And the smoke of her torment ascends forever and ever; and they have no rest day or night, who worship the beast and his image and whoever receives the Mark of his name* (14:11).

Throughout the generations of the kingdom of God, the saints of God laboured under intense opposition from the Babylonian beast and her Antichrist religious *harlot*. They were relentlessly persecuted throughout the history of the great tribulation which seemed endless, but they faithfully looked to the Captain of their soul, the Lord Jesus Christ. There has been a faithful testimony to Christ and His Gospel, so that those that have entered into a

Christless eternity are without excuse. For *here is the patience of the saints*. Through their faith in Christ, the very righteousness of Christ is demonstrated in practice to the watching world that knows that God is revealed in the faithful testimony of true believers that depended not on the flesh, but walked in the power of the Spirit of God, triumphant and true, *keeping the commandments of God and the faith of Jesus* (14:12).

PREACHING COMFORT TO THE FAITHFUL SAINTS

Verse 13 speaks this comfort: *Then I (the Apostle John) heard a voice from heaven saying to me, "Write: Blessed are the dead who die in the Lord…"* The words of the preacher are of the greatest comfort to the believers, for they are heavenly truth, and these things cannot be taken from them. Nothing comforts or provides balm for the soul more than words from heaven when the believer is so looking forward to his glorification with Christ.

This comfort is not based on man-centred philosophy of the self-help Gospel, or a motivational speech that "gees" people up to live in some positive mental framework. Living faith arises out of the hearts of those that have directly known the transforming grace of God in regeneration. It can deal with their sins through repentance and modification, but also sees the power of the grace of God. Those with living faith reconstruct their lives for the glory of God, and these people are profoundly comforted in nothing less than the truth from heaven. Disciples of Christ are dying men that *take up their cross daily*, but they are also living men who know the power of Christ's resurrection, and they live gloriously in Christ Jesus, the God of their salvation.

The Lord Jesus encouraged and taught His disciples extensively and with great diligence so that they should not be overwhelmed by the events that would come. The reaffirmation of the glorious

Gospel assures the people of God that their faith is not misplaced and that there can be no other salvation except in the Redeemer who is able to say, *I am the way, the truth, and the life. No one comes to the Father except through me* (Jn. 14:6). Assurance is given without any qualification to those who live by faith in the Lord Jesus. All the necessary resources for their work of faith will always be granted, and even if their bodies are taken from them, nothing can ruin their soul. The Holy Spirit is given without measure, and there will be no task that will be impossible for God as the disciple walks by faith in the Name of God Almighty and for His glory. The promise is that the Lord Himself will never leave or forsake them and that none would pluck them out of His Father's hand. Even if sin overwhelms us, God is there! And if failure devastates us for the lack of faith, God is there! If, because of the failure of wisdom and understanding, we have become lost sheep and we are in a place far from the will of God for us, God is there! If we have rebelled as Jonah and we find ourselves in the belly of spiritual depression, even there God takes us by the hand and vomits us out into a place for a particular testimony and useful work. Our pride is dealt with on such occasions and we are able to say, *And we know that all things work together for good to those who love God, to those who are the called according to His purpose* (Rom. 8:28).

This so-called fourth preacher does not speak to the dead but he speaks to the living who have lost a faithful brother, sister or child and he preaches the words from heaven through his physical lips, *Blessed are the dead who die in the Lord from now on* (14:13). The only explanation for Christian life is a special intervention of God based on the "Covenant of Redemption." This is effected by God the Holy Spirit, who gives His people unction from on high to live as resurrected ones. There is therefore 'no sting in death' and 'no victory' in that place called 'Hades'. There is therefore solid reasonable assurance that, *'"Death is swallowed up in victory..."*

But thanks be to God, who gives us the victory through the Lord Jesus Christ. Therefore, my beloved brethren, be steadfast, immovable, always abounding in the work of the Lord, knowing that your labour is not in vain in the Lord (1 Cor. 15:57-58). *Yes,* says the inner testimony of the Spirit witnessing within the believer's spirit personally and with great comfort, *they may rest from their labours, and their works follow them* (14:13). Thus, true comfort from God is granted so that we all ...*press toward the goal of the prize of the upward call of God in Christ Jesus* (Phil. 3:14).

EVANGELICAL PREACHING THAT ANNOUNCES THE LIMITS OF GOD'S SOVEREIGN MERCY

Verses 14-16 give us a glorious description: *Then I looked, and behold, a white cloud, and on the cloud sat One like the Son of Man, having on His head a golden crown, and in His hand a sharp sickle.* This picture is of the Lord Jesus ascended on high upon a *white cloud* with his royal *golden crown*. He is described in another place as being the *King of kings and Lord of lords* (19:16) and He is continuously surveying planet earth, harvesting here and harvesting there. However, reaping evangelistically unto life, or as the undertaker and 'grim reaper', death comes! *Blessed and holy is he who has part in the first resurrection. Over such, the second death has no power*...(20:6). The *first resurrection* occurs when a believer is born-again and regenerated at conversion so that thereafter the life of faith in Christ Jesus our Lord is always the mark of his life. Man is born into the death of Adam, being the first death, but the second death awaits him who has not received the *first resurrection*. But he who has received this regenerating resurrection need not fear the *second death* for he lives with the resurrected One, Jesus, the first-fruits of the *new creation*, who has granted him *eternal life*.

This picture of *the Son of Man coming on the clouds of heaven with power and great glory* (Matt. 24:27, 30-31, Lu. 21:27 Mk.

13:26-27) is found in the "Olivet Discourses" in each of the synoptic Gospels describing the destruction of the Jerusalem Temple and its city that took place in A.D. 70. For a full discussion on these passages, please refer to chapter 22.

The Lord Jesus is enthroned at the right hand of the Father and governs all things in His creation, and there is a constant harvest throughout the generations of the history of man. He gathers in every person that has ever been born and, we believe, even the unborn. The message of the preacher at this point is that, *It is a fearful thing to fall into the hands of the living God* (Heb. 10:31), who is sovereign and rules all things. The Gospel is God's mercy stretched out with great patience to the peoples of all the earth and *...whoever calls on the name of the Lord shall be saved* (Rom. 10:13) without exception. *But even if our Gospel is veiled, it is veiled to those who are perishing, whose minds the god of this age has blinded, who do not believe, lest the light of the Gospel of the glory of Christ, who is the image of God, should shine on them* (2 Cor. 4:3-4). *How shall we escape if we neglect so great a salvation,* says the writer to the Hebrews (Heb. 2:3).

This kind of preaching is effectual until death brings departure from this gracious free offer of the Gospel. Our Lord, while on the cross of Calvary, was able to speak the words of comfort to the thief on the cross beside Him. The thief was moved in his conscience to call upon the Name of the Lord in the words, *Lord, remember me when you come into your kingdom* (Lu. 23:42). The simple sermon that was given to the dying thief was, *Assuredly, I say to you, today you will be with me in paradise* (Lu. 23:43) and he was saved to the uttermost.

It says another angel, being yet the fifth kind of preacher and pastor, came out of the Temple. The Jerusalem Temple is long since gone, as the typological era of the Old Testament has passed away, and the new has come. This Temple from which the preacher proceeds is *...made of living stones, rejected indeed by man, but chosen by God and precious. You also* [all believers], *as living stones, are being built up a spiritual house, a holy priesthood, to offer up spiritual sacrifices acceptable to God through Jesus Christ* (1 Pet. 2:4-5). The preacher being at one with his Church is engaged in intercessory prayer to *...the Stone which the builders rejected (which) has become the Chief Cornerstone* (1 Pet. 2:7), the Lord Jesus Christ, the King and Head of the Church. The preacher knows that he converts nobody—it is only the Lord Jesus in His sovereign grace who shows mercy and gathers the harvest in His own timing, and yet He always uses prayer and preaching. The Church is the granary for this harvest and it is the place where the saints are discipled by the work of preaching and teaching in the fellowship of prayer for the saints. The Church earnestly prays and calls upon the Lord Jesus Christ: *Thrust in your sickle and reap, for the time has come for you to reap, for the harvest of the earth is ripe* (14:15). This is the Lord's harvest and the Lord is readier to bring in this harvest than the Church wishes to believe for this harvest. Therefore, the Lord says to His disciples, *Behold, I say to you, lift up your eyes and look at the fields, for they are already white for harvest and he who reaps shall receive wages, and gather fruit for eternal life, that both he who sows and he who reaps may rejoice together. For in this the saying is true: "One sows and another reaps," I send you to reap that for which you have not laboured; others have laboured, and you have entered into their labour* (John 4:35-38).

Verse 16 tells us, *So He who sat on the cloud thrust in His sickle on the earth and the earth was reaped.* The Lord Himself sovereignly attends the evangelistic work of the preacher and the prayers of the Church of God, in harvesting all that are Christ's. Christ the Lamb's atonement will be complete for *...none of them is lost...*

(John 17:12) from all nations and every generation of man, even the full number of the *hundred and forty-four thousand* (14:1), even to the end. The redeeming sacrifice of the Lamb is sufficient for every one of Christ's, who are *...chosen [elected] in Him before the foundation of the world, that we should be holy and without blame before Him in love, having predestined us to adoption as sons by Jesus Christ to Himself, according to the good pleasure of His will* (Eph. 1:4-5). The security of the redeemed in its full incomprehensible number of the *hundred and forty-four thousand* is an absolute, as the Lord Jesus Christ Himself gave *...them eternal life, and they shall never perish; neither shall anyone snatch them out of His or His Father's hand* (John 10:27-28).

THE PREACHER IN THE DAYS OF VENGEANCE AND THE REAPING OF THE GRAPES OF WRATH

In **verses 17-20**, The sixth and seventh angel messengers continue their work of preaching to make known the "days of vengeance" that come upon the earth, even to the end. Be it at the end of a season of war, famine, pestilence and natural disaster, or at the end of the epoch in history or at the visitation of death, every man, woman and child must face up to the consequences of their condition in sin, rebellion and transgression against their Creator who displays His grace and mercy at every point in their lives.

The startling aspect of this text is that the angel himself bears *a sharp sickle*. This suggests a certain directness in the issuing of vengeance in these days of greater wrath. Those of us who practise the exclusive use of psalmody in our worship of God will be startled when we use in our praise the prayers of the imprecatory Psalms [38] that lead the worshipper to praise God for terrible judge-

---

[38] http://en.wikipedia.org/wiki/Imprecatory_Psalms–Imprecatory Psalms, contained within the Ketuvim (wisdom literature) of the Hebrew Bible (תנ״ך), are those that invoke judgment, calamity, or curses, upon one's enemies or

ment upon the ungodly and unrighteous. In the providence of God and in the prayer life of the Church, there comes a time in the witness of the Church when there is an agreement between two or three gathered in the Lord's Name on earth who petition the Lord of heaven who says He has ...*give[n] (you) the keys of the kingdom of heaven, and whatever you bind on earth will be bound in heaven, and whatever you loose on earth will be loosed in heaven* (Matt. 16:19). When such prayer is offered according to the Word of God, such as in the imprecatory Psalms for example, God, who is sovereign, pours out from heaven the powers of God that bring torment and even death among man. So, the vengeance of God is poured out in direct relationship to the saints' petitions. It is true that ...*it is written, "Vengeance is mine, I will repay, says the Lord"* (Rom. 12:19), but God always remembers mercy in His wrath and always wishes to extend His mercy and grace to the very last drop of His patience. But then a *loud voice* cries out both in heaven and on earth ...*saying, "How long, O Lord, holy and true, until you judge and avenge our blood on those who dwell on the earth?"* (6:10). Then God's work is done, and it is well that we say, *Therefore since we are receiving a kingdom which cannot be shaken, let us have*

---

those perceived as the enemies of God. Major Imprecatory Psalms include Psalm 69 and Psalm 109, while Psalms 5, 6, 11, 12, 35, 37, 40, 52, 54, 56, 58, 69, 79, 83, 137, 139, and 143 are also considered imprecatory (link to full text of Psalms). As a sample, Psalm 69:24 states toward God, *"Pour out Your indignation on them, and let Your burning anger overtake them"* and Psalm 137:9, which declares *"Happy shall he be, that taketh and dasheth thy little ones against the stones."*

The Psalms (Hebrew: Tehilim, תהילים, or "praises"), considered part of both Hebrew and Christian Scripture, served as ancient Israel's "psalter" or "hymnbook", which was used during temple and private worship.

The New Testament contains passages that quote Imprecatory Psalms. Jesus of Nazareth is shown quoting from them in John 15:25, and John 2:17, while Paul the Apostle quotes from Psalm 69 in the Epistle to the Romans 11:9-10 and 15:3.

THE VICTORY OF THE KINGDOM OF GOD – REVELATION 14

grace, by which we may serve God acceptably with reverence and godly fear. For our God is a consuming fire (Heb. 12:28-29).

And another angel came out from the altar, who had power over fire... (14:18), which indicates that there is an agreement between two or three that the days of vengeance are upon the people who have known the witness of the faithful preacher, bearing the testimony of God that would lead them to salvation, but instead they blaspheme the Holy Spirit. This one comes out of *the altar* where the judgment of God is known in the sacrifice, but they have not believed in the redemptive power of the sacrifice of the Lamb and they have cursed life itself. Woe is man, woe is man, woe is he ... *who neglects so great a salvation...!* (Heb. 2:3) Then it is done! The imprecatory prayer is prayed in accordance with the purposes of God, so he cries with a *loud voice* to him who had the sharp sickle, *saying, "Thrust in your sharp sickle and gather the clusters of the vine of the earth, for her grapes are fully ripe"* (14:18). Nothing now will stop the judgement of God. The inevitability of torment begins, war breaks out, pestilence kills a third (8:10), famine destroys its third (8:7), blood pours out into rivers where the dogs lick it up to their full, the birds of the air take their feed from human flesh, and natural disaster (8:5) grips the people with terror. Their *babies are dashed against the rocks* (Ps. 137:9) and the *indignation of God* is vented (Psalm 69:4). So, they enter from the place of common grace and mercy into an eternity of torment and woe.

So the angel thrust his sickle into the earth and gathered the vine of the earth...(14:19). This is not simply something reserved for the very last day of history at the second coming of Christ, but is a process that is ongoing throughout history, and whenever a funeral service is conducted or a mass grave is constructed, or the furnace of a crematorium consumes the body, this *gather[ing] [of] the vine of the earth* is being performed by the "grim reaper." This is not the devil's work; this is God's work as everything that is God's returns to God and the devil is dispossessed. While these ungodly conspirators against the "kingdom of God" existed on the face of the earth, they were under the dominion of Satan, but now *It is a fearful thing to fall into the hands of the living God* (Heb. 10:31) who assigns judgement and indignation to all those who collaborated and abused their privilege as God's vice-regent of the earth.

These ripened grapes are without excuse and are ...*thrown into a great winepress of the wrath of God* (14:19). They enter into this eternal judgement from the day that they pass from time into eternity without God. Immediately, they will be in torment ...*cast out into outer darkness. There will be weeping and gnashing of teeth* (Matt. 8:12). But the real terror, if that is not bad enough, will be when, on the *last day* at the *general resurrection* (Jn. 5:28-30), the bodies of every human being will be raised. Each of these souls will possess a body that cannot die. It is then that these immortal souls will reside in an immortal body and will be assigned to outer darkness with a resurrected body. Such a body cannot die and will be in that place of utter lostness, torment and darkness, never to be redeemed, in a place called, *perdition* (2 Pet. 3:7). I think if we were to think about the implications of such a state for any length of time, we should go mad.

In the meantime, such people wish to say that there is no God and no accountability, but the word of God says otherwise. Prudence and wisdom should at least be given the benefit of the doubt–turn to God for He might just be right! Countless people, many of whom are highly intelligent, have looked to reason and opened the word of God and found this to be true.

And the winepress was trampled outside the city, and blood came out of the winepress, up to the horses' bridles, for one thousand six hundred furlongs (14:20). The bloodshed of these Days of Vengeance in the Grapes of Wrath goes on throughout the history of the world, in countless wars among men, genocide of brutal regimes, millions of unborn babies of the abortionist, millions of those lost to pestilence and famine, let alone the untold numbers that die in their old age.

Some wish to take this analogy and apply it to the blood-flow of the awful events of the destruction of the Temple and Jerusalem in A.D. 70.[39] As dreadful and as terrifying as that event was, it could not come anywhere near the magnitude of the blood-flow that is described here. The blood-flow out of this winepress of judgement is a river of blood that is at least five feet deep and 184 miles long. The blood-flow from the destruction of Jerusalem in A.D. 70 could be absorbed in the sands. However, the blood-flow here is describing the judgement of God on all the earth from the days when Cain murdered his brother Abel, and will not stop flowing until the Second Coming of Christ on the Last Day.

RJ Rushdoony puts it clearly, describing it as "1600 stadia (Roman measures), 4x4x100, i.e., the four corners of the world multiplied by itself and then multiplied by the fullness of 10, i.e., 100, a symbol of fullness itself. Thus the world as a whole is covered by the vengeance of God wherever it is uncovered by the atoning blood of Christ."[40]

---

[39] David Chilton, *The Days of Vengeance, an Exposition of the Book of Revelation*, Dominion Press, Texas 1987, pp 376-7

[40] R.J. Rushdoony, op. cit., p182.

CHAPTER 7.

THAT GREAT DAY OF GOD ALMIGHTY

At this point in the book of Revelation, there is a dramatic introduction of a new movement of revelation in history described in the words, *...that great day of God Almighty* (16:14). This is not to be confused with a much later event (20:11-15) described as the Last Day (Jn. 11:24; 12:48) at which time the Lord Jesus Christ Himself will bodily return to earth in the same manner that He ascended into heaven (Acts 1:9-11). At that point, the general resurrection and the final judgment will take place (Jn. 5:25-30).

Up to this point in the sequence of the book of Revelation, including chapter 14, the course of prophetic history is disclosed by recapitulation. Recapitulation is a literary device that interpreters use to describe historical events around prophetic themes that develop in parallel in terms of time. In the book of Revelation, after an introduction, chapters 2 and 3 describe the life and witness of the Church spanning the history of the kingdom of God from the first advent of Christ to His second advent on the Last Day.

After a prelude in chapters 4 and 5 describing the events in heaven in relationship to the spread of the Gospel to every corner of the earth, chapters 4 to 11 set forth, through a series of *Seven Seals* that are opened and *Seven Trumpets* sounded, the effect of the witness and powerful ministry of the Word of God throughout the Gospel history within this world. This is a full recapitulation within the prophetic history of the kingdom of God that further describes the Gospel era that will conclude with the final coming of Christ on the Last Day.

The next recapitulation is set around the theme of the great institutional opposition to the kingdom of God—the Dragon (that serpent of old, the devil or Satan) arises against Christ as the Antichrist in the form of a harlot; the beast that develops into Babylon the Great and the false prophet. There is a long period during which these Antichrist forces do battle against the kingdom of God and Christ's Church. Although the spiritual work of the kingdom of God, with material effect, advances progressively through the ages, Christ's Church is severely persecuted and the Antichrist forces appear to be consistently at centre stage. The true Church is, in varying degrees throughout history, relegated to the wilderness. This is to say that throughout this era of the Antichrist there has been no sustained Christian era, as promised in Scripture, in a millennial reign of the saints with Christ. Certainly, at times nations have achieved the name of being a Christian nation. Britain, since the Reformation and the eighteenth-century Revivals into the Victorian era, was noted as possessing Christian standards of public life. Likewise, the United States of America since the Puritan settlement in New England and other British colonial nation-states such as New Zealand, Australia, various African states along with some South Pacific island states, gained the name of being Christian societies. This no doubt saw a consolidation of a certain Christian culture that was advanced by the growth of the kingdom of God, but it is nothing like what is promised in the millennial reign of the saints in Christ where the nations in all the earth are no longer deceived by the forces of Antichrist and the rule of Christ in all the nations of the earth is sustained for a thousand years.

There is a decisive point in history when Christ intervenes and avenges the suffering saints throughout the era of the Antichrist forces (which continues to our day), and grants the consummation of the kingdom of God with the introduction of the millennial reign. The angel of the Lord Jesus Christ does this by His own providence through the natural order of the seven bowls filled with the seven last plagues (21:9) at what is known as *that great day of God Almighty* (16:14). How these *seven last plagues* are poured out by the seven angels in the end is a matter of fulfilment. However, we do have the precedent of the plagues of Egypt in the days of Moses where the natural order was invoked by the Lord God in His providence to bring the judgment of God against Egypt and her Pharaoh. (Exod. 7:14-11:10) Like the plagues of God on Egypt, they were sequential and swift in terms of time. The essential difference between the plagues of Egypt at the time of the Exodus and the plagues in Revelation is that the Egyptian plagues were localised, but here these *seven last plagues* that are spoken of in chapter 16 of Revelation are global. Such a comprehensive judgment of God was witnessed in the worldwide flood of Noah's day. (Gen. 7-8) Even though these *seven last plagues* are unleashed sequentially, they will probably be seen together as one event. If one were to live through this event it would be like a kaleidoscope of all the pieces or elements of each of the plagues that make up the whole event known as *that great day of God Almighty* (16: 14).

Therefore, chapters 15 to 19 are an historical event that takes place in a relatively short space of time and is not a recapitulation of history. The reasons for this interpretation will be presented in the discussion that follows.

Prelude In Heaven—Revelation 15

A Sign In Heaven

Verse 1 *John saw a sign in heaven*—the scene is set in heaven. *Great and marvellous* is not something to be feared by Christians because God is about to move decisively on their behalf. The heavenly sign was that the preserver and the providential carer of the natural order of creation, being the *four living creatures* (4:6-9), handed over their province (15:7) to the fearsome and awesome *seven angels* who now have in their hands *the seven last plagues*. In these plagues is found the complete *wrath of God* and therefore it is called, *the seven bowls filled with the seven last plagues* (21:9). This does not mean that God's wrath will not be seen in later periods of history, such as in the final judgment of God on the Last Day when he returns in the Second Advent. However, these *seven last plagues* are poured out by the *seven angels* at the end of an extended period. For some two thousand years, *the wrath of God is continually revealed against all ungodliness and unrighteousness of men who suppress the truth in unrighteousness* (Rom. 1:18) in a measured and merciful manner so that the mercies of God in the Gospel of Christ would be offered to the ends of the earth in the forbearance and patience of God. But now this decisive event, where *the wrath of God is complete*, will end an era that was dominated by the institutional enemies of God, being the Harlot, the Beast with Babylon the Great, and the false prophet. Also, it will usher in the glorious millennium where the saints reign with Christ for a thousand years.

The seven angels, being great angelic beings, do not appear to be the merciful message-bearing angels of the Word of God, the preachers of the Word of God in 10:7. These angels are poised to hurl the wrath of God in the natural order as described in chapter

16. These angels are to exercise the wrath of God in the form of the last seven plagues, *...for in them the wrath of God is complete*. This has the mood of the great deluge of Noah's day—not of water but a fire of plagues.

Verse 2 John *saw something like a sea of glass*, which is a picture of the very habitation of God's throne (see Rev. 4:6). The expression *... mingled with fire* means that the fire of purging is in the hand of God. As in the days of Noah, when *The Lord God said, "My Spirit shall not strive with man forever..."* (Gen. 6:3), He is poised to purge the earth of such high-handed iniquity, along with the spiritual forces that bring this malignancy in all the earth. Despite the patient call of the Gospel and the faithful testimony of the saints, which are everywhere martyred and endured every kind of persecution for the sake of Christ's Name and His righteousness (Matt. 5:10-12) they endured to the end and had *the victory over the beast*. The time has come and the iniquity of the nations of the earth is complete. At the conquest of the Promised Land by Joshua (Josh. 1:2-4), the iniquity of those that possessed the land was then *complete* after four hundred years, and four generations after God's promise to Abraham (Gen. 15:13-16); even so, the Lord God will purge with the fire of *the seven last plagues* the nations of the earth, to dispossess them and introduce the millennium where the saints reign with Christ for a thousand years (20:6).

Therefore *...those that have the victory over the beast* are all the saints that have come through what is called the *great tribulation* (7:14). To this date, these saints have lived faithfully according to the Word of Christ's righteousness, from the day that our Lord Jesus Christ ascended on high (Acts 1:9-11) and was seated at the right hand of the Father. This includes all ages ultimately until the Second Advent of Christ. *This is a great multitude which no man could number, of all nations, tribes, peoples, and tongues, standing* *before the throne and before the Lamb, clothed with white robes... These are the ones who come out of the Great Tribulation and washed their robes and made them white in the blood of the Lamb* (7:9, 14). These have been progressively gathered with Christ in what will be later called the New Jerusalem; (21:9ff) *And they cried out with a loud voice saying, "How long, O Lord, holy and true, till you judge and avenge our blood on those who dwell on the earth?"* (6:10).

The great tribulation is that long and arduous battle with the Beast, which is that Antichrist that becomes institutionalised in the massive religious socio-political edifice, whose origin is described in chapter 12 as the dragon that morphs into the beast of chapter 13. It is first illustrated in pagan Rome, and then seeks to take the place of Christ in Rome through the Holy Roman Empire, which is otherwise described as the Mother of Harlots (17:5). The beast becomes clearly represented in Roman Catholicism and its political inspiration through the Jesuit papal order, where the church and state become conflated. This socio-political system develops into what is called later *Babylon the Great* (17:5), which is secular humanism that became the all-consuming ubiquitous anti-Christian force throughout all the nations, until Christ avenges His saints in this event of the *great day of God Almighty* in *the seven last plagues*.

Another institutional anti-Christian force in world history is described in the book of Revelation as the *false prophet*. (16:13; 19:20; 20:10) This entity is something of a wild card because it is distinguished from the harlot, the beast and Babylon the Great. The false prophet arises at around 622 A.D. when the great Islamic leader Mohammed was proclaimed prophet around ten years before his death and is attributed with writing "The Koran." The distinctive call of Islam, "There is but one God Allah and Mohammed is His prophet" carries through the annals of history and now is uttered on a global stage. There are many false prophets in history but this one is the one that best describes what the book of Revelation presents as *the false prophet*, because the Islamic system represents a continuous historic religious socio-political anti-Christian force that runs down through history and is yet distinct from Roman Catholicism.

Interestingly, this *false prophet* arose at around the same time as the institution of the harlot and her children. In the year 600 A.D., Gregory the Great was proclaimed the Bishop of Rome and became known by the title "Pope," the Holy Father. Then in the days of the Italian Pope Vitalian (664-679 A.D.), the 664 A.D. Synod of Whitby falsely affirmed Roman claims that the Pope is the direct apostolic successor of the Apostle Peter, which is in person the Rock, upon which the Church is built and therefore claims to hold *the keys of the kingdom of heaven* (Matt. 16:18-19) to the exclusion of all others in the Church visible, creating an official schism between the Papal Romanists and others. From around 666 A.D. onwards, most of Europe and some of England, but not Ireland, Scotland and Wales, became increasingly Romanised, becoming a persecuting force within Christ's Church. Thus, the Romish Papal power or *horn* (Dan. 7:20; 24-25) became strong or *stout* and long sat and ruled in the Temple of God, while claiming to be His spokesman. However, the spokesman was in fact *the man of sin*, otherwise described as Antichrist (Dan. 7:25; 8:20-25; 11:36; 12:8-11; 2 Thess. 2:8-12; 2 Pet. 2:1-5; Rev. 13:11-18; 17:1-17) This *great multitude which no man could number* had gained the victory through the Gospel of the Lord Jesus Christ, not by merit in themselves but in Christ's righteousness alone, by grace alone, through faith alone. They did *not walk according to the flesh, but according to the Spirit for the principle of the Spirit of life in Christ Jesus set them free from the principle of sin and death* (Romans 8:1-2). It is according to faith in the Lord Jesus

Christ alone that they gained victory over the enemies of Christ and their false religion, and now glorified, standing in the very presence of God with their Saviour. They had testified against the Antichrist being, *the beast*, and refused to worship the religious form humanly constructed in the image of Roman Catholicism of *the harlot* that was not commanded in the truth of Scripture alone. They had refused the outward *mark of the beast* that was the non-scriptural sacramental system of the Romish Church. The great Protestant reformer, Martin Luther, declared in his controversial book that this sacramental system was "The Babylonian Captivity of the Church." These saints who were victorious and glorious refused to identify with the side of "the great schism" in the visible Church even though outwardly such Christianity was grander and more splendid in its religious appearance and system. Antichrist was formally entrenched as a system of the Papal Romanists in A.D. 666. To stand on the side of Biblical Christianity would force the believer to come under the lash of persecution that the Antichrist is renowned for throughout her bloody history in the Christian Church. However, a fuller discussion on the identity of *the beast* will be reserved for another place.

Those that had the Gospel victory are seen *standing on a sea of glass* being the habitation of God, the very throne of God in the presence of the triune God Himself.

In **verse 3** these saints were doing something that angelic beings could not do: sing! Although within the hymnody of human compositions angels are described as singing, there is nowhere in Scripture that they are recorded as singing; saying, but not singing (Luke 2:13-14). However, these saints are gathered in heaven and are singing *the Song of Moses...and the Song of the Lamb...* The song of the Lamb was the new song of redemption from the heart. Interestingly, they had *harps of God* not in their hand or instruments of their own making but harps that God had given them, nothing more and nothing less; they were singing with their lips and making melody in their heart to the Lord (Eph. 5:19). This gift of man is now heard in heaven; the Scripture pieces are sung in one song. These words are not the poetry of the saints' hearts but inspired portions of God's Word.

The content of the praise offered by the saints is summarised in the words of the Apostle John:

Great and marvellous are Your works,
Lord God Almighty!
Just and true are Your ways,
O King of the saints!
Who shall not fear You,
O Lord, and glorify Your name?
For You alone are holy.
For all nations shall come and worship before You,
For Your judgments have been manifested (15: 3-4).

This may well be a stand-alone scriptural song in the tradition of the "Magnificat"—the Song of Mary (Lu. 1:46-55)—or the "Nunc Dimittis"—the Song of Simeon, (Lu. 2:29-32)—which were a gathering of key verses from the Psalms that related to the focus of their praise. The saints here in heaven are not singing this hymn of praise as a mantra, over and over again, but as a collection of themes that are clearly extracted from Scripture and found replete in the book of Psalms that were sung continually leading up to this great event that was about to happen, *that great day of God Almighty*. They are applying God's word alone in their congregational praise before the throne of God as a prayer. This praise is not only continuous but also united and therefore the saints are not only the glorified saints in the Church triumphant but also saints that offered praise while in the Church militant on the earth, but gathered united for worship in heavenly places as one body in Christ.

Verse 5 tells us that *After these things...* the saints sing the portions of Scripture, particularly that which is contained in the Canon of Song known as *Psalms, hymns and spiritual songs* (Eph. 5:19; Col. 3:16) offering their petitions at the throne of God Himself. The Apostle John, *...looked, and behold, the temple of the tabernacle of the testimony in heaven...* This *temple of the tabernacle* is that of which the Lord Jesus said concerning the temple of Jerusalem that he would *destroy this temple, and in three days I will raise it up... speaking of the temple of his body* (Jn. 2:19; 21). When it would be raised up, on the third day after His redemptive sacrifice upon the cross of Calvary, it would be a heavenly spiritual work of God. As members of this body of Christ, the Apostle Peter describes each believer as *...living stones...being built up a spiritual house, a holy priesthood, to offer up spiritual sacrifices acceptable to God through Jesus Christ...*(1 Pet. 2:5). This temple made without hands is the resurrected "Body of Christ" Himself. The pure worship of the saints at worship both in heaven and on the earth, being in the same heavenly places, *in spirit and truth, for the Father is seeking such to worship Him*; (Jn. 4:23) leads to a remarkable *sign in heaven*, described as, *Great and marvellous* (15:1). An opening of *the temple and tabernacle of the testimony in heaven...*

In **Verse 6** we see that *...out of the temple came seven angelic beings having seven p*lagues... These are not the preaching kind, but the Gabriel kind. They are *Clothed in pure white linen*, having nothing iniquitous in them or pit-like or beastly about them. These are from God, having pure white wrath of God in their hand. They are glorious *..having their chests girded with gold bands*, which illustrates their righteous judgment.

Verse 7 introduces us to the *four living creatures* that are mentioned as the managers and providential keepers of the created order, particularly intervening in response to the ministry of the Word of God. They are approached by the seven angels that come out of the opening of *the temple and tabernacle of the testimony in heaven* (4:6-9; 5:6-8, 14; 6:1, 6; 7:11; 14:3 cf Isa. 6; Ezek. 1). These living creatures appear to establish the general providence of creation so that orderliness in all creation is properly served. Here we are witnessing a handing-over of this providence to the seven angels having seven golden bowls full of the wrath of God. This indicates that the order of the natural world will be dramatically disturbed and disaster is about to strike the earth. God will use these *seven golden bowls full of the wrath of God* of the physical created order for His mighty purpose revealing the greatest display of the wrath of God, *since men were on the earth* (16: 18).

In **verse 8** *The temple is filled with smoke from the glory of God and from His power*. As at the dedication of Solomon's Temple that *was filled with a cloud* (2 Chron. 5:13-14), there appears *a great and marvellous* (15:1) filling of the smoke of the glory of God in *the heavenly temple of the tabernacle of the testimony*. However, it happened in the dedication of Solomon's Temple that the cloud was a *black cloud* and on account of it the priests could not continue their ministry. Here in Revelation, *no one was able to enter the temple till the seven plagues of the seven angels were completed*. To have the temple in a state where it could not function as a *tabernacle* for the saints and a *testimony* of the Gospel for any length of time is unthinkable. These events therefore cannot be interpreted as a recapitulation of history as they are so often interpreted. These forthcoming events of the pouring out of the *seven bowls of God's wrath* are by necessity a relatively short time, because this temple in heaven is the focus of the saints in worship both on the earth and in heaven.

This would mean that Chapter 16 is a relatively short time-span as illustrated in the lesser plagues of Egypt. It would usher in a glorious new Exodus of global proportions.

CHAPTER 8

SEVEN ANGELS POUR OUT THE SEVEN BOWLS OF THE WRATH OF GOD – REVELATION 16

THE GREAT CRISIS OF WORLD HISTORY

NOW "THE BATTLE OF THE GREAT DAY OF GOD ALMIGHTY" (16:14) These acts of God's wrath comprise a sovereign intervention of God using the natural order of human disease so that *foul and loathsome sores came upon men* (16:2); a waterborne pandemic in the oceans and rivers of the world causes *every living creature in the sea to die* (16:3); an astrological event in the solar system causes *men to be scorched with fire* (16:8); some physical disaster that focuses on the geographical area of *the throne of the beast* brings a *great darkness over the beast's kingdom and they gnaw their tongues because of their pain* (16:10); some sort of drought or geographic event causes *the great River Euphrates and its water (to dry) up* (16:12), and finally a *great earthquake such as has not occurred since men were on the earth* (16:18), with *great hail from heaven fell upon man* (16:21). God's instruments are the seven mighty angels that came forth out of the opening of the heavenly temple of Christ's body, as discussed in the previous chapter

(15:5-6). These global events of natural disaster have a precedent in the great global deluge of the days of Noah.

These bowls of wrath appear as the plagues of Egypt in the days of Moses, but on a global scale. It is God intervening for the sake of the saints (6:9-11; 16:5-6), that they may see their deliverance and be brought into the victory of the kingdom of God. This dramatic event happens sequentially in this vision yet as elements of an entire event known as *that great day of God Almighty* in chapters 16-19.

THE FOCUS OF THIS GREAT WRATH OF GOD

The focus of this wrath of God is upon *the men who had the mark of the beast and those who worshipped his image* (16:2). It occurs after the seas and the rivers become *dead of every living creature*. The *angel of the waters* (16:5) testified that this judgment was for the sake of *the shedding the blood of the saints and prophets* (16:6). God's wrath was specifically, *...on the throne of the beast and his kingdom*, (16:10) and the nations of *the whole world* (16:14) that were arrayed against the Almighty and against *the cities of the nations* (16:19) that fell with Babylon the Great, along with everything that represents *the false prophet* (16:13). It follows that the saints in Christ will be typically preserved since the focus is not on them but on the institutional enemies of God: on the harlot, the beast and Babylon the great. Just as in the days of Noah during the great global flood, and through the plagues of Egypt, when those under *the blood of the Lamb* (Exod. 12:23) were passed over when the angel of death killed all the firstborn in Egypt (Exod. 12:29-30), so too the saints of Christ will be typically preserved.

Served over a relatively short period

Therefore, these seven bowls of God's wrath will be served over a relatively short period, just as were the plagues of Egypt in the days of the Exodus. It will be a prelude to a great movement of God for the full consummation of the kingdom of God that will usher in "the Millennium," where Christ and His saints will rule for a thousand years in covenantal fulfilment of the 'Covenant of Creation', also known as the "Covenant of Works." The refrain of *in one hour* of the descriptive passages that follow chapter 18:10, referring to the sudden fall of Babylon, (18:17, 19) adds weight to the idea that these plagues are served out in a relatively short period.

A comprehensive victory of the kingdom of God on earth

It must be said emphatically that this whole event in history is not some sort of doomsday prophecy, but is a prelude to a comprehensive victory of the kingdom of God on earth as it is in heaven, which will result in the introduction of the millennial reign of the saints with Christ for a thousand years. There remains a fundamental requirement of Biblical prophecy that is unfinished business. The foundation of all covenantal theology in the Bible is that Covenant that God struck with Adam at creation itself before the fall. As O Palmer Robinson puts it:

> By the very act of creating man in his own likeness and image, God established a unique relationship between Himself and creation. In addition to His sovereign creation-act, God spoke to man, thus determining precisely the role of man in creation.
>
> Through this creating/speaking relationship, God established sovereignly a life-and-death bond. This

original bond between God and man may be called the Covenant of Creation.

The creation bond between God and man may be discussed in terms of its general and its focal aspects. The general aspect of the Covenant of Creation relates to the broader responsibilities of man to his Creator. The focal aspect of the Covenant of Creation relates to the more specific responsibility of man rising from the special point of prohibition or testing instituted by God. (This aspect traditionally called the Covenant of Works)

The recognition of both these aspects in the Covenant of Creation has far-reaching implications. Because of an exclusive concentration on the specific test concerning 'the tree of the knowledge of good and evil,' the broader responsibilities of man as created in God's image frequently have been ignored. This narrowed perspective has been extended into considerations of the redemptive purpose of God. The result has been the development of a gaping deficiency in the church's concept of man's redemption. By thinking too narrowly about the Covenant of Creation, the Christian church has come to cultivate a deficiency in its entire world-and-life view. Instead of being kingdom-orientated as was Christ, it has become exclusively church orientated.[41]

The covenants of redemption that are the basis of the other enabling Covenant, being the eternal Covenant of Grace, find their foundation in this "Covenant of Creation." The Covenant of

---

[41] O Palmer Robertson, *The Christ of the Covenants*, Baker Book House, Grand Rapids, Michigan, 1980, pp 67-68

Grace that includes the redemptive covenants with Adam, Noah, Abraham, Moses, David and its consummation in the finished work of Christ our Saviour, would make no sense if God had not established the Covenant of Creation.

Much Evangelical Christian theology, in the interest of the redemptive purposes of God, has emphasised that which we need most, which is salvation. Of course, without salvation we cannot address the wider purposes of God that are found in the Covenant of Creation. It is only in this salvation that we find, through the Gospel of the Lord Jesus Christ, that we can address the wider purpose of God for men.

Also, we may, not so subtly, discount the Covenant of Creation because of the idea that mankind has broken this Covenant, and man consequently lives as though there is no remaining covenant. However, it would be erroneous for us to discount the Covenant of Creation on the grounds that it has become null and void due to our not keeping it. The fact is that even though we have not kept the Covenant of Creation (in particular the Covenant of Works), God has; His purposes are not frustrated because of human inability. Even as the Covenant of Grace is unfolded, the Covenant of Creation is the underpinning foundation of the Covenants of redemption. With the "commencement of the Covenant" with Adam, the universal creation ordinances of the Sabbath, marriage and labour are maintained because the Covenant of Creation with men is not abrogated on God's side. In the "Covenant of Preservation" struck with Noah, the same Covenant of Creation language is invoked. (Gen. 9:1-7) Even in the "Covenant of Promise" with Abraham, the ends of the earth are in perspective in terms of its extent. (Gen. 22:18) In addition, the concrete promise of the possession of a land that had specific boundaries (Gen. 15:18-21) was a foretaste of future possession contained in the promise of "inheriting the earth" (Ps. 37:11; Matt. 5:5; Rom. 4:13).

Furthermore, in the "Covenant of the Law" with Moses, not all individual Israelites were saved. Indeed, there were times within the history of Israel that it appears that she was so compromised by unregenerate unbelievers that she looked more like a pagan nation than God's special people (cf Rom. 11:2-5). However, the overall purpose of the nation of Israel was that she might be a righteous witness to the nations, one that was characterized as, *A chosen generation, a royal priesthood, a holy nation, His own special people, that you may proclaim the praises of Him who called you out of darkness into His marvellous light; who once were not a people but now the people of God, who had not obtained mercy but now have obtained mercy* (Deut. 7:6-11; 1 Pet. 2:9-10). This, of course, is also true for the new creation in Christ, the Church of God, yet the magnitude and the glory of the body of Christ are infinitely greater than that of the Old Testament Israel. The Covenant family under the sign and seal of baptism is a pledged people that will regrettably see some apostasies in this world. However, those that are in Christ, united to Him through the baptism of the Holy Spirit (Jn. 1:33; Acts 1:5), will be secured until the end, and this body of Christ will both grow on earth as it is in heaven, and form the ever-growing city of God, the New Jerusalem in heaven (Rev. 21:9-10ff). One of the chief differences between the Old Testament Israel and the New Testament Church is the role that *the beast* of Revelation 13 plays in subverting the Church's testimony: this beast, along with its harlot church, falsely poses as the true Church of God, deceiving the people on planet earth. But those that have a heavenly perspective, being indeed the children of God, are not deceived, although they are in large part condemned to *the wilderness* (12:14) and are heavily persecuted in what is known as the *great tribulation* (7:14) throughout the generations of the days of the Gentiles (for us now some 2000 years of Church and world history). The *throne of Satan* (3:13) is in Rome, officially declared in the year 666 (13:18), and her religious socio-political empire takes centre stage seeking to control the nations of all the earth. This Romish antichrist does not affect the true testimony of the body of Christ, as Christ Himself *...will build [His] Church and the gates of hades will not prevail against it* (Matt. 16:18). The body of Christ has an indissoluble spiritual union with Christ, who is the Head of the Church. He is directly and powerfully sustaining His body *...according to the good pleasure of His will, to the praise of the glory of His grace, by which He has made us accepted in the Beloved* (Eph. 1:5-6). Of course, those who are not of Christ will wither on the vine and perish, even if they are associated with the visible Church or trying their hardest to look like sincere Christians when they are, in the end, only nominal Christians and not actually Christ's.

Again, in the Covenant of the Kingdom struck with King David, David receives the promise, *I will establish the throne of his kingdom forever*. So, when the Lord Jesus Christ, the everlasting King, comes in His Messianic reign, the Kingdom of God is established. The rule of Christ *on earth as it is in heaven* (Matt. 6:10) begins with Christ's proclamation that *The time is fulfilled, and the kingdom of God is at hand. Repent, and believe in the Gospel* (Mk. 1:15). After laying down His life for the redemption of the full number of His elect, His rising from the dead to be seated at the right hand of the Father, and His ascension, Christ's rule expands progressively as *a stone made without hands* is cast from heaven to the earth and *grows into a mountain that fills the earth* (Dan. 2:34-35).

Many who wish to interpret the kingdom of God in purely spiritual terms, with no material effect in our physical world, appeal to our Lord's words to Pilate at His trial where Jesus answered, *My kingdom is not of this world. If My kingdom were of this world, My servants would fight, so that I should not be delivered to the Jews; but now My kingdom is not from here* (Jn. 18:36). They would therefore argue that the kingdom of God sees its growth in heaven only, holding that there is a parallel development of good and evil; there are God's righteous kingdom and Satan's evil empire, but the real progress of God's kingdom is in heaven with the gathering company of saints in the New Jerusalem. However, in the domain of Satan's earthbound empire, we can only expect a progressive falling away to Satan. To be sure, it is said, the whole apparatus of Satan's dominion on earth will be destroyed once and for all on the Last Day when our Lord returns in His Second Advent. There may be spiritual revivals and blessings of Biblical reformation within the church militant.

Nonetheless, there will be no final victory on earth, and the kingdom of God will endure defeat in this world; as the noted amillennialist J. Vernon McGee rashly concludes in the words of a well-known radio program in the United States in the early 1950s, in the pessimistic spirit of pre-millennial dispensationalism of a previous era, "You don't polish brass on a sinking ship." For such a view there is no triumph of Christ and His kingdom in history. There is no material advancement of Christ's rule of truth and righteousness over His creation.

Those who take this purely spiritual perspective need to read what the Apostle John says in the next verse to see a different perspective on this. John continues, Pilate *therefore said to Him, "Are You a king then?" Jesus answered, "You say rightly that I am a king. For this cause I was born, and for this cause **I have come into the world**, that I should bear witness to the truth. Everyone who is of the truth hears My voice"* (Jn. 18:37). That is to say, the very purpose of Christ's coming into this world was to have a more comprehensive material effect upon this world according to the "Covenant of Creation," as stated above. To put it in the Apostle Paul's words, ***All things*** *were created through Him and for Him. And He is before* ***all things****, and in Him* ***all things*** *consist. And He is the head of the body, the Church, who is the beginning, the Firstborn from the dead, that in* ***all things*** *He may have the pre-eminence* (Col. 1:15-18).

Although the progress of the kingdom of God in this comprehensive fulfilment has been continuing throughout the two thousand years of the Gospel age, it is at this point in prophetic history that there is a complete and general fulfilment of the Covenant of Creation, consummated through this event 'of that great day of God Almighty' in the restoration of covenantal glory.

The Scale of What is Described Has Yet to Be Fulfilled

Another point that could be made generally about this chapter is that the scope of what is described has yet to be fulfilled. The catastrophic events of natural disaster with *the seven bowls of God's wrath* are total. The natural disasters associated with the opening of the seven seals and the sounding of the seven trumpets in Revelation 6 to 11 are limited in scope to one-third of what could be destroyed.

With the dissemination of the Gospel throughout the Gospel age, there are always consequences for nations that do not receive the mercies and grace of God. As it says in Psalm 2, *The nations are Your possession. You shall break them with a rod of iron; You shall dash them to pieces like a potter's vessel*. In a measured way, God disciplines the nations so that they are awakened from their folly and ignorance and turn to Him. *Serve the Lord with fear and rejoice with trembling. Kiss the Son, lest He be angry. And you perish in the way, when His wrath is kindled but a little. Blessed are all those who put their trust in Him* (Ps. 2:8-12).

So as the trumpets of the Gospel are sounded in Revelation chapters 8 and 9, we witness the discipline of Christ's *rod of iron* in His ruling and providence. We are told, *...a third of the trees were burned up, and all green grass was burnt up* (8:7)...*a third of the sea became blood...*(8:8), *a third of the living creatures in the sea died, and a third of the ships were destroyed* (8: 9)...*A great star fell from heaven burning like a torch, and it fell on a third of the rivers and on the springs of the water* (8: 10). *A third of the waters became wormwood, and many men died from the water, because it was made bitter* (8:11). *A third of the sun was struck, a third of the moon, and a third of the stars, so that a third of them were darkened. A third of the day did not shine, and likewise the night* (8:12). *Also the four angels who are bound at the great River Euphrates were released to kill a third of mankind* (9:14-15). Events like these reoccur and history repeats itself frequently. They are characteristic of the Gospel age as the Gospel is preached to every generation and to the ends of the earth.

Contrast these with chapter 16, where we learn that, *the sea became blood as of a dead man and every living creature in the sea died* (16:3); *...the rivers and springs of water become blood* (16:4); *...the throne of the beast and his kingdom becomes full of darkness* (16:10); *...the great River Euphrates...was dried up* (16:12) and *a great earthquake as had not occurred since men were on the earth* (16:18). Historians can associate certain historical events with the devastations under the Gospel ministry, but nowhere in history have we seen *every living creature die in the sea* and *every river and spring turned to blood*, as it were. Nor have we seen the spectacle of the universal Romish church becoming *full of darkness*, and we certainly haven't seen the *Euphrates dry* *up* or a *great earthquake such as man has (n)ever seen since the beginning of man.*

SEPARATE EVENTS THAT HAVE DISTINCT PURPOSES TO FULFIL

The events of chapter 16, the seven bowls of God's wrath, and the cycle of events associated with the seven trumpets in chapters 8 and 9, are separate events that have distinct purposes to fulfil. These seven bowls of God's wrath usher in the long and sustained rule of the kingdom of God on earth in the millennial years that fulfil the original Covenant of God with man in the "Covenant of Creation." The cycle of events associated with Gospel preaching through the image of "the seven trumpets" sounding certainly extend the kingdom of God progressively throughout the Gospel age, but their purpose is one of discipline so that those that are being saved are brought out of their self-righteousness and their self-sufficiency into the mercies of God and grace in the Gospel of the Lord Jesus Christ.

It should also be noted that the instruments that God uses in each situation are different. The *golden bowls that were full of God's wrath* in chapter 16 were handed to seven mighty angels that came out of the temple in heaven by *the four living creatures* (15:7). However, as the seven seals are opened by the Lamb (the Lord Jesus Christ Himself), the four living creatures accompany the opening of the seals (6:1; 3; 5; 7) and the angels that sound the seven Gospel trumpets are the kind of angels that bear the message of the Gospel, being the called and anointed preachers of the Gospel (8:7). The fact that there are two separate kinds of administrators appointed by God to carry out these events indicates that these events are distinct from each other. Of course, the events associated with the preaching of the Gospel may well coincide with the events that are directly related to *the seven bowls of God's wrath*, because the Gospel call which began with the first coming of the Lord Jesus Christ will be heard throughout the history of the true Church, and will not end until the Last Day with His Second Advent.

SEVEN BOWLS OF GOD'S WRATH – REVELATION 16

Chapter 15 is a prelude to chapter 16. It is not a recapitulation but a move forward into the revelation of prophetic history. In chapter 15, the scene is set in the temple as a heavenly spiritual place where the saints are gathered with *the Lord God Almighty* (15:3). They sing *the song of Moses* that is a song of triumph and deliverance from Egypt and, as it were, *the victory over the beast, over his image and over his mark and over the number of his name* (15:2). That is to say, it is the triumph over the beast's heresy and deliverance of the true Church from the wilderness of the desert (12:6) and from her enemies. This Exodus is deliverance into the land of promise, as described in the "Covenant of Creation," where the kingdom of God is consummated with an international millennium of sustained righteousness and peace, where the saints reign with Christ for a thousand years. So, chapters 16 to 20 are an exodus on an international scale.

I (John) heard a loud voice from the temple saying to the seven angels, "Go and pour out the bowls of the wrath of God on the earth" (Rev. 16:1). We are not told whose voice this is, but it can be none other than the voice of the Lord God Almighty Himself (15:3) that has this kind of authority. These are sovereign acts of God. This command is from God, who is in the midst of His living temple, the very body of Christ, to the seven fearsome angels that administer the *seven bowls of God's wrath*. It is a single command in prophetic history, and this further indicates that this is a single event, rather than a recapitulation of events with the limited but terrible natural disasters associated with the sounding of the Gospel trumpets of chapters 8 and 9.

FIRST BOWL ON THE EARTH: SORE ON THE BEAST'S WORSHIPERS (16:2)

Foul and loathsome sores came upon the men who had the mark of the beast... This is very specific as the foul and loathsome sore is only upon the ungodly, particularly the marked man. This plague recalls the sixth of the Egyptian plagues, the plague of boils (Exod. 9:8-12; Deut. 28:27). As in Egypt, those that will be brought out of "the Babylonian Captivity of the Church,"[42] the very people of God, were not subject to this plague. True believers in Christ have nothing to fear from these plagues, just as the people of Israel in the days of the Egyptian plagues were not subject to these *foul and loathsome sores*. The holy, the saints—the separate ones—will be supernaturally preserved from such a pandemic.

Certainly, the psychological dispositions of those that have *the mark of the beast* are such that they have spiritual and mental sores that rob them of the peace of God and are plagued with the consequences of self-righteousness as they worship the *harlot*. These people are always plagued with self-complacency and they manufacture a religion that is *Antichrist* to placate a bad conscience. Such psychological dispositions can lead to mental disorders, and those people with these dispositions can find themselves confined within psychiatric institutions. However, it seems that this plague of *foul and loathsome sores* is more than a spiritual and mental disorder—there is an introduction of a physical outbreak of a pandemic that brings great physical distress and bewilderment. Most commentators want to interpret these plagues in spiritual terms

---

[42] Martin Luther, *The Babylonian Captivity of the Church*, 1520.

only, but one asks the question, "Why?"[43] The words are plain and straightforward and do not demand a spiritual meaning. When Moses heard the Word of the Lord in the days of the Egyptian plagues, I cannot imagine him interpreting the words in spiritual terms. If he had done so, he would have missed the entire purpose of his mission. Perhaps those who interpret this passage in spiritual terms want a bet both ways in case the plain meaning of these words is not fulfilled!

The first of these plagues is the lightest: *foul and loathsome sores* upon all the people of the beast (13:11-18). This is a specific first sign to indicate that these awful events of *the seven last plagues* are upon us. Just what the fulfilment of this event will look like is difficult to describe on this side of this particular event of *foul and loathsome sores* breaking out on those that have *the mark of the beast*. We have contended that the identity of *the beast* has been well stated in the Westminster Confession of Faith as follows: ...the Pope of Rome...is that Antichrist, that man of sin, and son of perdition, that exalts himself, in the Church, against Christ and all that is called God (Chapter 25, vi). It would seem therefore that this plague is uniquely a Popish plague. The Pope is depicted as *the great harlot* (17:1) riding the *scarlet beast* (17:3) and *on her forehead the name was written, "MYSTERY, BABYLON THE GREAT, THE MOTHER OF HARLOT'S AND OF THE ABOMINATIONS OF THE EARTH"...She was drunk with the blood of the saints and with the blood of the martyrs of Jesus...*(17:5-6).

Now there is suddenly a worldwide outbreak of *foul and loathsome sores* on all priests and clergy and the laity of the popish churches and all that hold to the popish doctrine, having the badge

---

[43] Rousas J Rushdoony, *'Thy Kingdom Come'*, Thoburn Press, Fairfax, Virginia, 1978, p188.

or the mark of the beast's sacramental system of baptism, confirmation, the mass, penance, orders, marriage and extreme unction: *those who worship his image* of the sacramental "host" of the mass.

Even though this plague is extremely offensive, there is no record that there is widespread death as, for example, with the AIDS epidemic. It leaves the patient with grossly offensive sores that will no doubt have social implications of isolation that will be entirely bewildering. Maybe even the institutions of the Roman Catholic Church, all around the world, will be set up to treat these grossly offensive sores. Just how this plague will be fulfilled remains to be seen. However, when it happens, it will be a sign to all those that believe the Word of God.

SECOND BOWL ON THE SEA: BLOOD AND DEATH (16:3)

The sea...became blood as of a dead man and <u>every</u> living creature in the sea died. This does not necessarily mean that the sea became red but that everything in the sea is dead as a dead man. The turning of water into blood reflects the first plague on Egypt, an actual physical historical event, when the water of the Nile turns bloody and *the fish that were in the Nile died... and the blood was through all the land of Egypt* (Exod. 7:21).

Some commentators who wish to find a spiritual parallel to the first plague in Egypt in the days of Moses speak of the origins of *the beast rising up out of the sea* (13:1). According to this view, the sea is the worldwide Roman web of trade and transport, which is the lifeblood of the Roman economy. In this plague, the heart of the Roman economy, its lifeblood, becomes dead. Such an interpretation seeks to demonstrate that the powerful and persistent preaching of God's Word will dismantle the beast, which is the Antichrist of the Roman Catholic Church, by killing its life support. If that is true, then it is still to be fulfilled because Roman

Catholicism is as powerful as it ever has been and its socio-economic-political monster of Babylon the Great, with its philosophy of "secular humanism," is ubiquitous, particularly when it is compared with Biblical Protestantism, its only historical opponent. The main difficulty with such an interpretation is that the analogy of the sea that is filled with death would not render the sea unnavigable; therefore, the spiritual analogy loses its spiritual application.[44] Furthermore, if this passage were interpreted along parabolic or analogous lines, then it would be expected that it would be written as a parable such as in Isaiah 5, when Israel is likened to an unfruitful vineyard. In such a case, the language is of a different character. In this passage, however, such linguistic devices are absent and all we have is sober prose.

In the first of the Egyptian plagues, Moses, ...*struck the water that was in the river, in the sight of Pharaoh and in the sight of his servants. And all the waters that were in the river turned to blood. The fish that were in the river died, the river stank, and the Egyptians could not drink the water of the river. So there was blood throughout all the land of Egypt* (Exod. 7:20-21). This is not parabolic or symbolic with a spiritual meaning, but is a real event. All the teeming life of the sea became dead. Presumably, all whales are dead, fish and sea life became *as a dead man* and *every living creature in the sea died*. This is not a limited death, as in the successive trumpets of chapter 8. The scale is total.

It would appear that some water-borne pandemic has caused this catastrophic event. To the modern mind, such an event is only too possible, considering our knowledge of the fragile nature of the ecosystem in the world's oceans. A relatively small event, whether

---

[44] Dennis E Johnson, *Triumph of the Lamb, A Commentary on Revelation*, Puritan and Reformed Publication, Phillipsburg, 2001, pp225-6.

it be man-made or a natural disaster, could poison the entire ecological structure of the oceans. Because of the interdependence of every part of the global economy, such an event would place everything into a precarious position.

Again, human losses in such a disaster are not mentioned, probably because there are no reportable human deaths. Such waterborne epidemics as cholera, which have high human mortality rates, are therefore not envisaged in this second bowl of the wrath of God.

THIRD BOWL ON THE RIVERS AND SPRINGS: THE WATERS TURN TO BLOOD (16:4-7)

The third bowl is *poured out on the rivers and springs of water*. These rivers and their sources also *became blood,* in the same way as do the oceans in the second bowl. These rivers are certainly the sources of life that sustain agriculture and provide drinking water, which is a staple for human survival. The picture presented by these water facilities becoming blood might be that every living creature in these rivers is struck down by this plague, as they were in the oceans. The water will probably not turn red, but everything will die. This judgment of God is striking very close to human sustainability. To access usable water for agricultural purposes, and freshwater for human consumption, will require special attention and human ingenuity to manage even the most basic human needs.

These events are followed by a single voice that the Apostle John hears arising from the waters as a messenger or an angel speaking as a poet:

You are righteous, O Lord,
The One who is and who was and who is to be,
Because You have judged these things (16:5).

It would seem that creation itself is testifying that this work of God's judgment is righteous, even though it is undergoing traumatic stresses. The reason for these righteous judgments of the eternal God is one of just vengeance and vindication on behalf of the suffering *saints and prophet* throughout world history for their patient testimony in the Gospel.

The angel of the water continues by saying:
For they have shed the blood of saints and prophets
And you have given them blood to drink.
For it is their just due (16:6).

The relentless and ruthless regime of persecution against *the saints and prophets* by the beast is incalculable. The blood of the martyrs is so extensive that rivers of blood are not an exaggerated image. Millions have shed their blood for the sake of Christ's name and His righteousness.

And I heard another from the altar saying, "Even so, Lord God Almighty, true and righteous are Your judgments" (16:7). This testimony coming from *the altar*, presumably part of the heavenly temple of Christ's body (15:5-8), is one voice of a great multitude concurring with *the angel of the water*. This heavenly altar has witnessed the suffering of saints, for under it the martyrs' souls await their vindication (6:9), and upon it the prayers of suffering saints have been offered as incense (8:3-4). From this altar, fire has fallen in limited judgments on earth's rebels (8:5) and the angel of the fire emerged to authorise the gathering of the wicked like grapes, to be crushed by God's righteous wrath (14:18-19). The altar's response echoes with variations of the song of the victors, *Just and true are Your ways* (15:3), and it will be picked up again in the shout of the great heavenly multitude, celebrating Babylon's destruction, by which God has avenged the blood of the saints' (19:2).[45]

FOURTH BOWL ON THE SUN: MEN ARE SCORCHED (16: 8-9)

Then the fourth angel poured out his bowl on the sun, and power was given to him to scorch men with fire (16:8). In the fourth trumpet, as the Gospel is sounded in all the earth *and a third of the sun was struck, a third of the moon, and a third of the stars*...(8:12), the result was darkness. But here, when the fourth bowl is poured onto the sun, there is heightened intensity in the sun's heat. The result is that the earth's rebellious inhabitants are scorched with fierce heat. Indeed, it is the angel that carries this great plague that uses the intense heat to inflict this searing pain, and this may be in the same measure and kind that *the beast* has inflicted upon *the saints and prophets* through the ages. It is surely a terrible prospect for the atheistic and godless society to be inflicted with the same vengeance that they have inflicted upon the incalculable number of *saints and prophets* that have suffered terribly for no other reason than that they simply loved their Lord and Saviour Jesus Christ.

This plague has no counterpart in the ancient plagues of Egypt. The fierce hostility of the created order against people who are hostile to the Creator turns the sun's light and warmth—in themselves necessary and delightful—into instruments of torture when taken to the extreme. This could be some astrological event, such as that which scientists concede could happen through black-spot activity on the sun, causing the temperature of the earth to rise so that the climactic conditions become intolerable. This has been popularized in a recent doomsday cinematic production called "2011." Of course, the whole production is fictitious, even ridiculous,

---

[45] Dennis E. Johnson, *'Triumph of the Lamb, A Commentary on Revelation'*, Puritan and Reformed Publications, Phillipsburg, New Jersey, 2001, p228

and has no resemblance to reality, but the storyline is built on the scientific knowledge that black-spot activity on the sun has enormous repercussions within the earth's climactic situation and weather outcomes.

And men were scorched with great heat, and they blasphemed the name of God who has power over these plagues; and they did not repent and give Him glory (16:9). *Men were scorched with great heat*... causing them to writhe in pain and to do what comes naturally to them: blaspheme the name of God. They curse and swear at God, ...*who has power over these plagues* (16:19), which is insane if they wish to survive. These godless and atheistic men do as they always did: Hate and curse God. They did not repent. Repentance is still open to mankind as this is still the Gospel age so it is still possible to come to salvation.

From a human perspective, you would expect that given the intensity of these acts of God in these bowls of God's wrath, great numbers would be jolted out of their self-sufficiency and self-righteousness and would cry out to God for mercy, which He would immediately give. The sinister thing about the theology of the Antichrist is that it twists truth so that it looks like truth but in fact it is a pernicious lie. It looks like medicine but in reality it is an inoculation, which administers a small dose of the virus. It has been said that Roman Catholic theology is designed to inoculate people against true Biblical religion. It is a restatement of Biblical doctrine that manipulates the truth of God's Word so that the Gospel is diluted and it cannot heal a sin-sodden soul. The terrifying thing about being inoculated against true Christianity is that, when you see true Christianity, you call it false and you cannot see it any other way. Such are the Gospel-hardened. Instead of repenting, they turn and characteristically curse God, *who has the power over the plagues* (16:9). This is the ultimate blasphemy against the Holy Spirit, which is an unforgivable sin (Luke 12:10; Matt. 12:32).

FIFTH BOWL ON THE BEAST'S THRONE: DARKNESS AND PAIN (16:10-11)

The throne of the beast (we would argue the Holy Roman See)...his kingdom (the vast real estate of the beast) became full of darkness....(16:10) (That would be physical darkness rather than spiritual because the other plagues are clearly physical, of the natural order). The people are so affected physically they *gnaw their tongues because of the pain* (16:10). This is a kind of prelude of hell, which is not a spiritual existence but a material and metaphysical reality.

This darkness of the beast's seat and kingdom has its illustrative parallel in the ninth plague on ancient Egypt. *So Moses stretched out his hand toward heaven, and there was thick darkness in all the land of Egypt three days. They did not see one another nor did anyone rise from his place for three days. But all the children of Israel had light in their dwellings* (Exod. 10:22-23). It is true that spiritually the beast's reign is shrouded in darkness for its foundation is a lie. This is a direct contrast with the truth affirmed in Moses' song: *Who is like You, O LORD, among the gods? Who is like You, glorious in holiness, fearful in praises, working wonders?* (Exod. 15:11). This kind of spiritual darkness is characteristic of the institutional enemy of God's people, the Antichrist, throughout the ages.

What we have in this plague is something that suddenly comes upon the beast's throne and his kingdom, just as the plagues suddenly came upon the Pharaoh of Egypt and his dominion. But as in the days of Israel's exodus from Egypt, where *all the children of Israel had light in their dwellings* (Exod. 10:23), so the saints on earth will somehow be provided with light through this plague that will envelop the entire earth.

The beast's throne is the Vatican and Rome. His kingdom is his universal church in all nations. These locations will become places *full of darkness*. Maybe that darkness is the torment of hell that is utter darkness. Just how this will occur is again a matter of fulfilment in terms of its detail. It is a targeted darkness on a specific person and groups of people associated with the throne and kingdom of the beast. Maybe the situation is that they will be gathered into the great real estate holdings that exist in Catholicism and other religious institutions. The corralling may be brought on by the effects of the previous bowls being poured out, because it can be imagined there is tremendous social dislocation everywhere. Every Roman Catholic piece of real estate would be packed with their marked-out people who were isolated by the first bowl of God's wrath being covered *with foul and loathsome sores* (16:2).

Now it says that this utter darkness will become so painful that *they gnaw their tongues because of the pain* (16:10). They blaspheme the God of heaven because of the torturous pains and their sores. It would seem that the effects of the first bowl on the people have not had time to be cured, and this darkness is sending them mad with pain. But they continue to be blasphemers because blasphemy is such a mark of Roman Catholic people. However, again repentance is available but they do not yield because their hearts are utterly hardened, as in the days of the Egyptian Pharaoh whose heart was hardened by the Lord (Exod. 10:27).

SIXTH BOWL ON THE RIVER EUPHRATES: RIVER DRIES UP AND THE ARMIES OF THE EAST MARSHALLED (16:12-16)

Then the sixth angel poured out his bowl on the great River Euphrates, and its water was dried up, so that the way of the kings from the east might be prepared (16:12). In the days of the Exodus just as the drying up of the Red Sea cleared the path for Israel's liberation from Egypt (Exod. 14:21-25), so here *the sixth angel poured out his bowl on the great River Euphrates and its water was dried up*. It was also a divine ambush of the armies of Egypt, *So the LORD overthrew the Egyptians in the midst of the sea. Then the waters returned and covered the chariots, the horsemen, and all the army of Pharaoh that came into the sea after them. Not so much as one of them remained* (Exod. 14:27-28).

The great River Euphrates and its water was dried up...(v.12) is a physical sign of impending doom that follows. It is like a red flag going up signalling disaster. This has as yet never happened, and when it does happen it will be an unmistakable sign. Some interpreters wish to interpret the drying up of the Euphrates in spiritual terms, referring to the geographical location of the Euphrates as being the seat of Islam with particular reference to the Turk, where the source of the Euphrates is located. This spiritualising suggests that there will be such powerful and persistent preaching of the Gospel across the Islamic countries that it will cause the Turk, being the Euphrates, as it were, to dry up and this will lead to the mass conversion of the Jews. The famous English Puritan, Thomas Goodwin says, "The fifth vial strikes at the throne of Romish Babylon. The sixth vial would destroy the Turks and convert the Jews to Christianity. And the seventh vial would destroy the united remnants of the antichristian Papists and the antichristian Turks. Revelation 16:10-17*f*."[46] This, of course, has yet to be fulfilled, as the powerful and persistent preaching of the Gospel within Islam has been fanatically resisted, to the extent that if the Euphrates is analogous to the strength of Islam, then the Euphrates

---

[46] Thomas Goodwin (Works, Miller, Edinburgh, 1891 rep., III:28).

will be in unprecedented levels of flood because Islam is a dominant socio-economic political-religious force across the globe.

The simple meaning of these words is as they are stated. The waters of the River Euphrates dried up. Why is it important to find spiritual analogies in these very plain concrete descriptions of physical disasters that have been brought about by successive interventions of God's wrath? Remember that these powers were handed over to the seven angels by the four living creatures that had providential power over all things on the earth as illustrated in seals with limited destruction. These angels bring about total devastation, not just the destruction of one third. It is well that Noah did not look for spiritual interpretations of prophetic pronouncements of the judgment in the days of the great flood. His preaching would have been in vain and he would not have prepared an ark for the physical disaster of the great deluge. We can be in danger of missing the boat, as it were, on this one if we do not look at the plain description of these prophecies.

The sign of the River Euphrates drying up signals that *the way of the kings from the east might be prepared* (v.12). The kings of the east are global world political and military powers that are marshalling for a major military showdown. Increasingly, such anti-Christian "beast-like," "Babylonian" and *false prophet* Islamic powers are crushing the saints that represent the kingdom of God, so that true Christians throughout the nations are being severely marginalised, and the capacity of these nations to form massive anti-Christian forces in military formation is here forecast. These forces that are marshalling in this geographical area of the Euphrates that has dried up are gathered because of their fascination for what is described as *the dragon...the beast...and the false prophet* (16:13). These forces are *Antichrist* military forces that are centred and focused on the geopolitical centre of the world, which is Israel. Even though Israel is not mentioned, these military forces are arrayed against something that they wish to annihilate. If anybody has been to the Middle East, they will know that Israel, who returned to her ancestral land in 1948, stands alone with the avowed intentions of every nation around her to exterminate Israel. When the River Euphrates dries up the nations of the east will amass with the same military intention that already exists in all Middle Eastern countries today: to exterminate Israel!

And I saw three unclean spirits like frogs coming out of the mouth of the dragon, out of the mouth of the beast, and out of the mouth of the false prophet (16:13). The spirit that lies behind these military forces that are gathered is one, a frog-like evil spirit that comes from the pit, out of the mouths of the dragon, the beast and the false prophet. It is given voice through their representative socio-political and religious institutions.

For they are spirits of demons, performing signs, which go out to the kings of the earth and of the whole world...(16:14). As in the days of Moses when he was in Egypt and the Egyptian sorcerers could replicate the miraculous signs of Moses (Exod. 7:11-12), so there will be great and impressive signs performed by *spirits of demons* that attract the *kings of the earth and of the whole world* (v.14) to this international military formation against Israel and her allies.

...to gather them to the battle of that great day of God Almighty (v.14). These Antichrist forces that hopelessly outnumber and probably outgun any opposing force are providentially herded together into *the place called in Hebrew, Armageddon* (16:16). The sovereign God orchestrates this climax, and this battle is the Lord's because it is called *the battle of that great day of God Almighty*. It is not the Euphrates drying up that enables these kings to transverse the land in battle formation but it is *the great day of God*

Almighty that providentially draws these powers into battle formation. Modern warfare is not affected by such things as rivers flowing or not flowing. The fact is that the sovereign God Almighty is about to intervene as he did when the people of Israel in the days of the Exodus crossed the Red Sea on dry land with the waters piled up on either side. The enemies of the people of Israel were killed *en masse* by being baptised by immersion.

In all the bowls of God's wrath to this point there has been no record of any mass human fatalities. No doubt the trumpets of the Gospel are being sounded concurrently through all these devastating plagues, which would be extremely frightening to live through. Yet there is no record of mass conversions as a result of these plagues. Although Israel as a national identity returned to her ancestral land in 1948, after nearly two thousand years of being dispossessed, Israel returned to the land in unbelief. God can *graft the natural branch* of Israel in again and their acceptance will *be life from the dead'* and *'so all of Israel will be saved* (Rom. 11: 11; 26).

Historic Protestant theologians with a commitment to reformed and Presbyterian theology generally interpret these verses in spiritual and allegorical categories. Nigel Lee has done an excellent job in cataloguing those that hold this position, and they are an impressive list: John Cotton, John Owen, Thomas Goodwin, Matthew Henry, Jonathan Edwards, John Brown of Haddington, Albert Barnes and William Symington, to name a few. All see the drying up of the Euphrates as a symbol of the effectiveness of the powerful and persistent preaching of the Gospel into all nations that will lead to the conversion of great numbers among 'the beast' of Rome Catholicism and *the false prophet* of Mohammedanism.

This spiritual River Euphrates dries up as a result of the power of the Word of God preached, thus cutting off the power of Rome and the Turk. This will leave the way open for 'the kings from the east' to cross over to come to the holy city of Jerusalem, the spiritual City of God. This would mean that 'the kings from the east' would find salvation through the Gospel. This geographical analogy is purely spiritual, and the great nations of the east such as China, India, Japan, Vietnam, Thailand and the Islamic nations in-between will be profoundly and comprehensively converted and be known as Christian nations for the first time in history. For example, Albert Barnes says:

> *This passage has reference to something in the future history of the Turkish dominions, and to some bearing of the events which are to occur in that history on the ultimate downfall of the Antichristian power referred to by the 'Beast'.... The Euphrates is represented as a barrier to prevent...'the Kings of the East' on their way to the West...*
>
> *Applying the symbol of the Euphrates as being the seat of the Turkish power – the meaning is, that that power is such a hindrance....In some way that hindrance is to be removed....It refers to what is still future. The kings of the East would be converted to the True Religion....There was some hindrance or obstruction to their conversion. That is, as explained, from the Turkish power...*
>
> *The destruction of that power, represented by the drying up of the Euphrates, would remove that obstruction.... The way would thus be 'prepared' for their conversion.... We should most naturally therefore look...for some such decay of the Turkish [or Muslim] power as would be*

followed by the conversion of the rulers of the East to the Gospel.[47]

If the interpretation of the Euphrates drying up refers to the Islamic powers no longer having power to disrupt the conversion of the nations in the east, their comments could very well apply, and as a missionary to India I would love to think that this is the case. But the emphasis in this passage is that these are antichristian forces that "blaspheme God," and it makes it unlikely that we can interpret this passage according to the above view. I am willing to accept that many people will be converted through these devastating events, and (God willing) there will be thousands, if not millions, that will be converted despite the general rule that the characteristic disposition will be a hardening of hearts among these antichristian forces. For instance, as already stated, it would seem that the conversion of the Jewish nation may be brought about as a consequence of these events, and Romans 11 may well be fulfilled at the time of the sixth bowl of God's judgment.

When the river dries up, it is suddenly dried up and there is no evidence of water flowing. The idea of a gradual drying out of the River Euphrates is not in the text as it says that the *water was dried up* ("an aorist passive tense," this means that it is "complete"). It is an event, not a trend towards an event. It is a sign that is manifested in the physical geographic Euphrates River.

If the *kings of the east* are converted at that *great day of God Almighty* by the direct ministry of Christ and his church militant, then such a glorious event would have been stated at this particular point. It does not say that the kings of the east are *prevented*, but

---

[47] A. Barnes, '*Analysis of Revelation 16'*, found in–Nigel Lee, *John's Revelation Unveiled,* Lamp Trimmer, The Historicism Research Foundation, El Pasco, 2001, p 217.

it does say that they are "prepared" for the great battle. This does not look to me like conversion but war.

Behold, I am coming as a thief. Blessed is he who watches, and keeps his garments, lest he walk naked and they see his shame (16:15). These words of Jesus are the third of seven blessings of encouragement that come directly from the lips of Jesus in the book of Revelation (1:8; 11; 1:17-3:22; 16:15; 22:7; 12-13; 16; 20). These blessings of encouragement are replete with the words *I am coming...quickly!* This is not a premillennial coming of Christ but words from heaven in like character to the words of the Father from heaven at the Lord Jesus's baptism, *This is my beloved Son, in whom I am well pleased* (Matt. 3:17). Also, at our Lord's Transfiguration on the mountain, the Father testifies concerning Jesus by saying, *This is My beloved Son, in whom I am well pleased. Hear him!* (Matt. 17:5). Again, the Father testifies from heaven to the Name of His beloved Son after his entry into Jerusalem by saying, *I have both glorified it and will glorify it again* (John 12:28).

The Lord Jesus directly intervenes to shore up the saints for a catastrophic event that is about to take place. The great need of the saints is to be watchful and expectant. Godliness is great gain, and holiness is our primary need. It will be very easy to be carried away by the media and events of the day and listen to the world that is under judgment rather than to the God that has saved us from the utmost to the utmost. Walking naked is our shame. Jesus had counselled the church at Laodicea to receive the white garments that he alone can give, so that *the shame of your nakedness may not be revealed* (3:18). Likewise, this promise is to the *"overcomer"* who avoids the weakness of the two weakest Asian churches, the drowsiness of Sardis and the illusory self-sufficiency of Laodicea. Soon the harlot Babylon's lovers, the rulers and merchants and the beast itself, which once shared her lust and luxury, will strip her naked, exposing her shame (17:16). This is no time to get into bed with the great cities' fast-fading beauty. This is no time for Jesus's followers to be lulled to sleep by the promise of pleasure and prosperity offered by a culture that rests on arrogance toward God and ruthless violence toward the church.[48]

SEVENTH BOWL INTO THE AIR: THE EARTH UTTERLY SHAKEN (16:17-21)

Kings in their military might will be arrayed in a geographical place called, in Hebrew, Armageddon. It would seem that this entire military force that is marshalled internationally, and that probably has no equal in history, has a Jewish focus. Although it is not mentioned in Revelation, this battle of Armageddon will probably never take place because of the events which are to follow. It may be this that Romans chapter 11 is speaking about when the natural branch will be grafted in place. This is, in fact, a divine ambush of the forces representing the Antichrist and the false prophet. Indeed, just when the whole situation looks hopeless in terms of the success and victory of the kingdom of God, Israel is grafted back onto the holy tree as a natural branch, and it will be *life from the dead* (Rom. 11:15). No wonder the voice from heaven of the sovereign Christ saying, *Behold, I am coming as a thief*...(16:15) suddenly changes the entire situation.

When Joshua and the nation of Israel crossed the Jordan on dry ground, even though the river was in flood, the way was opened up for conquest of the land, exposing the peoples of Canaan to the advancing armies of God (Josh. 3). In like manner, with the drying up of the Euphrates, John now signals the coming relief and release of the true Church and the defeat of its enemies.

---

[48] Dennis E Johnson, op cit, p232.

Then the seventh angel poured out his bowl into the air, and a loud voice came out of the temple of heaven, (place of Christ and His saints) from the throne, saying, "It is done!" (16:17). In heaven so on earth the spiritual has priority over the material matters of the earth. *The temple [in heaven] was filled with smoke from the glory of God and from his power, and no one was able to enter the temple until the seven plagues of the seven Angels were complete* (15:8). And so *a loud voice came out of the temple of heaven, from the throne, "It is done!"* Now the final plague is unleashed with awful outcomes. Just as our Lord's cry upon the cross of Calvary, *It is finished,* marked the completion of the Son of God's work of redemption, so here the decisive blow will be made against the enemies of the Kingdom of God.

At this point of time, *there were NOISES and THUNDERINGS and LIGHTNINGS, and there was a GREAT EARTHQUAKE, such a mighty and GREAT EARTHQUAKE as had not occurred since men were on the earth* (16:18). This could be apocalyptic language speaking of the fall of Jerusalem in A.D. 70, but the difference between this language and that applied to the fall of Jerusalem is that you will not find this quoted anywhere else, and the clause attached—*as had not occurred since men were on the earth*—sets it apart as unique and not a likeness of the past.

Noises and thunderings and lightnings remind us of the fearful days of Moses on Mount Sinai when the Law was given and the people of God were gathered. But this is a tectonic geographic global event that seems to have parallels with the great deluge of Noah's day. However, this one is by the fire of plague and not by water, as promised in Noah's day. If we see chapters 17 and 18 as descriptors of these events, then the earthquake that is spoken of here is a global event and the cities of the world will become as rubble.

This will be fleshed out in subsequent discussion in these pages, but it is at this point that there is enormous human carnage. The human losses of all previous plagues will be minimal, which emphasises the enormous forbearance and patience of God. I suspect there will be huge numbers that will be converted, but in proportion to the entire population of the world they will be a relatively small proportion.

The great city (Jerusalem) *divided into three parts, and the cities of the nations fell* (16:19) as a consequence of this global earthquake. The cities of the world are the great metropolises of Babylon, which are possessed by the spirit of the secular city — secular humanism thoroughly institutionalised in the *MYSTERY, BABYLON THE GREAT, THE MOTHER OF HARLOTS AND OF THE ABOMINATIONS OF THE EARTH* (17:5). These Sodoms and Gomorrahs will not be won by the preaching of the Gospel, but their *iniquity is made complete* and now it is time for a scorched-earth policy that obliterates the very institution of the BEAST.

The great city refers to modern Jerusalem. *Divided into three parts* is a specific prophecy that will be unmistakably fulfilled, and when we see it, it will be a clear sign. The great church father, Augustine of Hippo, in his book *The City of God*, defines two cities — the City of God, equated with Jerusalem, and the pagan and Secular City of Babylon, representing the cities of the world.[49] The great city of Jerusalem is *divided into three* but *the cities of the nations fell*. I would imagine that great cities all over the globe will report that this city has been reduced to rubble.

These geographic and tectonic global events are so great that, *then every island fled away, and the mountains were not found*

---

[49] St. Augustine, *City of God*, Penguin Books, London, 1994.

(16:20). The geographic landscape will be like another world because of this global earthquake *as had not occurred since men were on the earth.*

Then, if that's not enough, *great hail from heaven fell upon man...* The human losses will be incalculable. Again, this is real hail and possibly the atmospherics that surround these events will be severely checked to produce this phenomenon of *great hail from heaven.* Yet men are without the fear of God and have become utterly callous, so it records that, *Men blasphemed God...* (16:21) like the Egyptians in the days of Moses when they hardened their hearts and blasphemed God.

Great Babylon is a spiritual edifice of the secular city and the whole world system. The Roman Catholic spirit is everywhere (14:8; 17:5). And it is for this one-world system and all its institutions that a special *cup of the wine of the fierceness of His wrath* is reserved (16:19). The whole Babylonian system that is underwritten by *the beast* of Catholicism and its axis powers in left-wing socialism has waged war against Biblical Christianity with implacable hatred in the form of secular humanism, communism and all its institutions with its man-centred socio-political philosophies. Who is going to correct this? What is here in chapter 16 is but the beginning of the total subjugation of all these godless forces and the introduction of an entirely new era of a long and sustained millennial reign of the saints with Christ. This will be a Christian age where the truth of Christ's righteousness and peace will be consistently established in all areas of life in the consummation of the kingdom of God according to the Covenant of Creation.

THE PLACE FOR THE POWERFUL AND PERSISTENT PREACHING OF THE WORD OF GOD

The preaching of the Word of God, and particularly the Gospel, is an instrument of God's mercy, and it is the single instrument that brings about true salvation in the Lord Jesus Christ. It can be greatly used to bring about social changes and sound Biblical foundations to public institutions and public life. Through the instrumentation of the Word of God, the Kingdom of God makes great advances in the world and Christians should not be embarrassed about applying the principles of God's law in every area of life. However, in the providence of God, there have been times where the Word of God ceases and the judgment of God is introduced. It is not that the Word of God has returned without accomplishing its work, but it has become a situation where we, *Do not give what is holy to the dogs; nor cast your pearls before swine, lest they trample them under their feet, and turn and tear you in pieces* (Matt. 7:6). The focus of chapter 16 of Revelation is the judgment upon the institutional enemies of the beast, which is that swine that tramples under his feet the holy things of God and now *his iniquity is complete*. Judgment time has finally come! For, *After these things I heard a loud voice of a great multitude in heaven, saying, "Alleluia! Salvation and glory and honour and power belong to the Lord our God! For true and righteous are His judgments, because He has judged the great harlot who corrupted the earth with her fornication; and He has avenged on her the blood of His servants shed by her." Again they said, "Alleluia! Her smoke rises up forever and ever!"* (19:1-3).

If an evangelist in the days of the WWII had had the temerity and the zeal to preach the Gospel to Adolf Hitler (which Hitler no doubt did hear somewhere along the line) in the hope that he would change his mind on German military mobilisation, and Hitler rejected it, this would not indicate a failure of the Gospel but the failure of a man who would rather see millions of his own subjects senselessly killed because he could not and would not humbly submit to the *King of kings and Lord of lords* (19:16), Jesus Christ. The only solution was war, otherwise it would mean servitude and international misery. So too is the solution of dealing with *the beast* and *the false prophet*, (the institutional Antichrist) in all the ages of the great tribulation that stretched from the ascension of the Lord Jesus Christ to *this great day of God Almighty*.

Most Protestant and faithfully Reformed scholars believe that the powerful and persistent preaching of the Gospel is the instrument that God uses in chapter 16 of the book of Revelation. For instance, Dr. Nigel Lee writes:

> *In Revelation sixteen, we are told how this comes about. In addition to the mentioned* **powerful and persistent preaching of the Gospel** *to every nation And Kindred Unto The Conversion Of God's Elect, and the keeping of the Ten Commandments to the glory of God, there is also the outpouring of progressive punishments on those throughout the world who disobey the Gospel. Seven last vials and plagues are to be poured out on the Earth, before the completion of the Christianisation of the nations.*[50]

This is, of course, a motherhood statement for the Gospel age. But I reflect the teaching of chapter 16 of Revelation. There is no mention in the first six bowls of God's wrath of Gospel preaching until possibly the seventh bowl, when the Lord Jesus Christ Himself appears with a sword coming out of His mouth (if you accept Ch

---

[50] Nigel Lee, *'Christians Overcome Papacy and Islam'*, Electronic Edition, p107.

19: 11-21 as some sort of descriptive portion of the sixth and seventh bowls) which appears not of God's grace in the Gospel but the Word of judgment across the nations. There is no mention of the powerful and persistent preaching of the Gospel to every nation and kindred. This is a chapter about the wrath of God upon the beast, the harlot and the great Babylon. This is the focus of the entire passage and not the evangelical thrust of the Gospel.

> *First, faithless men are scorched with great heat. They blasphemed the name of God who has power over the first four plagues.*[51]

None of these people is affected by the Gospel preaching but remains Gospel-hardened to the end; that is the persistent theme of the entire chapter. It has the message of God's pronouncement concerning the Pharaoh of Egypt whose *heart was hardened* during the plagues at the time of the Exodus. It is simply jumping to conclusions without addressing the text.

> *Luther says: "In chapters 15 and 16 come the seven angels with the seven bowls" containing the seven plagues. Compare here the 1334-83 A.D. 'Black Death' and its accompanying plagues. "The Gospel increases, and attacks the Papacy on all sides by means of many learned and pious preachers....The throne of The Pope's power, becomes dark and wretched and despised...."*[52]

Taking a long-term interpretation of chapter 16 is confusing the historical movements described in the book of Revelation. With the outbreak of Biblical Christianity at the Reformation period, the

---

[51] Ibid, p 107.

[52] Ibib, p 108.

Gospel marched forward, gaining ground, and created an upward movement in Christian civilisation among the nations. The influence of the Gospel had an enormous effect in the advancement of knowledge with the civilising effects of that knowledge, but the Church has never experienced being at centre stage anywhere in history, and we cannot describe any part of history as being a Christian age, even though the Gospel has advanced powerfully and has seen a great multitude of converts coming into the church. There has even been a great legacy of Christian culture granted to many nations, but the Harlot, the Beast and the great Babylon, has always made his presence at centre stage throughout history. Believers in the Gospel of the Lord Jesus Christ, in the overall scheme of things, have always been in a tiny minority, although their influence has far outweighed their number through the kingdom of God and its growth.

For example, within one generation of the Reformation, the Counter-Reformation of the Roman Catholic Church caused it to regain its position over Europe through its education system that it introduced. Iain Murray makes an observation (at a conference) that historically speaking, after any major revival, there has followed a major war that has seen the deaths of many faithful believers, which had in effect counteracted the possible dawning of a Christian age. It could be said that the powerful work of the Gospel in the southern United States through the southern Presbyterians that had established a Puritan society was obliterated by the American Civil War when General Sherman used scorched-earth tactics on the Calvinistic southern states to obliterate the institutions of Calvinistic culture.

Many other examples could be quoted, such as the French Huguenots, that one historian said was the "most excellent school of Christ ever to exist." However, the beast with the harlot on the day of Bartholomew and subsequent relentless hounding and bloody persecutions by Catholic forces leaves France the enigma she is today.

The influence of the Great Awakening in Britain, America, South Africa, Australia and New Zealand with the commencement of the modern missionary movement had, by the 1960s, been brought to a standstill by two World Wars. These were brilliantly orchestrated by the German Theological Liberalism, French Revolutionary new political order (Marxism both in the west and east) and Hegelian–Darwinian Scientific and Social Theory. All these combine, resulting in the rise and rise of Secular Humanism, with Babylon the Great and the Beast and the Harlot being the inspiration behind this spiritual entity of Babylon.

> *The seven Angels, according to the Calvinistic Geneva Bible, include the Church's Preachers as "God's Ministers." And by the four living beings, "are meant all the creatures of God which willingly serve Him for the punishment of infidels." For "God gives us full entry into His Church, by destroying His enemies."[53]*

This comment in the Geneva Bible is without foundation. It is true that the angels in the earlier parts of the Apocalypse are referring to Gospel preachers in the form of God's ministers. These angels, however, have a completely different character and their work is distinctive in terms of their origin and works. These angels, like those that the prophet Daniel speaks about, and those found in Isaiah 6, are in heavenly places. It is true that the power of the Gospel preaching has glorious powers over the works of Satan and destroys the foundations of darkness. Here these angels are

---

[53] Ibid, p 110.

ministers of God's wrath, using the naked powers of the material universe for the furtherance of God's purposes of that Day of God Almighty (16:14).

APOSTOLIC EXPECTATION OF THESE EVENTS

It would seem that the writer of Hebrews brings this event into focus when referring to the events of Noah's day with the universal flood and the tectonic geological movement of the earth at that time. The author of the book of Hebrews says, *See that you do not refuse Him who speaks. For if they did not escape who refused Him who spoke on earth, much more shall we not escape if we turn away from Him who speaks from heaven, whose voice then shook the earth; but now he has promised, saying, "Yet once more I shake not only the earth, but also heaven"* referring to the ancient prophecy of Haggai 2:6 (Heb. 10: 25 – 26).

This catastrophic event, which is yet to come, that is promised through the writer to the Hebrews, is referring to the physical creation, being *as of things that are made* (Heb. 10:27). Now this *Yet once more* is referring to yet another like catastrophic, geological event left in history that will give a new beginning to planet earth. It is in our study of chapter 16 of the book of Revelation that describes this event, which is not some sort of doomsday event but an "exodus" type of event that will usher in the millennial reign of Christ with His saints, being the consummation of the kingdom of God on earth as it is in heaven.

Such a shaking will be like a sieve through which those eternal features of the kingdom of God that *cannot be shaken may remain* (Heb. 10:27). The kingdom of God was received in the days of our Lord Jesus Christ while He "tabernacled" amongst us in our own flesh and has been subject to violence throughout the Gospel age of the church (Matt. 11:12). But at this event of the *great day of God*

Almighty (16:14), deliverance will be granted and the victory of Christ's kingdom shall be complete. The rule of Christ will be established across all the nations of the earth, where a great mighty angel shall proclaim in heaven, saying, *The kingdoms of this world have become the kingdoms of our Lord and of His Christ's, and He shall reign for ever and ever!* (11:15). So, the writer of Hebrews gives a final exhortation in the light of these coming events, *Therefore, since we have received a kingdom which cannot be shaken, let us have grace, by which we may serve God acceptably with reverence and godly fear. For our God is a consuming fire* (Heb. 10:28-29).

If this event is a "Last Day" event, the victory of the kingdom of God would be fulfilled for just one day, but our study in the book of Revelation will give us indications that this victory is not for one day but for a long and sustained rule of Christ on earth as He rules in heaven. This sustained rule is a millennial rule of the entire earth and all her nations without exception. If we establish our understanding of the book of Revelation as a sequential unfolding of the purposes of God throughout history, then without doing violence to the text of Scripture, a natural flow in the description this millennial kingdom sits comfortably in the sequence of these events after the *great day of God Almighty* described in chapter 16, further expounded in chapters 17 to 19. Then the millennial passage of chapter 20 is found like a capstone in Christ's triumphant purposes for planet earth.

CHAPTER 9

THE DEMISE OF THE GREAT HARLOT-REVELATION 17

The focus of *the bowls of the wrath of God on the earth* was upon *the men who had the mark of the beast and those who worshipped his image* (16:1, 2). The fifth bowl was poured out directly and specifically *on the throne of the beast and his kingdom* (16:10). Then *a great earthquake, such a mighty and great earthquake as had not occurred since men were on the earth... and the cities of the nations fell* (16:18). Out of the genus of the beast, people attempted to God-proof themselves against the absolute sovereignty of God and *make a name for themselves* (Gen. 11:4) by creating the global Secular Humanist city-state of *the great Babylon* but *Babylon was remembered before God, to give her the cup of the wine of the fierceness of His wrath* (16:19).

Now, in chapter 17, the Apostle John is shown in detail *the judgment of the great harlot* (17:1). This malignant, dragon-like figure that sits in the Temple of God at the centre stage of world history up to this point is what the Apostle John describes elsewhere as the Antichrist (1 Jn. 2:18; 4:3) who sets himself up in the place of God, even bearing the names of God and audaciously calling himself, "the Holy Father (Father), the Priest and Mediator of God (Son) and the Vicar of Christ (Holy Spirit)." This substitute trinitarian harlot is now brought under the feet of Christ *and the God of peace will crush Satan under your feet shortly* (Rom. 16:20).

From the days of the First Advent of Christ, the Kingdom of God is ever-growing in its influence throughout the centuries, and now for some two millennia, so that its leaven develops a culture of knowledge, wisdom, and righteousness, with spiritual and material effects on earth as it is in heaven. This rule of Christ from heaven on earth is irrepressible, even under the great bloody persecutions perpetrated by the harlot, the beast and the false prophet of those centuries of great tribulation against the saints of God. The invisible work of the Kingdom of God is the civilising agency of God across every field of knowledge and enterprise throughout history, and its influence is ever growing so that, *the earth will be filled with the knowledge of the Lord as the waters cover the sea* (Isa. 11:9).

However, as the Master of heaven has sown the wheat of the kingdom of Heaven, the enemy has sown his tares (Matt. 13:24-30). So, the harlot, the beast, Babylon the great in the fullness of time, along with the false prophet, have exploited the civilising advances in the knowledge and wisdom that has been granted by God through the sciences, the arts and technologies and usurped these advances for the glory of man instead of for the glory of God.

Now in the fullness of time, God alone acts to avenge His saints against the harlot, the beast and the false prophet, *for they have shed the blood of the saints and prophets...for it is their just due* (16:6). As we read further, these events of *the seven last plagues* that indicate that *the wrath of God is complete* (15:1) lead to a mighty angel of God that captures the beast and with him the false prophet, and *these two were cast alive into the lake of fire burning with brimstone* (19:20). Then *an angel coming down from heaven, having the key to the bottomless pit and a great chain in his hand,* laid hold of the very spiritual power of wickedness himself, *the dragon, the serpent of old, who is the Devil and Satan, and bound him for a thousand years; and cast him into the bottomless pit and shut him up, and set a seal upon him, so that he should deceive the nations no more till the thousand years were finished* (20:1-3). These events will establish a great and sustained peace across the nations of all the earth where the reign of Christ the King with his saints as the Kingdom of God will be consummated.

The Apostle John is given a clear perspective on the reasons why *the bowls of the wrath of God* were specifically poured out against the great harlot who had *on her forehead a name was written: "Mystery, Babylon the great, the mother of harlots and of the abominations of the earth"* (17:5). During the events of the destruction effected by the Bowls of Wrath, a commentary is being presented to John by *one of the seven the angels who had the seven bowls* (17:1), and this is recorded for us in Chapters 17, 18 and 19. These bowls were unleashed in relatively rapid succession. This stands as an event in history, as did the plagues of Egypt in the days of Moses.

As the subject of chapter 17 is *the great harlot*, the chapter is broken up into two sections from the perspective of the landmark event of *the seven last plagues.* The first in verses 1-4 is a reflection on the history of this malignant character that has taken two millennia to complete, and therefore is a retrospective from the standpoint of these events. The second section in verses 5-18 is a prospective disclosure of *a great mystery* that looks into the distant future after the thousand-year banishment of *the Dragon, that serpent of old, who is the Devil and Satan* (20:2). This spiritual personality that formerly took the persona of the *mother of harlots* is released to rise out of the bottomless pit, then *deceives the nations, which are in the four corners of the earth* for a short time at the end. This will happen just before the Last Day when the bodily return of Christ is witnessed by every human eye that has ever existed, with the general bodily resurrection of every human being that has ever lived, in readiness for the Judgment of God (Dan. 12:2; Jn. 5:28-29).

By the time *the last seven plagues* are unleashed against the mother of harlots and her beast with the citizens of *Babylon the Great* and the false prophet, the iniquity of this Antichrist has thoroughly ripened and is complete (cf Gen. 15:16). The consolidation of the godlessness and unrighteousness, *who had the mark of the beast and those who worshipped his image* has now become established so that the hardness of their hearts makes them impervious to the Gospel. Therefore, during these last bowls of wrath, there have been no mass conversions referred to among those to whom they have been directed. Several times it mentions they are like the Pharaoh of Egypt in the days of Moses and that they *blasphemed the God of heaven* (16:9, 11, 21).

THE REVELATION OF THE MYSTERY OF THE GREAT HARLOT AND HER BEAST

THE CATHOLICITY OF THE GREAT HARLOT

Verse 1 tells us that one of the angels who had the seven bowls which were received from the four living creatures (15:7) shows John the judgment of the great harlot. She is described as sitting on many waters, which refers to 13:1 where she originally comes out of the sea in the form of the beast. That is to say, she arises out of the sea of paganism that is universal wherever the Judeo-Christian Gospel has not reached and where the Christian kingdom of God has not taken root. Here in chapter 17, she still has dominion *on many waters*, but now in the Christian persona of the antichrist. Truly, the leopard does not change his spots or the Ethiopian his colour. The harlot is here called the same beast, and she is antichrist in everything.

Wherever *the great harlot* has gone, she has taken the pagan world into her citadels to Christianise their populations so as to inoculate them with the form of Christianity that gives them enough truth to immunise them against the authentic Biblical Gospel, which is *the power of God to salvation for everyone who believes* (Rom. 1:16). As the Lord Jesus says of the scribes and Pharisees in His own day, *Woe to you, scribes and Pharisees, hypocrites! For you travel land and sea to win one proselyte, and when he is won, you make him twice as much a son of hell as yourselves* (Matt. 23:15). *These people draw near to Me with their mouth, and honour Me with their lips, but their heart is far from Me* (Matt. 15:8).

THE KINGS OF THE EARTH COMMITTED FORNICATION.

In **verse 2**, the great harlot is described as sitting on many waters having global and universal influence or dominion. The harlot and the beast are masters in politics and confound the roles of church and state, so that *the kings of the earth committed fornication with her* and entered into an unholy alliance. The harlot's church, that has the hearts and minds of the people in her control through religious fear and duty, has had a direct political influence across the nations because of her catholicity of religion. The kings of the earth would be little more than tribes if they did not have the mortar of the Roman Catholic Church to bind them together in a kind of "league of nations." Such alliances have made it easier for international trade and a strategic balance of international power to exist.

There have been dreadful persecutions throughout the history of the Papacy from 664-6 A.D. to our own day, but particularly through the days of the Protestant Reformation and the Catholic

Counter-Reformation. Millions were martyred and massacred because they were heretics in the eyes of the great harlot who piously committed this work on behalf of state authorities. In the many Inquisitions throughout the Holy Roman Empire, the Holy Order conducted the Inquisition through trials by torture and forced confessions by the harlot church's Inquisitor in one room, to be executed by the so-called State authorities through horrible slow and torturous deaths in the next room.

There were two movements at the time of the sixteenth and seventeenth centuries: The religious Reformation, and the Enlightenment known as the Renaissance. The civilising advancements of knowledge and wisdom that took place because of the Protestant Reformation could not be suppressed any longer by the old-world mediaeval power structures. The political powers of the tyrannical Machiavellian government structures that were controlled by *the antichrist* of Catholicism, could not match *the power of the Gospel* and the liberty that truth established. The old-world order of the mediaeval spiritual powers was shaken to the core.

For example, John Calvin, the Frenchman living in Geneva, promoted the Reformation throughout Europe. However, France was only partially open to Reformed evangelism. Religious and political hostilities, which also threatened Geneva, were a constant danger in France. Nonetheless, Calvin and his colleagues made the most of the small opening they had. The minutes of the "Company of Pastors" in Geneva deal with the supervision of the missionary efforts in France more than in any other country.[54]

---

[54] Robert M. Kingdon, *Geneva and the Consolidation of the French Protestant Movement* (Madison: University of Wisconsin Press, 1967), 31.

Reformed believers from France took refuge in Geneva. While there, many began to study theology. They then felt compelled to return to their own people as Reformed evangelists and pastors. After passing a rigorous theological examination, each was given an assignment by the Geneva "Company of Pastors," usually in response to a formal request from a French church needing a pastor. In most cases, the receiving church was fighting for its life under persecution. The French refugees who returned as pastors were eventually killed, but their zeal encouraged the hopes of their parishioners. Their mission, which according to the pastors, sought *to advance the knowledge of the Gospel in France, as our Lord commands,* was successful.

Reformed evangelistic preaching produced a remarkable revival. In 1555, there was only one fully organised Reformed church in France. Seven years later, there were close to two thousand. The French Reformed pastors were on fire for God and, despite massive persecution, God used their work to convert thousands. This is one of the most remarkable examples of effective home missions work in the history of Protestantism, and one of the most astonishing revivals in Church history.

Some of the French Reformed congregations became very large. For example, Pierre Viret pastored a church of 8,000 communicants in Nimes. More than ten per cent of the French population in the 1560s—as many as three million—belonged to these churches.[55]

During the St. Bartholomew's Day massacre of 1572, 70,000 Protestants were killed. Nevertheless, the Church continued. In the days and years after the St. Bartholomew's Day massacre, countless

---

[55] Joel Beeke, *Calvin's Evangelism,* (PDF Internet Article, 2004), 78-79.

numbers lost their lives for the Gospel's sake. Persecution eventually "ethnically cleansed" France of the French Protestants and, of course, history has been rewritten.

THE KINGS OF THE EARTH ... WERE MADE DRUNK WITH THE WINE OF HER FORNICATION.

Ignatius Loyola (1491-1556), with his Gestapo-like Jesuits, affected the counter-Reformation with brutal effect. Under the motto *The end justifies the means* and with political exactness, the Jesuits used terror and ethnic cleansing to gain the upper hand on the Reformation and establish an education system that captured the minds of the ruling classes with each successive generation. These young minds were inoculated against Christianity using the Christian vaccine of the sacerdotal Gospel of Rome with the promise of title, office and powerful careers in the best that the world can give.

The Jesuits, being the loyal subjects of the Pope of the Roman Catholic Church, answered the Reformation by setting up a spiritual kingdom that was the exact counterpart to the Kingdom of God. It would be built on the blessings of the true Gospel of Christ, as true believers shone *the light of the world* and became *the salt of the earth*, exhibiting the wisdom of God in every area of life. These anti-Christian powers of Rome usurped the knowledge of God and reorientated it so that man is at the centre and glorified, in place of God.

The emerging Humanist Movement that looked back to Roman society and Greek culture established a political and cultural system and, discovering in the Renaissance the civilising effects of the Reformation, then systematically built a spiritual kingdom of Babylon the great, hoping *to make a name for themselves* (Gen.

11:4) and God-proofing themselves against the absolute sovereignty of God.

By waging an all-out war against Protestant nations and Protestant elements within nations, using genocidal tactics of 'ethnic cleansing' and the institution of terror in the Inquisition, the Reformation was reduced to a refined remnant in Great Britain, Holland and other scattered locations in Europe. Using their tactical advantage, the Roman Catholic Church used its influence to secure her hegemony in the field of education and created—and where possible took over—Protestant institutions, institutions that were second-to-none in terms of Humanist excellence.

The Counter-Reformation also took advantage of the Renaissance of culture and the great advances in science, the arts, technology, economics, navigation and trade. The Counter-Reformation seized upon these things and erected a public education system that was controlled by the Roman Catholic Church and developed a Secular Humanist state where man was pre-eminent. From a humanistic point of view, these schools and universities, even to this day, are among the best in terms of gaining some of the best positions in society and orientating trades or professions so that Babylon the Great is erected. This strategy was hugely successful in giving birth to the 'Secular Humanist' state that would seize the ground of the advancing Kingdom of God.

THE INHABITANTS OF THE EARTH WERE MADE DRUNK WITH THE WINE OF HER FORNICATION.

Jesuit and Roman Catholic missions into the new world strategically colonised the vast continents to prevent Protestant missions from taking root. South Africa, North America, Australia and New Zealand were notable exceptions to the rule, at least until the early twentieth century.

After the massacres of the Calvinistic Huguenot French Reformed Church (1572), absolute power was given to the French monarchs, which gave way to the French Revolution (1789–1799). It became the model experiment for the socio-political doctrines of autocratic socialism that eventually vented itself in the "Communist Experiment." Marxism in the West (1916-1991) and Maoism in the East (1949-2005?) failed because there were no incentives in their economic theory.

With the fall of the Iron Curtain and rejigging of the Bamboo Curtain, secular humanism (with socialism as its cultural platform and statism as its political platform) and economic supply is put in place by re-establishing free enterprise as "a milking cow" to supply the Babylonian government through a taxation system so that everybody has to drink from its trough. This has the effect of apportioning absolute power to *Leviathan* (Isa. 27: 1).

IN THE SPIRIT AND IN THE WILDERNESS

As we come to verse 3, It must be remembered that, in spite of the ruthless opposition against the true Church of God, the *gates of hell did not prevail* (Matt. 16:18). The Church knew God's sovereign grace in the Gospel that is *the power of God unto salvation* (Rom. 1:16). This entails being justified by faith alone through grace; knowing the Scriptures as the Supreme Standard and authority of God; and worshipping God according to the regulative principle of worship, which is the Word of God alone that opens the heart of the true worshipper so that he *worships God in spirit and truth* (John 4:21-24). These Gospel believers refused to worship God by human artifices through the elaborate and sacerdotal system of priestcraft. The influence of the kingdom of God was breaking the defences of the antichrist through the establishment of the truth that sets free the soul of the true believer, even though they were being *killed all day long...(being) accounted as sheep for the slaughter* (Rom. 8:36).

The old orders of the harlot's beast had to be reinvented to counteract the advances of the kingdom of God in its invisible influence through its converted citizens, Gospel believers that established Christ's rule in every department of their lives, leaving the legacy of a Christian culture behind them. The harlot and the beast would grow apart, but will be possessed by the same spirit of iniquity. Babylon would be her intention for the modern world!

Babylon the Great is the political and social invention of the mother of harlots that is the exact sinister opposite yet a mimicking of the kingdom of God. As the kingdom of God is a spiritual rule of Christ from heaven, having material effect on earth due to its profound influence through the citizens of the kingdom of God, (Jn. 18:36) so too is Babylon the Great a spiritual entity that puts man at the centre so then man may seize any ground that the kingdom of God may gain. For instance, in the days of the Reformation, the Church regained sound Biblical doctrine and practices that affected its ability to advance the sciences and ascertain the knowledge of God so that the proper stewardship of that knowledge and wisdom may advance that which was promised in the Covenant of Creation (Gen. 1:28-30), to the end that all things spiritual and material would give glory to God.

THE KINGDOM OF GOD AND ITS ADVANCE

Protestant nations whose churches freely spoke a prophetic voice of God's word into the consciences of the people of these nations became *the light of the world* and *the salt of the earth*. This occasioned the advancement of a Christian Biblical culture where the law of God became the law of the land, and public life

THE DEMISE OF THE GREAT HARLOT-REVELATION 17

was chaste. Family life, which was seen the very fabric of society, was sacred and secure. Public education from a Christian perspective furnished these nations with outstanding leaders and dedicated servants across every field of endeavour, securing great liberty as the mark of national life. This did not mean there was no opposition against the churches of a Reformed and Protestant commitment, but there was a holy restraint so that even the ungodly and those that had vested interests were restrained and brought under discipline.

For example, in the Puritan period of England, and the time of the Presbyterian and reformed movement in Scotland and Northern Ireland, faithful churches were contested at every stage throughout their testimony for Christ by the kings and queens of the day, along with people in high places that hated the Biblical testimony of these churches. As Biblical standards were established within the Church, and greater Biblical unity was experienced across the churches, even though contrary churches holding to the spirit of Romanism were fighting a rear-guard action, the Puritans managed to establish the Long Parliament in Westminster.

The English Civil War (1642-1651) was a series of armed conflicts and political machinations between Parliamentarians (Roundheads) and Royalists (Cavaliers). The Civil War ended with the Parliamentary victory at the Battle of Worcester on 3 September 1651.

Constitutionally, the wars established the precedent that an English monarch cannot govern without Parliament's consent, although this concept was legally established only with the Glorious Revolution later in the century. The prominent young Scottish Presbyterian, Samuel Rutherford, against the background of the ancient ground-breaking constitutional document of the Magna

Carta (issued in 1215 and eventually passed into law in 1225), produced an influential treatise entitled *Lex Rex* (1644) which articulated the future settlement of Protestant church and state relations. It advocated limited government and constitutionalism in politics and the 'Two Sphere' theory of Church-State relations (which advocated distinct realms of church and state but opposed religious toleration).

The crown as the supreme human authority should be limited and governed by law rather than the so-called divine right of absolutism articulated as "the King is the law." The concept of the Law above the law was also propounded so that the law of the land is not a mere democratic device of the people but derived through due process of all departments of government vested in the crown, parliament and the judiciary being established under the law of God and expressed in natural law. The idea of liberty without anarchy was the object of such a Biblical view of government. It was also argued that defensive war and even pre-emptive war was the right of every citizen. Every citizen was required to be lawful and was subject to the judiciary so that justice was established for all citizens whether high or low, privileged or mean. Standing armies are to be used only for the defence of the realm and never against their own people for political ends or to terrify their citizens. The right to bear arms for personal protection is an inalienable right of all its citizens.

The Puritan faction in Parliament made five attempts to appoint an assembly between June 1642 and May 1643, but each time King Charles refused to sign the bill. A sixth bill was prepared and passed as an ordinance of the House of Commons; and, with the agreement of the House of Lords it became effective without the king's assent in June 1643.

The Westminster Assembly of Divines was appointed by the Long Parliament to restructure the Church of England which had the stench of Rome if not Papal sacerdotalism secreted across its life and practice. The Assembly met for six years (1643-1649), and in the process produced the documents which are the major Confessional Standards of the Presbyterian faith, including the Westminster Confession of Faith, the Westminster Larger Catechism, the Westminster Shorter Catechism, and the Directory of Public Worship. These documents, which had become known as the Westminster Standards, were a genuine reflection of the true Church of God in England, Scotland and Northern Ireland, the nations that formed the basis of the United Kingdom.

In later centuries, as the Church expanded into the Americas, South Africa, Australia and New Zealand and into the Pacific Islands and many other parts of the world, this benchmark of Protestant doctrine and the Reformation of the churches was set forth as the fullest and most mature foundations that the Church of Christ had had since the days of the Apostles. Similar victories were achieved in Europe, and particularly in the Netherlands, with very similar doctrinal standards: these were reflected in the Belgic Confession and the Heidelberg Catechism, and later in the addition of the Five Points of Calvinism that became known as the Three Forms of Unity.

Britain was largely spared the atrocities that befell mainland Europe, although she very very narrowly escaped the same fate of most other European nations, which had large Protestant populations, when the Spanish Armada failed to land on the shores of England. Due to the intervention of a fateful storm and excellent naval battle strategy used to great effect by British commanders with a maritime force that was inferior to that of the Spaniards, the day was saved for the burgeoning Protestant nation. "Jehovah blew with His winds, and they were scattered" (which may be an allusion to Exodus 15:10) is a famous phrase on the aftermath of the defeat of the Spanish Armada in 1588, when the Spanish (Catholic) fleet was broken up by a storm, which was also called the Protestant Wind. The phrase seems to have had its origin in an inscription on one of the many commemorative medals struck to celebrate the occasion.

Through the powerful work of the Gospel of the Lord Jesus Christ, the truth of God and the advances of the knowledge of God in the created order of existence released the powerful work in the kingdom of God that mysteriously established civilisation in the culture of mankind. God powerfully works primarily through the citizens of the kingdom of God, but He also works through whom he chooses. So, the wisdom of God is comprehensively advanced in all disciplines of learning: within the physical sciences of matter, in the spiritual and psychological power of the mind, in the mathematics of logic and technology, and the endeavours of substantial meaning and purpose in the light and life of truth and wisdom that expresses the comprehensive providence of God in all things. So as disciples of Christ are made through the Gospel and the promises of the Covenant of Redemption, and as Christ's disciples are visited with every good work that is born by walking in the Spirit, the Covenant of Creation is an emerging hope because *...the creation itself also will be delivered from the bondage of corruption into the glorious liberty of the children of God...*(Rom. 8:21). In a proportionate manner, during the now two millennia of the *great tribulation* (7:14) under the scourging lash of the harlot and her beast that morphs into a global secular humanist city state of Babylon the great and the false prophet, the disciples of Christ the King fulfil the great commission to make disciples of all nations (Matt. 28:19). At every point of history there have been nations that for a short season have known the light of Gospel culture and could be described as Christian or Protestant nations, such as Great Britain and the Netherlands and their dominions during the empire years.

However, *the great harlot ... with whom the kings of the earth committed (spiritual) fornication and the inhabitants of the earth were made to drink the wine of her fornication.*

"A Woman Sitting on a Scarlet Beast"

In **verse 3**, John the Apostle is carried away in the spirit into the wilderness and he sees *a woman sitting on a scarlet beast*, which is a description in Chapter 13 concerning the *beast coming out of the earth* (13: 1). She is now described as one possessing unbridled wealth, full of abominations and displaying the vilest and most filthy kinds of fornication, which is religious fornication and idolatry.

The Roman Catholic Church established a Reformed and Calvinistic relationship with church and state where the harlot church grew apart from the Babylonian woman, but always riding the scarlet beast, being the Roman socio-political religious entity of church-state. The Babylonian woman is all the time riding upon the beast of old but within separate spheres of church and state; then consistently propagating the Secular Humanist world and life view, and politically populating these institutions with people thoroughly prepared in this world and life view, that is man-centred and religiously atheistic in respect of true religion. In terms of regaining world hegemony and taking centre stage, the plan was brilliantly successful.

The sacred Beast *which was full of names of blasphemy*, probably refers to the companions of Roman Catholicism, which are in alliance with this Beast and share in the blasphemies of Roman Catholicism, but are known by other names such as Pentecostalism and the Charismatic Movement within contemporary Evangelical Christianity, Theological Liberalism of the twentieth century, Ecumenicalism of the World Council of Churches, Interfaith Dialogue between Catholicism and a Protestant agencies with Hindus, Muslims and Buddhists, and others.

The *seven heads and ten horns* motif is used in verse 7 and is a reference to the distant future that is tied up in the disclosure to the Apostle John, concerning *the mystery of the woman and of the beast that carries her*. This will be dealt with later, but note here that the same spirit of Antichrist of this era of her earthly dominion will also mysteriously be manifested in the far distant future, after the millennial rule of Christ and His saints, when *Satan will be released from his prison* (20:7) for a *little while* (20:3), just before the final return of Christ. The colour scarlet is such an appropriate description of Papal grandeur throughout her history.

Today Catholicism is by far the greatest general religious entity across the earth. It controls social order, politics, social welfare and education particularly within the world of western secular humanism that is largely a system of Roman Catholic politics. She has rapidly progressed and by her influence controls every department of society, to the near destruction of Biblical Protestant Christianity, but for the grace of God.

For this malignant universal powerbase to turn around, it will take a mighty intervention of God Himself. Roman Catholicism has become so *Beast-like* and its power is so comprehensive, the power of the Gospel through conversion is not for this purpose, which is judgment. The Gospel is a declaration of the mercy of God for the conversion of individuals, of the promotion of family religion and the establishment of Christian society. Many within the beast's grip will be touched by the Gospel and will be resurrected from spiritual death and gloriously saved. The Gospel is not an instrument of judgment but of mercy and grace. What is happening here is judgment, and the instruments of judgment are employed with great ferocity.

At times of war, such as the first and second World Wars, of our era, military might is God's solution to national problems. The Gospel was not the instrument of appropriate use. So too this thoroughly institutionalised godlessness will not be removed or destroyed by Gospel preaching. For Roman Catholic individuals, yes, but not this satanically designed system.

The solution is God's providential power as seen in chapter 16. A full commentary in chapter 18 describes the destruction of *Babylon the great*, when the three great historic institutional enemies of the kingdom of God will be delivered to judgment, and with white-hot wrath.

1. Beast – Babylon.
2. Harlot – Roman Catholicism.
3. False prophet – Islam and Muhammedanism.

That which lies behind all these enemies is the dragon, which is the personification of Satan himself.

THE WOMAN THAT POSSESSES THE WHOLE WORLD

In **verse 4**, the unbridled wealth and worldliness of this figure of the great harlot are portrayed. Roman Catholicism, with all her other companions, are enormously wealthy in this world, ...*arrayed in purple and scarlet...adorned with gold and precious stones and pearls*... The wealth of the Roman Catholic Church worldwide in terms of real estate and property is probably unequalled by any other organisation. That, along with its human resources inside her citadels, is one thing. However, the wealth and worldliness of the beastly institutions of Secular Humanism and its strategic and comprehensive control are such that it can be regarded as a one-world system.

Babylon the great, with its massive social welfare system, supplies every conceivable social need from "cradle to grave" through human and social engineering. The state's absolute power is attained through the strategies of attacking the cultural mandate of the family, church and community, and engendering dependency rather than self-sufficiency and freedom. This of course is done in the name of caring for the poor, disadvantaged, ignorant and dispossessed, but it widens the circle of dependency and increases the power of the state. Power is the name of the game, and as we know, illegitimate *power corrupts and absolute power corrupts absolutely*.

This strong drink of absolute power was entirely intoxicating and the hopeful prospect of not being accountable to God is such a relief to a wounded conscience of a rebellious and fallen people. Having medicines to give the Babylonian citizen when in God's providence He sends a Black Plague or some pandemic, being able to believe that science will discover a vaccine, is such a relief and empowers the pride of man. If it can be believed that poverty may be resolved by a welfare system, which galvanises society's dependence upon the state, then we will never have to pray to God for help or work faithfully before God. If we can believe that technology will find a solution to any natural threat to man or to human inadequacy; if problems of resource shortage, human slavery, navigation and communication barriers can be solved, so that the tyranny of distance and isolation will be broken, then the feeling of inadequacy before the all-sufficient God can be reduced. Therefore, man's accountability to God is also reduced, feeding the pride of man that does not need to give thanks to God. Being able to believe that it is possible as a Babylonian nation-state to use such technologies to invent military hardware and amass powerful military forces that would be able to wipe out other competing nations and further consolidate absolute power is intoxicating. Is it possible to not only ignore God, the Creator and Sustainer of all things, but also God-proof ourselves against His absolute sovereignty? Being able to believe that is personally empowering and establishes the kind of arrogance that is the ultimate blasphemy as it denies the very nature of human conscience and reality.

FULL OF ABOMINATIONS AND THE FILTHINESS OF HER IDOLATROUS FORNICATION

But, ...*(she has) in her hand a golden cup full of abominations and of the filthiness of her fornication*; which means that she is caught red-handed doing what she always has done. She has been wholly given over to her stock in trade: idolatry, which leads to all other *ungodliness and unrighteousness of men who suppress the truth in unrighteousness* in zealous persecution (Rom. 1:18).

Then the social agenda is engineered so that state dependency is normalised and family is reduced to an institution of convenience and personal choice. Sex is treated as just another appetite. Children are the responsibility of the state and therefore, by implication, the property of the state. Health and essential utilities are nationally based and therefore the family and local communities are treated as a dormitory, always looking to the central power. Pragmatic values that serve the convenience of the state and the cultural order of the man-centred Secular City prevail, so we soon see that abortion on demand, marriage as relationship and personal convenience, easy divorce, homosexuality as a matter of choice, state sanctioned gambling, pornography and prostitution as entertainment, and general decadence become values of discretion in the

Secular Humanist City State. Ethical standards of righteousness are regarded as a religious choice and therefore are not to be tolerated in the public square or imposed upon others in the Secular Humanist City State. Religion is encouraged in terms of multiculturalism and supported as a cultural entity in society. Religion has no place in the secular state and religious freedom is defined as a closed entity and kept private.

The Single, Sinister, Spirit with the Catholic Sign

In **Verse5**, the title on the forehead of the Great Harlot is:

1. MYSTERY = this is, in fact, one personality stretching its influence into many institutions throughout the earth. She morphs herself so that she has many faces and no one personage.
2. BABYLON THE GREAT = secular humanism, the design of Roman Catholicism.
3. THE MOTHER OF HARLOTS = of the Roman Catholic Church which is the religious entity of the beasts.
4. AND OF THE ABOMINATIONS OF THE EARTH = it is the abomination of the earth because it seeks to take the place of Christ. This is the ultimate abomination, the great usurper.

The personage of the Antichrist has been postulated as being represented by many personalities, from the Roman Emperor Nero to Hitler or Stalin or even Mao. There is only one that has consistently, throughout history, fulfilled the description of the harlot described here. All other candidates have been momentary manifestations of a greater evil, but none has been in the same class as the Roman Catholic Church that has morphed into Babylon the Great, the Mother of Harlots. She has been consistently the abomination of the earth. She is a master of inoculating everything that touches her against Christianity. Throughout the ages, she has consistently persecuted the true Church. The true church has been mainly in the wilderness under its domination (not dominion because there is only one that has dominion—the Lord Jesus Christ), throughout the ages of the kingdom of God.

The further description in verse 6 of the great harlot is particularly apposite to the Roman Catholic Church because the history of the papacy is filled with rivers of blood, particularly those of believers in the Lord Jesus Christ who are described as "saints" by the Apostle Paul. Here the great harlot is described as being *drunk with the blood of the saints*. The martyrs are described as dying with the Church of Jesus Christ, that is the body of Christ, and when she has spilt her blood it is, as it were, the blood of Jesus himself. This Harlot of Roman Catholicism is the ultimate perpetrator of abominations because the anointed of Christ has been the continual focus of her persecution—the very body of Christ. For example, throughout some 200 years of the Reformation and counter-Reformation, the harlot church reacted with unprecedented violence against the Protestant Church. By massacre and inquisition, there were more than 68 million that were judged as heretics within the European nation-states.[56] The thing that made John the Apostle

---

[56] David A. Plaisted, *Estimates of the Number Killed by the Papacy in the Middle Ages*, 2006 -http://webwitness.org.au/estimates.html This extensive and well-documented paper is a thorough treatment of this question of the very bloodthirsty nature of the Papacy tracing the subject through respected historians that lived closer to these atrocities that had access to material that is buried by modern popularized works of revisionist historians that don't want to believe the awful facts of history. Plaisted then verifies these figures by a very thorough treatment using statistical analysis of the demographics throughout the Middle Ages that also include the Reformation years and the counter-Reformation and beyond. These figures not only verify the extraordinary numbers that were persecuted unto death by the Papacy but would indicate that the death toll is in fact a lot higher than the respected historians of former times have indicated by their own computations from available

marvel with great amazement was the sheer audacity of this personage who was openly drunk with the blood of the martyrs of the most sacred and the most loved of Christ the King.

DISCLOSURE OF THE MYSTERY OF THE WOMAN

In **verse 7** *The angel*—who is one of the angels that held one of the Seven Bowls of God's Final Wrath—took John the Apostle down the corridors of history to see the latter end of this personage, the Great Harlot. He should not have been amazed at the constant and continuous persecution of the saints by the harlot because our Lord Jesus said in the Sermon on the Mount that there is one sure thing that every believer will encounter: persecution for the sake of righteousness and for the Gospel. Maybe it was the sheer extent and scale of these atrocities and their sustained nature that staggered the Apostle? For us it is impossible to see what the Apostle John saw by studying history books and recorded accounts of these atrocities because such accounts will not, may not, or do not wish to have the ability to tell the whole story. The testimony of the saints will be fully told as we gather in the company of the saints of the New Jerusalem in heavenly places.

The Angel goes on to say, *I will tell you the mystery of the woman and of the beast that carries her...* The Beast that carries the Harlot is the Great Babylon, which is a secular humanism or

---

documentary records of the day. It is probably an impossible task to gather every record ever written that would establish the exact figure. Even if we could, it would not change the terrible conclusion that the Papacy as it welds together its alliances with nation states that there is no other institution anywhere in history and throughout history that can equal the atrocities of the great harlot church. The blood lust and the sinister lust for power has no parallel in history, and even taking into account modern figures such as Joseph Stalin, Adolf Hitler, Mao Zedong or Pol Pot, although the rates of genocide under such regimes may be higher than what the Papacy perpetrated, the sheer numbers throughout history that can be placed at the feet of the Papacy and the brutality under the Inquisition really has no parallel in history.

the secular state, the socio-political manifestation of man-centred religion. This beast carries the Great Harlot which is the religious persona manifested in Roman Catholicism.

The statement in verse 8 that *the Beast that you saw was, and it is not, and will ascend out of the bottomless pit and go to perdition* speaks of the final judgment of the Beast that carries the woman or Great Harlot which is fully described in chapter 18 which is about the fall of Babylon the Great. The question is what is meant by *the beast that you saw* which presumably is referring to *a scarlet beast* in **verse 3** and *it is not* which properly refers to its judgment described in chapter 18 and is therefore an extended period, namely through the years of the millennium described in chapter 20. He then *ascends out of the bottomless pit* which is also described in 20: 7-10 at the end of the millennium years. He rises from *the bottomless pit* to receive his final judgment and is assigned to *perdition* forever and ever.

The fall of Babylon is also described in 14:8. The preachers of the Gospel to all nations, tribes, tongue, and people are encouraged by those that hear the Gospel that the final judgment is sure and certain, and another angel, which probably refers to Gospel preachers, says, *Babylon is fallen, is fallen, that great city, because she has made all nations drink of the wine of the wrath of her fornication.*

Why should this spiritual personage of Satan be released *to deceive the nations* (20:8) for a short time after the years of the millennium are complete, or toward its end? Human reasoning cannot explain this and it is therefore a great mystery that is known to God alone.

And those who dwell on the earth will marvel, whose names are not written in the Book of Life from the foundation of the world...

This is a reference to the event associated with this mystery, *the beast that was, and is not, and yet is*, that will be acted out after the years of the millennium in the distant future. Throughout the years of the millennium, there exist *those that are not written in the Book of Life from the foundation of the world*, but they will enjoy the bliss of sustained peace and manifest righteousness in a time when the kingdom of God is consummated and consistent Gospel life is experienced in all the earth. The millennium is not a time where sin no longer exists. For that we will have to wait for the full redemption of our bodies and our translation into ...*the Father's house of many mansions* (John 14:2ff). It will be what Isaiah describes in Isaiah 65 generally, but specifically in verse 17: *For behold, I create new heavens and a new earth; and the former shall not be remembered or come to mind*; which is a reference to and a synonym for the kingdom of God.

Maybe this is the purpose of the release of the Beast and of the False Prophet under the sinister initiative of Satan—to call for rebellion and sedition making a final grab for power by *surrounding the camp of the saints and the beloved city* (20:9). This will expose these unbelievers for what they are, rebellious moles within the company of God's people.

We are told in **verse 9**, *Here is the mind which has wisdom:* Wisdom is putting Christ and his Word first so that all things may have the pre-eminence for the Glory of Christ. If we interpret Scripture with Scripture, this is the kind of wisdom of which this verse speaks. *The seven heads are seven mountains on which the woman sits...* This is a clear reference to the Vatican City which is reputed to exist on seven mountains. It is referred to in the Fifth Bowl of God's Wrath (16:10) as *the throne of the Beast*.

Gog and Magog, To Gather the Nations Together to Battle at the End of the Millennium

Verse 10 tells us *There are also seven kings...* the seven kings with seven successive dominions of the beast. *Five have fallen, one is* (which is the sixth). The sixth king is the one that exists at the time of the fulfilment of this prophecy, which I would place at *the pouring out of the Bowls of the Wrath of God on the earth* 16:1ff. *...and the other has not yet come*, which is the seventh king.

World and Church history tells us who these six kings were. Any historian would refer to the great empires of the old world as being the *five (that) have fallen*. These absolute rulers of those days were the ancient Egyptian, Babylonian, Assyrian and Medo-Persian and Roman Empires. The pagan Roman Empire being the fifth fell in A.D. 475. The beast had been *wounded* (13:3) for a season but regained her strength by taking her seat inside the Temple of God, the church Catholic. By the year 666, the church Catholic had a unifying papal personality: The Holy Father, the sacerdotal priestly "head" as mediator representing Christ in the sacrament and claiming to be the very Vicar of Christ, the trinitarian representative of God in the mother church. This sixth beastly head is referred to in Revelation chapter 13 as the beast that comes *out of the earth* (13:11). This is the Holy Roman Empire, who *had two horns like a lamb and spoke like a dragon* (13:11). These two horns are the institutionalised religious power of the church Catholic (the Mother of Harlots 17:5) and the socio-political power exercised through the state (the Beast that carried the Harlot, 17:7 which also morphs into Babylon the Great, 17:5).

This sixth head, having great spiritual power with material effect in all the earth, is put away for a thousand years, and is described to the Apostle John as *the beast that was and is not* (17:8). From the Apostle John's perspective, seeing the events of *the great day of God Almighty* (16:14) as a result of *the seven last plagues* (15:1; 21:9) outlined in chapter 16 and further described in chapters 17-19 of the Apocalypse, victory is gloriously granted to Christ *King of kings and Lord of lords* (19:16). The Apostle John sees definitively:

That the beast was captured and with him the false prophet who worked signs in his presence, by which he deceived those who received the mark of the beast and those who worshipped his image. These two were cast alive into the lake of fire burning with brimstone. And the rest were killed with the sword which proceeded from the mouth of him who sat on the horse. And all the birds were filled with their flesh. Then I saw an angel coming down from heaven, having the key to the bottomless pit and a great chain in his hand. He laid hold of the dragon, that serpent of old, who is the devil and Satan, and bound him for a thousand years; and he cast him into the bottomless pit, and shut him up, and set a seal on him, so that he should deceive the nations no more till the thousand years were finished. But after these things he must be released for a little while (19:20-20:3).

After the events of the great day of God Almighty, a long and sustained period of peace shall be established of millennial proportions with the original Covenant of Creation established with Adam in the garden of Eden. This was broken by man but established by God, who is not frustrated by the fall of man or his inability. Through the purchase by Christ of the "Covenant of Redemption," man is enabled to be redeemed and to be *the salt of the earth* and *the light of the world* (Matt. 5:13-14). Man is released to become the zenith among all mankind as they exercise their vice-Regency under the "Covenant of Creation." As the Apostle Paul puts it in Romans chapter 8 and verses 19 to 22, *For the earnest expectation of the creation earnestly waits for the revealing of the sons of*

God. For the creation was subjected to futility, not willingly, but because of Him who subjected it in hope; because the creation itself also will be delivered from the bondage of corruption into the glorious liberty of the children of God. For we know that the whole creation groans and labours with birth pangs together until now (Rom. 8:19-22); there is a comprehensive rule of Christ through man, His vice-regents, of all the earth as originally "foreknown" by God under the decree of God's providence.

After this glorious millennial age, where the kingdom of God is fully consummated and the Church delivered from the two millennia of *the great tribulation* (7:14), the seventh beastly head or king is mysteriously released from the bottomless pit. *And when he comes, he must continue a short time* (17:10). This is referring to the outworking of the mystery that is pointed to in the previous verse. This seventh king is yet to come, will come in the distant future from this prophecy, after the years or toward the end of the millennium, when the beast is released from his prison, to ascend out of the bottomless pit, and this king ...*will deceive the nations which are in the four corners of the earth, Gog and Magog, to gather them together to battle*...(20:8). The reason for this happening is undoubtedly in the mind of God Himself and is therefore a great mystery. However, the events of this sudden appearance of what the Apostle John says in his first letter to the Churches generally, indicate that this is the *last hour* when *the Antichrist is coming* (1 Jn. 2:18), even as there are *many antichrists* that exist at the time of the Apostle and throughout Church history in the form of *the mystery of lawlessness* (2 Thess. 2:7) in the successive history of the Papacy.

But this seventh head that arises after the time when he *is not and yet is* (17:10) is of another order. When this *lawless one will be revealed*...*is according to the working of Satan with all power, signs and lying wonders* (2 Thess. 2:8-9). How this will look is a matter of fulfilment, but the context of this appearance of the lawless one is significant. This coming of the lawless one is just before the final and second coming of the Lord Jesus Christ. When we say "just before the second advent," we mean a matter of years. We find from the prophet Ezekiel that the cleaning up of the war debris after the battle of Gog and Magog will take some *seven years* (Ezek. 39:9, 12). The great deception of this personage, *the Antichrist* (1 Jn. 2:18), will be that he will appear as some sort of messianic figure who fraudulently presents himself as the returning Christ. It would seem that as the millennial period advances, many presumptuously assume that their salvation in Christ, and that of many God-fearing unbelievers, existed within the population of the nations. The most serious problem in this millennial period will be nominalism. Many nominally belonging to Christ and appearing as Christians are not actually Christ's children. This appearance of the lawless one will be an international phenomenon. He will present his appearance as the authentic return of the long-awaited glorious and triumphant *King of kings and Lord of lords* (19:16). This will reveal a great apostasy among the people of all nations and their national churches. As the Apostle John puts it, *The ten horns,* or kings, *who have received no kingdom as yet, but (who) receive authority for one hour as kings with the beast* (17:12) are led by *Gog and Magog to gather together to battle, whose number is as the sand of the sea. They went up on the breath of the earth and surrounded the camp of the saints and the beloved city* (20:8-9). ...*For this reason God will send a strong delusion, that they should believe the lie, that they all may be condemned who do not believe the truth but had pleasure in unrighteousness* (2 Thess. 2:11-12). It will be the ultimate act of blasphemy committed in world history. There will be an attempt by Satan to usurp the very position of Christ in His second advent.

How this will happen is a great mystery. But one thing is sure: the entire world population will be sifted like wheat. Only ...*they [that] overcame him by the blood of the Lamb and by the word of their testimony, and they [that] did not love their lives to the death* (12:11) will be saved. These are those that have been truly redeemed by the blood of the lamb and *do not walk according to the flesh, but according to the Spirit* (Rom. 8:1), who are truly baptised by Christ with the Holy Spirit and who powerfully walk in the righteousness of Christ, patiently as *saints ...[as] those who keep the commandments of God and the faith of Jesus* (14:12).

It specifically says, ...*a short time*. This means there is a strict time limit on this treacherous act. The Beast along with the False Prophet will certainly not have time to regain the domination that he had before the millennium. God will personally intervene by sending, *fire down from God out of heaven to devour them* (20:9).

Verse 11 reveals that *The Beast that was, and it is not, is himself also the eighth* king. This is a continued reference to the mystery (v7) which is referring to the satanic rebellion after or towards the end of the years of the millennium. God Himself will crush this rebellion. In this act of sedition, there are actually two kings: the Beast and the False Prophet. The eighth king is that false prophet working in the alliance with the seventh king of the Beast and is one power. On this occasion, these enemies of Christ, which is the Antichrist, is going to *perdition,* and that is referred to in chapter 20:10: *the devil...was cast into the lake of fire and brimstone where the Beast and the False Prophet are. And they will be tormented day and night forever and ever.*

Verse 12 reveals that *The ten horns which you saw are ten kings who have received no kingdom as yet, but they receive authority for one hour as kings with the Beast.* Although there needs to be more study on this verse, the cue is the mystery that the angel is disclosing to John the Apostle. This mystery refers to the satanic rebellion *after the thousand years have expired* (20: 7). Satan will be released for a short time, *to deceive the nations which are in the four corners of the earth, Gog and Magog, to gather them together for battle...*(20:8).

Ezekiel 38 and 39 deal with these prophecies relating to Gog and Magog that are arrayed against Israel. These forces that are gathered *Whose number is as the sand of the sea* (20:8) at the time of this satanic rebellion *surrounded the camp of the saints and the beloved city* (20:9). We think it is safe to take *the beloved city* as the physical city of Jerusalem. In the prophecy of Ezekiel 38, this alliance of Gog and Magog names ten kings (Gog, Magog of the land of Magog, Rosh, Meshech, Tubal, Persia, Ethiopia, Libya, Gomer and Togarmah—ten in all) that are arrayed against God's people. This would indicate the *ten kings who have received no kingdom as yet, but they receive authority for one hour as kings...* In the prophecies of Ezekiel, the judgment against Gog and Magog is extensive, but the kind of thing is stated in Ezekiel 38:22: *And I will bring him to judgment with pestilence and bloodshed; I will rain down on him, on his troops, and on many peoples who are with him flooding rain, great hailstones, fire, brimstone.* This language is not dissimilar to chapter 20:9: *And fire came down from God out of heaven and devoured them.* If the fulfilment of the prophecy in the Revelation is that which Ezekiel speaks about, then the prophecy about these ten kings that have no kingdom, yet who are given authority for an hour, which is a very short time, would be perfectly fulfilled at this time of history not long before the Judgment Day at the Great White Throne (20:11ff).

In **Verse 13**, these forces are determined because it is very apparent to them that this is the last opportunity for the forces of darkness to gain a foothold to exercise the dominion of the serpent of old. The violence of this short time comes right out of the pit and is a desperate suicidal grasp for power. So, these ten kings of Gog and Magog are of one mind and they give their power and authority to the Beast, who of course predictably uses such power against *the saints and the beloved city* through is waging war by proxy against the *Lamb*.

Verse 14 tells us that *These will make war with the Lamb...* The context of this insane rebellion against the *Lord of lords and King of kings* is senseless, particularly when it takes place at the end of *the thousand years* (20:7) when life was at its best—under proper Biblical governance, with a godly community within their hearts and growing in righteousness and holiness, secured as a state of peace and even joy. This kind of society will restrain the evildoer (there remain unregenerate and non-elect people during the millennial reign) even though they will not prosper as the righteous.

It would appear that the unregenerate and the non-elect are considerable in number because when the satanic rebellion takes place *the saints and of the beloved city* are greatly outnumbered and surrounded by the multitudes of Gog and Magog that are in a number *...as the sand of the sea*. After the Lamb's intervention, Ezekiel's prophecy says that it will take seven months to bury the dead that are left of Gog and Magog's army (Ezek. 39:12).

THE LAMB AND HIS SAINTS

Those that remain faithful to the Lamb may still not number in the majority, but throughout Church history the three great enemies of the Christian Church, have been the Harlot, the Beast and Babylon. Despite these enemies, a Christian civil society was experienced and the nations were governed by the Word of God such that the Law of God became the law of the nations. Historically, minimal numbers of regenerate people have transformed society to such a degree that these societies could be called Christian. However, not until the millennial reign, where the saints reign with Christ for a thousand years and the kingdom of God gains its victory *on earth as it is in heaven* (Matt. 6:10), do we witness a Christian age. Nowhere in Church history can we call a particular period in history a distinctly Christian age. Not even of the Reformation and the Puritan era of British history or American colonisation can it be said that, "Here was a Christian age." The Gospel has been increasingly influential throughout the history of the Christian Church, and the influence of Biblical and spiritual principles have been responsible for great liberty in some locations and times within history. More recently, within a single generation, the three great enemies of the Christian church have regained centre stage and have usurped gains in knowledge to employ such advances for exploitative purposes, and usually against God's anointed in persecuting principles. Everything before the millennial reign promised in chapter 20 is a pre-Christian age.

BRIEF RETROSPECTIVE AND REMINDER!

Verse 15 begins with another focus relating to the demise and judgment of the Harlot, which is the Roman Catholic Church, and the religious identity of the Beast. From verses 7-14, we have been taken up with the disclosure of the mystery that focuses on the satanic rebellion *when the thousand years have expired*. However, the focus now returns to chapter 13 concerning the rise of the beast that was in the beginning *out of the sea, having seven heads and ten horns, and on his horns ten crowns, and on his heads a blasphemous name* (13:1). This is pre-Reformation history; however, we will not enter into a specific interpretation of the symbols here as they may be studied under that section of these notes. The seven heads represent the seven successive world empires about which the prophet Daniel speaks. These are the Egyptian, Assyrian, Babylonian, Medo-Persian, Pagan Rome and the modern Roman Papal Empire.

...The ten horns and on his horns ten crowns... represent the ten kingdoms of the beast exercising political and cultural dominion. As the Roman Empire moves to Western Europe after the breakup of imperial Rome in A.D. 476, and before the rise of the Papacy from 606-666 onward, the ten crowns are the Western European nations of England, France, Germany, Switzerland, Portugal, Spain, Italy, Austria, Central Europe, and Eastern Europe. On the beast's head is a blasphemous name, taking the names and rights of Christ to himself, Holy Father, Mediator of Christ and the Vicar of Christ — the Holy Spirit. He seeks to take the place of God, being the great usurper which is the character of the devil himself. He is "anti" which means "in the place of." His blasphemy is that he seeks to be Christ doing the ministry of the Triune God, but all the time he is Antichrist. This establishes the historical identity of the beasts.

The context of this prophecy is the Seven Bowls of God's Wrath which are directly focusing on *the men who had the mark of the beast* (16:2), *the one who is, and who was, and who is to be* (16:5), which refers to the mystery that has been discussed above, *the throne of the beast and his kingdom* (16:10), and the great Babylon (16:19). History moves into the events of the Seven Bowls of God's Wrath, and the house of the Beast becomes divided. The reference to ten nations is probably symbolic at this point in history, because these nations have colonised all parts of the earth and left the legacy of the beast and the harlot in the culture of these nations. The harlot sits among *many peoples, multitudes, nations, and tongues* with the universality of Roman Catholicism indisputable.

Verse 16 reveals that ...*The ten horns which you saw on the beast*... are the ten kingdoms identified in the long history of these antichrist institutions. These institutions become "a divided house" because *the horns of the beast hate the harlot*, the Roman Catholic Church. The political arm of Roman Catholicism takes the form of secular humanism and its more radical manifestation of the Marxist command economics that was inaugurated at the time of the French Revolution. It has become atheistic, anti-clerical, and greedy, regarding the church as irrelevant to the politics of the states. This hatred manifests itself right across Catholicism and secular humanism even in our own day. The Communist States hated any manifestation of religion and saw it as "the opium of the people," but the statecraft of the beast remained firmly in place. The role of the Church has suffered a severe decline in such countries. The ten horns, we are told, *make her desolate and naked, eat her flesh and burn her with fire*, and she joins the ranks of those persecuted—the true church. However, as the Iron Curtain fell, and as the Bamboo Curtain falls, the hunger for religion becomes insatiable and the harlot regains her favoured status at centre stage.

Verse 17 reveals that through such behaviour the Beast has unwittingly furthered the cause of God's purposes. *God put it into their hearts to fulfil His purpose, to be of one mind, and to give their kingdom to the beast...* This looks as though the secular humanist beast has driven a wedge between church and state so that the parliamentary system of government in the form of republicanism has affected the way in which the church plays politics, and it would seem that the Roman Catholic system has to compete against all other interests and therefore does not enjoy the same degree of influence that it used to. The control of the nations is still very much in the hands of the Beast, but not under the direct hand of the harlot.

In **verse 18**, the unbridled power of the woman is described. She *reigns over the kings (political powers) of the earth*. She does so through that great city, Babylon the great.

CHAPTER 10

THE FALL OF BABYLON THE GREAT-REVELATION 18

SOME SPECIAL CONSIDERATIONS

As we approach this chapter, we find an inspired commentary on the events relating to chapter 16 that described the pouring out of the seven bowls of God's wrath on the earth, with particular focus on the fall of Babylon. We are given such cues as, *Therefore her plagues will come in one day* (18:8). We are then told, *The seven plagues of the seven angels were completed* referring to, *the bowls of the wrath of God.*

The events of this chapter take place quickly with cues that arise several times: *in one hour your judgment has come* (18:10) *For in one hour such great riches came to nothing* (18:17); *For in one hour she is made desolate* (18:19); and *Thus with violence the great city Babylon shall be thrown down, and shall not be found anymore* (18:21).

The identity of Babylon the great is that secular city state that has developed through the political machinations of the *Mother of Harlots*, being the Papal system of Roman Catholicism, which is *the abomination of the earth*. Babylon the Great is yet another metamorphosis of the beast which is the socio-political child of the Harlot. It could be described as the political, economic and commercial system that makes man independent, which foolishly leads him to believe that he is autonomous from God. The ancient symbol of Babylon the Great is the Tower of Babel with its audacious claim to flood-proof itself against any repeated calamity of God's judgment in such things as the great deluge of Noah's day. It is the personification of man-centred religion.

A reference to this event is made back in chapter 14 verse 8 that is announced by the preaching kind of angel to encourage beleaguered believers in the face of Babylon's all-consuming power and influence against Biblical Christianity. The preacher declares, *Babylon is fallen, is fallen, that great city, because she has made all nations drink of the wine of the wrath of her fornication* (14:8). Believers in previous generations, as we do today, look forward to the fall of Babylon the Great when true unencumbered Biblical religion will be recovered and enjoyed.

Chapter 17 is a kind of prelude to chapter 18, as chapter 17 describes the situation of the Mother of Harlots in terms of her future and her history which is one of demise and judgment. This is the situation of the Harlot as history moves toward the events of chapter 16 which describes the Seven Last Plagues.

Many would wish to place a spiritual interpretation on this chapter and cast all the geographical, tectonic events described in this chapter in the same "apocalyptic language" that is employed in the Gospels when the Lord Jesus Christ describes the destruction of the temple and Jerusalem which occurred in A.D. 70. For example, in Matthew 24:29-30, He says *Immediately after the tribulation of those days the sun will be darkened, and the moon will not give its light; the stars will fall from heaven, and the powers of the heavens will be shaken. Then the sign of the Son of Man will appear in heaven, and then all the tribes of the earth will mourn, and they will see the Son of Man coming on the clouds of heaven with power and great glory.* As the Lord Jesus describes the events of the pending destruction of the Temple of Jerusalem, the disciples were looking upon the Temple from the vantage point of the Garden of Gethsemane. As Jesus was using this familiar apocalyptic language, they were able to understand the impending destruction of this beautiful Temple in terms of the destruction of the historical Temple of Solomon during the conquest of Nebuchadnezzar. These verses are laced with apocalyptic language similar to that used in Isaiah's prophecies concerning the destruction of Jerusalem during the conquest of Nebuchadnezzar the king of Babylon in March 597BC (Isa. 13:10). On both occasions, God's very own covenanted people were afflicted.

The language in this chapter of Revelation is momentous but it is not employing the apocalyptic style as it is a sober recounting of real physical events. These are judgments of God when He intervenes in the historical situation of the day. It is the white-hot vengeance of God against the ungodly. As in the days of the great deluge at the time of Noah, these momentous events will be witnessed in the fullness of time. Those who take this language as apocalyptic language and claim that all that is described in this chapter will be brought about by powerful and persistent preaching of the Word of God are confusing the purpose of preaching and the purpose of God's providential judgments. The purpose of preaching is to make known the mercies of God, which are preached with great patience and perseverance. However, there comes a time when preaching is finished with and the iniquities of the nations are *complete* (Gen. 15:16), so that God *gives them up to desolation* (2 Chron. 30:7) and destruction.

BABYLON THE GREAT IS FALLEN, IS FALLEN!

In **verse 1**, *after these things* means after the description of the demise of the Mother of Harlots (that is set as a prelude to the seven last plagues), then the destruction of the Beast and Babylon along with the False Prophet, and now we are going to be treated to a full description of the fall of Babylon the Great that takes place during the seven last plagues.

I saw another angel coming down from heaven, having great authority, and the earth was illuminated with his glory. The identity of this great personage, having great authority, would appear to be a theophany of Christ Himself, intervening personally at the point of the sixth bowl of God's wrath. If this is what chapter 16 verse 15 is describing, using the very words of the Lord Jesus Christ, *Behold, I am coming as a thief. Blessed is he who watches, and keeps his garments, lest he walk naked and they see his shame*, then we have here a coming of Christ in like manner to His appearances at crucial times throughout the history of revelation of both the pre-incarnate Christ in the Old Testament and appearances of our Lord after His resurrection in the days of the Apostles. The testimony of Christian literature speaks of special comings of Christ in times of judgment—such as in AD 70 at the destruction of Jerusalem and its temple—and revival (Jonathan Edwards speaks of this in his treatment on the revivals in New England in the 1730s and 1740s which, although not theophanies as such, are also supernatural presences of Christ). It is not suggested here that we are talking about the Second or Final Coming of Christ at the end of history. However, this was certainly a very unusual angel and was distinct from the mighty angels, pouring out the bowls of God's wrath, as it describes him as *another angel*. His authority is equal to the task that he is about to perform, which is the destruction of Babylon the Great. This angel's presence illumines the earth with his glory. All these facts would indicate that this is no ordinary angelic appearance but that we have a special coming of Christ that is specifically related to the destruction of Babylon the Great.

In chapter 19 verse 11, there is an opening of the eternal habitations and a revelation of Christ seated on *a white horse*. This takes place after the destruction of Babylon the Great because that revelation of Christ from heaven happens after *a great multitude in heaven* (19:1-10) give praise to God for, among other things, the *judgment of the great harlot*. This revelation of Christ from heaven could not be the same thing as the angel coming down from heaven because the purpose here is the destruction of Babylon the Great, and when Christ is revealed riding *the white horse*, His purpose is the inauguration of the millennial reign of Christ and His saints.

The angel in **verse 2**, *cried mightily with a loud voice, saying, "Babylon the great is fallen, is fallen..."* This sudden announcement resounds throughout the earth and it spells the imminent, sudden and swift destruction of its godless man-centred empire. The corruption of Babylon is so extreme and so highly developed that the angel describes the condition of this evil empire as *a dwelling place of demons, a prisoner of every foul spirit, and a cage of every unclean and hated bird*. This secular state that claims to be religiously neutral, even atheistic, is nothing of the kind, and Roman Catholicism, as the inspiration of the "secular city," can be described in the very same words. It has synchronised and accommodated every conceivable religious invention and idea known to mankind because the cult of Roman Catholicism knows only too well that human beings need religion and it is their business to make sure everyone gets the Babylonian kind.

Verse 3 makes it clear that this world system of Babylon the Great has comprehensively drawn all the nations into one, interdependent world-order, through its economics and commerce. *All the nations have drunk the wine of the wrath of her fornication.* The distinctive ingredient of secular humanism is self-sufficiency—which is the blasphemy of idolatry—that precludes faith in the *King of kings and the Lord of lords.* Idolatry is drinking the wine of God's wrath which will lay up certain destruction as in the days of Sodom and Gomorrah (Isa. 13:19). Committing fornication with Babylon is a simple matter of sharing in her secular humanist philosophy of life that puts man first and living out her world-view.

The merchants of the earth have become rich through the abundance of her luxury. The commercial power of Babylon is the genius of the system as she keeps her citizens' loyalty by feeding the insatiable desire for the proverbial "more, please." In this world, goods and services are based on the principle of covetousness. Greed is promoted as a virtue because man's greed gives another man a job, and so the cycle of interdependence is achieved. If you scratch my back, I'll scratch yours, so commerce is made possible, and if we can get into the "major league," then luxury and the good life follow.

Verse 4 relates that *...I heard another voice from heaven...* This may be the voice of the gathered saints that is described in 19:1 *as a great multitude in heaven...* speaking from their experience and knowledge of the Scriptures. *"I will dwell in them and walk among them. I will be their God, and they shall be My people." Therefore "Come out from among them and be separate, says the Lord. Do not touch what is unclean, and I will receive you." "I will be a Father to you, and you shall be My sons and daughters, says the LORD Almighty"* (2 Cor. 6:16-18)—so this voice of exultation from heaven says, *Come out of her, My people, lest you share in her sins, and lest you receive of her plagues.* Biblically reforming an institution such as Babylon the Great is a vain and hopeless task as the institution is ripe for just judgment. We should not be lured into the idea that we can reform such institutions. They are synagogues of Satan and we have no place in them.

Biblical separation is paramount and we are responsible, ...*to come out of her*... We may have had a long history of association with the Babylonian churches and institutions and there may be many practical reasons to continue such associations, but if we do we will share in her sins, and we may receive the plagues that are about to be poured out on her. If we linger in Sodom and Gomorrah, even if not physically but in our heart and soul, we will be like Lot's wife and turned to a pillar of salt (Gen. 19:26).

This call for holiness is illustrated well by the people of Israel. When they came out of Egypt, they were to be separated to God under the blood of the Lamb, who is our Passover. So too, the people of God, who are described here as, *My people*, must come out of Babylon the Great–the secular society with her world-view and lifestyle. To do that we must be joined to a faithful, Biblically-orientated church and fellowship that is able to keep the Biblical doctrine of Christian living firmly in place so that our homes and educational institutions pastorally lead us obediently to serve God alone.

Verse 5 declares that ...*her sins have reached to heaven, and God has remembered her iniquities*. There comes a time when the sins of a particular nation (or an institution in this case) have overreached God's patience and mercy. There is a point when just judgment must be executed so that the integrity and the wisdom of God Himself will be preserved for His greater glory. For example, when the Lord promised Abraham that a nation would come forth from his own loins through Isaac and that they would possess the land of his sojourn, He said, *But in the fourth generation they shall return here, for the iniquity of the Amorites is not yet complete* (Gen.

15:16). In the case of Babylon the Great, at this juncture of history her iniquity is complete and judgment is about to be poured out in full measure. The time is now right for the *grapes of wrath*.

So, in **verse 6**, God commands, *Render to her just as she rendered to you, and repay her double according to her works; in the cup which she has mixed, mix double for her*. The parallel verse in Revelation 16:9, where this prophecy is fulfilled under the seventh bowl of God's wrath, states, *And great Babylon was remembered before God, to give her the cup of the wine of the fierceness of His wrath*. Of course, what follows is a description of these prophecies. There is no mercy shown and the judgment is complete.

Verse 7 proclaims that *In the measure that she had glorified herself and lived luxuriously, in the same measure give her torment and sorrow; for she says in her heart, "I sit as queen, and am no widow, and will not see sorrow."* The destruction of Babylon the Great is only the beginning of her woes. Her destruction would be an unthinkable event in the Babylonian spirit, but for those disciples of Babylon who possess an immortal soul, the parable of 'Lazarus and the rich man' has particular application in this event. There is a spiritual dimension of everlasting torment that is spoken of in this portion of Scripture that would indicate that repentance is not witnessed, although possible, because we are still living in the Gospel age, and the deep *torment and sorrow* will be measured out in like manner to the parable of "Lazarus and the rich man" (Lu. 16:19-31).

In the Babylonian spirit of godless self-sufficiency, man has worked hard and smart. He arrogantly believes that he is able to "God-proof" himself so that he is never accountable to God, at least in this life, and refuses to consider his mortality. He wants to think that he is a mere animal of a higher order and, like animals, he simply stops existing. If there is an eternal state, it is for the 'holy other' and not for him. So, he says to himself, *I sit as queen, and I am no widow, and I will not see sorrow* because I am a self-made man. He is like the rich fool who says to his soul, *"Soul, you have many goods laid out for many years; take your ease, eat, drink, and be merry." But God said to him, "Fool! This night your soul will be required of you"* (Lu. 12:19-20).

Verse 8 warns, *Therefore her plagues will come in one day...* The suddenness of these plagues is underscored several times in this chapter. In one fateful day, the wrath of God shall fall upon the entire Babylonian system. Chapter 16:18 describes this event: *And there were noises and thunderings and lightnings; and there was a great earthquake, such a mighty and great earthquake as had not occurred since men were on the earth...and the cities of the nations fell...and the mountains were not found. And great hail from heaven fell upon men, each hailstone about the weight of a talent* (16:18-21). With the fourth plague, scorching heat and fire accompany these events (16:8-9). This all comes upon Babylon the Great suddenly as in one day in duration. It may take longer, but it will be swift and sudden. Also, in the days that follow, *Death and mourning and famine...she will be utterly burned with fire, for strong is the Lord God who judges her.*

These days are momentous and the scope global. These momentous days are reminiscent of the great deluge in the days of Noah. It would seem that, just as in the great deluge, the geographical features of the earth will be significantly altered and there will be parts of the earth's landscape that will be unrecognisable.

THE WORLD LAMENTS FOR GREAT CITY BABYLON

In **verses 9-10**, the saints rejoice at the fall of Babylon, which is certainly a feature that is recorded in chapter 19:1-10. However, the world that is represented here will soon weep and mourn, as we see explicitly in this passage. *The kings (the captains of industry and the powerful players of the old exploitive economy)....who commit[ted] fornication and lived luxuriously with her will weep and lament for her, when they see the smoke of her burning.* The world's Tower of Babel is no longer their sure and certain hope because the foundation of their faith is no longer materially there. They are exposed in their atheism, and in their insanity they will still *...blaspheme[d] God because...the plague...was exceedingly great* (16:21). The only sane thing for these Babylonian refugees to do is to turn to the God of the plagues, get right with God and seek His mercy. They would have found mercy; instead they blasphemed God.

...when they see the smoke of her burning, standing at a distance for fear of her torment, saying, "Alas, alas, the great city Babylon, that mighty city!" Here we observe survivors, who are not believers in the only Redeemer Jesus Christ the Lord, as they see these great calamities that have happened on a universal scale. They are lamenting and weeping as they witness the total destruction of one of the great cities of the nations. These people are too frightened to go into the city because of the fierce burning and destruction of the whole city. *A great earthquake, such a mighty and great earthquake as had not occurred since men were on the earth...* (16:18) sees the city in rubble and fires break out from all quarters throughout the city precincts. These witnesses see great plumes of smoke rising out of the city rubble indicating the unthinkable—utter destruction! As the observers look on with horror at the reality of the destruction of the city, *great Babylon was remembered* (16:19) as a figure of history, and they say, *Alas, alas, that great city Babylon, that mighty city! For in one hour your judgment has come.* All this comes suddenly, without warning, as in the days of the great universal flood at the time of Noah, where the inhabitants of this world were caught unprepared for this kind of judgment.

Verse 11 reveals the merchants of the earth also weeping and mourning because they cannot trade their goods. The economic and commercial component of the Babylonian system is no more. The human carnage in such a disaster is unthinkable and incalculable; without people, there can be no trading and therefore the economic system of co-dependence is no longer. The old economy is in deep depression and there is no recovery possible in terms of the Babylonian solution because Babylon is no more.

The picture of the commercial world of Babylon continues in verse 12: *merchandise of gold and silver, precious stones and pearls, fine linen and purple, silk and scarlet, every kind of citron wood, every kind of object of ivory, every kind of object of most precious wood, bronze, iron, and marble...* This is a picture of any shopping mall of our Babylonian age where everything is accessible with the plastic credit card which is totally "maxed out" because of unbridled covetousness, which is idolatry.

Verse 13 adds to this list of merchandise, naming all the things that feed the body and pleasure the flesh, such as, *cinnamon and incense, fragrant oil and frankincense, wine and oil, fine flour and wheat, cattle and sheep, horses and chariots*. We can go to the supermarket and fill our shopping trolleys to overflowing and cart them off to the kitchen to feast and revel to our hearts' content. The citizens of Babylon have such an insatiable desire for the good life that they *have drunk of the wine of the wrath for her fornication... have committed fornication with her* (18:3), thus becoming like the children of Israel at Mt. Sinai who bowed down to the golden calf, committing idolatry, (Exod. 32:2-6). Thus, by fornicating with Babylon, they become fit for the plagues of God's wrath on Babylon.

The focus is upon the merchant banks and moneylenders of all kinds who trade in *bodies and souls of men,* who make people slaves to debt so they must slavishly work for the Babylonian chiefs. The credit card industry, mortgages for housing, and loans of all kinds so heavily burden the covetous consumer that he can do nothing else but serve the Babylonian beast that has called for his soul on the basis of depreciating and obsolete goods and services.

Verse 14 says, *The fruit that your soul longed for has gone from you...* The system of avarice will no longer exist. The good life that the soul longed for has evaporated. The world-view that rendered man a practical atheist though God was on his lips when it was convenient—the belief that God is irrelevant and passé—is now utterly exposed. He is nothing more than a dead man walking. He is empty and superficial in spiritual things.

... all the things which are rich and splendid have gone from you, and you shall find them no more at all. The ever-increasing gross national product of nations that was promised by Babylon the Great has gone in the space of one day under these calamities. The riches of western society, with those who aspire to it in the east, and the splendid opulence of modern Babylonian life are suddenly extinguished and are only a memory within the mind of the haves of its society. It has been said that the living standard and conveniences of a family in the average suburban western city are higher than those of a king and prince 100 years ago. Such is the achievement of Babylon the Great when it has risen to its zenith in the year 2000 A.D.

In **verse 15**, we observe that the businessmen and the merchants of the old economy *who became rich by her (Babylon the great), will stand at a distance for fear of her torment...* Again we are observing survivors of these momentous events gathered in a relatively safe place, observing the destruction and carnage of the fall of Babylon because no one would be safe if they approached such a city. These captains of industry in the past were obdurate businessmen but are now *weeping and wailing* because of their great loss of property and personal effects, and also for the loss of family members, friends and business associates.

In **verse 16**, there is great mourning. *Alas, alas, that great city that was clothed in fine linen, purple, and scarlet and adorned with gold and precious stones and pearls!* Such was the citizenry of Babylon with her fashion industry presenting such a culture of decadence, ostentation and personal presence of outward show; but it is now no more. The inward reality of perversion, vainglory, covetousness and idolatry was the ugly reality of life.

Verse 17 conveys the suddenness of these events. *For in one hour such great riches came to nothing...* The sudden character of these events is yet again underscored at this point. For these offences to be spiritually realised as a result of a long history of Gospel preaching is simply not taught in these verses.

Verse 17 continues, *Every shipmaster, and all who travel by ship, sailors, and as many as trade on the sea, stood at a distance* for it would be too dangerous to venture anywhere near these great cities that were built around the great shipping destinations and ports of commerce.

Verse 18 elaborates on this. In the day of her visitation those in the transport industry that are caught between ports, seeing the billowing smoke pillars that arise from the cities marvel and say, *What is like this great city?* Again, the suddenness of these events is underscored because the seafaring people depart from one port of call and arrive at their destination only to find that the city is in a state of absolute calamity and on fire.

Verse 19 shows how such survivors become unhinged at the sight of such devastation *They threw dust on their heads* and like other witnesses *Cried out, weeping and wailing, and saying, "Alas, alas, that great city, in which all who had ships on the sea became rich by her wealth!"* Babylon the Great delivered immense wealth and was a kind of tower of Babel where the whole world became united, staking their faith on something of their own making. But God has now brought it to an end.

All this happens so suddenly and without any warning, *For in one hour she is made desolate.* Babylon is stripped of her wealth and atheistic lifestyle, made naked so that all can see her shame, made to render back to God the product of God's earth that has been used for man-centred gain.

Verse 20 tells us that woe and misery is the response of this world, but in heaven all are, *Rejoic[ing] over her, O heaven, and you holy apostles and prophets, for God has avenged you on her!* The hallmark of the Beast, and in turn Babylon, is one of utter hatred of all God's servants. Babylon stood by as the saints were being martyred for the name of their Saviour Jesus Christ. She would exclude Christians in the workplace and therefore deny them any means of making a living. Babylon did everything she could do to frustrate the extension of the kingdom of God. She persecuted and did violence to the body of Christ whenever she had the opportunity. Whenever the Church established a righteous institution, Babylon would take the initiative and make it into an atheistic institution, such as in the field of education and welfare. She opposed the Christian institution of marriage and family and sought to tear it apart by introducing unfair exploitive work practices and obliterating the Sabbath Day. Babylon made pleasure an art form so that the senses were overwhelmed by her music, food, sporting entertainment and recreational lifestyle activities that fed the secular mind and emotions with every conceivable pleasure so that the distinction between right and wrong, true and false, beauty and ugliness, light and darkness became so blurred and so altered that everything became relative and there was no such thing as truth. Such is the state of the secular mind.

These momentous events are taking place for the single reason that *God has avenged you on her!* Throughout the centuries of the patient endurance of Christ's anointed true Church, she has been persecuted for the Gospel's sake and for righteousness. The blood of the martyrs has been a feature of the entire Gospel age and the three great institutional enemies in all that time have been the mother of harlots, the beast and Babylon the Great. These three have been at centre stage in terms of power throughout this age. The Church has been characteristically driven into the wilderness, being preserved and protected by the Lord God our Saviour Jesus Christ, but it has been a titanic struggle throughout the years of her sojourn. The kingdom of God has indeed been ever-growing as *leaven leavens the whole lump* of dough (Gal. 5:9) in terms of its influence in this world. To that extent, these great enemies are increasingly being frustrated as history marches on through the centuries, but these institutions remain at centre stage. It is not until these events suddenly come to pass that there will be a change of guard and Christ, with His saints, will then take centre stage in the years of the millennial reign. Now that the iniquities of these diabolical institutions are complete, the hour of vengeance is upon her.

God's Final Vengeance upon Babylon the Great

Verse 21 begins the final vengeance. *Then a mighty angel took up a stone like a great millstone and threw it into the sea...* This final event against the Babylonian empire is a compounding event that is associated with a *great earthquake as had not occurred since men* *were on the earth*. It has caused the secular cities across the nations of the earth to become rubble and a cauldron of fire. The event spoken of here will compound these events and spell the utter destruction of the Babylonian empire. What this event is cannot be determined definitively, but it does appear to be a cosmic event involving a stone—maybe a meteor that plunges into the sea and causes further seismic and geographical events that destroy these institutions of iniquity. Chapter 16 and verse 21 describes how *great hail from heaven fell upon men, each hailstone about the weight of a talent*. Perhaps a meteorological event such as a meteor plunging into the sea creates this great hail storm described here.

Thus with violence the great city Babylon shall be thrown down, and shall not be found anymore. Again, it is with violence that this city is dealt with, not through the instrument of mercy and grace, which is the powerful and persistent preaching of the Word of God through the ministers of the Gospel. These are real physical events and not idealistic hopes of some future Gospel revival and reformation that will convert this satanic-inspired institution. Such idealistic hopes may include wishing the devil himself to be converted. Such expectations are simply not taught in Scripture.

It might be said that a physical judgment of this kind will not deal with the spirit of Babylon that will exist in any surviving citizen of the Babylonian empire. This criticism may have some justification, but because of their comprehensive nature, the extent and scope of these titanic and momentous events will see the extermination of the great multitude that had served Babylon the Great. Even a sudden general revival and reformation that could see the interpretation of these passages in spiritual terms will never be able to exterminate the Babylonian spirit in the heart of man entirely. Every saint in the kingdom of God will struggle with his sins in some way or other, even in a millennial reign of Christ and His saints. Even if there were such spiritual events as a general global revival and reformation that went so deep and was so extensive that almost the entire population of the world was caught up by such a revival in true conversion, that event does not seem to be taught in these passages. We would have to turn to other passages of Scripture to construct such an understanding, such as Romans 11.

Verse 22 makes clear that the events of the fall of Babylon are so complete and so far-reaching that there is nowhere on earth that the lifestyle of former days will be experienced. *The sound of harpists, musicians, flautists, and trumpeters shall not be heard in you anymore...* No doubt there will be good music heard when things return to normal in the years that follow, but not in the Babylonian spirit of rock'n'roll.

No craftsman or any craft shall be found in you anymore, and the sound of a millstone shall not be heard in you anymore. The trades and the wheels of industry will always be needed for the proper stewardship of God's resources for the glory of God and for the service of man's need while remaining in this finite world. But the exploitative and corrupt industry of the old economy will be no more, and the slavery of the underclass will be no more, the institution of the family and the Lord's Day will not be neglected anymore, and the principles of self-sufficient autonomous wealth gathering will be no more. Amassing property and real estate to the exclusion of others, and establishing autonomous kingdoms of avaricious wealth that take advantage of others, will be no more. In all these activities, the spirit of Babylon will never be experienced again.

Verse 23 elaborates on this. The Babylonian empire controlled all utilities for its own advantage such as the power grid, water supply, sewerage, communications and transport and did all these things so that the control was in no one else's hands. No doubt the restoration of these utilities will take some considerable time as they will all have to be rebuilt. But these things shall not be the sole preserve of Babylon the great. However, *The light of a lamp shall not shine in you anymore, and the voice of bridegroom and bride shall not be heard in you anymore. For your merchants were the great men of the earth, and by your sorcery all the nations were deceived.*

These things will continue after the fall of Babylon, but not in Babylon, and there will be a spirit of righteousness and holiness that will permeate all activities so that God is given the glory. The captains of industry and the powerful men of the world will never again be allowed to exercise their sorcery to deceive the nations. Justice and equity will be the features of the new economy and the new order.

Verse 24 elaborates further. All this happened to Babylon because, *In her was found the blood of prophets and saints, and of all who were slain on the earth.* As the blood of Abel cried out to God from the ground after being murdered by Cain his brother, so *the souls of those who had been slain for the word of God and for the testimony which they held…cried with a loud voice, saying, "How long, O Lord, holy and true, until You judge and avenge our blood on those who dwell on the earth?"* (Rev. 6:9-10). *The blood of the prophets and saints has cried to God saying, "Vengeance is Yours," so God has avenged you on her!* (18:20).

CHAPTER 11

A GREAT MULTITUDE IN HEAVEN REJOICES- REVELATION 19

SOME SPECIAL CONSIDERATIONS

Like the flood in the days of Noah, God's great wrath of chapters 16 and 18 is over. God has judged Babylon the Great because He *avenged you on her [for]...the blood of prophets and saints, and of all who were slain on the earth* (Rev. 18:20, 24). The fall of Babylon the Great is described in chapter 18. These events are descriptive of the fourth and seventh bowls of God's wrath, with particular emphasis on the seventh.

The Mother of Harlots is the subject of chapter 17, but this chapter is a review of the condition and position of the harlot which is a picture of Roman Catholicism in its most mature form just before the pouring out of the seven last plagues of God's wrath. The harlot is severely judged during the last plagues, particularly during the first five plagues. It is not until after the plagues that the Rider of the white horse, of whom it is said that He is *called Faithful and True, and in righteousness He judges and makes war* (Rev. 19:11), takes up the harlot, the beast and the false prophet and casts them alive into the lake of fire burning with brimstone. We

A GREAT MULTITUDE IN HEAVEN REJOICES—REVELATION 19

have seen that after the years of the millennium, a satanic rebellion occurs for a very short time, when *Satan will be released from his prison and will go out to deceive the nations...* (Rev. 20:7) and will *(surround) the camp of the saints and the beloved city* (Rev. 20:8). He will then finally be judged and cast into perdition. So, it would seem then that the harlot and the false prophet will be imprisoned in the lake of fire and brimstone until their final judgment on the last day. They will not harm the saints any longer throughout the years of the millennium, except during that final satanic rebellion which will be crushed quickly by the "King of kings and Lord of lords."

19:1-10 is a window into heaven that begins with John hearing *a loud voice of a great multitude in heaven...* (Rev. 19:1). These are all those who are gathered with Christ in the eternal habitations of God, those that have gone to be with the Lord throughout the generations of the kingdom of God, those who are called saints. Also, the twenty-four elders in verse 4 with the four living creatures are all at worship and praising God. Now verse 7 presents a difficulty because it speaks of *the marriage of the Lamb...His wife...arrayed in fine linen...for the fine linen is the righteous acts of the saints*. The whole number of the saints—the bride of Christ, otherwise described as the body of Christ—will be brought to the Bridegroom, which is Christ Himself. But there is a marriage supper that is set for the Lamb. When John sees this revelation, he falls to his face to worship his heavenly interlocutory, but is corrected and told not to do such a thing.

The difficulty is that this wedding feast is at a place in the Revelation that is unexpected. The answer can be found in the fact that this vision is but a call to the marriage supper and to be prepared for this occasion, but it is not the occasion of the marriage supper itself. The reason for this line of argument is as follows:

- Immediately after this announcement where we see Christ riding on the white horse *He judges and makes war* (19:11), which means that Christ is not in the state of holy matrimony but is positioned as Commander and Judge.
- After the millennium and after 20:11, Christ was seated on the *great white throne. And the dead were judged according to their works...* (Rev. 20:12). There is no evidence at this point of the proceedings that the wedding feast has taken place.
- The consummation of the kingdom of God had come, for in Revelation 21:1 we read of *a new heaven and a new earth, for the first heaven and the first earth had passed away* (Cf 2 Pet. 3:10-13).
- Then we see *the holy city, New Jerusalem, coming down out of heaven from God, prepared as a bride adorned for her husband* (Rev. 21: 2), at which time great praise breaks out. This is clearly the precise point at which the great wedding feast is positioned, after the millennium.
- A description is given of the bride, the Lamb's wife, as the great city, the holy Jerusalem (see 21:2 and 21:10 ff).
- The marriage of the Lamb and the bride (church) is described in Ephesians 5:32 as a perfect and indissoluble union which is a great mystery.

Unanimous Chorus of Alleluia! in Heaven and Earth

The picture of the heavenly hosts responding to the glorious righteous judgment in the seven bowls of God's wrath is a marked contrast to the weeping and wailing of the citizens of Babylon in the previous chapter. This heavenly host rejoices that the Lord God, *...Judged the great harlot...and...has avenged on her the blood of His servants shed by her.*

In **verse 1**, the harlot and Babylon are the focus of the great multitude's exultation because smoke rises forever and ever. This refers to the fourth and fifth bowls of God's wrath described more fully in chapter 18.

Although it is at times difficult to trace the historical connections within world and Church history, the Apostle John now reveals that all Antichrist institutions merge to become one. It is one of the anomalies of history that the *mother of harlots*—i.e., the Roman Catholic Church with her sacerdotal Gospel—has throughout history been the most bloody institution of all. Indeed, she is soaked in the blood of the saints. She has also been at the centre of geopolitics as *the beast*. Furthermore, she has taken control of global educational institutions and has, from one generation to the next, prepared a man-centred geo-political system that has been hostile to the Biblical concept of the kingdom of God.

As history has proceeded, this beastly system of international politics has challenged the advancement of the Church at every point of history by creating situations of war, revolution and persecution in order to destroy the citizens of God's kingdom. In chapter 19, the day of reckoning has come for this 2,000 years of institutional terror against the saints, and there is *a loud voice of a great multitude in heaven, saying, "Alleluia! salvation and glory and honour and power belong to the Lord our God! for true and righteous are His judgements, because he has judged the great harlot who has corrupted the earth with her fornication; and he has avenged on her the blood of his servants shed by her."*

The False Prophet (Islam) is not mentioned here but is taken up with the subsequent events with the *white horse rider*. The resounding *Alleluias* are the praise of the heavenly hosts of the *great multitude in heaven...*

Alleluia! Salvation and glory and honour and power belong to the Lord. This is not referring to the former times of the Gospel preaching of the seven seals and the seven trumpets but to God's direct intervention through the seven angels of the last plagues because it goes on to say, *true and righteous are His judgments* (v. 2) which is a direct reference to the seven bowls of God's wrath — *because He has judged the great harlot who corrupted the earth with her fornication* (v. 2)

It should be noted that in the latter stage of the Gospel age in which the kingdom of God has been advancing, this figure of the Roman harlot has been at centre stage exercising her Jezebel-like dominion, corrupting the whole earth. Any idea of a Christian age where a Biblical theocratic dominion is established before the intervention of the seven final plagues should be questioned. We are living, not in a post-Christian age, but in a pre-Christian age where the harlot has been the corruptor of the whole earth, and the history of the Papacy and Roman Catholicism is an eloquent commentary on that fact.

The Gospel age of the kingdom of God is characterised by the motif of the persecution of the saints. It is the bloody story of the harlot's history with a tally of incalculable millions dead under the holy order of the Inquisition and the Jesuit regime.

Salvation and glory and honour... is a unique word that Christians express because they know their salvation from sin and death and have been brought into the marvellous salvation of the Lord Jesus Christ. These are saints that give us this new song of praise, who have experienced the salvation of God and the wonderful eternal habitations of their inheritance. Salvation means deliverance as the Lord has intervened at the point of the harlot's zenith of power on the earth. He destroys Babylon the Great, who is a child of the mother of harlots, and has delivered the kingdom of God in preparation for the consummation of the kingdom under the millennial rule of Christ and His saints.

This is achieved by the naked power of God Himself for there is no other authority under heaven or upon earth that can give such a glorious deliverance.

Verse 2 speaks of God's judgments. There is no question of the integrity and the righteous judgment of God in these great calamities of the seven final plagues. Although the entire superstructure of Babylon the great has become rubble, a burning cauldron, and the human carnage is incalculable, the Lord God is absolutely just in His judgments. It says that He has *judged the great harlot who corrupted the earth with her fornication.* The citizens of the kingdom of God are the *light of the world* and *the salt of the earth* (Matt. 5:13-16) and everything they touch is cleansed and sanctified for the greater glory of God. On the other hand, everything that the citizens of Babylon touch is fornication, idolatry and a factory of every imaginable sin known to mankind.

He has avenged on her the blood of His servants shed by her. The blood-soaked image of the harlot *...drunk with the blood of the saints and with the blood of the martyrs of Jesus* in chapter 17:6 is the cause of these great calamities, for the Lord says that, *Vengeance is mine, I will repay* (Rom. 12:19).

In verse 3 we are told, *Again they said, "Alleluia! Her smoke rises up forever and ever!"* The smoke referred to here is the burning of the cities of the nations that have become rubble. They are *burned with fire* (18:8). *They saw the smoke of her burning, saying, "What is like this great city?"* (18:18). The great multitude is rejoicing over the thorough and complete destruction of the

Babylonian empire that was ubiquitous in all the earth and making the earth unclean by her fornications.

Verse 4 describes *...the twenty-four elders...* referring to the whole company of the Church in the Old and New Testaments that have gathered in the eternal habitations with the Lord Jesus Christ, waiting for the redemption of their bodies. *...The four living creatures...* refers to forces of providence in creation, that is, the total sovereignty of God.

The sight of these great and glorious righteous judgments elicits the only appropriate response that the elders and the creatures can make. Falling down and worshipping God on the throne saying, *Amen! Alleluia! Amen!* is the expression of their complete accord with these righteous judgments. **Verse 5** gives rise to a question. Whose is this *...voice...saying, "Praise our God, all you His servants and those who fear Him, both small and great!"*? It comes from the throne where God is seated. But God Himself does not need to tell worshippers to praise Him. The words of exultation to praise come from another. The work of the Holy Spirit is to enable the saints to worship and praise God throughout the ages of the kingdom of God, and He enables this heavenly host of saints, both small and great, to give praise to God.

This exultation is related to *the marriage of the Lamb*. This exultation is the kind that is spoken of in the Parable of the Ten Virgins (Matt. 25:1-13). In verse 8 of this passage, the Holy Spirit is calling the saints to be ready, *arrayed in fine linen, clean and bright*. These are *the righteous acts of the saints* in the Holy Spirit that are to be replete in the wife of the Lamb. It is the Holy Spirit that brings about the union of the bride (the Church) with Christ. The exultation is from the glorified saints that are gathered before the throne. Their number is so great and innumerable that their sound was the sound of many waters. They were made *small and great* as they differed in glory according to their works.

Verse 6 continues the praise and adoration. *And I heard, as it were, the voice of a great multitude, as the sound of many waters and as the sound of mighty thunderings, saying, "Alleluia! For the Lord God Omnipotent reigns!"* Again, the praise to God from this great gathered multitude in heavenly places is focusing on the unrivalled power of the reigning monarch, the Lord Jesus Christ.

THE CHURCH'S RENEWED HOPE HAS COME

This rejoicing in **verses 7-8** takes a new theme and moves from the great display of God's power in the execution of judgment of the last great plagues to *the marriage of the Lamb (that) has come, and His wife (the true Church) has made herself ready*.

This doctrine of the body of Christ being united to Christ in marriage is a progressive work throughout the Gospel age and will be completed only at the end of the age when the full number is brought in—none will be lost. This reference is to the days of her betrothal being nearly over—*the marriage of the lamb has come*... in the sense that it is imminent. The climax of this event is described in the actual union of Christ and the bride, His wife, in 21:9 ff. In this passage, the metaphors are extending and emerging. The New Jerusalem and the major themes are coming together. A study of this will follow when this passage is dealt with.

What can be said at this point is that as a result of the seven last plagues (the great intervention of the seven angels), to her it *was granted to be arrayed in fine linen...for the fine linen is the righteous acts of the saints*. This intervention of the Lord has cleansed the Church and the refining of the bride is of great significance.

The Church today is in a disgraceful state. She is overwhelmed by worldliness because of the Babylonian captivity through secular humanism. The intervention of the seven last plagues will in fact purify the true church of Christ.

In **verses 9-10**, the Apostle John is specifically instructed to *Write: "Blessed are those who are called to the marriage supper of the Lamb!"* These words cause John, in verse 10, to *fall at his (the angel's) feet to worship him.*

This statement is, in fact, the sum of all true theology—our union with Christ. All truth of theology should lead to this one doctrine: our union with Christ. The grace of election has its beginning in all eternity in the glory of the wisdom of God alone, and its final destination and purpose are this: *He made us accepted in the Beloved* (Eph. 1:6).

The purpose of our generation in the creation is adoption where *the earnest expectation of the creation eagerly waits for the revealing of the sons of God...* (Rom. 8:19-22). Our effectual calling is a work of God the Holy Spirit where we are raised from the estate of death, called personally by the Triune God, regenerated, and united to Christ through conversion by faith and repentance. We are renovated continuously by dying to sin and living unto the righteousness of Christ, bearing the image of Christ as our union with God is effected in holiness, godliness and righteousness. We have been justified by faith in Christ by which *we have redemption through His blood, the forgiveness of sins, according to the riches of His grace* (Eph. 1:7).

Our glorification is but one thing: our final union with Christ. Baptism is all about our union with Christ (Col. 2:11-12; Rom. 6:3). *Do you not know that...many of us...were baptised into (united with) Christ...* The Covenant of Grace has its origin in the unilateral sovereign purposes of God's grace. Its end is our restoration to Christ so that that which was lost in the fall might be restored as Christ's own possession.

In **verse 10**, John is instructed not to worship any other being than God Himself. The person speaking to John describes himself as, a *fellow servant, and of your brethren who have the testimony of Jesus*. This is referring to one of those in verse 6, the *great multitude...* who in verse 8 are arrayed *in fine linen, which is the righteous acts of the saints*.

This statement, *the testimony of Jesus is the spirit of prophecy*, is establishing that all Scripture or prophecy has one subject, Jesus, who is the sum of all things.

THE BATTLE OF THE GREAT DAY OF GOD ALMIGHTY

HEAVEN OPENED REVEALING THE CONQUERING CHRIST SEATED UPON A WHITE HORSE.

The decisive moment has now been reached where Christ Himself is revealed and heaven is opened, revealing the conquering Christ seated upon a white horse. When heaven opens, the omnipotent power of God Himself is revealed in the figure called *Faithful and True...The Word of God...KING OF KINGS AND LORD OF LORDS* who rides the white horse. This signals the end of the seditious reign of the harlot, the beast and Babylon along with the false prophet.

There is no doubt about the identity of this figure—it is Christ Himself. The names given to the figure can be attributed only to Christ. Is this the second coming of Christ before the millennium? It is certainly a revelation of Christ's omnipotent power and authority. The term *second coming* is not a term that is found in Scripture but it is a commonly used theological expression. The incarnation and Christ's witness and work of redemption are regarded as the first coming. The coming of Christ for the final judgment when He sits upon the great white throne is regarded as the second coming of Christ. This is a little misleading because holy writ speaks of many comings of Christ throughout redemptive history, starting with the theophanies of the Old Testament, such as Genesis 12:7; 13:18. Abraham met the Lord here and built an altar, just as he did wherever and whenever he personally met the Lord. See also Genesis 15:17; 17:1; 18:1; 22:1, 15. Another theophany is His coming and sojourn to accomplish the work of redemption on behalf of the elect (Matt. 2:1-4; Acts 1:9-11). There is also the coming that took place at the destruction of Jerusalem with its Temple in A.D. 70 (Matt. 24:29-30). There are also those records in Church history that speak about baptisms in revival, with the sovereign and

A GREAT MULTITUDE IN HEAVEN REJOICES—REVELATION 19

personal interventions of Christ in Gospel blessings. There are also sovereign interventions of the judgment of God for the sake of the kingdom of God. These may not be regarded as bodily returns of Christ, but they are personal interventions of Christ. The comings of Christ should be distinguished from the final coming of Christ in the final judgment when He sits upon the white throne (20:11-15).

Neither is it a pre-millennial coming of Christ, because although the saints reign with Christ during the millennial years (20:4), Christ remains at the right hand of the Father in all heavenly glory, and these years will be a kind of Paradise Restored in the likeness of the garden of Eden before the fall, where the saints are Christ's Vice-regents or "redeemed Adam" as it were. When we arrive at these passages, a more detailed discussion will be presented.

This opening of heaven and revelation of Christ can be associated with the sequence of events at the end of the pouring out of the seven final bowls of God's wrath, and especially the sixth bowl, which has to do with *the battle of that great day of God Almighty* (16:14) where the Lord Jesus speaks directly saying, *Behold, I am coming as a thief. Blessed is he who watches, and keeps his garments, lest he walk naked and they see his shame* (v. 15). This revelation of Christ is unannounced as His coming is like a thief in the night. The exhortation is to all the saints, that they are to have their lamps trimmed, being replete in all the graces and works of God the Holy Spirit. The exhortation is to be sanctified and clothed in the garments of our Lord Jesus Christ.

The seventh bowl of God's wrath is the context of this coming of Christ, but it is at the end of the sixth bowl that the *Kings of the earth and of the whole world…gather…to the battle…to the place called in Hebrew, Armageddon* (Rev. 16:14, 16). It is at that point that seismic tectonic events occur. It speaks of *a great earthquake, such a mighty and great earthquake as had not occurred since men were on the earth...every island fled away, and the mountains were not found. And great hail from heaven fell upon man* (16:18-21). These events are directed at Babylon the great, to pour out on her a special, *cup of the wine of the fierceness of His wrath* (16:19), which is also further described in chapter 18. In chapter 19:1-10, these events are being witnessed by the heavenly host with the successive *Alleluias!* being offered up in praise as these events unfold or when they are about to be accomplished. This great multitude in heaven is a spectator of the events that unfold and they see the vengeance of God for the sake of their own blood.

Now I saw heaven opened... in **verse 11**. Heaven is that dimension above all and yet over all, unseen by the finite eye. Yet it may be seen by revelation, but only at God's disclosure. The Apostle John saw into eternity a long time into the future. From our perspective, this history has been something like 2,000 years in coming as these events have not yet occurred and they remain as unfulfilled prophecy. With this opening of heaven, John sees a white horse ready for battle to strike the nations for the purpose of *ruling them with a rod of iron*, being poised for *the fierceness and wrath of Almighty God* (19:15). Jesus sits as commander-in-chief ready for battle where He *judges and makes war*.

This figure on the *white horse*, which is a symbol associated with the generals and commanders-in-chief in ancient days, would usually be seated upon the throne high above all authority, but this authority is transferred to the battlefield, where He is seen riding on a white horse, and exercising all authority and power. His name is called *Faithful and True...* He is *Faithful* because He keeps His Word of the Most High and the Covenant. He is *True* because the integrity of His actions is in accordance with absolute righteousness and justice. There are unsettled matters of justice and unresolved lawlessness that must be dealt with. The purpose of this warfare is justice. This is truly a just war because the issues at stake are not measured according to the counsel of men but according to the righteousness of God.

"HE HAD A NAME WRITTEN THAT NO ONE KNEW EXCEPT HIMSELF"

Verse 12 uses the description *His eyes were like a flame of fire...* This is a term used in chapter 1: 14 and it identifies Him as the Son of God who can see into the hearts of men so that no hidden thing is able to go unrevealed. *...On His head were many crowns*, which means that He has no rival in terms of His authority. The mysterious nature of this personage is past finding out in that, *He had a name written that no one knew except Himself.* This description in this context is essential because in Chapter 1 we see a revelation of Christ that is understood and unmistakable, but here we are dealing with a revelation of God as it was in the days of Moses at Mount Sinai, at a distance. Jeremiah the prophet sees a generation of God's people that will know the Lord personally without the mediation of prophets or priests. The Lord says, *"I will make a new covenant... not according to the covenant that I made with their fathers...But this is the covenant that I will make..."* says the LORD: *"I will put My law in their minds, and write it on their hearts; and I will be their God, and they shall be My people...for they all shall know Me, from the least of them to the greatest of them, says the LORD. For I will forgive their iniquity, and their sin I will remember no more"* (Jer. 31:31-34). So, we will learn the knowledge and revelation of God through Christ, and only as we are united in Christ. This knowledge is complete in terms of the revelation of God to man. However, because God is God, there is an "unknowability" concerning God that must be left with God Himself.

The Lord comes to avenge his suffering saints throughout history. These believers will recognise him instinctively and intuitively, because they are able to cry out to God in the Spirit of adoption, *Abba, Father* (Rom. 8:14). But to the citizens of Babylon the Great, this fierce figure of judgement is altogether mysterious and unknowable to them because of their hardness of heart. Therefore, in the community of Babylon the Great, the appearance of Christ the Sovereign King is described thus: *He had a Name written that no one knew except Himself.*

"HE WAS CLOTHED WITH A ROBE DIPPED IN BLOOD, AND HIS NAME IS CALLED THE WORD OF GOD."

Verse 13 reveals that *He was clothed with a robe dipped in blood, and His Name is called The Word of God.* This is a reference to the violence perpetrated against the entire body of Christ through the incessant and ruthless persecution of the saints throughout the age of the Gospel, particularly by the Harlot, the beast and Babylon the Great. The Apostle Paul speaks of completing the sufferings of Christ., *I now rejoice in my sufferings for you, and fill up into my flesh what is lacking in the afflictions of Christ, for the sake of His body, which is the church...* (Col. 1:24). The horrific persecutions against the body of Christ—whether through the official mechanisms of the Roman Catholic Church in the Inquisition, or by the incitement of hatred within communities against the pious believers in Christ, or by the relentless anti-Christian system of the secular humanists of Babylon the Great—is a direct assault on Christ Himself as the blood of the saints is spilt. We see a picture of Christ dripping in blood because of the monstrous and disgraceful treatment of the body of Christ throughout the generations of the Church's witness to the grace of Christ. Christ says, *Assuredly, I say to you, inasmuch as you did it to one of the least of these My brethren, you did it to Me* (Matt. 25:40).

The attributes describing this glorious figure sitting on the white horse are now bound up in one name, *The Word of God.*

This Word is revealed from all eternity as God the Creator, who stamps His image across the entire creation, revealing Himself in His handiwork that is known as the universe. He entered into Covenant so that He revealed the plan of salvation progressively throughout the Old Testament. He bound Himself to His Word written, and required this redemptive work as a single sacrifice necessary for our salvation. He is so united to us on the basis of the Word of the Covenant that He personally receives the sufferings of the saints and will recompense them entirely in the righteous vengeance of God.

Verse 15 tells us *Now out of His mouth goes a sharp sword...* This is a reference to the Word of God spoken by Christ, but this Word is a word of justice in vengeance for the blood of the saints. The Saviour is now dripping in the blood of the saints, as the *great Day of God Almighty* (16:14) has come.

...that with it He should strike the nations. As Christ brought into existence the creation by the power of His Word, so He brings about justice and avenges His persecuted people who have borne the stripes in Christ's Name. He does this by striking the nations according to His righteous judgment. The nations that have been under the control of the Harlot, the beast, and Babylon the Great bear the punishment for striking God's anointed, the very body of Christ.

...He (Christ) Himself will rule them with a rod of iron is a reference to His intervention at the *great day of God Almighty* (16:14), into the years of the millennium where the direct rule of Christ and His saints will be established for the sustained season of the millennium (20:1-6), even to the end of the millennium when the Satanic rebellion (20:7-10) arises shortly before the end, and the

final judgment takes place when Christ will be seated on *the great white throne* (20:11).

VENGEANCE IS MINE, I WILL REPAY

He Himself treads the winepress of the fierceness and wrath of Almighty God. Because the Lord says, *"Vengeance is Mine, I will repay"* (Rom. 12:19; Deut. 32:35), Isaiah refers to the words of Christ, *I have trodden the winepress alone, and from the peoples no one was with Me. For I have trodden them in My anger, and trampled them in My fury; their blood is sprinkled upon My garments, and I have stained all My robes. For the day of vengeance is in My heart, and the year of My redeemed has come...I have trodden down the peoples in My anger, made them drunk in My fury, and brought down their strength to the earth* (Isa. 63:3-6). This does not mean that the Gospel age is over but that the time is very short and the patience of God is diminished. Many, including the Jews (Rom. 11:15 ff), may respond to the Gospel in these days, but these days will be noted for the fierce wrath of Almighty God upon the nations that will be wielded with righteous force, and He will be seen *ruling them with a rod of iron*. His purpose in exercising His wrath against the nations is to demonstrate that the nations are His inheritance and the ends of the earth His possession, and therefore He *break[s] them with a rod of iron* (Ps. 2:8-9) to restore them as His own possession.

THE KING OF KINGS AND LORD OF LORDS

Verse 16 gives the full disclosure of the identity of the figure upon the white horse as One who has on His *'blood-drenched'* robe, and who has on His thigh a name written: KING OF KINGS AND LORD OF LORDS. This, of course, is an unmistakable reference to the Lord Jesus Christ who has the sovereign power over all authorities in all the earth; any authority on earth is first derived from the Lord Jesus Christ and those who wield authority are accountable to

Him in the final estimate. Psalm 2 declares, *The nations rage, and the people plot a vain thing. The kings of the earth set themselves, and the rulers take counsel together, against the LORD and against His Anointed, saying, "Let us break their bonds in pieces and cast away their cords from us."* In rebellion, they may rise against the King of kings but *The Lord shall hold them in derision... He shall speak to them in His wrath, and distress them in His deep displeasure:* because God has set His King on His holy hill of Zion (Ps. 2).

"It is Done!"

John then, in **verse 17**, sees *...an angel standing in the sun...* This is a distinct figure in the heavens, an angel that is distinguished from the Lord Jesus Christ. This is probably the seventh angel that pours out his bowl into the air because he is identified with a loud voice that came out of the Temple of heaven that says, *It is done!* (16:17). The voice is *from the throne,* hence it is the voice of God the Holy Spirit, for His dwelling place is with God Himself. He is God speaking the very Words of God. So, with that, *there were noises and thunderings and lightnings; and there was a great earthquake, such a mighty and great earthquake as had not occurred since men were on the earth* (16:18). The human carnage from this event is probably incalculable. So, the angel standing in the sun *Cried with a loud voice, saying to all the birds that fly in the midst of the heaven, (or literally, the air) "Come and gather together for the supper of the great God..."*

Mobilisation In Battle Formation in the Place Called, in Hebrew, Armageddon

Verse 18 says, *...that you may eat the flesh of kings, the flesh of captains, the flesh of mighty men...* This may refer not only to the carnage of *the great earthquake as had not occurred since men were on the earth* but also to these military men and national leaders that have fallen during the *great day of God Almighty... gathered...to the place called in Hebrew, Armageddon* (16:14, 16).

Caught up in this carnage is also found *the flesh of horses and of those who sit on them, and the flesh of all people, free and slave, both small and great.* This is a description that is understandable to readers throughout the ages. It describes the battlefield and a place of a natural disaster of proportions that are so great that it resembles the global tectonic shaking of the earth that took place in the days of Noah and the great deluge. Horses, for example, are the symbol of mighty battles throughout history. Although they are not used in modern warfare, and are unlikely to be seen on the battlefield when such an event takes place, they are symbolic and represent the Apocalypse to the readers. The cavalry of modern warfare is the mobile weapons of war—the tank brigades, which of course cannot be eaten by the birds of the air. All fallen flesh of this titanic event of earthquakes and even the battle of Armageddon will become food for the birds of the air.

Verse 19 continues this theme: *And I saw the beast, the kings of the earth, and their armies, gathered together to make war against Him who sat on the horse and against His army.* The cue for this event is the drying up of *the great River Euphrates... so that the way of the kings from the east might be prepared* (16:12) during the pouring out of all the six bowls of God's wrath. The kings from the east are the unrighteous nations that are represented by the beast, and who have set themselves against the King of kings and Lord of lords. The spirit of Antichrist drives them, the child of the Harlot called the beast, which is the political manifestation of the harlot that also morphs into Babylon the Great. These nations gather together for war against Christ and His armies. Many commentators such as Barnes[57] would suggest that this is the point at which the Jews, having returned in 1948 (though in unbelief) to the land promised to Abraham, are now gathered and grafted back into the vine as *the natural branch*. The Land of Promise was won for them through Joshua, then dispossessed in A.D. 70 (Matt. 24:3 ff), and has been without a King for two millennia (Hosea 6:2), which hence, this event will be *life from the dead* (Rom. 11:15; 24), as their conversion will happen suddenly and sovereignly under God's hand.

...against Christ and His armies refers to more than one army. If the army of Israel is included, it will be attached to other allied armies that are not angelic hosts but material human formations in battle array. These allies will be known only on the day, but it would seem that nations deeply affected by the influence of the kingdom of God through the leavening work of the Gospel may well be in a position to form an army in alliance with Israel on the side of *Christ and His armies* for *the battle of the great day of God Almighty* (16:14).

The process of polarisation in global politics in our own day between the so-called Christian nations and Islamic nations may well be a factor in determining who will have the political nerve to side with *Christ and His armies*. This may not be a simple identification with historic Christian nations, because the process of multiculturalism, with rapid immigration to the west from nations of the east and the open door that has been created by Babylon the Great through secular humanism may render impotent many of these nations that could side with the armies of the Lord, and they may not have the substance of the matter in them on that particular day.

---

[57] Alfred Barnes, *Notes on the New Testament – Revelation*, Online Bible edition, Rev 19:19.

If the day is near for these events—and present global politics is lining up for such an event—we will no doubt be surprised by which nations fail to become numbered with the allies of *Christ and His armies*. We can be sure that Islamic nations will line up against Israel and hardline persecuting nations of the Christian church, such as China, Russia and even India may well line up against *Christ and His armies*, but such judgments may surprise us when the real situation occurs. Those nations that have a history of warring against Islamic nations may well have the nerve to become allies with Israel on that *great day of God Almighty*. Maybe the purpose of God in the recent advance of Islam worldwide is to test the resolve of nations one way or the other.

In **verse 20,** *...the beast was captured, and with him the false prophet...* It may seem strange that Roman Catholic-dominated nation-states will be found allied with Islamic nations because historically the beast and the false prophet have been opponents in the political sense throughout the history of the world. However, the same spirit exists in both, i.e., the spirit of Satan. In "the great day of God Almighty," these traditional enemies will unite in a *place called in Hebrew, Armageddon* (16:16). Religiously, these two are the same; their persona is different for the sake of deception. In the west under the Harlot and her child, the Beast is manifested and born in the days of the French Revolution by the inspiration of Erasmus, the Roman Catholic, and the Jesuit movement that produced the left-wing political theory that underwrites Communism in Russia's Stalin regime in the west and China's Marxist revolution in the east.

What is meant by the capture of the beast and with him the false prophet is that they are strategically cornered in a specific place so that they are corporately dealt with by Christ and His armies. What causes this strategic gathering of all the enemies of Christ is not described. Some offence to Islamic powers and the religious sensibility of papal Rome may have occurred. The mere existence of Israel in its land is enough to offend the sensibilities of Islamic powers that exist at every quarter around the nation of Israel. Year by year, the pressure on Israel in its land mounts, and the Islamic powers around Israel have openly declared that the only thing that will satisfy their offence is the total annihilation of Israel and its people. However, this on its own, albeit a tinderbox and a political flashpoint in world politics, is not sufficient to bring these powers as one in battle formation to this geographic place called, in Hebrew, Armageddon. If something like a total desecration of sacred places of Islam occurs—such as the desecration of Mecca and Medina—in a time when they are growing increasingly fanatical, this could draw the entire Islamic world out of all the nations of the earth to one place. Furthermore, such desecration in their eyes would draw papal Rome to side politically with such Islamic outrage and the two will become one politically and militarily.

As these forces mobilise and posture in battle formation under the pouring out of the sixth bowl of God's final plagues, the Apostle John sees, *three unclean spirits like frogs coming out of the mouth of the dragon (Satan), out of the mouth of the beast, and out of the mouth of the false prophet. For they are spirits of demons, performing signs, which go out to the kings of the earth, and of the whole world, to gather them to the battle of that great day of God Almighty* (16:13-14). What these signs will be is not disclosed, but they will be so powerful and supernatural that they will catch the eye of the entire world. The world media will be in a frenzy! The entire general population of all the nations of the earth will side for or against *Christ and His armies*.

CAPTURED

The beast...and with him the false prophet who worked signs in his presence, by which he deceived those who received the mark of the beast and those who worshipped his image. This is a description that will weld such a synergistic oneness between the two that it will be like a magnet which will unite Islamic and Roman Catholic peoples in this common course of doing battle against *Christ and His armies.* This will be a crisis of world war proportions. Strategically, they will be clearly defined for what they are: A manifested human collective face of the beast and the false prophet, in a geographic place and therefore exposed militarily and in the words of our text, *captured.*

There is no record that this battle of Armageddon takes place, but we are told that, *then the seventh angel poured out his bowl into the air, and a loud voice came out of the temple of heaven, from the throne, saying, "It is done!" And there were noises and thunderings and lightnings; and there was a great earthquake, such a mighty and great earthquake as had not occurred since men were on the earth* (Rev. 16:17-18). This great Antichrist military formation is swallowed up in the great earthquake of the seventh bowl of God's great wrath. *These two were cast alive into the lake of fire burning with brimstone* (Rev. 19:20), which is described in chapter 17:8 as *the bottomless pit and ...perdition.* The bodies of this great military multitude are cast alive to their death, but the spirit of Antichrist, the beast and the false prophet is assigned to *the bottomless pit* (17:8) that is *the lake of fire burning with brimstone.* This *lake of fire burning with brimstone* is in the other order of existence that is separate from the finite, in the eternal and spiritual which is the ultimate order of existence. It is in this order of existence that the general resurrection will be accomplished. The bodies of all humanity will be raised from the dust of death into a spiritual body that is incomprehensible—in the likeness of the resurrected body of Christ, being a real body bearing the physical attributes of the material body, but spiritual and not bound by the finite and which can never die. (John 5:28-30; Dan. 12:2) On the Last Day, the Lord Jesus Christ is seated upon the *great white throne before which the dead, small and great standing before God...are judged according to their works...are cast into the lake of fire...which is the second death* (20:12-14).

According to **verse 21**, apparently not all are swallowed up alive by the earthquake of the seventh bowl of God's wrath as *...the rest were killed with the sword which proceeded from the mouth of Him who sat on the (white) horse.* This reference to Christ who sits on the white horse with heaven opened encompasses all the remaining survivors *who received the mark of the beast and those who worshipped his image* (19:20). It is achieved by sending out a word of vengeance for the blood of the saints. Those that are not on the great battlefield of Armageddon will not be overlooked, and there will not be a remnant left for the beast and the false prophet to regain their influence; not one who has the mark of the beast will be spared. These people will be like fugitives and will not be able to flee the awful wrath of Christ the victorious commander, seated upon the white horse, who kills the remainder that either survives the earthquake or does not arrive for the battle against *Christ and His armies*.

These people will have no graves but will be in the open for the birds of the air to be filled with their flesh.

CHAPTER 12
AN OVERVIEW OF MILLENNIALISM

Our view on the Biblical themes of Covenant and kingdom theology will largely determine how we approach the doctrine of the millennium. If we accept Covenant theology, we will find a unifying purpose in Holy Scriptures. The Gospel of the Lord Jesus Christ will be at the centre of our understanding, and all related teaching of Scripture will be drawn into an organic, unitary whole. Scripture itself then provides its own agenda for fulfilment and there will be no need to impose a theological construct or, for that matter, any other system to explain the purpose and plan of God for His people and His world. The doctrine of the millennium is that the earthly rule of Christ promised in the Old Testament[58] and revealed in the New Testament is the coming of the kingdom of God.[59] So the various colours and shades in the theological spec-

---

[58] E.g., Genesis 1:26; 8:20-22; Psalm 104:1-35; 2 Samuel 7:12-17; Isaiah 2; 9:8-7; 11 and 12; 65:17-25; 66; Jeremiah 31-33; Ezekiel 36-48; Daniel 2:7-12, etc.

[59] Matt. 3:2 Announcement by John the baptizer; Matt. 4:17 Announced by Jesus; Matt. 5-7 Teaching of the Kingdom of God; Matt. 10 Powers of the kingdom and earthly opposition; Matt. 13 Kingdom parables; Matt. 19:16-30 The Gospel and the kingdom; Matt. 21 The King's final coming to Jerusalem; Matt. 23-25 Israel rejects the King and is to bear the judgement of for a long season; Matt. 27:25; 27:45-54 The King as Priest provides redemption for all

trum in this area will play out in any theological discussion concerning the millennium.

PREMILLENNIALISM

Premillennialism can be defined as the belief that the kingdom of God on earth will only occur after our Lord Jesus Christ comes in His Second Advent (Rev. 19:11-16). When that kingdom comes, Christ will personally be on earth for 1,000 years. The believers only, both the dead and the living, will be bodily resurrected (1 Thess. 4:16-17; 20:6) at the premillennial coming of Christ. These saints will rule with Christ on earth in the millennium. Premillennialism can be divided broadly into two camps: Historic premillennialism and premillennial dispensationalism.

Historic premillennialism looks forward to the evangelisation of the nations, the great tribulation, the great apostasy or rebellion, and the appearance of the Antichrist in person before Christ's premillennial return. There will be a comprehensive and complete conversion of all Jews at this time, as they will have returned to the land promised to their ancestral father Abraham. The natural olive branch of Israel is grafted back in when the days of the Gentiles

---

the citizens of the kingdom; Matt. 28 The authority and resurrection power of the King is also assigned to the citizens of the kingdom; Acts 1:9-11 The risen King ascends to His throne at the right hand of the Father fully glorified in heaven; Acts 2:1-4 God the Holy Spirit comes from heaven to enable the citizens of the kingdom in their spiritual service on earth; Acts 1:4-8 The promised anointing of the citizens of the kingdom for kingdom service beginning at Jerusalem, then to all Judea and Samaria even to the end of the earth which took place in Jerusalem, (Acts 3:1-8:1) Cornelius's household (Acts 8:1-12:25) and Rome (Acts 13:1-28:31) with the signs of the Holy Spirit. The distinction between the Gospel ministry and the kingdom of God is established in Acts 20:24-25.

have been completed and the two, both Jews and Gentiles, become one people of God.⁶⁰

A form of historic premillennialism became very prominent at the end of the nineteenth century and during the twentieth century. This was known as Premillennial Dispensationalism and was popularised by the Scofield Bible, first published in 1909 and later revised by a committee of nine dispensationalist theologians as the New Scofield Bible of 1967.⁶¹ Dispensational premillennialism has been the dominant fundamentalist viewpoint in America since the publication in 1879 of the anonymous "Jesus Is Coming."⁶²

According to this view, before the millennium there will be a seven-year tribulation⁶³ during which the Antichrist will appear, (Ezek. 38-39) and there will be a rapture⁶⁴ (1 Thess. 4:16-17) of

---

⁶⁰ Historic premillennialism believes that there will be a Great Tribulation of the church (not by the church) immediately prior to Christ's bodily return. There are very few Historic Premillennialists writing or preaching today. The two most famous ones in this century have been Carl McIntire, who in his nineties is still writing, and his one-time disciple and subsequent defector, Frances A. Schaeffer, who died in 1985. Francis A. Schaeffer, *A Christian Manifesto (1981)*; and, by the same author, *The Great Evangelical Disaster (1984)*, both published by Crossway Books, Westchester, Illinois.

⁶¹ Published by Oxford University Press, which trademarked the title Scofield Reference Bible because it could not keep control of the still highly lucrative copyright after 1984.

⁶² Written by W. E. B.: William E. Blackstone.

⁶³ Dispensationalism teaches that just before the Great Tribulation, Jesus will return secretly, resurrect dead Christians, and raise all living Christians into the sky in an event called the Rapture.

⁶⁴ The doctrine of the pre-Tribulation Rapture was first articulated in 1830 by a 20-year-old Scottish woman during a trance. On this see Dave MacPherson, *The Great Rapture Hoax* (Fletcher, North Carolina: New Puritan Library, 1983); and, by the same author, *The Rapture Plot* (Simpsonville, South Carolina: Millennium III, 1995). Belief in the pre-Tribulation Rapture is the

the faithful overcoming saints (7:14) before, midway or after the tribulation, depending upon which school of premillennialism is followed. Those left behind will then go through a war when the Antichrist leads the world's armed forces against helpless Israel for at least three-and-a-half years.[65] The seven-year period which follows is a fulfilment of the 70th week of Daniel's prophecy (Dan. 9:24-27). Dispensationalists hold that though the 69th week of this prophecy was fulfilled at the time of Christ's first coming, the prophecy about the 70th week (v 27) will not be fulfilled until after the rapture. The Great Tribulation will be national Israel's disaster, not that of the true Church, since the true Church will have been raptured to heaven.[66] The raptured believers (1 Thess. 4:16-17; 20:5-6) go to be with Christ to celebrate the marriage feast of the Lamb with Him for seven years (19:9).

In the meantime, cruel judgements fall upon the inhabitants of the earth during the cruel rule of the Antichrist, who demands to be worshipped as God. Yet a remnant of Israel will turn to Jesus as the Messiah—the 144,000 sealed Israelites of Revelation 7:3-8 (cf. 14:1)—and begin to preach the *Gospel of the kingdom*. This Gospel has as its central message the establishment of the coming Davidic kingdom, but includes the message of the cross and the

---

basis of the bumper stickers that say, "Warning: In case of Rapture, this car will go out of control."

[65] Gleason L. Archer, et al., *The Rapture: Pre-, Mid-, or Post-Tribulational* (Grand Rapids, Michigan: Zondervan Academie, 1984). Why the combined armies of the entire world cannot defeat the nation of Israel in three and a half years remains something of a mystery.

[66] Ironically, dispensational leaders who are vocal supporters of the State of Israel do so, on the basis of an eschatology which teaches that two-thirds of all Israelis will inevitably die during the Great Tribulation. See John F. Walvoord, *Israel in Prophecy* (Grand Rapids, Michigan: Zondervan Academie, [1962] 1988), p. 108.

need for faith and repentance. Through the witness of this Jewish remnant, an innumerable multitude of Gentiles will also be brought to salvation (Revelation 7:9). The kings of the earth and the armies of the beast and the false prophet now gather to attack the people of God in the Battle of Armageddon (16:16).

In the second half of this tribulation (Dan. 9:27), known as the Great Tribulation, Christ will effect a great victory at the Battle of Armageddon (16:16) and He will inaugurate the glorious reign of Christ on earth in the millennium.[67] As Christ the *King of kings and Lord of lords* (19:16) touches down on earth in the same way and at the same place from whence He Ascended, (Lu. 24:51) with His glorified resurrected saints in train, the person of the Antichrist is *bound and cast him into the bottomless pit*, and his oppressive reign is brought to an end (20:1-3).

The Temple of Jerusalem will be rebuilt (Ezek. 40-48) with all its sacrificial ceremonies because this will be a time when the Jewish nation will return to Christ.[68] Dave Hunt, the accountant who became the leading dispensational author of the 1980s, has described the coming New World Order: "During his thousand-year reign, Christ will visibly rule the world in perfect righteousness from Jerusalem and will impose peace upon nations... Justice will

---

[67] Most dispensationalists believe that resurrected and "raptured" Christians will return in sin-free, indestructible bodies. Thomas D. Ice announced hopefully in 1988: "My blessed hope, however, continues to be that Christ will soon rapture his Bride, the church, and that we will return with him in victory to rule and exercise dominion with him for a thousand years upon the earth. Even so, come Lord Jesus!" Thomas D. Ice, "Preface," in H. Wayne House and Thomas D. Ice, *Dominion Theology: Blessing or Curse?* (Portland, Oregon: Multnomah Press, 1988), p. 10.

[68] Charles L. Feinberg, *The Prophecy of Ezekiel, The Glory of the Lord,* Moody Press. Chicago 1974, pp. 245-279.

be meted out swiftly."[69] While some academic dispensationalists believe that resurrected Christians will not return with Christ to rule on earth during the millennium, but will remain instead in heaven,[70] this theory is never mentioned in popular dispensational literature.

The dispensationalists' kingdom goal is the exercise of power, but at least this power will reside in the hands of sin-free people under the command of the Messiah. Absolute power will not corrupt sin-free people absolutely, but it will surely make them insufferable for sinners, which is why the non-Christians will revolt after a millennium of this benevolent despotism.[71]

However, near the end of the millennium, Satan, who will have been bound during this period, will be loosed and will go out to deceive the nations once again (20:7). He will gather the rebellious nations together for the Battle of Gog and Magog (20:8), and will lead them in an attack upon the *camp of the saints*. (20:9) But fire will come down from heaven on the rebellious nations (20:9), and Satan will be cast into the *Lake of Fire* (20:10).

---

[69] Dave Hunt, *Beyond Seduction: A Return to Biblical Christianity* (Eugene, Oregon: Harvest House, 1987), p. 250.

[70] Cf. J. Dwight Pentecost, *The Relation between Living and Resurrected Saints in The Millennium*, Bibliotheca Sacra, vol. 117 (Oct. 1960), pp. 331–41; John F. Walvoord, *The Rapture Question, rev. ed.* (Grand Rapids, Michigan: Zondervan, 1979), p. 86.

[71] Problem: What would persuade a person who can be killed or maimed to attack an army of sin-free, death-free bureaucrats who have emigrated from heaven? Some parts of dispensationalism's version of the millennium still seem a bit fuzzy, which is why no one except dispensationalism's critics ever mentions them.

After the millennium, Christ returns for judgement. This is when the "general resurrection" (Dan. 12:2; John 5:25-29; 20:13) of all unbelievers and carnal believers who were *left behind* (Matt. 25:1-13; 20:5) in the rapture are separated into the sheep and goats (Matt. 25:32-33). All must appear before the *great white throne* upon which Christ is seated to judge and condemn those that failed to believe in Christ, whose names are not found in the *Book of Life*—they are assigned to hell (20:11-12). Satan and all the enemies in spiritual places are finally assigned to the bottomless pit forever (20:1-3).

Until the arrival of the millennium, however, premillennialists do not expect very much except continuing ridicule by sceptics. As there is no likelihood of reforming an ever-more morally corrupt world, social action programmes are, at best, holding actions. It takes divine power to shape up society, and such power will be denied to Christians until the millennium.

The primary appeal of dispensational premillennialism is the hope of death-free living, and the abolition of the old rule that "nobody gets out of life alive." If Jesus will appear soon—and popular dispensationalists have preached this continually[72]—then those Christians who are alive today may not have to taste death. Dispensationalists believe they probably have been issued a kind of cosmic Monopoly card: "Do not pass death; do not collect the wages of sin."[73] But this intense personal hope in the imminent

---

[72] Dwight Wilson, *Armageddon Now! The Premillennial Response to Russia and Israel Since 1917* (Tyler, Texas: Institute for Christian Economics, [1977] 1991).

[73] Hal Lindsey, whose *Late, Great Planet Earth* (1970) sold over 35 million copies, making him the best-selling Protestant author of the 1970s, followed with *The Terminal Generation* (1976) and the 1980s: *Countdown to Armageddon* (1980).

return of Christ creates a remarkably short cultural time horizon. There is not sufficient time remaining to reform society.

It will be noticed that for both historic and dispensational premillennialism there are two resurrections, (20:6) one at the second coming of Christ to establish the millennial kingdom of God, and the other at the final coming of Christ on the Day of Judgement. Also, the kingdom of God is only spiritual with Christ in heavenly places, and to some degree found within the church which is besieged on all sides during the Church Age before the millennium.

There was a kind of theological vacuum created by the onslaught of Theological Liberalism within the mainline denominations throughout the world that effectively and comprehensively disenfranchised the Church of the Bible. There was hardly a mainline denomination anywhere in the world that had not come under the spell of Theological Liberalism from the 1890s to 1990 and even to our own day. The Bible to their minds was no longer *the pillar and ground of truth* (1 Tim. 3:15), but was reduced to a man-made document that was based on religious myth and tradition. Bible-believing evangelicals were in retreat. They had lost sight of reformed theology with its Biblical Covenant theology that understands the Bible as having its own canonical centre that establishes an organic unity to Biblical revelation. Reformed theologians have championed this covenantal canonical centre to the Bible since the Protestant Reformation in the sixteenth century.[74]

As a result of Theological Liberalism, the Bible-believing churches were hurled out into a faraway wilderness place in terms of their Gospel witness. The bearers of the Biblical testimony were

---

[74] Johannes Oecolampadius who was contemporary with John Calvin, is recognised to be the father of covenant theology.

found in the Baptist churches, Brethren Assemblies, independent churches, and a multitude of missionary agencies that were Gospel-only ministries. There were isolated "separated brethren" from the historic denominations scattered to "the four winds" that maintained the historic reformed faith, but only in disparate minorities.[75] The theological discourse of the Church had become undisciplined and fragmented and that gave birth to many extremes. Premillennialism flourished among these bodies and became the orthodoxy among Bible-believing churches.

Premillennialism has no firm commitment to Covenant theology and therefore Scripture is segmented between Old Testament and New Testament, Israel and the Church, law and grace. Dispensationalism also segments the Bible historically and maintains different administrations of the Gospel in these dispensations, whose number can range from only two to seven or more. In most cases, these administrations of the Gospel, in the end, become different Gospels for different ages. For example, when Christ institutes the millennium, so too will the Temple in Jerusalem be rebuilt, and the entire sacrificial system will be reinstituted. The Apostle Paul, when rebuking the Galatian churches of his day who were in danger of returning to Judaism, said that any return to the former things of the Old Testament would be *to turn again to the weak and beggarly elements* (Gal. 4:9) of the former Gospel that had not

---

[75] An example of this is found in Australia during this period of Theological Liberalism and the story is recorded for us in the well-documented, *The Bush Still Burns, The Presbyterian and Reformed Faith in Australia 1788-1988*, by Roland S Ward, self-published in Melbourne, 1989. The mainline denominations of the Methodist Church of Australia, Australian Congregational Church, and Presbyterian Church of Australia, the emergence of the Uniting Church of Australia by 1977 and even to a lesser degree the Baptist Churches of Australia were completely under the spell of Theological Liberalism during these years. Mainline Protestant churches were paralysed by Theological Liberalism and Roman Catholicism seized the opportunity and advanced to a dominating position in Australia during this period of history.

come to its majority or maturity. Any returning to the sacrificial system is a denial of the complete and perfect redemptive work of Christ on the cross that was done once for all those that believe (Heb. 10:29).

There are different understandings of how these dispensational periods are presented in Scripture, but all present a segmented view of Biblical history. At one end of the spectrum, Scofield asserts seven dispensations, while the other less speculative dispensational theologians only mention two dispensations. The Old and New Testament are contrasted: the law of the Old Testament with the grace of the New Testament; the sacrificial worship of the Tabernacle and Temple with the spiritual worship of the Gospel dispensation. Almost all premillennialists believe that the Temple will be rebuilt and all the sacrifices will be introduced in the millennium when Christ comes and rules for 1,000 years on earth.

Many, seeing the enormous theological problems of dispensationalism, developed what is called Covenantal Premillennialism,[76] that maintains the historic premillennial plan that Christ's return will be the consummation of the kingdom of God in the millennium. Until then, the kingdom of God is purely spiritual, with Christ in heaven and among believers on earth in the Gospel age. The Old and New Testament Gospel is the same. The Gospel is by grace through faith in Christ alone, but by a different stewardship of God's grace, which is entirely orthodox. However, they divide the eternal Covenant into two, and in the New Covenant (Heb. 8:7-13), there is no substantial continuity between the two; they are separate and distinct and therefore come close to falling under the two-Gospels concept. Historic premillennialism will speak of a

---

[76] J Oliver Buswell, *A Systematic Theology of the Christian Religion,* Zondervan Pub. House, Grand Rapids, 1976, pp 406ff.

third Covenant with Israel; they maintain that Israel will be saved in an exceptional way and that this will be expressed in the re-introduction of the Temple with its worship. So, there is a sense in which all premillennialism is dispensational for want of a reformed view of Covenant theology.

AMILLENNIALISM

According to this view, the millennium is symbolic of the spiritual rule of Christ. The earthly theatre of the Church militant is in a constant state of "ebb and flow" in terms of Christ's rule on earth.[77] Generally, the earthly Church is in a state of conflict and persecution where the saints are continually establishing their spiritual credentials for their place in heaven.[78]

The book of Revelation is interpreted using the literary device called "idealism." This approach lays aside all chronological or predictive concerns in order to treat the book as an artistic exposition of the ongoing battle between good and evil. Revelation is a drama that profoundly touches the longings and fears of the human heart. One of the difficulties of this is the number of troublesome verses that do not sit well with a general and spiritual interpretation.

---

[77] The amillennial tradition claims that the millennial reign of Christ is neither geographical nor physical; it is exclusively spiritual, tracing its beginning to Pentecost, when the New Testament era's institutional church began. This amillennial view has been the dominant eschatological viewpoint of Roman Catholicism, Lutheranism, Episcopalianism, with their "high church" liturgies, and also the view of Continental (Dutch) "mid-church" Calvinism/Presbyterianism.

[78] Amillennialists argue that attempts at social reform are morally valid but not Biblically mandatory. Furthermore, all such attempts will inevitably fail to permanently change the secular realm of politics. Dark days lie ahead for Christians: the coming Great Tribulation of the Church.

The kingdom of God is purely a spiritual kingdom in the words of Jesus, *My kingdom is not of this world. If My kingdom were of this world, My servants would fight, so that I should not be delivered to the Jews; but now My kingdom is not from here* (John 18:36). On earth, the kingdom of God is found in the believer's heart (Luke 17:21), and if the believer is successful he may establish a Christian presence and influence in the world to some degree, but we should not get our hopes up too much because in the end, *Our citizenship is in heaven* (Phil. 3:20). Christians belong to the Jerusalem which is above, *...for here [on earth] we have no continuing city, but we seek the one to come* (Heb. 13:13-14). Are we not called to *lay up for yourselves treasures in heaven, where neither moth nor rust destroys and where thieves do not break in and steal? For where your treasure is, there your heart will be also?* (Matt. 6:20-21). *But now we desire a better, that is, a heavenly country...for He has prepared a city for them* (Heb. 11:16).

So, the real and spiritual, yet symbolic, millennium of the rule of Christ's kingdom is being gathered into a "realised millennium" in heavenly places only (Rev. 20:4-6). There is no particular plan for Christ's spiritual rule on earth except for an evangelical purpose and for the body of Christ to maintain her clear testimony during her earthly pilgrimage. There is no earthly millennium, no particular victory of the kingdom of God on earth. In fact, the spiritual power among *the principalities and powers, the rulers of the darkness of this age, the spiritual host of wickedness in the heavenly places* (Eph. 6:12) is of greater dominion than the Church militant, until of course the Second Coming of Christ. Until then, planet earth is the scene of a veritable battlefield that might resemble the World War I Western Front but without a victory.

There is a new form of amillennialism called "optimistic amillennialism." The historical reality of spiritual revivals and their effect in society generally, which is well-documented,[79] has led many who hold to amillennialism to a more optimistic view of history. Maintaining the spiritual nature of the kingdom of God in heavenly places, but its spiritual effect on earth, the Church has prospered and Christian revival has breathed life not only into the Church but also into society. There is a realised kingdom of God of millennial proportions, even an upward movement, throughout history that influences human affairs in "godliness and righteousness." It is believed that there have been high points in the history of the world during this New Testament era between the advents of Christ that could be described as "Christian society" such as Reformation Europe, Puritan England, post-George Whitfield Britain and post-Jonathan Edwards America, and the blossoming of world mission in the modern missionary movement since William Carey of India.

This "optimistic amillennialism" is often confused with historic postmillennialism because it agrees with postmillennialism on so many points. The realised millennial teaching of optimistic amillennialism does place such a spiritual millennium before the Second Advent of the Lord Jesus Christ. Therefore, such amillennialists hold to a postmillennial return of Christ. The optimism that is characteristic to postmillennialism is also apparent but the "optimistic amillennialists" fall short of a sustained millennial peace which is seen as merely spiritual and indicative rather than actual.

However, Covenant Theology is essentially studied separately from the doctrine of the millennium. That is to say, the amillennial view of Covenant Theology stands alone and does not impact on an amillennial view of eschatology. So, a reformed Baptist view

---

[79] Iain Murray, *The Puritan Hope, Revival and the Interpretation of Prophecy*, The Banner of Truth, London, 1971.

of Covenant Theology that makes a sharp distinction between the Old and New Covenants, as expressed in their view of baptism, is able to hold to an amillennial view of eschatology without any inconsistency.

This system of eschatology is pliable enough to hold strongly to all the orthodox doctrines of eschatology, which for many is their primary concern. The spiritual counsel that the message of the book of Revelation provides is steadfastness and faithfulness. The bodily resurrection of all the saints is firmly confessed. The belief in the Biblical millennium is defensively maintained. The Second Advent of Christ is faithfully taught and believers are exhorted to look for the coming of Christ as the Scriptures teach. The Biblical teaching of heaven and hell is maintained without any compromise. The final judgement is asserted strongly and with Biblical soundness. Covenant Theology is maintained and the unitary nature of Scripture is upheld. Even difficult passages in the book of Revelation such as the teaching on Antichrist are explained in a way that is defensible and Biblical. Millennialism throughout Church history has captured the imagination of crackpots, cranks, extremists, fanatics, and outright heretics, and amillennialism provides a safe, moderate ship to navigate through these complex issues.

PRETERISM

In recent years, there has been a tendency on the part of Protestant theologians to adopt a certain Roman Catholic interpretation of eschatology, which has resulted in a view called preterism. The term "preterism" comes from the Latin *praeter*, meaning "ahead of" or "beforehand." This view claims that almost everything in the Book of Revelation describes the events from the birth of Christ to the fall of Jerusalem and the destruction of the Temple in A.D.

70. There has historically been general agreement that the Jesuit Luis De Alcazar wrote the first systematic preterist exposition of prophecy during the Counter-Reformation.[80] Preterist Moses Stuart noted that Alcasar's preterist interpretation was of considerable benefit to the Roman Catholic Church during its arguments with Protestants; and preterism has been described in modern eschatological commentary as a Catholic defence against the Protestant historicist view which identified the Roman Catholic Church as a persecuting apostasy.

Preterism has almost always been associated with postmillennialism because it holds to the belief that Christ's coming will be after the millennial reign. Also, Preterists believe in a realised kingdom of God "on earth as it is in heaven" that begins with the destruction of the temple of Jerusalem in A.D. 70 and is fully consummated with the Second Advent of Christ. Preterism is committed to the belief that, as the saints of Christ, we are strongly committed to the cultural mandate of the original 'Covenant of Creation' that may be described as the "Covenant of Works" with Adam (man), and we are in the process of "reconstruction" so that the righteousness of the law is established across all areas of society and the Covenant

---

[80] It has been usual to say that the Spanish Jesuit Alcasar, in his *Vestigatio Arcani Sensus in Apocalpysi* (1614), was the founder of the Præterist School', Farrar, Frederic,'*The Early Days of Christianity*, volume 2 (1882).

Alcazar was the first to apply Preterism to the Apocalypse with anything like completeness, though it had previously been applied somewhat to Daniel': Froom, Leroy Edwin, *The Prophetic Faith Of Our Fathers*, volume 2, page 509 (1954).

It might be expected that a commentary which thus freed the Romish church from the assaults of Protestants would be popular among the advocates of the papacy. Alcassar met, of course, with general approbation and reception among the Romish community': Stuart, Moses *A Commentary On The Apocalypse*, page 464 (1845).

in Eden is realised (Gen. 1:26-28).[81] However, it is not the same as historic postmillennialism. In fact, preterism has more in common with amillennialism, as most preterists hold to the idea that the millennial reign of Christ started after the destruction of Jerusalem in A.D. 70, and is a symbolic period that will be completed on the last day when the Final Judgment of Christ is instituted. Everything in the book of Revelation up to the beginning of chapter 20 has been entirely played out and fulfilled with the destruction of the Jewish Temple.[82]

---

[81] David Chilton, *Paradise Restored, A Biblical Theology of Dominion*, Dominion Press, Texas, pp 23-63. Chilton has mounted an excellent case for the Theology of Dominion, which is otherwise known as Reconstruction Theology and this book is by far his best but in my opinion his eschatology is also a reconstruction that is imposed upon the Reformation doctrine of Postmillennialism. There is an unwitting adherence to Jesuit designs in Preterist eschatology. Another 'Reconstructionist' theologian, R. J. Rushdoony does not share Chilton's eschatology but propounds historic Postmillennialism that particularly came to light in the days of the Reformation. Rushdoony's historic postmillennial eschatology is well expounded, though briefly, in his book; R. J. Rushdoony, *Thy Kingdom Come, Studies in Daniel and Revelation*, Thoburn Press, Virginia, 1978.

[82] K. L. Gentry, *The Beasts of Revelation*, American Vision, Georgia, 1995. Gentry establishes the case for the Preterist view that the book of Revelation has been already fulfilled, tying the Olivet discourses of Jesus and the prophecies of Revelation together and identifying that everything in the book of Revelation up to the end of chapter 19 is best seen as happening before and with the destruction of the Temple of Jerusalem in A.D. 70.

Gentry, in his book, *Before Jerusalem Fell, Dating the Book of Revelation*, American Vision, Powder Springs, GA, makes a strong case that the entire Canon of Scripture including the book of Revelation was closed by A.D. 70 which brings the apostolic age to its conclusion. This masterly work is, I believe, sound and true but was mounted to buttress the Preterist eschatology of the Reconstructionists as the dating issue was a deep impediment to the Preterist position and I believe Gentry has answered the case well. However, to the historic Postmillennialist this is not the issue, although we are grateful to Gentry's contribution to the discussion.

So, Revelation 20 to 22 is a description of the powerful work of the Kingdom of God throughout the history of the Gospel Age from A.D. 70 through to the last day. Such a view sees the advancement of the kingdom of God as the victory of Christ's kingdom as all-victorious 'on earth as it is in heaven' (Matt. 6:10). However, most amillennialists do not share this highly optimistic perspective of the preterist form of millennialism. The Preterist view leaves the Church without a predictive prophetic word from A.D. 70 through to the final return of Christ at the end of history, which should be a problem for the preterists.

POSTMILLENNIALISM

Postmillennialism is the belief that the kingdom of God, *on earth as it is in heaven* (Matt. 6:10) in a robust rule of Christ from heaven with His saints in heaven and on earth[83] (Isa. 9:6-7; Matt. 13:33; 19:28; Luke 18:28-29; 22:29-30; Eph. 2:6) will, in the fullness of time, be consummated with a sustained peace in millennial proportions (Rev. 20:4-6; Isa. 2:5-21; 11:1-9; 12:5; 65:17-25). After the millennium, Christ will return in His final glory on that Last Day (Acts 17:31; 2 Cor. 5:10; Rom. 2:16; Matt. 12:36).

Christ announced the kingdom of God the King at His First Advent, demonstrated in the resurrection of Christ (Rom. 1:4), established in His ascension and enthronement at the right hand of the Father, proclaimed through the preaching of the Gospel both in Word and Spirit, and advances throughout the Gospel age. The growth of the kingdom of God is continuous and relentless throughout the Gospel age.

---

[83] The imperfect church which is redeemed by the blood of the Lamb and is in the world throughout all generations of the Gospel era (described in the book of Revelation as the seven churches), gains the victory (Rev. 2:1-3:22)

The kingdom of God begins with the destruction of the Old Testament world empires of the Babylonian, Medo-Persian, Macedonian and Roman Empires in the like manner of *a stone that was cut without hands*. The kingdom was cast from heaven and struck the old-world order to its own destruction, and that little *stone* of the kingdom of God grew into *a great mountain that fills the whole earth* (Dan. 2:35). Christ's kingdom, like a *mustard seed* at the beginning, becomes the greatest tree in the garden of all the earth (Matt. 13:31-32). *For the earth shall be full of the knowledge of the Lord as the waters cover the sea* (Isa. 11:9). It may be likened to a grain of *leaven* that is placed in the dough of this world and it *leavens the whole lump* (Matt. 13:33).

THE WARS AGAINST THE KINGDOM OF GOD

This kingdom of Christ will not go unchallenged. Indeed, throughout the history of this kingdom of God, there is a titanic spiritual battle being continually waged in heavenly places, the battle affects everything that this kingdom on earth does. *The field* of *the world*, is sown with *the good seed of the sons of the kingdom*, but the enemy *sows tares*, which *are the sons of the wicked one*. This sinister work of *the devil* is allowed to remain until *harvest*, at which time there will be a gathering of the tares so that the wheat remains. *Therefore as the tares are gathered and burned in that fire, so it will be at the end of this age* (Matt. 13:37-40).

The institutional figures that are spoken of in the book of Revelation will arise in the course of the history of the kingdom of God and challenge the authority of the *King of kings and Lord of lord* at every point. The tares are the children of *the harlot* (17:3-6). They are marked with the mark of the beast, bearing the number of the Antichrist, 666, (13:16-18; 1 Jn. 2:18; 2 Thess. 2:3) *Babylon the great* (16:19; 17:5; 18:1-24) and the *false prophet* (16:13-14). These enemies are focused against the citizens of the kingdom of

God, being the believers or saints of Christ. The battle of the saints persists for a long time and is a bloody, life-and-death struggle that is the *Great Tribulation* (Rev. 7:14). As the Apostle Paul says, *For your sake we are killed all day long; we are accounted as sheep for the slaughter. Yet in all these things we are more than conquerors through Him who loved us* (Rom. 8:36-37). Jesus says, *And blessed are you when they revile and persecute you, and say all kinds of evil against you falsely for my sake. Rejoice and be exceedingly glad, for great is your reward in heaven, for so that they persecuted the prophets who were before you* (Matt. 5:11-12).

BEING CITIZENS OF THE KINGDOM OF GOD

This kingdom begins in the hearts of its citizens who are regenerated (John 3:3-8), justified by faith in Christ (Rom. 3:21-26), and sanctified, being renewed continually through the ministry of the Word of God and its sacraments and by walking by faith in Christ according to the Spirit (Rom. 8:1-11).

Postmillennialism lays stress on the Reformation doctrine of sanctification. The Reformation doctrine of justification by faith gave liberty to the believer, but sanctification both cleanses and creates. Biblical sanctification is how the believer deals with sin (by mortifying sin). It is established in the righteousness of God in the heart such that the entire life of the believer is renovated, along with his world. In this way, sanctification becomes the powerhouse of the kingdom of God on earth and the disciple of Christ is the *light of the world* and *the salt of the earth*.

The Biblical Christian is both a citizen of the kingdom of Christ and a citizen in this world, with particular loyalty given to the nation in which God has placed him. The kingdom of God is not identified merely with the Church but is the spiritual rule of Christ through 'the priesthood of all believers' in this world. The influence of this spiritual rule of Christ through the citizens of the kingdom of God is profound and culture-forming. The legacy of the influence of 'the priesthood of all believers' not only influences the immediate world that they are involved in but also leaves a legacy for the future. Very often, such a legacy has profound effects even upon unbelievers who are also regulated and gifted in such a way that their influence can be effectual for the sake of the kingdom of God. Such people have been greatly used of God because they have been so influenced and supported by the Christian culture surrounding them. This does not make them citizens of the kingdom because only those who know the Gospel and are regenerated and sanctified as saints are true citizens of the kingdom of God. Christ's kingdom is therefore a blessing to believers and nonbelievers, for wherever the kingdom of God is, so also there is peace, righteousness and holy order.

COVENANT OF CREATION

This does not go against the grain even for unbelievers as the work of the kingdom of God is nothing less than the fulfilment of the original Covenant with Adam that is sometimes described as the "Covenant of Creation." The unregenerate are at odds with this original Covenant because they have broken the stipulations of this Covenant, called the "Covenant of Works." However, the natural order is inherent in every human being and even the creation itself. For postmillennialism, this is at the very foundation of the postmillennial view. Despite mankind having fatally broken the "Covenant of Works," God has not failed or forsaken His "Covenant of Creation" with man and creation. Postmillennialism believes that this Covenant will find its fulfilment through the advancement of the kingdom of God and will find complete consummation of millennial proportions to the end. Christ our King will accomplish His purpose not only in heaven but also on earth. God has not failed, even if man has.

This is not a Gospel of works, because the "Covenant of Creation" is the foundation of the gracious "Covenant of Redemption" with the various disclosures throughout the history of Biblical revelation. The "Covenant of Redemption" can be described as the enabling Covenant of the "Covenant of Creation." That is to say, the "Covenant of Creation" is made possible through the "Covenant of Redemption" that only Christ can fulfil. The fatal rebellion of man could only be resolved through the redemption and resurrection in Christ. That Trinitarian work of salvation finds its fulfilment not merely in the evangelical cause of Christ's kingdom but also in its '"Cultural mandate" across the whole earth.

O. Palmer Robinson says, "Man, as part of creation, is responsible to obey the ordinances embedded in creation's structure. Three ordinances, inherent in God's creational orders, deserve particular attention. They are the Sabbath (Gen. 2:3), marriage (Gen. 2:18), and labour (Gen. 1:27-28). Each of these creational orderings stands as an inviolable principle inherent in the structure of the world as God has ordained it."[84] These creational ordinances are at the foundation of the whole creation whether "fallen" or redeemed. In fulfilment of this Covenant, when the kingdom of God is consummated for a sustained millennial period, these ordinances shall form the framework of this godly and righteous order, as they do to varying degrees throughout the history of the kingdom of God. The righteous law of God as enunciated later in the Ten Commandments (Exod. 20:1-17) are written on the conscience of every human being (Rom. 2:15) and will prosper in true liberty and orderly conduct if the righteousness of God is so expressed in the kingdom of God on earth.

---

[84] O. Palmer Robertson, *The Christ of the Covenants,* Baker, Grand Rapids, Michigan, p 68.

Protestant Reformation and the Renaissance

For example, there were two movements at the time of the sixteenth century: The religious Reformation and the Enlightenment, known as the Renaissance. The ancient mediaeval power structures could no longer suppress the civilising advancements of knowledge and wisdom that took place as a result of the Protestant Reformation. The power shift from the tyrannical, Machiavellian government structures that were controlled by "Antichrist" of Catholicism could not match *the power of the Gospel* and the liberty that truth unleashed. The old-world order of the mediaeval spiritual powers was shaken to the core.

Ignatius Loyola, with his Gestapo-like Jesuits, effected the counter-Reformation using brutal methods. Believing that *The ends justifies the means*, the Jesuits used terror and ethnic cleansing techniques with political exactness to gain the upper hand on the Reformation and establish an education system that captured the minds of the ruling classes along each successive generation. These young minds were inoculated against Christianity using the Christian vaccine of the sacerdotal Gospel of Rome, being enticed by the promise of title, office and powerful careers in the best that the world can give.

As the knowledge of the Lord was being emancipated in matters of both faith and life through Christian revival and the theological Reformation, the dominion of the Lord emerged in nations that established a Biblical Christian culture of truth, righteousness, holiness, loving-kindness, goodness and mercy. This in turn reaffirmed the original creational ordinances of true worship, social cohesion, stability of family life, and productive enterprise in the equity of work and economics.

Protestant nations developed national governments that were orderly and free. They limited the power of rulers to make them serve the state and be accountable to the body politic. There was one righteous law for everyone; the evildoer was to be justly punished and the righteous honoured.

Under this system, the power of "Magistrates" (a technical term for those belonging to the ruling class) is divided and responsibilities apportioned so it is not centralised or tyrannical. A system of "checks and balances" is established. These divisions of power provide for the office of Head of State (that is preferably not hereditary) who represents the law of God as God's Vice Regent, and who reviews law but has no power to initiate law. The body politic consists of the Legislative (Parliament) and the Executive of Ministers (Elders) that are assisted by the Bureaucracy of Civil Servants (Deacons).

The judiciary manages its own affairs without interference or influence from other levels of government, applies the laws of the realm and enforces these laws justly and righteously, while remembering mercy. In the interests of justice, and the expeditious delivery thereof, descending levels of courts exist so that doubtful cases may be heard at a higher level and lesser cases do not clog the system. Each case requires credible witnesses and competent presentation of the case from both sides. Where necessary, a case is heard and declared by "common people of peers" (Jury). The judge declares the verdict with the penalty if the charged person is found guilty.

True religion is propagated and the irreligious are not permitted to institutionalise their system of false religion. Diversity within true religion is granted freedom and liberty of conscience, but it must find its explanation in the Word of God alone or by necessary consequence.

Church and State are separate as ordained institutions by God. The mutual support of each sphere is according to the Establishment Principle. The Church, having religious powers related to the Gospel, determines its own affairs, including Church discipline and the payment of stipends. The State, having the power of the sword in established civil legislation, maintains just law enforcement and provides for defence for the commonwealth.

Social and community welfare has its mainspring in the family unit, being the central social institution of society. Common natural resources are for the common good of the nation that is committed to the citizens of the realm, who in turn display responsible stewardship of such resources without resorting to exploitative practices. Common utilities such as water, sewerage, waste management, local community planning, power and communication facilities, health and education are not owned by the government but are community-owned in dedicated "trusts" or family enterprises. They are therefore profitable but are managed for the common good and the preservation of basic human rights. They are also regulated so that profiteering is effectively punished. There is fair competition between existing enterprises and new starters in any enterprise may freely enter on a level playing field.

Wealth generation is for the common good of the family and the community properly accesses unutilised reserves through the utility of banking services. Education is the responsibility of the family, and common educational institutions are accountable to the family (parentis locus).

Every individual is to be gainfully employed. Welfare support is a family responsibility, and if the family is too poor, then the 'common purse' meets the needs of the circumstances and in payment for work that is deemed just and reasonable and for the common good of the local community. Lending and borrowing are based on the ability to pay back the loan, and the principle of jubilee is enforced so that no-one becomes enslaved indefinitely.

The instruments of the national government are responsible for the commonwealth, defence and justice of the nation. The head of state is the commander-in-chief of the defence forces, but the payment for defence is made from the common purse by the national government. Defence forces are only to be used for the defence of the realm and deployed at the borders and never deployed against the citizens of the realm. A citizens' police force is directed only to matters of justice within the realm and is used for law enforcement and the keeping of justice and peace. The police force is accountable to the judiciary for every individual abuse of power.

The Secular Humanist and Babylon the Great

The Jesuits, being the loyal subjects of the Pope of the Roman Catholic Church, answered the Reformation by setting up a spiritual kingdom that was the exact counterpart to the Kingdom of God. It would be built on the blessings of the true Gospel of Christ, as true believers shone as *the light of the world* (Matt. 5:14) and became *the salt of the earth* (Matt. 5:13), exhibiting the wisdom of God in every area of life. The anti-Christian powers of Rome usurped the knowledge of God and reorientated it so that man was at the centre and glorified in place of God.

The emerging humanist movement that looked back to Roman society and Greek culture established a political and cultural system. Discovering in the Renaissance the civilising effects of the Reformation, they then systematically built a spiritual kingdom of Babylon the Great, hoping *to make a name for themselves* (Gen. 11:4) and to God-proof themselves against the absolute sovereignty of God.

By waging an all-out war against Protestant nations and Protestant elements within nations, using genocidal tactics of "ethnic cleansing" and the institution of terror in the Inquisition, the Reformation was reduced to a refined remnant in Great Britain, Holland and other scattered locations in Europe. During the 200 years of the Reformation and the counter-Reformation, it has been estimated that 68 million souls lost their lives because they were declared to be heretics.[85] Using their tactical advantage, the Roman Catholic Church used its influence to capture the field of education and create institutions that were second to none in terms of humanist excellence.

The Roman Catholic Church established a reformed and Calvinistic relationship with church and state. It then consistently went about propagating the secular humanist world and life view and politically populating these institutions with people thoroughly prepared in this world and life view. This world view was man-centred and religiously atheistic with respect to true religion. In terms of regaining world hegemony and taking centre stage, the plan was brilliantly successful.

Jesuit and Roman Catholic missions into the new world strategically colonised the vast continents to prevent Protestant missions from taking root. South Africa, North America, Australia and New Zealand were notable exceptions to the rule. After the

---

[85] Please refer to my study under Revelation chapter 17 and verse 6 particularly concerning the bloody history of Roman Catholicism.

French massacres of all the Calvinistic Huguenot French Reformed Church, absolute power was given to the French monarchs. This eventually resulted in the French Revolution (1789-1799). This became the model experiment for the socio-political doctrines of autocratic socialism that ultimately manifested itself in the "Communist experiment." Marxism in the West (1916-1991) and Maoism in the East (1949-2005?) failed because there were no incentives in their economic theory.

With the fall of the iron and the bamboo curtains, secular humanism—with socialism as its cultural platform and statism as its political platform—established economic supply by re-establishing free enterprise as "a milk cow" to supply the Babylonian government through a taxation system, so that everybody has to drink from its trough and absolute power is apportioned to *Leviathan* (Isa. 27:1). The massive social welfare system, where every conceivable social need is supplied from the cradle to the grave through human and social engineering, attacks the cultural mandate of the family, Church and community, engendering dependency rather than self-sufficiency and giving absolute power to the state. This, of course, is done in the name of caring for the poor, the disadvantaged, the ignorant and the dispossessed, but it widens the circle of dependency and increases the power of the state. Power is the name of the game, and as we know, illegitimate *power corrupts and absolute power corrupts absolutely*.

The social agenda is then engineered so that state dependency is normalised and the family is reduced to an institution of convenience and personal choice. Sex is treated as just another appetite. Children are the responsibility of the state and are therefore, by implication, the property of the state. Health and essential utilities are nationally based, and thus the family and local communities are treated as a dormitory, always looking to the central power.

Pragmatic values serve the convenience of the state and the cultural order of the man-centred Secular City so that abortion on demand, marriage of convenience, and homosexuality are a matter of choice. State-sanctioned gambling, pornography and prostitution as entertainment, and general decadence are values of discretion in the secular humanist city-state. Ethical standards of righteousness are regarded as a religious choice and therefore not to be tolerated in the public square or imposed upon others in the secular humanist city-state. Religion is encouraged in terms of multiculturalism and supported as cultural entities in society. Religion has no place in the secular state, and religious freedom is defined as a closed entity and kept private.

CHRIST'S KINGDOM CONSUMMATED – THE MILLENNIUM

However, there are events in Christ's providence that bring about the consummation of His kingdom, and all the nations of the earth will become the kingdom of God (Dan. 7:27; Rev. 11:15). The institutional enemies of God will be assigned to the bottomless pit to deceive the nations no more (Rev. 20:2-3), and a sustained millennial peace will become a reality (Rev. 20:4). Just what these events will be is discussed rigorously among postmillennial theologians.

In 1850, John A. James, in his book entitled *The Church In Earnest*, states the issue as follows

> *In the foregoing pages, we have glanced at the state of the Christian church from its commencement to the present time; and we have seen the imperfections and corruptions which, in its best condition, have hitherto weakened its strength, impaired its beauty, limited its extent, and hindered its usefulness. An interesting enquiry now presents itself: "Will it be always thus, till it*

is swallowed up of life, glory, and immortality? Is there no hope that it will arise from the earth, shake off the dust, put on its beautiful garments, and array itself as a bride adorned for her husband?" It were a melancholy thing, both for herself and the world, if there were no such expectation. It were a painful thing to look down the vale of time, and see the same divisions, errors, worldliness, and feebleness, ever within the church; the same Paganism, Mohammedanism, Judaism, and Popery, around it; and no provisions for better things and advancing to supplant these scenes of the moral world. If what we have seen, or read, is all that Christianity is to do for our race–if the world is never to be converted to Christ, nor the church is brought into a near conformity to the New Testament–then would infidelity be triumphant, and exultantly affirm that the Son of God had not destroyed the works of the devil–that the Gospel had been partial, and to a great extent, a failure, and therefore was a fable. We have no apprehension that such a ground of triumph will ever be given to the enemies of our faith. A brighter era is destined to arrive; a golden age is to draw upon us, when the predictions of prophets, and the descriptions of Apostles, are all to be fulfilled, and the earth is full of the knowledge of the Lord.[86]

Augustine of Hippo (354-430) stood as a watershed in the Church's understanding of the millennium. Eusebius and others had adopted what was known then as a chiliast view of the millennium, which we would describe today as historic premillennialism. Augustine viewed the kingdom of God as spiritual but

---

[86] J. A. James, *The Church in Earnest*, pp 283, 284.

with its roots firmly planted in this world and therefore like "a mustard seed planted" with the ascension of Christ in His first Advent, growing throughout the generations of the Gospel until the second Advent. It has become fashionable for amillennialists to identify Augustine as one of their own. To the extent that Augustine did hold to the entire Gospel era as being millennial, they are right.[87] Augustine was one that believed in the continual existence of the kingdom of God and represented the millennial rule of Christ. However, Augustine believed that the kingdom of God was the most powerful influence in the finite material world as it is in heaven. He believed that the Lord Jesus Christ is the sovereign King throughout the generations of the Gospel and that the influence of the kingdom of God would ever increase on earth throughout the ages and it was just a matter of time until the world hegemony of Christ would be realised.[88] This view was directly against the chiliasts, who believed that the kingdom of God was reserved for the 1000-year millennium after Jesus's premillennial return. Until then, the Church would be assailed by Satan.[89] In this, Augustine was a realised Postmillennialist, not an amillennialist without any concrete advancement of the kingdom of God on earth. Augustine believed that the Antichrist would be revealed as a person in earthly terms in the future.[90] He witnessed the fall of the Roman Empire, which represented the civilised world under the

---

[87] Augustine of Hippo, St Augustine, City of God, Penguin Classics, 1972, Book XX.7, pp 906-10.

[88] ibid, Book V, pp179ff.

[89] ibid, Book XX, p908.

[90] Op cit, p 919ff The existence of the Antichrist shall emerge among the peoples of the City of Man but will assume the place of the City of God. This City of God will gain the ground of the kingdom of God but at the end for 3.5 years the manifestation of Gog and Magog will be revealed, being that Antichrist spoken of in the Apocalypse and in Daniel 12:7.

converted Emperor Constantine, and its sacking by the barbarians.[91] However, he saw that the City of God was essentially unmoved by this event and that the Gospel would continue to march forward according to the decree of Christ the King.

The Antichrist would arise from within the Church in 664-6 A.D. with the formal schism in the Church at the Synod of Whitby in the year 664. The schism occurred between the evangelical Bible-believing Church and the sacerdotal church of the papal regime of Catholicism.

In about the year 621, a sectarian anti-Christian cult arose under a man named Mohammed, whose movement ravaged the Christian Church. Although the Revelation does not identify the false prophet (16:13; 19:20), the nature of this religious, socio-political, anti-Christian movement is such that its leader, who is called "The Prophet" by his followers, meets all the criteria for this personage. There is no proof text to identify him definitively, but we know of no other such movement in world history that so closely fits the description. Mohammedanism has as its foundational tenet, "There is no god but Allah, and Mohammed is the prophet of Allah." The longevity of Mohammedanism has its only equal in Roman Catholicism. No other political ruler or empire has had the same longevity as these two movements. Other religious ancient movements such as Hinduism and Buddhism have made no pretence at being Christian or claimed any attachment to Christ. Mohammed,

---

[91] The sack of Rome by Alaric in 410. Instead of arguing that the Parousia ushers in a new kingdom, Augustine believed that the City of God and the City of Man coexist through time but remain completely separate. Earthly kingdoms come and go; but the City of God endures forever. In that way, Augustine countered the charge that Christianity had weakened the once invincible Roman Empire and thus caused its fall to more robust barbarians.

on the other hand, attempted to reform what he regarded as corrupt Christianity.

The antichrist that we identify as the Roman Catholic Church with her many illegitimate children is not sectarian as it is orthodox in many respects, but it comes into the Church surreptitiously to establish *Satan's throne* inside the temple where the saints *dwell* (2:13). The same spirit of "antichrist" is also manifested in Mohammedanism, sometimes referred to as the 'antichrist' of the east, who also rides a beast of a political nature called Islam. The "beast" (13:11-18) of the west in Roman Catholicism and the 'beast' of the east called Islam are always at war throughout history, but where these political interests come together, they find unholy commonality as they engage in the persecution of the saints in "the wilderness" (12:14).

These events took place more than 230 years after the death of Augustine. However, these prophesied spiritual forces would shake the City of God to its core. There was a great expectation that the consummation of the kingdom of Christ that may begin the millennium would take place around the year A.D. 1000 by an emerging Christian culture that would assume the central position among the nations. These hopes were dashed by the rise of Roman papalism and the politicisation and corruption within the visible church, as well as by the emergence of militant Mohammadenism under the false prophet Mohamed and his rampaging military exploits that prompted the Crusades.

The Medieval Church sank into deep corruption and ignorance. Martin Luther, in the opening days of the Reformation, saw that the powerful and sustained preaching of the Word of the Gospel would bring the millennium into being. The logical conclusion of the Reformation would be the millennium. The counter-reformation put paid to that hope. The counterparts of the English puritans were the Pilgrims who went to the New World in North America and saw their new society with a Biblically Reformed Church and State being constituted outside the reach of the Roman Antichrist. The Puritans and Pilgrims would be the pioneers of this new world to establish a society that would lead into the world-wide dominion of the kingdom of God.[92] In the second and third generations, this

---

[92] David W Hall, *Calvin In The Public Square, Liberal Democracies, Rights, and Civil Liberties*, P & R Publishing, 2009. David Hall gives an excellent historical description of how the reformers during the Reformation developed the theology of Church and State that was a Biblical approach to discipling the nations under the rule of Christ. He shows that Geneva became a clear though imperfect model of Church and State governance. The economic theory that lay behind the challenge of caring for the thousands of refugees that came to Geneva became an economic model that reflected Biblical principles of stewardship. The ecclesiastical arrangements of Presbyterian church government established Gospel order within the nations that the Gospel was going out to. The reformed doctrine was being codified into reformed confessions of faith both in Europe and Great Britain. The relationship between the churches' consistory and the Genevan civil Councils became a model for the 'establishment principle' between Church and State. The politics of reformed and Presbyterian people within the world was in principle reformational as opposed to revolutionary. They perfected the art of the possible and brought about change from unBiblical practices to Biblical practices and they did this from the top of society down rather than in the reverse. The Calvinistic evangelistic and missionary thrust of the reformed churches brought the Gospel into the world and kingdom of God was thus realised. David Hall also shows how the disciples of John Calvin gave great attention to these issues and carried these principles from the 16th century into the 17th century despite heavy persecution, genocide and military terror. David Hall, in his description in chapter 5 entitled *'Calvin's Disciples in the Public Square, 1540-1640 and Beyond'* p. 129 establishes reformed and Calvinistic political thought and maintains that Samuel Rutherford's generally accepted book called 'Rex Lex' was saying nothing new but summarised reformed political theory. Men like Pierre Viret, Martin Bucer, Heinrich Bullinger, John Ponet, Christopher Goodman, John Knox, Peter Martyr Vermigli, Francois Hotman, Theodora Beza, Junius Brutus, George Buchanan, Lambert Daneau, and Johannes Althusius all wrote extensively, evolved sensibly, coherently and were remarkably single-minded in what reformed politics looked like.

hope began to unravel as these subsequent generations did not adhere to the convictions of the earlier generations.

Later, men like Jonathan Edwards, seeing the force of genuine spiritual revival again, believed that the millennium would come quickly.[93] The American Civil War, which became the prototype of

---

[93] Jonathan Edwards, *History of Redemption*, Collected Works, Vol 1, p 606-7. The so-called millennium will be brought about, not by the visible return of Christ to set up a temporal throne and kingdom, but by the Holy Spirit restraining the power of Satan in some unknown way, and by giving unwonted efficacy to all the ministrations of the Gospel, and the means of grace. What if the power of the Papacy to corrupt and delude mankind, and to oppose the spread and reception of the Gospel were set aside; and along with it should come to an end the power of the Muhammadon system to fetter and enslave mankind; what if all the direct influence of Satan in causing or perpetuating *slavery, war, intemperance, lust, avarice, greed, oppression of the poor, skepticism, and social injustice* were checked and stayed, and the heathen nations were evangelized! Would it not justify the language of Scripture that Satan was bound with a chain? And what if at the same time, a marvellous and unwonted power of the Holy Spirit should send vast waves of ever-recurring revival power around the earth, converting and sanctifying uncounted multitudes of people throughout the entire world! What if the spiritual condition that occurred in Northampton, Mass., during the ministry of Jonathan Edwards in 1745 should spread from town to town, from land to land, from continent to continent! Might it not be said that the millennium had come?

Jonathan Edwards, *Thoughts On The Revival*, Collected Works, Vol 1, p 376. "Presently," says Edwards, "a great and earnest concern about the great things of religion and the eternal world became universal in all parts of the town, and among persons of all degrees and ages: all the conversation in all companies and upon all occasions, was about these things only, unless what was necessary for carrying on their ordinary business. They seemed to follow their worldly business more as a duty, than from any disposition they had to it. The only thing in their view was to get the kingdom of heaven, and every one appeared pressing into it: the engagedness of their hearts in this great concern could not be hid: It appeared in their countenances. The work of conversion was carried on in a most astonishing manner, and increased more and more: souls did, as it were, come by flocks to Jesus Christ. From day to day, for many months together, might be seen evident instances of sinners brought out of darkness into marvellous light. This work of God, as it was carried on, and the number

warfare for the First World War in Europe and the Second World War in Europe and Asia, dealt a harsh blow to such aspirations. Theological Liberalism overwhelmed the Church and she bowed the knee to so-called scientism with the advent of Darwinian evolutionary scientific theory. However, there is a host of Reformed theologians that have maintained the testimony of Reformed theology through these difficult days without wavering from postmillennialism. This is confirmed in Old Testament prophecies speaking of a glorious age of the Church upon earth through the preaching of the Gospel under the power of the Holy Spirit. Such postmillennial hope looks forward to all nations becoming Christian and living in peace one with another. Only after the triumph of Christianity throughout the earth does postmillennialism look for the second coming of the Lord.

Charles Hodge, with his son A. A. Hodge, writes:

> *The scriptural doctrine, therefore, is consistent with the admitted facts that separate nations, and the*

---

of true saints multiplied, soon made a glorious alteration in the town: so that in the Spring and Summer following, in the year 1745, the town seemed to be full of the presence of God: it never was so full of love and joy, and yet so full of distress as it was then. There were remarkable tokens of God's presence in almost every house. It was a time of joy in families on account of salvation being brought to them: parents rejoicing over their children as new-born, and husbands over their wives, and wives over their husbands...Our young people when they met were wont to spend their time in talking of the excellency and dying love of Jesus Christ, the gloriousness of the way of salvation...God has in many respects gone out of, and much beyond, His usual and ordinary way. The work in this town and some others about us has been extraordinary on account of the universality of it, affecting all sorts of people, sober and vicious, high and low, rich and poor, wise and unwise. A loose and careless person could scarcely find another in the whole neighbourhood: and if there was any one that seemed to remain senseless or unconcerned, it would be spoken of as a strange thing. Now who shall say that the Holy Spirit is not able to repeat such a state of things in ten thousand towns around the world, and keep on doing it?"

human race as a whole, has made great advances in all ages of knowledge and in all the parts of life. Nor is it inconsistent with the belief that the world under the influence of Christianity is consistently improving, and will ultimately attain, under the rule of Christ, millennial perfection and glory.[94]

B. B. Warfield writes:

Surely, we shall not wish to measure the saving work of God by what has already been accomplished in these unripe days in which our lot is cast. The sands of time have not yet run out. And before us stretch, not merely the riches of the ages, but the infinitely resourceful reaches of the promise of God. Are not the saints to inherit the earth? Is not the recreated earth theirs? Are not the kingdoms of the world to become the kingdom of God? Is not the knowledge of the glory of God to cover the earth as the waters cover the sea? Shall not the day dawn when no man need say to his neighbour, "Know the Lord," for all shall know him from the least to the greatest. To raise your eyes, raise your eyes, I beseech you, to the far horizon: let them rest nowhere short of the extreme limit of the divine purpose of grace. And tell me what you see there. Is it not the supreme, the glorious, issue of that love of God which loved, not one here and there only in the world, but the world in its organic completeness; and gave his son, not to judge the world, but that the world through him should be saved.[95]

---

[94] Charles Hodge, Systematic Theology, Vol. II, p 94.

[95] B. B. Warfield, The Saviour of the World, p. 129.

Archibald Alexander and Joseph A. Alexander, when commenting on Isaiah 2:2-4, says, *The Prophet sees the Church, at some distant period, exhausted and conspicuous, and the nations resorting to it for instruction in the true religion, as a consequence of which he sees war cease and universal peace prevail.*[96]

The Princeton tradition was then broken, with Gerhardus Vos introducing the amillennial position. He was followed by Cornelius van Til, and initially John Murray (who became post-millennial after writing his commentary on Romans), who regrouped from Princeton to the Westminster Theological Seminary.

The Southern Presbyterian Church theologian and leader, J. H. Thornwell, when writing against premillennialism says,

> *If the church could be aroused to a deeper sense of the glory that awaits her, she would enter with a warmer spirit into the struggles that are before her. Hope would inspire harder. She would even now arise from the dust, and like the eagle plume her pinions for loftier flights than she has yet taken. What she wants, and what every individual Christian wants, is faith – faith in her sublime vocation, in her divine resources, in the presence and efficacy of the Spirit that dwells in her – faith in the truth, faith in Jesus, and faith in God. With such a faith, there would be no need to speculate about the future. That would speedily reveal itself. It is our unfaithfulness, our negligence and unbelief, our low and carnal aims that retard the chariot of the Redeemer. The Bridegroom cannot come until the bride has made herself ready. Let the Church be in earnest after greater*

---

[96] J. A. Alexander, Prophecies of Isaiah, Vol. I, p.96.

holiness in her own members, and in faith and love undertake the conquest of the world, and she will soon settle the question whether her resources are competent to change the face of the earth.[97]

R. L. Dabney in his *Syllabus for Systematic Theology* also has this to say,

Before this second Advent, the following events must have occurred. The development and the secular overthrow of the Antichrist (2 Thess. 2:3-9; Dan. 7:24-26; Rev. 17, 18), which is the papacy. The proclamation of the Gospel to all nations, and the general triumph of Christianity over all false religions, in all nations (Ps. 72:8-11; Isa. 2:2-4; Dan. 2:44, 45; 7:14; Matt. 28:19, 20; Rom. 11:12, 15, 25; Mark 12:10; Matt. 24:14). The general and national return of the Jews to the Christian Church (Rom. 11:25, 26) and then a partial relapse from this date of high prosperity, into unbelief and sin (Rev. 20:7, 8).[98]

H. Witsius says, concerning the conversion of the Jews, which is universally held by postmillennial theologians:

...when the fullness of the Gentiles is brought in, all Israel shall be saved, that is, as our Dutch commentators well observed, not a few, but a very great number, and in a manner the whole Jewish nation, in a full body... As this is not yet accomplished, as to the whole body of the Israelites, and yet the Scripture must be fulfilled, the

---

[97] J.H. Thornwel, *Collected Writings (1871)*, Vol. II, p. 48.

[98] R.L. Dabney, *Syllabus for Systematic Theology*, p. 837.

Apostle has justly inferred that in the last times it will be perfectly fulfilled (Rom. 11:25-27)...To this restoration of Israel shall be joined the riches of the whole Church, and, as it were, life from the dead, Romans in 11:12. The Apostle intimates that much greater and more extensive benefits shall redound to the Christian Church from the fullness and restoration of the Jews, than did to the Gentiles, from their fall and diminution: greater, I say, intensively, or with respect to degrees, and larger with respect to extent...For there is a certain fullness of the Gentiles, to be gathered together by the successive preaching of the Gospel, which goes before the restoration of Israel, of which ver. 25, and another richness for the Gentiles, that comes after the recovery of Israel.[99]

In more modern times, there has been a quiet regathering of Church leaders that adhere to Reformation principles, which is a growing movement across the world. There is, in fact, a returning to postmillennial eschatology, and if not postmillennial then amillennial eschatology and particularly those that believe in a more optimistic history of the kingdom of God.

As indicated in previous chapters in these notes, it is thought that significant events in the natural order will occur that are spoken of in chapter 16. If this is indeed the mechanism where the existing world order of Babylon the Great will be shaken and even destroyed, there will be extraordinary human loss during these disasters. What is left afterwards would require everything that the church has learnt throughout the history of the kingdom of God in order to establish the kingdom of God in its consummated form in all the earth.

---

[99] H. Witsius, *Economy of the Covenants (1775)*, Vol.III, p. 352.

These things are, in the end, a matter of fulfilment, and probably the truth is that all these spiritual forces of the kingdom of God will be used by God to effect His purposes. Augustine's vision of a Christian culture taking centre stage will be experienced. The European Reformation vision of Luther, Zwingli, Bucer, Calvin, Viret, Beza, Ponet, Knox, Bullinger, Hotman, the English Puritans and Rutherford along with the Westminster Divines all believed that the powerful and continuous preaching of the Word to establish the Biblical principles of Church and state would lead to nations' being discipled in godliness and righteousness to establish a new world society. Also, powerful spiritual revival such as Jonathan Edwards experienced, along with many others throughout Church history, will be required for any consummation of the glorious Golden Age to be affected. It is clear from Scripture that any such consummation of the kingdom will include the Jews and their remarkable conversion, which is yet to be seen. As John Milton puts it in his monumental work called *Paradise Lost*:

> *Here shalt thou sit incarnate, here shalt reign*
> *Both God and Man, Son both of God and Man,*
> *Anointed universal King; all power*
> *I give thee, reign forever, and assume*
> *Thy merits; under thee as Head Supreme*
> *Thrones, Princedoms, Powers, Dominions I reduce:*
> *All knees to thee shalt thou bow, of them that bide*
> *In heaven, or earth, or under the earth in hell.'*
>   John Milton, *Paradise Lost* [3.315-22]

WHAT WILL THE MILLENNIUM LOOK LIKE?

This millennium will be a culmination of everything that has gone before it. There will not be resurrected indestructible saints that rule on the earth with Christ: like some alien immigrants from heaven who rule with some sort of despotic benevolence.

The Christians before the millennium will be the same Christians after the start of the millennium. Death will still exist in "Paradise Restored," though life will be extended *as the days of a tree* (Isa. 65:22) and therefore the relentless last enemy of death (1 Cor. 15:36) still exists because *the sting of death is sin* (1 Cor. 15:56). Only on the last day shall the last enemy, death, be overcome *so in Christ all shall be made alive...Christ the firstfruits, afterwards those who are Christ's at His coming* (1 Cor. 15:22-23). It will not be a sinless society but it will be a regulated society that establishes liberty and is rid of the spirit of Antichrist so that *the nations will not be deceived any longer* (Rev. 20:3).

In this new heavens and new earth (Isa. 65:17), regular living will go on and be sustained where, *They shall build houses and inhabit them, they shall plant vineyards and eat their fruit* (Isa. 65:21). There will be marriage and succeeding generations shall be born, and they shall not, *bring forth children for trouble; For there shall be descendants for the blessed of the Lord. And their offspring with them...*(Isa. 65:23).

The Lord Jesus says regarding Satan, *No one can enter a strong man's house and plunder his goods, unless he first binds the strong man. And then he will plunder his house* (Mark 3:27). Satan is likened to a strong man, who is designated as the spiritual *prince and power of the air, the spirit who now works in the sons of disobedience* (Eph. 2:2). Once the strong man has been bound, his subjects are now unprotected and exposed, but these subjects do exist both in the spiritual world and upon the earth. The dominion of Satan is now divided with his *being bound for a thousand years and cast ... into the bottomless pit and shut ...up and set a seal on ...*(Rev. 20:2-3). The lesser demons are not cast into the bottomless pit with Satan but they still exist and therefore they will seek to seduce the saints in much the same way as they have always been doing, so the saints will be tempted. Not all people will be converted in *the new heavens and the new earth* (Isa. 65:17) and *there will be sinners (who) being one hundred years old shall be accursed* (Isa. 65:20). Such people will no doubt stumble badly and sin outside the culture of the day because evil spirits will have seduced them.

Even though the institutional enemies of the harlot, the beast, Babylon the Great and the false prophet are destroyed and Satan is bound and will not be permitted *to deceive the nations any longer*, the Christian will still be required to wage personal war. This war will be against spiritual powers of darkness, the inner enemy of the flesh that is crucified with Christ, and the outward enemy of the world, albeit the enemy will be greatly restrained because of the profound Christian culture prevailing.

No longer will the instruments of war, terror and genocide be used after Christian revival has been effected. Indeed, *The wolf and the lamb shall feed together. The lion shall eat straw like the ox. And dust shalt be the serpent's food* (Isa. 59:25). *A nursing child shall play by the cobra's hole. And the weaned child shall put his hand in the viper's den. They shall not hurt nor destroy in all My holy mountain* (Isa. 11:8-9). No longer will war kill and demoralise the Christian flower of nations. Indeed, warfare has ended. *They shall beat their swords into ploughshares, And their spears into pruning hooks; Nation shall not lift up sword against nation, Neither shall they learn war any more* (Isa. 2:4). No longer will godly institutions be established and be taken over to establish purely secular institutions by the enemies of the kingdom of God and the Gospel. In fact, *They shall not build and another inhabit, they shall not plant and another eat* (Isa. 65:22). No longer will scientific and technological breakthroughs that are granted by God be exploited by the Babylonian juggernaut for its own political ends, as *the earth shall be full of the knowledge of the Lord, as the waters cover the sea* (Isa. 11:9).

It will be possible to rebuild a society that reflects the original Covenant of Creation with Adam in paradise where true worship is found. The society that is built on Biblical standards of family life, and features true enterprise of work and sound economics, will be forged over time. The society will be enduring and it will be a Christian age of millennial proportions. The institutions of God, Church and State, shall be established in peace and godly order. Babylon the Great will be no more, the whole world system will yield to the reorientation of society so that God is glorified and the dignity of man is found in the fact that he has been created in the image of God and not autonomous from God. Faithful stewardship of God's gifts will be established so that exploitation and greed are controlled. International borders will be safe and a strategic balance between nations will be found so that peace is established between nations.

This will not just happen; it will take hard work and wise application of the knowledge and wisdom of God, and it will probably take generations to build sustained and mature institutions that will serve the needs of subsequent generations. However, there will be success and everything will be established so that Christ is pre-eminent in all things. All fields of knowledge, be it the arts, sciences, technologies, literacy and linguistics, mathematics and astronomy, will be regarded as sacred because the whole of creation is God's and sustained by the Word of His power continually.

AN OVERVIEW OF MILLENNIALISM

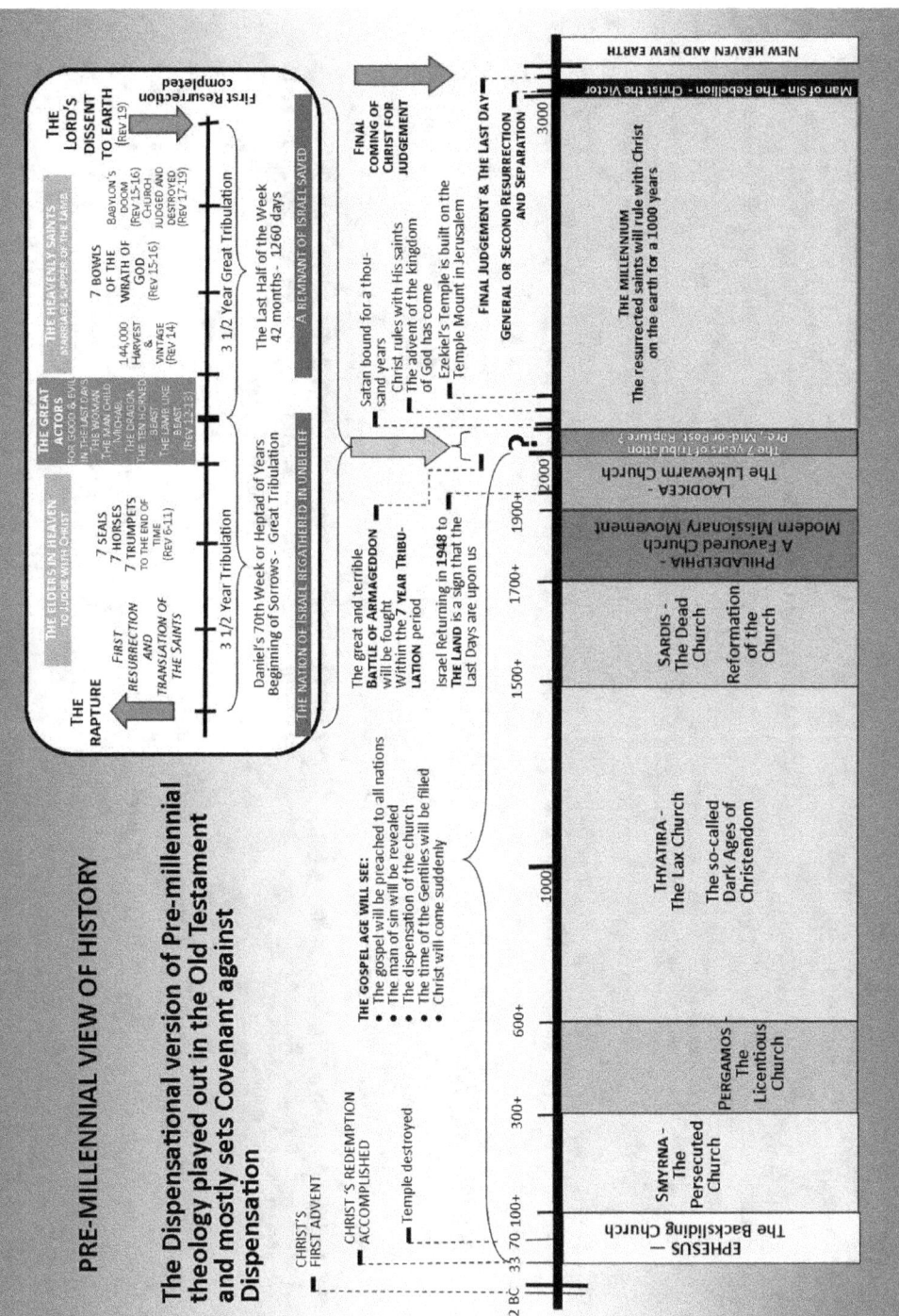

THE QUEST FOR MILLENNIAL HOPE

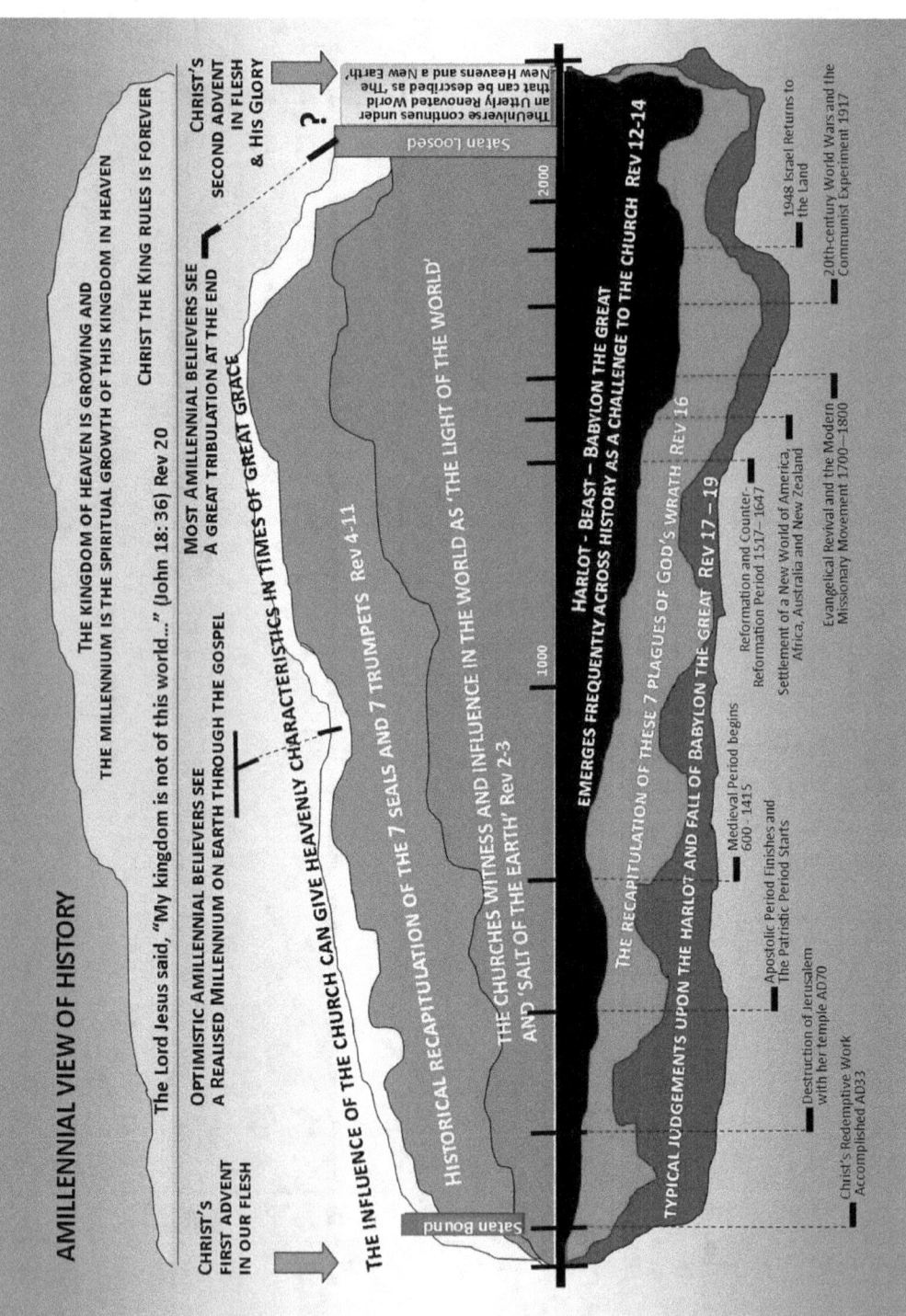

AN OVERVIEW OF MILLENNIALISM

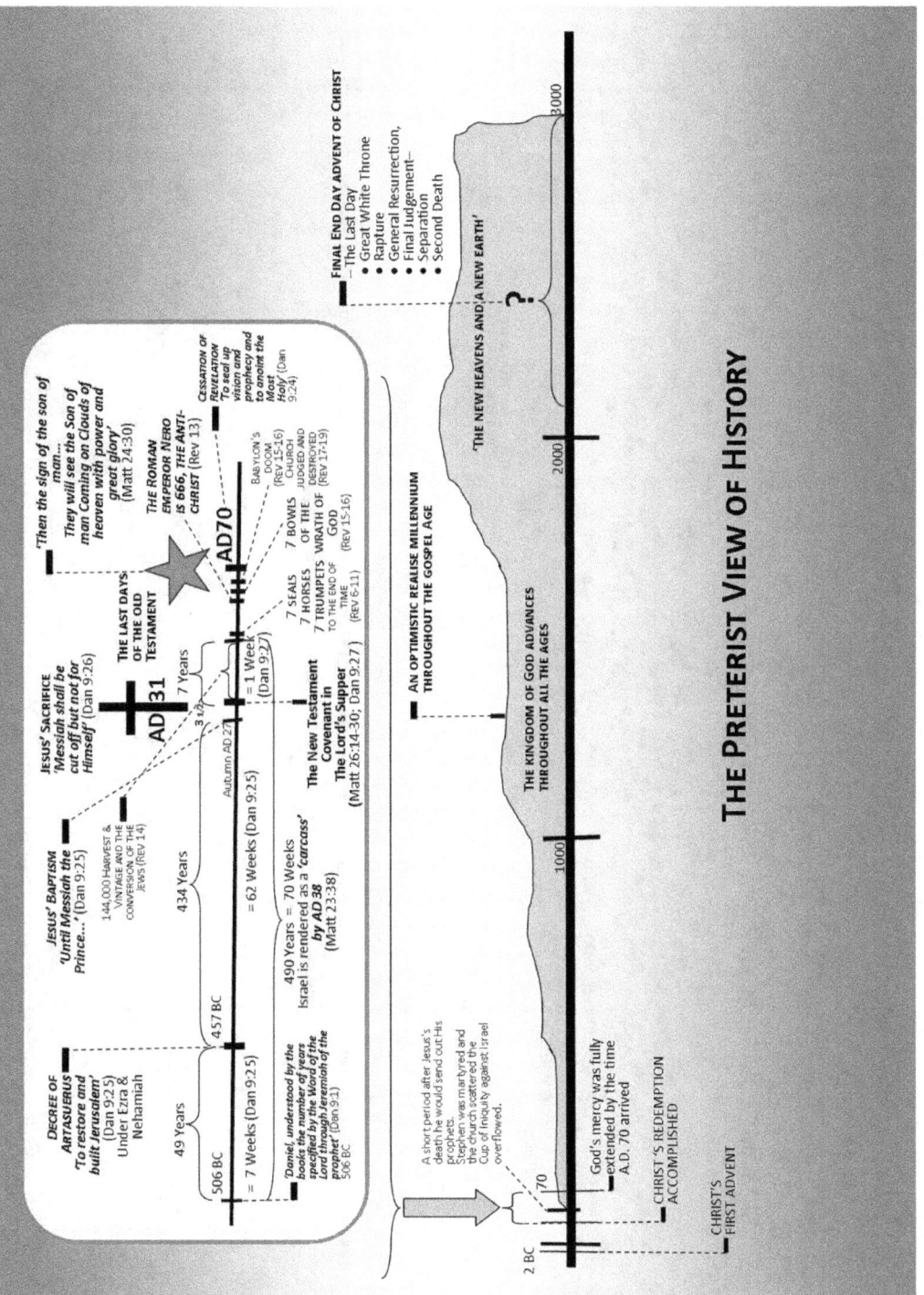

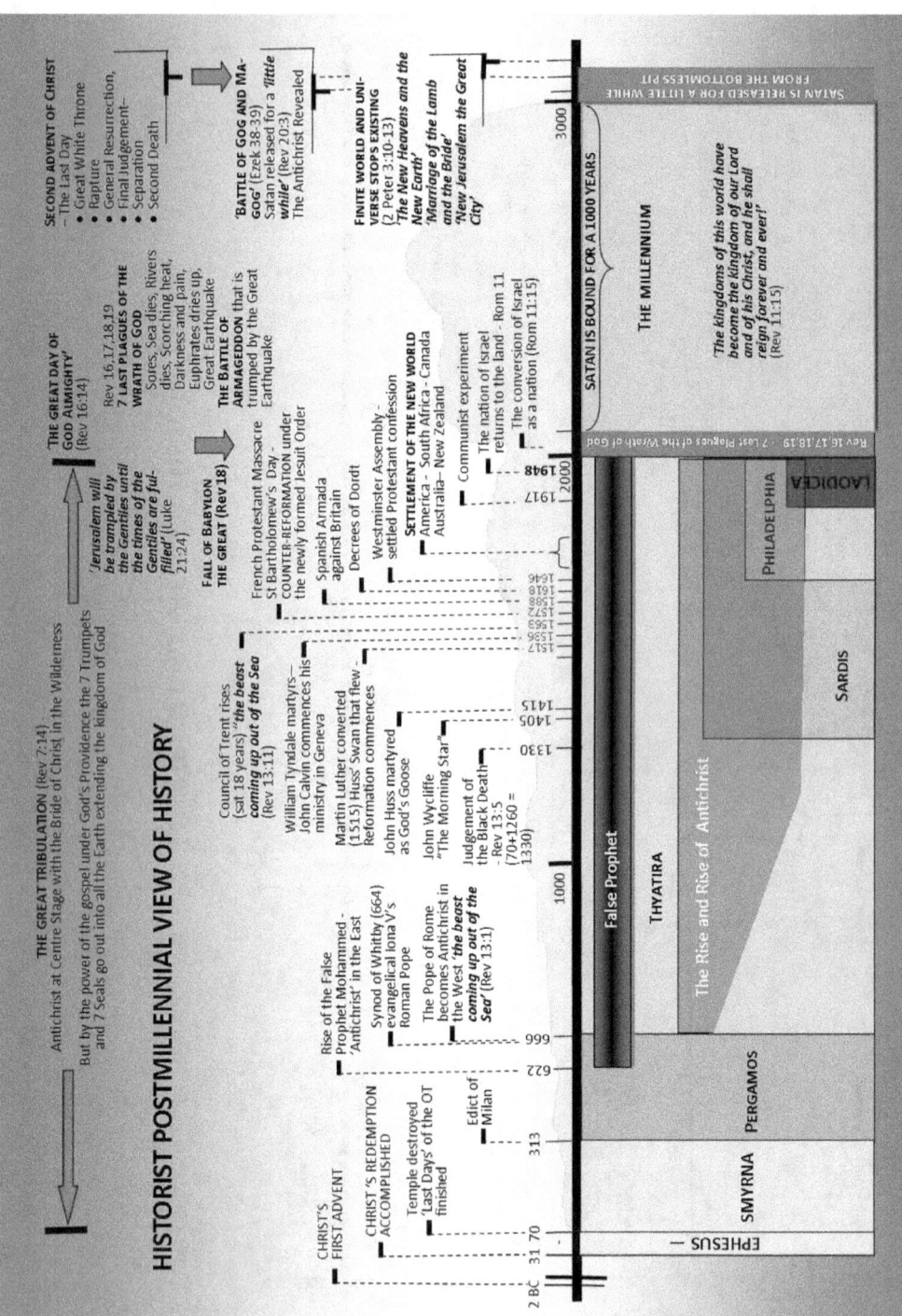

CHAPTER 13

THE MILLENNIUM– REVELATION 20

This section of Scripture has been the subject of endless discussion, and it is not my intention to say anything original or new about it. Because of the preceding chapters where I have described the events as taking place at the "top" of history, rather than as a recapitulation of history, the interpretation of this passage will follow a consistent line—that these events constitute a continuation of history rather than a recapitulation of history. This interpretation will be consistent with what is known as *post-millennial* eschatology, as opposed to *amillennial* and *premillennial* eschatology.

COMMON GROUND OF 'HISTORICISM'

We have had 2,000 years of Church history, and—whatever perspective one takes on Church history—we have been in a long continuum of Christ's providential rule from the right hand of the Father in heavenly places. The one stubborn fact which is often overlooked in the millennial debate is that *the gates of Hades [have] not prevailed* over the Church that is established and sustained by the King and Head of the Church, the Lord Jesus Christ (Matt. 16:18). Throughout Church history, there have been sharp differences of opinion on the role of the millennium in the interpretation of the Apocalypse. In Protestant circles, the millennial question has generally been a matter that is allowed to be challenged and debated. The Confessions of the Church have allowed liberty of opinion on the millennial question, as it is not seen as an article of faith. Certainly, the historic Reformed Confessions, such as the Westminster Confession of Faith, have defined essential things that we must believe because they enter into the substance of the Gospel and salvation. Issues such as the state of men after death, the resurrection of the dead, and the last judgment are Biblical essentials. In reality, there is more common ground among the three historic millennial views that include these essentials than is often stated. For example, the three views have all seen that the Book of Revelation is a book of prophecy that relates to the entire Gospel age of the rule of Christ within the Kingdom of God. The events of the Revelation are historical, or events that are yet to be seen in the future course of history. Generally speaking, this common ground is called "historicism."

Prophetic history is for our assurance because our Lord has said, ...if it were not so, I would have told you (John 14:1).

The message of the Book of Revelation is that there is a solid, confident, Bible-based assurance that, before the Second Coming of Christ, the Gospel of the Lord Jesus Christ and His Kingdom will be victorious throughout the world. The history of Christendom has been marked by all-out war in heavenly places and in earthly theatres of battle where *the King of kings and the Lord of lords* who now sits at the right hand of the Father establishes His purposes with infallible decrees. The rule of Christ through the righteous saints of God has been profound and effective; though always comparatively small in number, the saints have been triumphant in purpose. The sanctified believer, without the force of arms but possessing all the spiritual graces of Christ, secures the crown rights of King Jesus, progressively conquering at the cost of extraordinary persecution and suffering throughout all the ages of the inevitable domination of the kingdom of God, which is like ...*a stone made without hands* (Dan. 2:34) that is cast from heaven upon all the kingdoms of this earth. It grows into a great and glorious *mountain that fills the whole earth* (Dan. 2:35). The prophet Daniel, looking forward to when this old world of the Babylonians will be followed by two other great empires (the Medo-Persian and Greco-Roman empires), and then to these events of the *Latter Days* that begin the new world of the kingdom of heaven, says to Nebuchadnezzar: (Dan. 2:28) *And in the days of these kings the God of heaven will set up a kingdom which shall never be destroyed; and the kingdom shall not be left to other people; it shall break in pieces and consume all these kingdoms, and it shall stand forever* (Dan. 2:44).

AMILLENNIAL RECAPITULATION

Historicist amillennialism notes that the term "millennium" is found only in the book of Revelation, and that to understand the book we must understand that it is replete with Biblical symbolism. This symbolism derives particularly from the Old Testament. Therefore, it is a symbolic term that refers to the Gospel age, which is also the age of the Kingdom of God, where Christ rules from heaven; and it spans the period between the first and the second advents of Christ.[100] William Hendriksen is an excellent exponent of this view in his book *More Than Conquerors*, which has become a standard commentary on the book of Revelation. He divides Revelation into seven distinct sections, and uses a term called "Progressive Parallelism" which sees each of these sections as a recapitulation of the history of the Gospel age; with each recapitulation a more complete revelation is painted on the canvas of history.

---

[100] William Hendriksen, *More Than Conquerors*, Inter-Varsity Press, pp34-36

The amillenarian interprets this chapter as a recapitulation of the entire history of the Gospel age from Christ's First Advent to His Second Advent at the great Judgment Day. The amillennial interpretation maintains that an angel ...*laid hold of the Devil and Satan, and bound him for a thousand years; and he cast him into the bottomless pit, and [God] shut him up, and set a seal upon him, so that he should deceive the nations no more till the thousand years were finished* (20:2-3). This event is supposed to have happened at the death of Jesus Christ, His resurrection and ascension. The millennium is regarded as the entire Gospel age; and the thousand years' reign of Christ spoken of in chapter 20:4-6 is the long and extended rule of Christ that is figurative in terms of time. Even though there are 'ebbs and flows' in the extent of this rule of Christ through the advancement of the Kingdom of God that commenced with Christ and continues throughout all the Gospel age into eternity, the essential characteristic is one of Satanic restraint, which is expressed at the beginning of chapter 20.

The difficulty with such an interpretation is that the history of the Gospel age has been characterised by all-out war, as described throughout the book of Revelation. If this is an analogy of Satan's being bound in some general sense for a thousand years, then why is the more specific description of this event added that says...*he cast him into the bottomless pit, and shut him up, and set a seal upon him, so that he should deceive the nations no more till the thousand years were finished* (20: 3)? This is describing more than Satan's being bound and restrained. It is a complete locking-up of his satanic power and influence. This amillennial generalisation is not a true reflection of the teaching of The Revelation, as the battle throughout has been intense and relentless, revolving around the institutions of Satan, which are the *Harlot*, the *Beast* and *Babylon the Great*, along with the *False Prophet*, who have throughout the age of the Gospel been at centre stage. Yes, this battle has indeed

THE MILLENNIUM-REVELATION 20

seen its victories, and there is a certain restraint on Satan and he has never been autonomous, as the Sovereign Christ has always been in control, but it could not be said that his influence and power have been *locked up*. Indeed, the contrary is true!

PREMILLENNIAL FUTURISM

In the historicist *premillennial* interpretation of Chapters 19 and 20, it is maintained that, in Chapter 19:11-21, we are told that Christ will return bodily to the earth in *like manner as you saw him go into heaven* (Acts 1:9-11), and that throughout Chapter 20, He will continue in His bodily presence, establishing His physical rule for a thousand years (20:4-6). This interpretation is known as "premillennialism" because it teaches that Christ will come back in a bodily form *before* the millennium. The difficulty with this interpretation is that when the Apostle John writes that he *..saw heaven opened, and behold, a white horse. And He who sat on him was called Faithful and True, and in righteousness He judges and makes war...*(19:11), there is no actual evidence that the Lord Jesus Christ comes forth out of heaven. There is no going-forth of Christ into the earth. As Commander-in-Chief, He is seated upon the white horse issuing commands. *...out of His mouth goes a sharp sword, that with it He should strike the nations. And He Himself will rule them with a rod of iron* (19:15). It is not Christ personally who goes to battle, but the armies of Christ (19:14) carry out the commands of *the King of kings and the Lord of lords* (19:16). The inference is that this refers to the Second Coming of Christ before the millennium is introduced. It is a mighty intervention of the Lord Jesus Christ; but it is not a bodily return.

What does come is an angel from heaven *having the key to the bottomless pit and a great chain in his hand* (20:1), who casts Satan into *the bottomless pit* (20:3) — the kind of place mentioned earlier: *...The beast was captured, and with him the false prophet...were cast* *alive into the lake of fire burning with brimstone* (19:20). In this time, the *King of kings and the Lord of lords* remains in heaven until the Last Day. However, even though the transcendence of the King of heaven and earth is maintained, His immanence is always exercised in His power and glory. This is in much the same vein as the debate over how the bodily presence of Christ in the Lord's Supper is perceived. In the Calvinistic perception, Christ's real presence in the Supper is found, not in the material physical presence, as in Roman Catholicism's *transubstantiation*, or extended in space and time, as in the Lutheran *consubstantial* presence, but is exhibited in space and time by the power of God the Holy Spirit and through the angelic hosts of *the armies in heaven* (19:14). In the Calvinistic perception, Christ the King is intimately and directly involved in all these events; and He intervenes even more powerfully, if that is possible, at the time when these great crises occur.

DISPENSATIONAL SPECULATIVE MILLENNIALISM

A further development of premillennialism is *dispensational premillennialism* that sees in Scripture seven neat, successive "dispensations" or "stewardship ages" of Gospel grace throughout Biblical history. It is not necessary to expound the intricate details of dispensational premillennialism, because not all exponents of the view agree on the details (and the details can be very intricate). For our purposes, we can describe the premillennial view as tending to be literalistic. This literalist interpretation has suggested that the Temple of Jerusalem will be rebuilt in greater glory along the lines of Ezekiel's Temple vision in Ezekiel Chapters 40-48, and that the sacrificial system will be reinstated when the Lord Jesus Christ comes in his millennial reign that will be, of course, before the millennium. This is a serious misinterpretation of Scripture and cannot be regarded as orthodox, because introducing such a sacrificial system would be a denial of the finished work of Jesus

Christ on the Cross of Calvary, which was perfect and complete for all believers in all ages (Heb. 10:12).

PRETERIST REALISED MILLENNIALISM

In Postmillennialism, Christ's coming in His final judgment on the Last Day will be *after* the millennium. Historic postmillennialism has always, until recently, interpreted Scripture along historicist lines. As stated earlier, the Preterists subsumed postmillennialism because their system saw a symbolic thousand years as the millennium that commenced at the fall of Jerusalem in A.D. 70 and ended with the final Coming of Christ at the Last Day. Additionally, they believed that the kingdom of God would continue to increase in its influence and transforming power across all areas of society and into every nation, so that the kingdom of God would come on earth *as it is in heaven*. They maintained that the millennium is a present reality as described in Revelation 20 to 22.

HISTORICIST POSTMILLENNIALISM

Historicist postmillennialism has a very optimistic outlook concerning the entire Gospel age. Its proponents believe that the Olivet discourses of our Lord Jesus Christ in Matthew 24-25, Mark 13, and Luke 17: 20-37 and 21 are all fulfilled in the destruction of Jerusalem with its Temple in A.D. 70, and that the entire Book of Revelation is successive history in a prophetic genre of the Gospel age and describes the growth of the Kingdom of God. This approach gives the Church a prophetic word of encouragement throughout the Gospel age, which was its intended purpose (1:3). There is a similarity between some postmillenarians and amillenarians in that they view the millennium in figurative terms. However, the postmillenarians see a definite consummation of the millennium, as described in Revelation 19-20, as involving the ingathering of ethnic Jews according to the Gospel of Jesus Christ and their grafting back into the Vine as a natural branch (Rom.

11). Other postmillenarians see the advancement of the Kingdom of God throughout the Gospel age as described in the Kingdom parables such as the Parable of the Mustard Seed (Matt. 13:31-32) and the Parable of the Leaven (Matt. 13:33). However, they believe that it is not until the intervention of the mighty power of God as described in Revelation 15 to 19, which will include the ingathering of the Jews, that the millennium will be instituted as in chapter 20. This millennium will be a long and extended period where the saints reign with Christ, when Christ Himself will be bodily upon the throne of heaven where He ascended after His resurrection. Whatever it will be, A.W. Pink suggests it is a simple matter of what we shall see in the fullness of time:

> *There is an important Scripture in Hosea 6:2.*
> *After two days, He will revive us.*
> *In the third day He will raise us up, that we may live in His sight. For almost two thousand years–two days with God (2 Peter 3:8) - Israel has been without a king... But the second day is almost ended...*
> *When the third dawns..., **renaissance** shall come!* Arthur W. Pink, 1974 A.D.[101]

A more literal millennial reign may be witnessed when it is instituted.

---

[101] A.W. Pink: *Exposition of the Gospel of John* (2:1), Zondervan, Grand Rapids, 1973, p. 81.

TEXTUAL COMMENT:

THE INTERVENTION OF A POWERFUL ANGELIC BEING AND NOT THE "ANGEL OF THE LORD."

In **verse 1**, we are told, *Then I saw an angel coming down from heaven...* This angel is not the "Angel of the Lord" which would be a theophany of Christ, but a powerful angelic being—possibly an angel that is part of *the armies in heaven, clothed in fine linen, white and clean, that followed Him on white horses* (19:14); this mighty angel breaks ranks to follow his Commander-in-Chief's commands, and has *the key to the bottomless pit and a great chain in his hand*. The bottomless pit is some intermediate and terrible place that resembles hell itself. In chapter 17:8, the *bottomless pit* is mentioned as that place from which the beast ascended and went to another place called *perdition*, which suggests a final place of torment that is secured, known as hell. Satan's time had now been fulfilled, with the institutions of his influence and mischief destroyed; the beast and the false prophet (19:19-20)—the instruments of his power—are dismantled, and the angel who was in charge of the bottomless pit (as he had the key and a chain for Satan's imprisonment), is gone.

THE SPIRITUAL IDENTITY THAT LIES BEHIND THE INSTITUTIONAL ENEMIES OF THE CHURCH AND THE KINGDOM OF GOD IS BOUND AND DISPOSED OF DURING THE MILLENNIAL PERIOD.

Verse 2 continues, *He laid hold of the dragon, the serpent of old, who is the Devil and Satan...* This spiritual heavenly being took hold of the fallen angel, the serpent of old who had played mischief in the Garden of Eden with Adam and Eve, who sought to be the usurper of God's sovereignty. This is the father of lies who, at every turn, distorted the truth, and he is now is to be assigned to something worse than death: a millennium of utter torment.

There is a parallelism that fully describes this creature, *the dragon...the devil and the serpent of old...Satan*. It emphasises the Biblical identity of one person—that sinister spirit that possesses no material body, but is an embodied fallen angelic being. This many-faced, schizophrenic personality is bound for a thousand years. He will be released when the thousand years are complete as he instigates his final rebellion for a short time, after which he will be assigned to perdition, where the beast and the false prophet are. Otherwise, it is described as *the lake of fire and brimstone where... they will be tormented day and night forever and ever* (20:10).

Verse 3 gives further confirmation: *...and he cast him into the bottomless pit, and shut him up, and set a seal on him, so that he should deceive the nations no more till the thousand years were finished*. This casting away of Satan so that he does not deceive the nations is a complete shutting out of his influence and power in absolute terms rather than in relative terms.

At this point, the amillennialists[102] want to make a general comparison between the Old Testament dispensation and the New Testament economy of God's grace. The Old Testament era indeed was, as Paul the Apostle says, *weak and beggarly* (Gal. 4:9), waiting for its consummation. The New Testament economy bears no resemblance to the Old as regards the effectiveness of God's power and the graces that are at work in the Gospel; but the enemies of the Church and the Kingdom of God that are described throughout the Apocalypse leave the Church in a wilderness-defensive posture

---

[102] *Cornelis P. Venema, Christ and the Future,* (Banner of Truth, 2008) p. 119 ff.

with the institutional instruments of Satan having the upper hand in the purposes of God.

THE SAINTS' WEAPONS OF WARFARE ARE NEVER CARNAL BUT SPIRITUAL (EPH. 6: 10-20)

Unlike the four great institutional opponents of the true Church of God (the harlot, the beast, Babylon the great and the false prophet), the Lord has never permitted the Church to mount a physical army. God has used instruments of the state, which ultimately are servants of God, as armies to fulfil His purposes. The true Church of God has never been able to exercise vengeance against her enemies. Vengeance is God's work, and when it comes, it will be measured out in no uncertain terms. The work of the Gospel requires the approach of dependence upon God's grace and His spiritual provision throughout the Gospel age, and therefore, strategically, the Gospel ministry must be conducted as if by those going out into the field without the weapons of this world's warfare but with spiritual weapons that deal with spiritual forces as "lambs among wolves." The great characteristic of the New Testament is the rule of Christ through the history of the kingdom of God which amillennialists wish to call a "realised" millennium in heaven with the gathering of the saints in heavenly places throughout the Gospel age. The apparent defeat of the Kingdom of God on earth is only apparent and not actual, as the *King of kings and the Lord of lords* is still on the throne at the right hand of the Father. This apparent "hollow rule" of Christ in His Kingdom on earth is simply a process of "ebbs and flows" in the cycle of prophetic history.

This is not a description of Christ's millennial reign here in this chapter of the Apocalypse. It may be a description of the history of the kingdom of God in the Gospel era in which we live before the final consummation of Christ's Kingdom, but it is not a description of the millennium. We should and must expect more than "ebbs and flows" in Christ's rule in such a consummated Kingdom. This binding and shutting out of Satan has the result of him *not deceiving the nations for a thousand years*.

Can it be said that throughout the "realised" amillennialist millennium, the nations are not deceived? I think not! The progress of the Kingdom of God has undoubtedly had an enormous positive influence, and a great restraint on evil has been witnessed. It could be said that, in a temporary sense, such nations were so governed by the wisdom and knowledge of God that some would describe a nation as being a Christian nation. Certainly, the effects of the Reformation on European nations and the missionary movement into pagan nations fall into this category. It is true that the kingdom of God unerringly advances so that the Gospel is heard in all nations, and the social effects of Christ's Kingdom have advanced the civilising influence of Christ in His mercy.

THIS WORLD HAS REMAINED "ANTICHRIST" WITH ITS INSTITUTIONS AT CENTRE-STAGE.

However, the overwhelming characteristic disposition of this world has remained "antichrist" with its institutions at centre stage— the harlot, the beast and Babylon the Great, along with the false prophet in Islam. The *beast* in the form of Roman Catholicism has deceived almost every nation throughout the history of the Gospel age. *Babylon the Great* in the form of secular humanism is the most prominent philosophy in all the earth and, under its ruthless and seductive demeanour, the Church is almost irrelevant, having been made a department of society at best. Indeed, we have never seen a Christian age in any sustained period that approaches a thousand years. To say that we are now living in a post-Christian society is a total misunderstanding of the real situation, because we are living in a *pre*-Christian era and not in a *post*-Christian period. The prophetic motif of books like Isaiah, Daniel and Revelation reveal that far more is promised.[103] Not until the Lord Himself intervenes and Satan is cast into the bottomless pit will the new order be introduced.

The amillenarians are so affected by this nebulous, generalist view of the millennium that some of the bolder and more forthright proponents of this view have attempted to describe the immediate days of current history as being those of Satanic rebellion after the 'realised' millennium of Revelation 20:7-10. Such a scenario would be a defeat to the kingdom of God with no sustained extensive era of a glorious victory as described in 20:1-6.

THE KINGDOM OF GOD AND ITS MILLENNIUM

The Apocalypse is saying far more to *those who had been beheaded for their witness to Jesus and for the word of God, who had not worshipped the beast or his image, and had not received his mark on their foreheads or on their hands...*(20:4) than describing it as a kind of amillennial heavenly retirement, looking upon the earth and *reign[ing] with Christ*, with a kingdom never to see its comprehensive victory, except at the Last Day. These souls of the *first resurrection* (20:6) that are corporately united to Christ in His bodily resurrection are real saints with real authority, having *judgment...committed to them* (20:4), *liv[ing] and reign[ing] with Christ for a thousand years* (20:4).

But after these things he (Satan) must be released for a little while (20:3). This is referring to that satanic rebellion (20:7-10) after the thousand-year reign which will be for a *little while*. The

---

[103] Isa 11: 1 – 10; 11: 6 – 9; 65: 17 – 25; Dan 4: 34 – 35; 7: 13 – 14; Rev 20: 4.

millennium will not be a sinless paradise and will not be a place for believers only. It will be a paradise restored (Gen. 2) where the King of kings and Lord of lords will be in control; and there will be great Godly, righteous order and prosperity. But those who are not of the elect will be tested and found wanting when they join forces with Satan when he is released from the bottomless pit. This *little while* means that Satan will never be able to reinstitute his institutionalised instruments of power. However, God's purposes will be fulfilled in preparation for the final judgment on the Last Day.

The fully-orbed progress and purpose of the Kingdom of God that will be consummated with the specific intervention of God and His armies, and in the fullness of time instituted in the millennium, can be otherwise described in terms of *a new heaven and a new earth* (21:1). The Kingdom of God is an associated theme of a new creation (2 Cor. 5:17), as the first day of the week was immediately instituted as the Lord's Day for those in Christ, knowing the resurrection of Christ, worshipping Christ as part of the new creation. We are seeing in the millennial reign of Christ and His saints a consummation that can be described as the Kingdom of God—*a new heaven and a new earth*. In Revelation 21:1 it says there will be *...a new heaven and a new earth, for the first heaven and the first earth had passed away*, which indicates that the millennium is not eternal and will be brought to an end by these postmillennial days of apostasy (20:3).

THE MILLENNIUM AND THE "PARADISE THEME"

We need to remember one of the most basic lessons of the "paradise" theme—that salvation is a *re-creation*. When Noah and his family stepped out of the ark, they were entering into a new world. When the children of Israel were released from the house of bondage in Egypt, they were to enter the Promised Land *flowing with milk and honey*. As the Gospel of Christ's resurrection inaugurated the kingdom of God, we entered a new creation. When God spoke through Isaiah, prophesying the earthly blessings of the coming kingdom (Isa. 65:17-25), he was not speaking of heaven or of a time beyond the end of the world; for in the consummation of the kingdom of *a new heaven and a new earth*, there still exists death, even though the citizens of the millennium may be very advanced in age—perhaps like the antediluvial saints of the old world who could achieve the lifetime of a tree (Isa. 65:20). People in this consummated era of the kingdom would be building (Isa. 65:21), planting (Isa. 65:22), working (Isa. 65:21-22), and having children (Isa. 65:23). The point that can be stated is that the term *new heavens and a new earth* is a statement about this earthly arena *before* the end of the world (2 Pet. 3:13). Isaiah is describing the blessings of Deuteronomy 28:1-14 in what is probably their greatest *earthly* fulfilment.

THE EXPRESSION "A NEW HEAVEN AND A NEW EARTH" AFTER THE MILLENNIUM

The reason for raising the Biblical expression *a new heaven and a new earth* (which is taken up at the beginning of the next chapter, but in an entirely new light), is that the old expression that describes the advancement of the kingdom of God throughout the Gospel era is found in the millennium as the consummation of the comprehensively victorious Kingdom of God. So, the expression *new heavens and a new earth* is a description of the kingdom of God within the Gospel age, which *includes* the millennium. This old expression that is used by the Apostle Peter (2 Pet. 3:13), and which is picked up from Isaiah, is transformed at the conclusion of the millennium and the Day of Judgment, which is that Last Day when the quick and the dead will be finally judged.

As glorious as the consummated kingdom will be in the millennium, it will never equal what Jesus is *preparing* for the time beyond the Last Day. He is referring to *My Father's house* (John 14:2), which will be far greater than anything that previously existed, both, either on the earth or in heaven. This place will be fit for the Bride of Christ and her Husband; and two symbols come together to describe this place. The marriage supper and the *new heavens and a new earth* combine to manifest *New Jerusalem* that has *no Temple* as Christ the Lamb is that Temple. That is to say that the kingdom of God symbolised in the *new heavens and a new earth* finds its zenith and its most complete fulfilment in the long-awaited finale of the marriage of the Bride and the Lamb for which Christ prepares nothing less than *My Father's House*.

CHRIST'S DECREE IN HIS PROVIDENCE, THE KINGDOM OF GOD AND THE MILLENNIUM

The preaching of John the Baptist and that of the Lord Jesus Christ Himself both announced that the Kingdom of God was at hand in the first advent of Christ. Daniel the prophet announced in the interpretation of the dream of Nebuchadnezzar that *a stone... cut out without hands* (Dan. 2:34) would strike the Greco-Roman Empire of the old world at the time of the first advent of Christ, and that this stone was like the Kingdom of God which would grow to become *a great mountain* that would fill *the whole earth* (Dan. 2:35). The Kingdom of God is a spiritual work of God's rule that is within the heart of man, and not a political movement or an outward Empire, but is *like leaven, which a woman took and hid in three measures of meal till it was all leavened* (Matt. 13:33). The Kingdom of God was of insignificant origins, but it would grow throughout the days of the Gospel era *...like a mustard seed, which a man took and sowed in his field, which indeed is the least of all the seeds; but when it is grown it is greater than the herbs and *becomes a tree, so that the birds of the air come and nest in its branches* (Matt. 13:31-32).

Nonetheless, the Lord Jesus spoke of the Kingdom of heaven, which will *suffer[s] violence, and the violent take it by force* (Matt. 11:12). *The violent* briefly spoken of here is a reference to the enemies of the kingdom of God as *the Antichrist* which was made manifest in *the last hour* (1 John 2:18), the *last hour* being that of the Old Testament era, which is represented by John the Baptist. But this Antichrist is first mentioned in the description of *many antichrists* that *went out from us [the true Church of God]* (1 John 2:18, 19). They were not of the true Church of God but were apostate, rejecting Christ yet having a form of the name of Christ that was called *the Antichrist*. This enemy is *the dragon* that *stood before the woman* (Mary, the mother of Jesus) *who was ready to give birth, to devour her Child (Christ) as soon as it was born* (12:4). It was also *a beast rising up out of the sea (13:1)* and changes into another *beast coming up out of the earth* (13:11). In the fullness of time, these figures that do violence against the kingdom of God are manifested as the *mystery, Babylon the Great, the Mother of Harlots and of the Abominations of the earth*, being *the woman drunk with the blood of the saints and with the blood of the martyrs of Jesus* (17:5-6). Daniel the prophet summarises the violent opposition to the Kingdom of heaven ...*those great beasts, which are four, are four kings, which arise out of the earth. But the saints of the Most High shall receive the kingdom, and possess the kingdom forever, even forever and ever* (Dan. 7:17-18).

However, this will be gained only through a long period of violence against the saints and the Kingdom of heaven. As Daniel watched the history of prophetic drama unfold, he wrote ...*and the same horn [Antichrist] was making war against the saints, and prevailing against them, until the Ancient of Days [Christ Jesus] came, [cf 20:1-3] and a judgment was made in favour of the saints of the Most High, and the time came for the saints to possess the kingdom* (Dan. 7:21-22). Daniel gives a full description of this victory of Christ's kingdom as the saints take possession of the kingdom at its consummation by the special intervention of Jesus Christ who is described as the *Ancient of Days* (Dan. 7:23-28).

THE THRONES IN HEAVEN, AS CHRIST SO THE ASCENDED SAINTS.

In **verse 4,** John tells us, *And I saw thrones...* which follows the theme that these thrones are not on the earth but in heaven as Christ was in heaven on a white horse (19:11) conducting Himself in His role as Commander-in-Chief of the armies of God. With Him are the saints in heaven who, like Christ, are sitting on thrones exercising vice-regency granted by the Sovereign. Their souls enjoy transcendence and Christ, and the imminently active role of rulership (judgment) is committed to them. These godly souls are holy saints that are not joined with their resurrected body, but they are highly-ranked because of their consistent testimony to Christ.

To be more specific, these thrones that the Apostle John saw were set up at the beginning of the millennium and should not be confused with the Great White Throne that will be seen at the end of the millennium after the satanic rebellion is crushed and the Final Judgment is executed. It seems to be clear to the Apostle John who would occupy these thrones, but it is not clear to us. There is a certain assumption that his contemporary readers understood what he was referring to.

Not all the great multitude of saints in heaven is in focus here (19:1). The saints that have gathered in heavenly places through the centuries of the Gospel age, including the saints of old that were released by Christ to be with Him between His death and resurrection (1 Pet. 3:18-22; Eph. 4:9-10) are not referred to as being the occupiers of these thrones. They are set up so those who occupy them exercise *judgment [that] was given to them.* A particular kind of saint is being referred to—a saint *who had been beheaded for their witness to Jesus and for the word of God, who had not worshipped the beast or his image, and had not received his mark on their foreheads or on their hands.*

At the end of the recapitulation describing the churches in chapters 2 and 3, we come to the beginning of the millennium. Chapter 4 stands as an interlude describing *a door standing open in heaven.* There is a description of a vision into heaven revealing *a throne...* And *...One sat on the throne...* but *...around the throne were twenty-four thrones, and on the thrones I saw twenty-four elders sitting, clothed in white robes; and they had crowns of gold on their heads* (4:2, 4). An elder is a representative, which may refer to the twelve tribes of Israel representing the Old Testament economy of the Gospel and the twelve Apostles representing the New Testament Gospel age. Certainly, the twelve Apostles, if we include the Apostle Paul as the replacement of the Apostle Judas Iscariot, were great testimonies to Christ; and all of them, if history is correct, were in fact martyrs. The fathers of the twelve tribes of Israel did not have such a clear testimony, but many great examples in the Old Testament that represent true faith gained for them a *better resurrection* through their holy testimony as Old Testament martyrs (Heb. 11:35). These would be great representatives among the saints to represent the Church of all ages in this *judgment that was committed to them* (20:4).

These twenty-four thrones will probably be occupied by specific New Testaments saints that represent the new creation in Christ, because these saints were *beheaded* for their stance against *the beast* and his *mark*, which has been a particular enemy of the Gospel age since the resurrection of Christ. Who these exalted holy ones are will be revealed in the fullness of time, because if the Apostles are representative and are included, their number would not make up the twenty-four that appear here, and therefore they may well represent a wider body of many more thrones. Whoever they are, this select group will have intimate and personal knowledge of a particular kind of evil that was perpetrated against the saints that led to their martyrdom. This sinister spiritual power is institutionalised in the Mother of Harlots, the Beast, and transforms into Babylon the Great (17:5). These conspired together as *The kings of the earth set themselves, and the rulers take counsel together, against the LORD and against His Anointed, saying, "Let us break their bonds in pieces and cast away their cords from us"* (Ps. 2:2-3). And this Antichrist *...shall speak pompous words against the Most High, shall persecute the saints of the Most High, and shall intend to change times and law. Then the saints shall be given into his hand for a time and times and half the time* (Dan. 7:25). After this, a high court bench of judges shall sit in the fullness of time, at the beginning of the great millennium, for the benefit of all saints and for the consummation of the kingdom of God. Daniel the prophet goes on to say, *But the court shall be seated, and they shall take away his [Antichrist's] dominion, to consume and destroy it forever. Then the kingdom and dominion, and the greatness of the kingdoms under the whole heaven, shall be given to the people, the saints of the Most High. His kingdom is an everlasting kingdom, and all dominions shall serve and obey Him* (Dan. 7:26-27).

This a High Court Bench of Judges with a certain kind of *judgment [that] was committed to them*—a judgment that is distinct from the ultimate general judgment of the Lord Jesus Christ, when He takes His place on the Great White Throne, at his bodily return to earth, at the conclusion of the millennium, which will be a judgment of all mankind according to *their works* (20:12). This judgment will be specifically against the harlot and all her children who have been hell-bent on destroying the saints. All its bloody history shall be brought under the light of truth and justice in much the same way as the Nuremberg Trials for war crimes against Germany was conducted after the Second World War. However, in these trials against *the beast*, the evidence will not be able to be suppressed. Everything will be laid bare in the full light of justice so that judgment will be clearly seen and executed. The beast and her children will be judicially cast alive into the lake of fire with brimstone, and cast into the bottomless pit with great chains. They will be shut up with a seal set upon them for a thousand years, and there will be weeping and gnashing of teeth in unquenchable pain and misery in perfect execution of justice.

And they lived and reigned with Christ for a thousand years. The identity of **they** *[who] lived and reigned...* are *the souls of those who had been beheaded...* mentioned at the beginning of this verse. These are those saints, it would appear, that are distinct from those who were given the *judgment* of the beast (please see the discussion above as conclusions are drawn on the basis of cross-references to the Book of Daniel). If that is so, it would appear that this group of souls was a far greater group who had the privilege of what is described later on in verse 6: *Blessed and holy is he who has a part in the first resurrection*. Just who these souls are will be discussed later, but here we say that there is a select and privileged group that is described as comprising souls who are wider in number and who will *live and reign with Christ for a thousand years*. These souls in Christ are distinguished by their role as *living and reigning with Christ* as opposed to that very select group of saints to whom *judgment was committed*.

As stated earlier, the prophet Daniel discloses that *...the kingdom and dominion, and the greatness of the kingdoms under the whole heaven, shall be given to the people, the saints of the Most High* (Dan. 7:27). The Apostles were taught that the saints would judge the world, although at first the early disciples misunderstood the content of this teaching. Fragments of His teaching are found in such places as the Parable of the Talents (Matt. 25:14-30), where those who have been faithful stewards are granted the privilege of far greater responsibilities in the coming kingdom in terms of their ruling dominions on the Lord's behalf—presumably as vice-regents. Sensing the gravity of the moment, the mother of Zebedee's sons (James and John), whose ambition was excited, came to Jesus and pleaded with Him, *Grant that these two sons of mine may sit, one on Your right hand and the other on the left, in Your kingdom* (Matt. 20:21). Far from dismissing such a request, Jesus said that the request was beyond her comprehension and was the peculiar province of *My Father*. He corrected her misconceptions about exercising God's authority, as great authority would be granted to the saints in the fullness of time.

The Apostle Paul, writing to the Corinthian churches during the Gospel age after the resurrection of Christ, corrected a practice of Christians taking other Christians to the civil courts and reminded them that this practice was below their dignity. He wrote, *Do you not know that the saints will judge the world?* (1 Cor. 6:2). This future work of the saints will occur after a probationary period to which all the saints throughout all the generations will be subject. In the fullness of time, they will be granted their vice-regencies both here on earth and in the kingdom to come—the consummated kingdom of God of the millennium and beyond.

SPIRITUAL COSMOLOGY AND ITS EARTHLY EFFECTS

I would suggest that the spiritual cosmology was dramatically altered between the Old Testament age and the New Testament Gospel era. With the coming of the kingdom of God that was inaugurated at the resurrection of Christ, the saints in Christ were in the new creation, so that they were no longer in the "department for the righteous" in Sheol, but were now with the resurrected and ascended Christ in heavenly places. However, throughout the history of the kingdom of God in the Gospel age, because of the evangelistic work of the Gospel, the sons of God are being revealed. The Apostle Paul asserts this even further by saying *...for the earnest expectation of the creation...was subjected to futility...in hope; because the creation itself also will be delivered from the bondage of corruption into the glorious liberty of the children of God* (Rom. 8:19-21). Throughout the Gospel age, the expanding influence of the rule of Christ has liberated earth from great darkness and has had immense civilising powers throughout the earth. But Satan, the usurper, has exploited such advances for his own sinister purposes. Successive generations of the saints, who have laboured throughout the Gospel age, have suffered in *this present time*; but such *sufferings...are not worthy to be compared with the glory which shall be revealed in us* (Rom. 8:18).

The spiritual cosmology of the millennium will undergo seismic changes as *the devil and Satan* are *cast ...into the bottomless pit* (20:2-3). As we look further at the Apostle Paul's words in Romans 8:22 where the focus is on the whole creation *that... groans and labours with birth pangs together until now*, we see that the *until now* refers to the inauguration of the Kingdom of God in the new creation, which took place at the resurrection of Jesus. We also see the leavening effect of this kingdom. However, the ecological groaning of the whole creation does not cease until the consummation of the Kingdom through the direct intervention of Christ Himself. Romans 8:23 bears this out, as the perspective of these verses in Romans is the entire rule of Christ throughout the Gospel age that begins with the first advent of Christ and extends to His second advent. The statement that ...*we also who have the first-fruits of the Spirit, even we ourselves groan within ourselves, earnestly waiting for the adoption, the redemption of our body*, is a direct reference to the final General Resurrection of both the living and the dead on the Last Day after the millennium.

As mentioned earlier, the millennium will be, as it were, a paradise restored where the rule of Christ and His saints will be the consistent and continuous rule of Christ's righteousness, truth and justice through godly institutions and instruments of true governance. Although this will not be a society of believers only or a society without sin, it will be a society where the fear of God will be known even amongst the ungodly. How this will look can only be indicated rather than delineated in distinct terms. The rule of Christ will continue in much the same way as it has throughout the history of the kingdom of God. Christ is seated at the right hand of the Father exercising his offices of Prophet, Priest and King, and the division of powers will be maintained, with the Church on the earth representing the spiritual powers of the kingdom; also, the powers of civil government will be in complete accord with Christ the King. Biblical law and righteousness will be held in place in every institution of society such as marriage and family, work and industry and their proper stewardship; education will be conducted according to Biblical principles; public behaviour will be conducted with appropriate decorum; and consequences of misbehaviour will be effectively enforced. The notable absence will be the harlot, the beast, Babylon the Great, and the false prophet that has traditionally usurped the rule of Christ and His saints, but who will no longer be deceiving the nations:

The kingdoms of this world have become the kingdoms of our Lord and of His Christ, and He shall reign forever and ever! (Rev. 11: 15).

THE SAINTS IN HEAVEN AND ON EARTH REIGN TOGETHER WITH CHRIST WITHIN THE KINGDOM OF GOD.

There is a less obvious matter that needs to be addressed at this point. How are these souls, who are with Christ in heaven, going to reign together with the saints on earth who still possess a mortal body? I would suggest that it would look like this: Christ, through the kingdom of God, in a particular and distinctive way, has been exercising His reign from the right hand of the Father and effecting His sovereign purposes throughout all the ages; but He has done this with particular and special effects since the coming of the kingdom of God in the new creation since the resurrection of Christ.

Since the creation of the world, there has been a kind of symbiotic relationship between the spiritual or the heavenly and the physical or the finite. In the day of the creation before the Fall, this symbiotic relationship was extremely close and could be described as an ideal relationship reminiscent of paradise. After the Fall, this symbiotic relationship was severed and the creation was left with a deeply-scarred relationship with the God of providence. The relationship of man with God was dead and broken. The creation *groaned and travailed* under the enveloping evil of sin during the antediluvian era, and the consequences of global flood altered the topography of the earth. From the days of Noah to the Coming of Christ, the redemptive purposes of the Covenant of Grace were being played out until the Day of Christ in His first advent, when the ransom was paid and the sons of God appeared and continue to appear throughout the Gospel age, when the Kingdom of God advances and the symbiotic relationship between heaven and earth is once again restored. The ideal relationship and the consummation of God's kingdom are fully realised in the millennial reign of Christ and His saints.

The saints in heaven, who do not yet have a redeemed and resurrected body, nonetheless, in Christ will enjoy the resurrected body of Christ and rule with Christ in His body. Indeed, the Heidelberg Catechism goes as far as to say in answer to Question 49, ...we have our own flesh in heaven—a guarantee that Christ our head, will take us, His members, to Himself, in heaven... The saints on earth, like the saints in heaven, do not have a redeemed and resurrected body but possess their natural body which is described as *earthen vessels that the excellence of the power may be of God and not of us* (2 Cor. 4:7). The saints on earth are in Christ, united to Christ in the body of Christ, which is otherwise known as the Church of God. The division between heaven and earth is still there, but the symbiotic relationship between the two is very close and the presence of God can almost be reached out to and touched. The saintly *souls* (20:4) in heaven, who enjoy the most intimate presence of Christ, are commissioned to rule with Him in heavenly places. However, during the millennial reign of Christ and His saints, the strong symbiotic relationship between heaven and earth will be so real that the saintly *priests*, (20:6) who are Christ's vice-regents on earth, will have a united and coordinated *reign with Him (Christ) a thousand years* (20:6). This will be reminiscent of the days of Adam before the Fall in the Garden of Eden (Gen. 1:28; 2:8-25). The creation itself will come into the liberty of the saints, and all true believers will know the profound presence of God in all the means of grace. The non-elect and unbelieving, who will not profess to be unbelieving, will not know the reality of the saint's relationship with their Saviour, the Lord Jesus Christ. They will express a God-fearing disposition and exercise their natural gifts for the benefit of the created order as they will know that, in such service, true freedom is found.

THE DEAD WITHOUT CHRIST REMAIN IN THE PLACE OF THE DEAD UNTIL AFTER THE MILLENNIUM.

Verse 5 speaks of *...the rest of the dead (that) did not live again until the thousand years were finished*. These are those who died without Christ throughout the history of mankind. They are not a subset of God's elect who were the least in the kingdom of heaven or Old Testament saints before John the Baptist. Neither are they carnal Christians, or non-spirit-filled Christians or even Christians who had failed to overcome. All such divisions are known Biblical categories that have been invoked by modern Christianity because of the embarrassing phenomena of false professions of Christ within the Church. I do not want to take up the subject here, but for those who wish to follow this issue through, it is recommended that you read, Tom Wells's book, *Christian: Take Heart!* (1987 Banner of Truth). These are dead people and cannot be likened to saints who are alive in Christ. These are nonbelievers, who enter into eternity without Christ, *who are dead in trespasses and sins in which they once walked according to the course of this world, according to the prince of the power of the air, the spirit who now works in the sons of disobedience...in the lusts of our flesh, fulfilling the desires of the flesh and of the mind, and are by nature children of wrath* (Eph. 2:1-3). These souls remain in the place of the dead without Christ, as they lived in this world, waiting for a time after *the thousand years were finished*, and of course, for all that time until the millennium has commenced. This place of the dead is best described in the parable of "Lazarus and the Rich Man" (Luke 16:19-31). This place is a place of *torments in Hades* (Luke 16:23)—a place that is separated by *a great gulf fixed* (Luke 16:

26), so that there can be no passing between the place of the dead and the dwelling place of the saints in Christ.

THE FIRST AND SECOND RESURRECTION

Of the dead who do not live until the millennium is finished, Daniel the prophet says ...*those who sleep in the dust of the earth shall awake, some to everlasting life, some to shame and everlasting contempt* (Dan. 12:2). This is describing a general resurrection of the living and the dead, which is a bodily resurrection of the same kind as the resurrection of Jesus. The Lord Jesus gives extensive teaching on this general resurrection in the Gospel of John where he says, *Most assuredly, I say to you, the hour is coming, and now is, when the dead will hear the voice of the Son of God; and those who hear will live* (John 5:25). This is also reflected in the words of the Apostle John: *This is the first resurrection...* which means being resurrected with Christ and made alive through the preaching of the Gospel. The precise time of this first resurrection is given to us by the Lord Jesus: *The hour is coming, and now is.* This refers to the entire Gospel age, from the resurrection of Jesus and the establishment of a new creation, to the end of the millennium at which the Lord Jesus Christ will undertake the last great event of the final judgment Himself, seated upon the great white throne (20:11). The first resurrection is experienced only by those who have heard the Gospel of Jesus Christ and who are transformed in regeneration, being united to Christ and His resurrection. As the Lord Jesus states in the Gospel of John: *Most assuredly, I say to you, he who hears My word and believes in Him who sent Me has everlasting life, and shall not come into judgment, but has passed from death into life* (John 5:24). The amillenarian position makes a fundamental error of interpretation at this point, which is understandable because of the position of the words, *This is the first resurrection.* This appears to be referring to what is preceding these words, namely *...the rest of the dead.*[104] As discussed above, the implications of such an interpretation would be a two-tiered Christianity where some were qualified to reign with Christ, while others would not qualify. The subjects of the first resurrection are the saints that live with Christ, and if we do not live with Christ we are dead and have no part with Him. Therefore, the words, *This is...* refer to what follows, which further expands on what the first resurrection is.

However, the rest of the dead who do not live again until after the millennium must await the general resurrection of the living and the dead. The Lord Jesus continues to teach in John's Gospel: *Do not marvel at this; for the hour is coming in which all who are in the graves will hear His voice and come forth – those who have done good, to the resurrection of life, and those who have done evil, to the resurrection of condemnation* (John 5:28-29). Those who have done evil have no part of *the first resurrection* but will now be subjected to what is called *the resurrection of condemnation*. This resurrection will be like to that of Christ's resurrection, which will be a bodily resurrection of an incomprehensible nature with a body that will never die; and in this resurrected body the whole person will be brought before the *great white throne* for judgment and condemnation.

Verse 6 promises: *Blessed and holy is he who has a part in the first resurrection.* The amillenarian commentator, William Hendriksen, sets forth the classic amillenarian interpretation of the first resurrection. It is, he says, The translation of the soul from this sinful world to God's holy heaven. It is followed by Christ's second coming—by the second resurrection when the body, too, will be

---

[104] Kim Riddlebarger, *A Case for A-millennialism: Understanding the End Times*, Baker Books, 2003, p 217).

glorified.[105] Dying and going to heaven is wonderful; but for all its benefits it is not a resurrection. The first resurrection is *a blessed and holy* estate, whether it be on earth or in heaven. In the millennium, there will be *souls* in heaven with Christ and saints on earth who are described as, *priests of God and of Christ, who together shall reign with Him (Christ) for a thousand years*. This passage cannot be describing disembodied saints in heaven, as the context of the millennium is set on earth. The satanic rebellion after the millennium is cast in geographical places that are known only to the earth; namely, *the four corners of the earth* (20:7-9).

A lot of space has been given to this discussion on what the *first resurrection* is; but we should establish conclusive arguments. We cannot refer to the bodily resurrection of the last day, as we have established that there can be only one general resurrection of the living and the dead. To find the answer, we must go back to Genesis, which tells us of the first death: *And the LORD God commanded the man, saying, "Of every tree of the garden you may freely eat; but of the tree of the knowledge of good and evil you shall not eat, for in the day that you eat of it you shall surely die"* (Gen. 2:16-17). Adam and Eve did not die physically on the day that they ate the fruit of the tree of the knowledge of good and evil. That was the day of their *spiritual* death and their alienation from God that would consequently lead to their final physical death. This spiritual death was inherited by the children of Adam (Rom. 5:12-14) so that we are all born *dead in trespasses and sins* (Eph. 2:1). The first death is this spiritual death. Then the first resurrection is spiritual as well *...even when we were dead in trespasses, [He] made us alive together with Christ (by grace you have been saved), and raised us up together, and made us sit together in the heavenly*

---

[105] William Hendriksen, *More Than Conquerors: An Interpretation of the Book of Revelation*, Inter-varsity Press, 1973, *p 192*.

places in Christ Jesus... (Eph. 2:5-6; cf. Col. 2:11-13; 1 John 3:14). The bodily or physical resurrection will take place at the Last Day, when there shall certainly *be a resurrection of the dead, both of the just and the unjust* (Acts 24:15). But would the Apostle John use the term *resurrection* in two radically different senses in the same passage? Yes, and with excellent precedent, because Jesus Himself did so – as recorded by the Apostle John. The first resurrection is stated by the Lord Jesus as follows *...he who hears My word and believes in Him who sent Me has everlasting life, and shall not come into judgment, but has passed from death into life* (John 5:24). He then further describes the general resurrection by saying *...for the hour is coming in which all who are in the graves will hear His voice and come forth – those who have done good, to the resurrection of life, and those who have done evil, to the resurrection of condemnation* (John 5:28-29). So those of us who have heard the Word of God and believe have eternal life and have passed from death to life, and are already partakers of the first resurrection. Our first resurrection is that regeneration that leads to justification and adoption; and the power that is at work in our members brings about that sanctifying grace that unites us to Christ and His resurrection. *Over such the second death has no power* because the second resurrection is, in fact, our glorification, since the works of faith are replete with the works of God who *...does good to the resurrection of life,* completing the full redemption of our bodies.

The partakers of the first resurrection—the priests of God and Christ on earth, and the souls in heaven with Christ—are blessed and holy and the second death has no power over them. The Apostle John began Revelation by informing us that all Christians are priests. He says that Christ *...has made us kings and priests to His God and Father, to Him be glory and dominion forever and ever. Amen* (1:6). Throughout the history of the kingdom of God, those of the first resurrection, who are all true believers, reign with Christ, and as the Bible says, we are now seated with Christ, reigning in His kingdom (Eph. 1:20-22; 2:6; Col. 1:13; 2 Pet. 2:19). We need to understand that, although we are speaking of the millennium in this passage, it would be a great mistake if we failed to recognise that it speaks about this present age that spans the history of the kingdom of God. The Bible is clear that, as partakers of the first resurrection, we have been resurrected to eternal life and rule with Christ *now in this age*. The only variation to the spiritual truth for those that battle in the pre-Christian era of the Gospel age and the Millennium is the *extent* of this rule of Christ and His saints within the kingdom of God. In this Gospel age, the influence of the kingdom of God is ever increasing; and in the millennial age this rule will be comprehensive.

CHAPTER 14

SATAN'S RELEASE FOR A LITTLE WHILE - REVELATION 20

GOG AND MAGOG

The final Satanic rebellion, here disclosed as occurring after the thousand-year reign of Christ and the saints (see the discussion on chapter 17:7-18), looks through the corridor of prophetic history in relationship to the destruction of *the Mother of Harlots*. During the afore mentioned discussion, we saw the parallel description between the figure of *Gog and Magog* and the king or power *not yet come* (17:10). When he comes, he must *be released* and continue *a little while* (20:3), being that seventh king (17:10) who is manifested at the end of the millennium, and who is *...the beast... and with him the false prophet...These two were cast alive into the lake of fire burning with brimstone* for a thousand years (19:20). We also saw in this discussion that there is a lengthy parallel description of this event by the prophet Ezekiel in Ezekiel chapters 38 to 39. In Ezekiel's prophecy, there is a graphic description and specific material of this sinister attempt to snatch authority and usurp God's rule. However, in Ezekiel's prophecy, the timing of this event is not clearly revealed and is somewhere in the distant future. Here, in Revelation 20:7, it is very clear that *when the thousand years have* *expired, Satan will be released from his prison.* The description of Gog and Magog in Ezekiel's prophecy (Ezek. 38:2; 39:1, 6) is that culmination of Satan hatching his sinister reptilian eggs through the Mother of Harlots into the Beast and the False Prophet, who is otherwise described in another place as *the man of sin...the son of perdition* (2 Thess. 2:3), and we will see that it is *the Antichrist* that comes in the last hour (1 Jn. 2:18).

Our purpose here is not to repeat the earlier discussions, but to draw together the various themes into an overall developed picture that is disclosed in this portion of Scripture.

THE THOUSAND YEARS HAVE FINISHED.

Verse 7 gives a time cue. *Now when the thousand years have expired.* This time cue specifically identifies when the event that follows, that is, the satanic rebellion against *the camp of the saints and the beloved city* will begin (20:9). The nations have well and truly recovered from the tectonic events of God's intervention through the seven final plagues outlined in the 16th chapter of the Revelation a thousand years earlier. Looking through Old Testament eyes, the prophet Isaiah describes these days of the millennium in several places such as Isaiah chapters 2 and 65, where the nation of Israel is physically and symbolically at centre stage, with true worship being practised: *Many people shall come and say, "Come, and let us go up to the mountain of the LORD, to the house of the God of Jacob; He will teach us His ways, and we shall walk in His paths." For out of Zion shall go forth the law, and the word of the LORD from Jerusalem* (Isa. 2:3). Wars cease as justice is established between all nations, weapons of warfare are turned into tools of production, and industry engages in peaceful activities, where *they shall beat their swords into plough-shares, and their spears into pruning hooks; nation shall not lift up sword against* *nation, neither shall they learn war any more* (Isaiah 2:4). The whole earth has been repopulated and a Christian culture of righteousness and social responsibility is solidly established across all instruments and institutions of society. There is the godly stewardship of knowledge and resources, where industry and welfare are harmonised and the social order does not exploit the exploitable and the initiatives of the gifted are not used to gather wealth for the sake of having wealth.

This millennial world order will suddenly be disrupted by a hideous event yet to take place for the sake of God's glory. Satan will be released from his prison, which is the bottomless pit (20:3). Satan did not escape from his prison of torment of a thousand years, but was released under God's authority. Satan is released to *sift...as wheat*, (Luke 22:31) as it were, the souls of the unregenerate to rid them of any self-righteousness. During the generations of mankind living in the millennial years, where people were not always pressed to their extremity, God often used instruments in the effectual calling process, so that they call upon the name of the Lord for salvation.

The timing of these final events at the end of history was announced by the prophet Daniel in Chapter 12. It would be difficult to interpret Daniel's prophecy without these words of the Apostle John: *Now when the thousand years have expired, Satan will be released from his prison*. This release will be confined to what is described by John as *a little while* (20:3). After that short period will occur the general resurrection described by John (20:13). This is also described in Daniel's prophecy: *And many of those who sleep in the dust of the earth shall awake, some to everlasting life, some to shame and everlasting contempt* (Dan. 12:2). Then Daniel asks, *How long shall the fulfilment of these wonders be?* (Dan. 12:6), and he is given a cryptic answer: *...that it shall* *be for a time, times, and half a time; and when the power of the holy people has been completely shattered, all these things shall be finished* (Dan. 12:7). Then Daniel ventures to further ask ....*what shall be the end of these things?* (Dan. 12:8), and the answer is given that these prophecies are sealed, *till the time of the end* (Dan. 12:9), which is clearly stated by the Apostle John as at the end of the thousand years, at the conclusion of the satanic rebellion which is crushed by the Lord Himself when ...*fire came down from God out of heaven and devoured them* (Rev. 20:9; cf Dan. 12:16). This is also marked, in terms of time, by the general resurrection of the godly, as well as the ungodly, in readiness for the final judgment at the Great White Throne, upon which the Lord Jesus Christ sits in judgment of the living and the dead (20:11). Daniel was given the answer to his question about when these momentous events would take place at the end of time with the words ...*time, times and half a time* (Dan. 12:7) we are now able to establish these events with the second coming of Christ after the thousand-year reign of Christ and His saints.

Hosea is helpful at this point when he writes: *After two days He will revive us: on the third day He will raise us up, that we may live in His sight* (Hos. 6:2). Hosea here is speaking to Israel concerning their long period without a king, as the Gospel is handed to the Gentiles *until the fullness of the Gentiles has come in* (Rom. 11:25), which is referring to a two-day period. As A.W. Pink puts it: "For almost two thousand years – two days with God (2 Pet. 3:8) – Israel has been without a king...But the second day is almost ended...When the third dawns...**renaissance** shall come!"[106] Therefore, with this disclosure found in the Book of Revelation, there is a coalescence in terms of time revealed to John, Hosea and

---

[106] AW Pink, *Exposition of the Gospel of John* 2:1, Zondervan, Grand Rapids. 1973 p. 81.

also Daniel when he receives the time cue of these days' prophecies ...*time, times and half a time* (Dan. 12:7). A *time* is referring to a *day* of a thousand years and there are two *times* (which is two thousand years), which marks the beginning of the millennium; *half* of that time is of the thousand-year millennium. Then come these momentous events at the end of the millennium that marks *the time of the end* (Dan. 12:9). Whether these events will be presented in the future precisely as stated is a matter of fulfilment, as no one will know the exact *day and hour* of our Lord's coming (Matt. 24:36), but the markers in prophetic history have been set in these passages.

Satan's sinister final work and the appearance of the Antichrist

Verse 8 shows clearly that Satan, as a fallen angel, is a spiritual personage that requires the agency of human presence to carry out his dark schemes of wickedness. So, as Satan is released from the bottomless pit and reaches into every corner of the earth, he *...will go out to deceive the nations which are in the four corners of the earth*. Satan then will no longer have the formal institutions of power that he once had: The Mother of Harlots (with the long tradition of the Antichrist of the papal system and its like); and the Beast (that socio-political edifice that controls matters of state), which is transformed into Babylon the Great (that secular, humanist man-centred world order). He will not have time to construct such a system again as we are told that he will be *released [only] for a little while* (20:3).

Satan goes *to and fro on the earth* and walks *back and forth on it* (Job 1:7). He is able to search out the real spiritual condition of those without Christ, and seduce and organise them into the armies of Antichrist. The clue given here is that the figures of *Gog and Magog* are the human leadership of the released Satan who will make the last and final grab for power on earth. However, this is all under the sovereignty of Christ the King, as it separates and cleanses the company of the saints from the unregenerate who have been quiet in self-righteousness and clothed in false humility. Ezekiel puts it this way: *Thus says the Lord GOD...*"*Thus I will magnify Myself and sanctify Myself [the whole Body of Christ], and I will be known in the eyes of many nations. Then they shall know that I am the LORD"* (Ezek. 38:17, 23). Added to this, Daniel speaks of a great sanctification and this event: *Many shall be purified, made white, and refined, but the wicked shall do wickedly; and none of the wicked shall understand, but the wise shall understand.* (Dan. 12:10).

During the millennial years, Gog and Magog, along with the other eight kings described in Ezekiel 38 and a host of unregenerate non-believers, will exist at peace under the righteousness of the consummated Kingdom of God. The world for a long time will have been demilitarised, the people of the nations will have been governed with great liberty under the Law of the Lord, trust will have been established and there will have been genuine regard among the people. However, as soon as Satan, the father of lies, the usurper (Matt. 8:44) of the authority of Christ the anointed Messiah, is released from the bottomless pit, the non-elect will be herded into the camps of Antichrist. The speed and ferocity of the mobilisation of the forces of Gog and Magog are staggering, and the numbers that are gathered are overwhelming *(...as the sand of the sea)*. Indeed, his strategic weapon is speed and ferocity. The Apostle Paul, in his second letter to the Thessalonians, calls this, *the falling away* that must *come first* before *that Day* of the Lord's Second Advent for the final judgment (2 Thess. 2:3).

Again, the prophet Daniel has revealed this Antichrist as the final and peculiar Antichrist. The strategic campaign is described in Daniel 11:40-45, and a further, more complete description is found in Ezekiel 38 and 39. Daniel gives us a time cue saying, *at the time of the end* (Dan. 11:40), which is clearly a reference to the end of history, namely the end of the millennial era, where the Apostle John marks this Satanic rebellion before the general resurrection and the establishment of the Great White Throne of judgment. The Apostle Paul makes a specific reference to this end-time figure that must come first, which is the end-time revelation of the *man of sin...the son of perdition, who opposes and exalts himself above all that is called God or that is worshipped, so that he sits as God in the Temple of God (the church), showing himself that he is God* (2 Thess. 2: 3-4).

Daniel records that initially there is a division within the forces of Satan where there is *the king of the south* and *the king of the north* (Dan. 11: 40). The king of the south stages an act of provocation by attacking the king of the north. Ezekiel states that *the LORD GOD* speaks to the king of the north: *On that day it shall come to pass that thoughts will arise in your mind, and you will make an evil plan* (Ezek. 38:10). Then the king of the north, otherwise known as the *Gog and Magog*, will respond with the full force of military might against the king of the south *...like a whirlwind, with chariots, horsemen, and with many ships; and he shall enter the countries, overwhelm them, and pass through* (Dan. 11:40). This will have the effect of galvanising one world military force that will appear invincible, ruthless and set on one mission only – *the Antichrist* that will annihilate *the camp of the saints* (20:9).

This situation is further fleshed out by the prophet Ezekiel when he says: *Thus says the Lord God: "On that day when My people Israel [saints] dwell safely, will you not know it? Then you will* *come from your place out of the far north, you and many peoples with you, all of them riding on horses, a great company and a mighty army. You will come up against My people Israel [saints] like a cloud, to cover the land. It will be **in the latter days** that I will bring you against My land, so that the nations may know Me, when I am hallowed in you, O Gog, before their eyes"* (Ezek. 38:14-16).

Ezekiel then describes a figure that was the subject of many prophecies in former times concerning Gog. He says, *Thus says the Lord GOD, "Are you he of whom I have spoken in former days by My servants the prophets of Israel, who prophesied for years in those days that I would bring you against them?"* (Ezek. 38:17). The Apostle John, in 1 John 2: 18, makes a specific reference to this figure that arises at *the last hour* describing him as *the Antichrist... coming*. He elaborates thus: *...even now many antichrists have come* (in the past, probably referring to Daniel's prophecy concerning Antiochus Epiphanies). In the Apocalypse, John further traces Antichrist in the mother of Harlots, the Beast, and Babylon the Great that was a succession of Papal heads who have usurped for themselves the central place that is rightfully Christ's. But John then says that this Antichrist is coming *...by which we know that it is the last hour* (1 Jn. 2:18). This unmistakable event at *the last hour* will be an audacious final grab for power and destruction of *the camp of the saints and the beloved city* (20:9).

THE FINAL BATTLE OF GOG "THE ANTICHRIST" AGAINST THE SAINTS AND THE BELOVED CITY

Verse 9 relates how *They went up on the breadth of the earth and surrounded the camp of the saints and the beloved city.* Ezekiel gives a description of Gog that shows how it has become all-powerful in terms of military might. Gog sees a soft target in what Daniel sees as *the Glorious Land* (Dan. 11:41). Gog, the Antichrist, says, *"I will go up against a land of unwalled villages; I will go to a peaceful people, who dwell safely, all of them dwelling without walls, and having neither bars nor gates"* – *to take plunder and to take booty, to stretch out (my)hand against the waste places that are again inhabited, and against a people gathered from the nations, who have acquired livestock and goods, who dwell in the midst of the land...to take great plunder* (Ezek. 38:11-13). This King of the north, Gog, rampages through nation after nation as Daniel says, *...many countries shall be overthrown; but these shall escape from his hand: Edom, Moab, and the prominent people of Ammon. He shall stretch out his hand against the countries, and the land of Egypt shall not escape. He shall have power over the treasures of gold and silver, and over all the precious things of Egypt; also the Libyans and Ethiopians shall follow her at his heels* (Dan. 11:41-43).

Gog's military campaign is redirected, *...but news from the east and the north shall trouble him; therefore he shall go out with great fury to destroy and annihilate many* (Dan. 11:44). Gog, filled with absolute arrogance and pride, laying a trail of blood and misery of monumental proportions in his wake, will be defeated: *And he shall plant the tents of his palace between the seas and the glorious holy mountain; yet he shall come to his end, and no one will help him* (Dan. 11:45). In God's sovereign purposes, Gog the Antichrist is now in a geographical position between *the sea and the glorious holy mountain* (Jerusalem) and *...he surround[s] the camp of the saints and the beloved city*, which is on the glorious holy mountain. It would seem that the saints who have served faithfully during the millennial years as God's vice-regents, and who are separated and cleansed from the non-elect and unregenerate, are about to be annihilated by the seemingly invincible armies of Gog.

Suddenly the Lord God intervenes when ...*fire came down from God out of heaven and devoured them* (v. 19)—that is, the armies of Gog the Antichrist. A fuller description of this event is received by the prophet Ezekiel in (Ezek. 38:18-22):

> *¹⁸ "And it will come to pass at the same time, when Gog comes against the land of Israel," says the Lord GOD, "that My fury will show in My face. ¹⁹ For in My jealousy and in the fire of My wrath I have spoken: Surely in that day there shall be a great earthquake in the land of Israel, ²⁰ so that the fish of the sea, the birds of the heavens, the beasts of the field, all creeping things that creep on the earth, and all men who are on the face of the earth shall shake at My presence. The mountains shall be thrown down, the steep places shall fall, and every wall shall fall to the ground. ²¹ I will call for a sword against Gog throughout all My mountains," says the Lord GOD. "Every man's sword will be against his brother. ²² And I will bring him to judgment with pestilence and bloodshed; I will rain down on him, on his troops, and on the many peoples who are with him, flooding rain, great hailstones, fire, and brimstone."*

This description continues right into Ezekiel 39 until verse 16, which is a horrifying description of God's final intervention on behalf of His people against the Antichrist. Some commentators think that this description is of a different character from that of the Apostle John in Revelation 20:9, because the only common thing that is mentioned is that *the fire came down from God out of heaven and devoured them*. In Ezekiel 38 and 39, we have *a great earthquake* (38:19-20), *every man's sword will be against his brother* (38: 21), *pestilence and bloodshed, rain[ed] down...flooding rain, great hailstones, fire, and brimstone* (38:22), which is also mentioned from a different standpoint in our text in Revelation.

In Ezekiel 39 the Lord says that He *...will knock the bow of out of your left hand, and cause the arrows to fall out of your right hand*. The whole number of Gog's army will *fall upon the mountains of Israel* and *birds of prey of every sort* and *the beasts of the field* will devour them as food (39:3-4). The Lord will also send fire on Magog, who has made an alliance with Gog as an inferior force, and *those who dwell in the cities of Israel will go out and set on fire and burn* their weapons of warfare and it will take seven years to complete (39:9). It will take seven months for the house of Israel to bury the armies of Gog in the Valley of Hamon *to cleanse the land* (39:13-16). This description is not of a different character but is couched in the era of Ezekiel's prophecy and time. He was using descriptions of instruments of warfare of his own day rather than weapons of the future.

Prophecies such as these will present in ways that will surprise us as there will be a lot of noise going on around them. However, these details will be recognisable as God fulfils them very specifically as recorded. We have demonstrated how the time cues in these prophecies coalesce, and how they all relate to the general resurrection in the last hour at the end of history. The context dictates that these passages in Ezekiel are simply a fuller description of this momentous event of the last rebellion in the personage of Gog the Antichrist.

SATAN IS NOW FINALLY ASSIGNED TO PERDITION

Verse 10 describes how *The devil, who deceived them, was cast into the lake of fire and brimstone where the beast and the false prophet are.* The devil, or Satan, is now assigned to perdition, which is described here as *the lake of fire and brimstone*. The *bottomless pit* to which Satan was bound and thrown for a thousand years was a place of torment, but only a temporary holding pen. *Perdition*, which is eternal hell, is a place of utter darkness and torment of fire where there is no end and no escape. Being of the eternal order, it will contain the immaterial spiritual beings even when the natural order of *the heavens will pass away with a great noise, and the elements will melt with fervent heat; both the earth and the works that are in it will be burned up*. (2 Pet. 3:10). This will not annihilate hell and all it contains. This place must have pre-existed because it is for this place and to this place that the beast and the false prophet were *captured ...[and] cast alive* (19:20). *And they will be tormented day and night forever and ever*. Whatever way we hear it, these are stubborn words. If we were to think about the full implications of such a place, we would soon enter a state of mind like those who are cast into this place—we would become stark, raving mad. These words are Scripture and therefore the very Word of God, not some mediaeval invention.

The effect of this casting out of Satan will be to immediately restore order among the nations and peoples that are still alive. However, their real condition is a proven condition. The non-elect are seen for what they are—reprobate and without excuse. The elect will have demonstrated the excellencies of Christ even under extreme provocation. Technically speaking, the passages are still in the era of the Gospel, and there may be final conversions made even at that late hour, but we are not told about them. It would seem that all is complete and the last hour is upon us. It would seem from the prophecies of Ezekiel that there were some years to pass because we are told it took 'seven months' for Israel to bury Gog's army *in order to cleanse the land* and *seven years* to burn Gog's weapons of warfare (Ezek. 39:9, 12). It is truly the ultimate fulfilment of the risen sovereign Saviour, who sits at the right hand of the Father, and the words of Psalm 110:1 resound across the entire history of the world:

*The LORD said to my Lord, "Sit at My right hand, **till I** make Your enemies Your footstool"* (Psalm 110:1).

CHAPTER 15

THE FINAL JUDGEMENT – REVELATION 20

The Last Day

The doctrine of the Final Judgment is a foundational doctrine of the Scriptures and has been included in every orthodox Confession of Faith throughout the history of Christendom. Scripture is replete with references to this Final Judgment that takes place on the last day after everything is complete.

For example, the last chapter of the Westminster Confession of Faith contains these words:

> **Of the Last Judgment**
> I. God has appointed a day, wherein He will judge the world, in righteousness, by Jesus Christ, to whom all power and judgment are given of the Father. In which day, not only the apostate angels shall be judged, but likewise all persons that have lived upon earth shall appear before the tribunal of Christ, to give an account of their thoughts, words, and deeds, and to receive according to what they have done in the body, whether good or evil.

II. The end of God's appointing this day is for the manifestation of the glory of His mercy in the eternal salvation of the elect, and His justice in the damnation of the reprobate, who are wicked and disobedient. For then shall the righteous go into everlasting life, and receive that fullness of joy and refreshing which shall come from the presence of the Lord; but the wicked who know not God, and obey not the Gospel of Jesus Christ, shall be cast into eternal torments, and be punished with everlasting destruction from the presence of the Lord, and the glory of His power.

III. As Christ would have us to be certainly persuaded that there shall be a day of judgment, both to deter all men from sin, and for the greater consolation of the godly in their adversity, so will He have that day unknown to men, that they may shake off all carnal security, and be always watchful, because they know not at what hour the Lord will come; and may be ever prepared to say, Come, Lord Jesus, come quickly. Amen.

To properly understand this passage, we do need the assistance of other related Scriptures to unlock the sequence of events that takes place at the second coming of the Lord Jesus Christ and the Final Judgment of *the quick and the dead*. When we put together the scriptural material, we are left in no doubt that this is the point of the Lord's second and final coming. Yet in this passage it is not explicitly mentioned. Details relating to the general resurrection are left to other passages which describe it more fully.

THE GREAT WHITE THRONE APPEARS

In **verse 11**, John relates, *Then I saw a great white throne...* The focus of this passage in Revelation 20:11-14 is on the Final Judgment itself; but other related events are going on around this focal point. As suggested earlier, the situation had normalised since the great rebellion of Gog and Magog and the casting of Satan into perdition. It could have been described as the millennial era reformed, but in the economy of God, it was now in the past. The Apostle Paul says *...that the day of the Lord so comes as a thief in the night. For when they say, "Peace and safety!" then sudden destruction comes upon them, as labour pains upon a pregnant woman. And they shall not escape* (1 Thess. 5:2-3). This grand finale of the Lord Jesus Christ's coming and the opening of heaven's portal will strike all the residents of the earth with the greatest suddenness. *A great white throne* that is gloriously great will become visible. It is a white, fiery throne of the Judge of all the earth with its spiritual principalities and powers.

THE SECOND ADVENT

The Apostle Paul continues his description: *For the Lord Himself will descend from heaven with a shout, with the voice of an archangel, and with the trumpet of God* (1 Thess. 4:16). This is not a scene in heaven, but it is Christ's bodily return to earth in precisely the same manner as He ascended into heaven before the very eyes of the gathered multitude on the day of the ascension (Acts 1:11). The great difference between Christ's ascension into heaven forty days after His resurrection from the dead, and His Second Coming will be the overwhelming grandeur of the Coming. It will be a grand entry, and the whole of heaven will commence the royal procedure that is fitting for *the King of kings and Lord of lords*. The grandeur of this glorious event is uniquely described by the Apostle John in this text when he says ...*from whose face the earth and the heaven fled away. And there was no place found for them* (v. 11). This is to say that as the sun rises in the east, its brightness sends the stars and the moon beyond our vision, and we do not know their place anymore in the sky; when the Son of God comes, the sheer glory and grandeur of His presence will make *the earth and heaven flee away.* They will still exist but they will be so out-ranked in terms of their presence that they *flee away.* It will be, as it were, as if the natural order of the earth and heaven will be in suspense in anticipation of the command that will be made by the Word, the very Son of God, who created all things out of nothing by the Word. It is at that time that the Apostle Paul's words in his letter to the Philippians are fully realised: *Therefore God also has highly exalted Him and given Him the name which is above every name, that at the name of Jesus every knee should bow, for those in heaven, and of those on earth, and those under the earth, and that every tongue should confess that Jesus Christ is Lord, to the glory of God the Father* (Phil. 2:9-11). The regenerate and unregenerate, believer and unbeliever, saints and sinners alike will all bow the knee to the Lord Jesus Christ. The dissonance in the wicked will be so strong that his natural craving will be to hide, as Adam hid from the presence of the Lord after the Fall. But there will be *no place for them* [to hide] (20:11).

THE RESURRECTION

Because the Apostle John is focusing on the Final Judgment in this passage, some aspects leading up to the Final Judgment are not mentioned here. The General Resurrection is necessary at this point for what is depicted in verse 12—the assembly of *the dead, small and great, standing before God.* John teaches in his Gospel that *...the hour is coming in which all who are in the graves will hear His voice and come forth – those who have done good, to the* *resurrection of life, and those who have done evil, to the resurrection of condemnation* (Jn. 5:28-29).

We have already seen, in a discussion relating to the souls in verse 4 of this chapter, that those who die in Christ have received eternal life through the Gospel of Christ. When they pass from this world into eternity, their soul goes immediately to be with Christ. As the believer is organically united to Christ in the body of Christ on earth, so he is in the eternal habitations with Christ in heavenly places. His soul is united with the incomprehensible resurrected body of the Lord Jesus Christ and therefore he is not left as a bodiless soul. The Apostle Paul clearly states that the natural body that is left in the grave is yet to receive its redemption because *...The body is sown in corruption, it is raised in incorruption. It is sown in dishonour, it is raised in glory. It is sown in weakness, it is raised in power. It is sown a natural body, it is raised a spiritual body...* (1 Cor. 15:42-44). This redeemed body will be united to the soul upon the Second Coming of the Lord Jesus Christ. Paul continues by saying *...we shall all be changed – in a moment, in the twinkling of an eye, at the last trumpet. For the trumpet will sound, and the dead will be raised incorruptible, and we shall be changed* (1 Cor. 15:51-52). It will be at this point that the final victory is won, because the *last enemy* that Christ overcomes is death (1 Cor. 15:26), and while the dead corpses of the saints lie in the grave, the moans of the devil and his multitude of demons against the sovereignty of Christ can, in a sense, be heard, saying, *We have at least got their lifeless bodies in the pangs of death*. But no such claim can be made against Christ.

This resurrection is in the exact likeness of the resurrection of the Lord Jesus Christ. It was not like the resurrection of Lazarus (Jn. 11:43-44) — that was a resurrection which led to further corruption. Christ's resurrection led to incorruption — to a glorious, powerful, and spiritual body. On the first Resurrection Day, Christ rose from the dead and passed through the material grave-clothes, leaving them in their place, undisturbed, with the face-cloth folded and set aside in a separate place. This was more than a ghost or a spirit; and it could not have been resuscitation. It was truly a bodily resurrection. John, who witnessed this evidence in the tomb where Christ had been laid three days earlier, wrote that he *...saw and believed'* that Christ had truly risen from the dead (John 20:8). This is incomprehensible—a body being a spiritual body yet handling the material world and therefore necessarily being of a material substance; able to eat a meal of fish at the Sea of Galilee; able to pass through closed doors in the upper room and to show His disciples signs of His crucifixion—comprehended by the disciples at times and not recognised by them at other times.

All flesh will be raised on the last day and given an incomprehensible resurrected body. As we have seen in Daniel 12:2, *...many of those who sleep in the dust of the earth shall awake, some to everlasting life, some to shame and everlasting contempt.* However, there is an order that will take place on that day. As Christ appears and is still in the air descending to the earth, there will be *a shout, with the voice of an archangel, and with the trumpet of God. And the dead in Christ will rise first...* (1 Thess. 4:16). The bodies of the saints in Christ will rise from the earth where they lie, and will be united to their souls that are in the body of Christ that is in the air at this particular point. The Apostle Paul continues his description by addressing those that are alive at the moment of Christ's return by saying; *Then we who are alive and remain shall be caught up together with them in the clouds to meet the Lord in the air. And thus we shall always be with the Lord* (1 Thess. 4:17). So those saints that live in their natural bodies that have not been assigned to the grave receive their resurrected body in that *moment, in the twinkling of an eye* (1 Cor. 15:52). Christ knows His own and His own know Him, and there is no culling of the multitudes. So, follows the scene of Christ's triumphal entry to earth with His saints fully redeemed with their resurrected bodies.

THE SECOND OR "GENERAL RESURRECTION" AND THE "RAPTURE"

Verse 12 indicates that there is to be another process at work that begins with Christ's touching down on the earth. This is known as the "general resurrection" previously referred to. There will be the immense multitudes of unbelievers who are all raised into an incorruptible body on the last day. This body will never die, and will be inhabited by an eternal soul. All the dead who are separated from Christ will come forth from the dust, along with those that are present, both *small and great, standing before God.*

Matthew's Gospel records the words of Jesus: *When the Son of Man comes in His glory, and all the holy angels with Him, then He will sit on the throne of His glory. All the nations will be gathered before Him, and He will separate them one from another, as a shepherd divides his sheep from the goats. And He will set the sheep on His right hand, but the goats on the left* (Matt. 25:31-33). The separation process is not a culling process but a selection of the sheep from the goats. "The sheep" is a clear reference to the saints. They are distinguished by their being united to Christ already, because they are selected by being resurrected from their graves among the dead, and the living are lifted into the air from among the masses of the living dead who are separated from their Creator and God.

THE BOOK OF LIFE IS OPENED

And another book was opened, which is the Book of Life. The Book of Life contains the names of all the saints who are secure in the redeeming work of Christ the Saviour. The saints, by their resurrected constitution, are already set to Christ's right side away from any final judgment. There will be a judgment and a reckoning based on their stewardship of God's grace, and there will be vast differences amongst the saints that will be determined by the reckoning of Christ alone. The Apostle Paul says, *For we must all appear before the judgment seat of Christ, that each one may receive the things done in the body, according to what he has done, whether good or bad* (2 Cor. 5:10). This reckoning, albeit a fearful thing, is not unto damnation, but it will be the determining factor in deciding our place in the eternal kingdom prepared for the saints (Matt. 25:34).

And books were opened, which indicates that every thought, word and deed has been recorded, and that nothing is hidden from the God of heaven, for everything that was done to His anointed saints throughout history has been done to Christ Himself, because the company of His people is the very Body of Christ. Every sin is recorded and every detail is established in righteousness and truth. There will be no glossing over of any detail. All will be made clear and nothing will be forgotten or can be forgiven.

THE SCALES OF JUSTICE ARE ABSOLUTE.

And the dead were judged according to their works, by the things which were written in the books. The scales of justice are absolute. God's law is written both in the Word of God and in the created order that bears the stamp of the Creator, including the very conscience of man that has the law written on his heart. And the works of every individual known of God are judged. It must be remembered that all these that are standing before God – both small and great from every nation—have been resurrected in a spiritual body as the saints have. There will be no inability to comprehend or to recall every offence against God. The sheer justice will be incontestable and absolutely true, and there can be no disagreement and no plea; only the words, "Guilty as charged!" These judgments, handed down in true justice, will vary from person to person, because it says that they *were judged according to their works.* All the works of the flesh are sinful, but some are more sinful than others. How this is worked out is left to the wisdom of Christ Himself, but it will be perfect. Hell is an unimaginable place, but there must be some more unimaginable places than others to which some go and others do not.

ALL THE DEAD OUTSIDE CHRIST ARE RAISED WITH AN IMMORTAL BODY.

Verse 13 continues, *The sea gave up the dead who were in it....* Not only will the land-based graves yield their dead in the general resurrection, but the watery graves of the sea will also yield their dead, which would amount to an unimaginable number. We are then told that, *death and hades delivered up the dead who were in them.* This includes the souls of all those departed outside Christ that were in this place called *Death and Hades.* As the bodies of the dead are resurrected from the earth and the sea, so their souls are raised from death and hades to be united with a spiritual body. The subterranean, immaterial, spiritual regions are the dwelling place of the *principalities and powers* (Eph. 6:12), the demons who had dominion but who will yield their fiendish personalities that have already been cast into perdition in *the lake of fire and brimstone* with the devil (20:10). *And they were judged, each one according to his works.* None can escape. All—small and great, rich and poor, bond and free, privileged and squalid—are brought to this place of the Final Judgment.

The logistics of this extraordinary undertaking of the Final Judgment in terms of time is beyond our comprehension, but it will be a perfectly executed procedure, and it will be a matter of fulfilment which every one of us will witness personally.

JUDGMENT IS EXECUTED IN "THE SECOND DEATH."

Verse 14 informs us *Then Death and Hades were cast into the lake of fire*. This means that all the resurrected dead have received their judgment which is executed without undue delay, and the unbelievers are cast into perdition—the *lake of fire*, where the devil, the harlot, the beast and the false prophet have already been cast. *This is the second death*. There is nothing more frightening than the prospect of the second death, because it is a death from which there is no escape. In the most horrendous hell-like situations throughout history, human beings have despaired so greatly in this life that the relief of suicide has been viewed as a far better option. In this situation, however, there is *no* such option, and anything in this world that knew the constant supply of God's common grace and mercies ranks far better than this place called the *lake of fire and brimstone*; for the worm will never die. There will be no release even after a thousand years or a hundred thousand years, for it will grind on and on into all eternity.

OUR NAMES AND THE "BOOK OF LIFE"

Verse 15 continues with this theme. *And anyone who is not found written in the Book of Life was cast into the lake of fire*. The Lord Jesus said this to His disciples after he had sent seventy of them on the mission to teach in Christ's name. When they returned, they saw the powers of the kingdom at work—even the demons were subject to them in Christ's name. The Lord Jesus corrects the priorities of the disciples by saying *...do not rejoice in this, that the* *spirits are subject to you, but rather rejoice because your names are written in heaven* (Luke 10:20). Here we see the reason for exaltation. If our names are not found in the Book of Life, then we have run in vain, because who can save us from such a fate as the lake of fire? As the Lord Himself says, *Not everyone who says to Me, "Lord, Lord", shall enter the kingdom of heaven, but he who does the will of My Father in heaven. Many will say to Me on that day, "Lord, Lord, have we not prophesied in Your name, cast out demons in Your name, and done many wonders in Your name?" And then I will declare to them "...depart from Me, you who practice lawlessness!* (Matt. 7: 21-23).

Our election in Christ has been made sure in His redemptive work for us in calling us, and in allowing us to taste salvation in *the first resurrection* of regeneration, *Over [which] the second death has no power* (20:6). In this alone let us rejoice and be glad!

CHAPTER 16

ALL THINGS NEW– REVELATION 21

NEW HEAVENS AND A NEW EARTH

V 1: In our discussion on the millennium, we looked at the term, *new heavens and a new earth*, and concluded that this is one of many descriptions of the Kingdom of God (20:3). The Kingdom of God is the rule of Christ on earth as well as in heaven, and He renews everything under its influence according to the pattern of Christ's righteousness and holiness on earth as it is in heaven. As to the temporal world of this earth, the best expression of the Kingdom of God on earth will be during the years of the millennium, which is a consummation of the Kingdom of God. Even when the Kingdom of God finds its earthly zenith in *the new heavens and the new earth*, as it were, that is as good as it will be in this temporal world.

In Revelation 21, another heaven and earth are revealed. It is of an entirely different order from that of the temporal world, and is fit for the Son of God, the Christ, and His Bride in the habitation of God Himself, otherwise known as the New Jerusalem.

PASSING AWAY OF THE 'FIRST HEAVEN AND THE FIRST EARTH'

Now that the Final Judgment is complete, the Apostle John sees *a new heaven and a new earth* (21:1), which is an eternal and glorious place that far exceeds any renovated or renewed finite material heaven or earth. The Kingdom of God is eternal and passes into the eternal habitations of God with her citizens and their good works (Matt. 6:19-21). However, that which is not eternal but is, by definition, finite matter, *passes away*. As the Apostle John puts it, *...for the first heaven and the first earth passed away* (21:1). This is to say that it no longer exists. As the creation of the material universe was called into existence out of nothing by the power of the Word in the person of the Lord Jesus Christ, this finite material creation *passed away* into non-existence whence it came. The components of matter, space and time that make up this material universe are, by definition, finite and therefore have a beginning and an end. Such an end is here announced after the Final Judgment when all previous habitations of man here on earth and the material heavens *passed away*. The *first heaven and the first earth* are not to be renewed or renovated, but they simply *'passed away'*, having fulfilled their purpose.

The question may arise, *How is this passing away of the "first heaven and the first earth" going to happen?* The Apostle Peter, in his second letter, says, *...the heavens will pass away with a great noise, and the elements will melt with fervent heat; both the earth and the works that are in it will be burned up* (2 Pet. 3:10). This is a startling piece of Scripture, as at face value it seems to say that the earth at least will simply dissolve or implode into non-existence, and that may well include the entire temporal universe. This verse would seem to be somewhat isolated within Holy Writ. Most commentators are scrambling away from the plainest meaning of this verse, as it is difficult in our modern atheistic, scientific culture to think of this planet melting with fervent heat into non-existence, let alone the heavens of the physical universe passing away with a great noise. It is certainly true that the Apostle Peter states this matter of the *passing away* of the *first heaven and the first earth* in the clearest and most dramatic form of words. However, its teaching is a fundamental premise of Biblical teaching and prophecy that world history and the natural order of this earth will be brought to an absolute end.

Those who wish to interpret the Book of Revelation along amillennial lines speak of the earth continuing as a thoroughly renovated earth, which *is a new earth*, and the heavens, in the physical sense of the word, continuing in exactly the same way as always. The *new heaven* is heaven as we know it in Scripture, which is the place of God, but now *new* in the sense that the glorious drama of redemption is now complete, with the bride of Christ now in her place beside Christ the King. So the passing away of the *first heaven and the first earth* is a spiritual reference to the old world that underwent the redemptive process in Christ and has been entirely renovated or glorified in Christ.[107] This is a kind of post *Day of the Lord* millennium of an earthly reign of Christ and His saints. This interpretation is consistent with a consuming desire to be moderate in our interpretation of the Word of God—like wax that can be modelled to fit our reasonableness in matters eschatological.

---

[107] Kim Riddlebarger, *A Case for Amillennialism, Understanding the End Times*, IVP, England, 2009. Pp 137-8, and Cornelius P. Venema , *Christ and the Future, the Bible's Teaching About the Last Things*, Banner of Truth, Edinburgh, 2008, pp 205-224. Kim Riddlebarger gives only a brief explanation of this view and connects the term, "the new heavens and the new earth" as a renovated earth with Romans 8:18-25. However, the best exposition of this amillennial position is properly made by Cornelius Venema who gives a very complete description of this amillennial construction of the world after the final judgement of God.

The reasoning runs something like this: science has revealed the extraordinary, almost eternal, and even infinite dimensions of our world and is plumbing into the extraordinary vastness of the universe, and to think that they will simply implode into non-existence is absurd to a degree, and any rational or sensible person could only scoff at such an idea.

This interpretation raises more problems than it solves, as it leaves the text of Scripture dancing around the issues. By definition, the temporal material universe is finite and therefore was never intended to be eternal. The doctrines of evolution, which is a construct of Charles Darwin, see the universe in eternal dimensions and fails to understand the metaphysical dimensions that are out of reach of scientific analysis. Such Darwinian evolutionists have just as much difficulty in believing the Biblical account of the creation of the heavens and the earth, where there is no doubt in Scripture that the earth and the heavens of the physical universe were called into existence out of nothing by the power of the Word of God. The reason they have this difficulty is explained by the writer of the Hebrews who says, *By faith we understand that the worlds were framed by the Word of God, so that the things which are seen were not made of things which are visible* (Heb. 11:3). The Biblical evidence for God's creation of the world is as clear as it could be, but without faith in that Word and testimony from God Himself there can be no understanding. Even atheistic scientists concede that the physical material of the universe, which includes the part that we know best, i.e. planet earth, must, by logical definition, have had a beginning, as Isaac Newton's Laws of Thermodynamics require. The physical order of existence is by definition limited in terms of space, matter and time; no matter how vast space is, how large matter becomes, or how long the time is, by the definitions of science itself it is limited and therefore requires an end.

In the amillennial interpretation (even if they do not directly address it), by inference, at this point, heaven and earth are split into two orders of existence, but this is not what the text is teaching. "Heaven" refers to the constellations of the material universe, and earth is part of the universe, as the material of one is the same material as the other, which is otherwise described as the natural order and is under the ravages of corruption and decay. This material universe as an entity passes away, being *the first heaven and the first earth.* To spiritualise this would be inconsistent with what we find in the text. Of course, the earth could conceivably melt with fervent heat and leave the universe as it is, but that is not what the Scripture says. It says explicitly that *the heavens will be dissolved, being on fire, and the elements will melt with fervent heat* (2 Pet. 3:12). When the text refers to a *new heaven and a new earth*, it is referring to the kingdom of God that began with the resurrection of the Lord Jesus and His ascension to the right hand of the Father where *He must reign till He has put all enemies under His feet* (1 Cor. 15:25). At this point, the Lord Jesus Christ has finally come in His glory and the general resurrection has now been effected, which means that *The last enemy that will be destroyed is death* (1 Cor. 15:26). *Then comes the end,* says the Apostle Paul, *when He delivers the kingdom to God the Father, when He puts an end to all rule and all authority and power* (1 Cor. 15:24). The Kingdom of God is that spiritual entity that has its ultimate fulfilment in heaven, which is translated into *a new heaven and a new earth* as a spiritual entity that is also the greatest reality of existence.

So it would seem that it is necessary for the old, finite created natural order to *pass away*. Like a giant seed, it is buried to give way to a resurrected order known as *the new heavens and the new earth,* that will be more glorious than the seed that is disposed of. As the Apostle Paul states it, ...*the creation itself also will be delivered from the bondage of corruption into the glorious liberty of the children of God* (Rom. 8:21). The word "resurrection" as applied to the *new heavens and the new ea*rth is not too strong because the creation in this new order that is spiritual will be established in the likeness of *the glorious liberty of the children of God* that now have an incorruptible resurrected body, which is like the resurrected body of the Lord Jesus. The old seed of the temporal creation has *passed away* and the new spiritual, resurrected universe of another kind of material has blossomed into unsurpassable glory. So, this *passing away* is not the annihilation of life but resurrection that establishes the eternal heavens and earth. This probably assumes the place of the finite in much the same way as Jesus's resurrected body assumed the place of the finite but was gloriously incomprehensible to the finite.

This text in Revelation announces such an end with the words, *...for the first heaven and the first earth had passed away* (21:1). If it doesn't pass away at this appointed time then it must, by logical necessity, pass away in some other appointed time. The difficulty at this point for many Christians is not so much that God has created the heavens and the earth according to the Genesis account of creation, but that this creation is also upheld personally, in all its details, by God the Creator through *the word of His power* by which *all things* consist. (Heb. 1:3) The character of God is consistent; therefore, the so-called laws of nature are consistent, but it is God who maintains that consistency due to His character, otherwise nothing would exist. As the Apostle Paul says, *He is the image of the invisible God, the firstborn over all creation. For by Him all things were created that are in heaven and that are on the earth, visible and invisible, whether thrones or dominions or principalities or powers. All things were created through Him and for Him. And He is before all things, and in Him all things consist* (Col. 1:15-17). So, it is by God's decree alone that heaven and earth exist, and if that decree is suddenly brought to an end, then all things cease to exist. The laws of nature are not perpetual but entirely dependent on their source—the Sustainer in whom 'all things consist'.

THE PASSING AWAY AND RESURRECTION OF THE HEAVENS AND THE EARTH

So, we return to the question, *How will these things take place?* The Apostle Peter answers in unambiguous terms: *...the heavens will pass away with a great noise, and the elements will melt with fervent heat; both the earth and the works that are in it will be burned up* (2 Pet. 3:10). He then repeats this event in similar words: *Therefore, since all these things will be dissolved, (we are)...looking for...the coming of the day of God, because of which the heavens will be dissolved, being on fire, and the elements will melt with fervent heat* (2 Pet. 3:11-12). This speaks of the passing away of the material universe. As a seed is thrown into the ground, so it gives way to the more glorious plant which, *according to His promise*, will be a *new heavens and a new earth in which righteousness dwells* (2 Pet. 3:13). The *heavens will be dissolved* and *the elements will melt with fervent heat*. This describes the very nature of this passing away. The very building blocks of creation itself, the elements of the material universe that we may scientifically describe as the atomic makeup of its material, dissolve and *melt with fervent heat* (2 Pet. 3:12), imploding into non-existence. God Himself decreed that He would no longer sustain the creation of the old order but would institute a more excellent order of greater glory.

Isaiah the prophet foresaw this event and records these words of God, *Lift up your eyes to the heavens, and look on the earth beneath. For the heavens will vanish away like smoke, The earth will grow old like a garment, and those who dwell in it will die in like manner; but My salvation will be forever, and My righteousness will not be abolished* (Isa. 51:6). And later He says, *"For as the new heavens and the new earth which I will make shall remain before Me," says the LORD, "So shall your descendants and your name remain"* (Isa. 66:22).

The Lord Jesus Christ gave much of His teaching with the understanding that the world in its finite existence will end. In the Sermon on the Mount, for instance, where He refers to the absolute enduring truth of God's Word, He says, *For assuredly, I say to you, till heaven and earth pass away, one jot or one tittle will by no means pass from the law till all is fulfilled* (Matt. 5:18).

Just in case we are left in any doubt, the Apostle John sees this distinctive *new heaven and new earth* being of an entirely different order of existence, having *no more sea* (21:1). No matter how thorough the renovation is, this cannot refer to a renovated heaven and earth since it says that such a *new heaven and new earth* had *no more sea*. Some believe, and with good reason, that the ante-diluvial world before Noah was a world without seas and oceans. For that world to be restored, the geological and climatic conditions of earth before the universal flood would have to be completely restored, which is less likely than what our text is saying: *...the first heaven and the first earth passes away,* and it gives birth to a kind of *new heavens and new earth* that will never pass away.

NEW JERUSALEM, COMING DOWN OUT OF HEAVEN FROM GOD

In **verse 2**, the scene is set on "the terra firma" of the new heavens and the new earth that exceedingly surpasses in glory the seed of the old universe, since it is a kind of resurrected heaven and earth that is of the order of the spiritual resurrected body of Christ and His saints. This is incomprehensibly different from the old order of the temporal, finite, material heaven and earth. In this eternal place ...*John, saw the holy city, New Jerusalem, coming down out of heaven from God...* The figure of Jerusalem in the Scriptures is that holy convocation of the saints of God, united into the holy doctrine of the faith, in communion and union with Christ, the sum of all worship and holy discourse. The great church father Augustine of Hippo entitled his book on systematic theology, *The City of God* This title derives from the idea that all true Christian doctrine defines the people of God as saints united to Christ.

This *holy city, New Jerusalem* is that spiritual order that now exists, therefore it is *new*. It is *coming down out of heaven from God*, which means that the very throne of God is still transcendent above *the new heavens and the new earth* even in its most glorified condition. The holy city, New Jerusalem, is a personification of the glorified body of Christ, the Church of God fully redeemed and translated into Christ. The figures of the New Jerusalem and the bride of Christ become one, as conveyed in the description of her as, the *New Jerusalem, coming down out of heaven from God, prepared as a bride adorned for her husband*. The bride of Christ is now fully adorned in the doctrine of Christ with the full number of the elect and is prepared for her husband. The final act of union between Christ and His glorified Church is now consummated. The long-awaited marriage supper has now taken place in heaven.

The appearance of Christ the Husband, together with His bride, to whom He is now united, speaks of the fact that *the marriage of the Lamb has come, and His wife has made herself ready* (19:7). It is a glorious sight that can be likened to a young couple setting out upon their marriage, going to their honeymoon destination, *the new heavens and a new earth*. There is no lengthy description in Scripture of *the marriage supper of the Lamb* (19: 9), but this marriage is solemnised in the very presence of God the Father and God the Holy Spirit in the most sacred place of the Most High.

Such a marriage could only take place after the bodily resurrection of the saints and before the coming of Christ and His Bride to *the new heavens and new earth*. Please refer to the discussion on the Wedding Supper of the Lamb and the Bride under chapter 19:7-9.

Truly, Holy Matrimony

Verse 3 records that *I heard a loud voice from heaven saying, "Behold, the tabernacle of God is with men..."* This voice from heaven is a heavenly announcement of a new order in God's relationship with men. God has tabernacled with His people according to the Covenant of Grace in the wilderness wanderings in the days of the Exodus, where he tented in the midst of the camp of Israel. Later, when Israel became a settled nation, He dwelt in the land of promise until the days of Solomon, when the true and living God resided in the Temple made with hands in the midst of the nation of Israel. After the resurrection of Jesus Christ, He tabernacles spiritually with the Church, the body of Christ, which is a Temple made without hands, made of *living stones...being built up a spiritual house, a holy priesthood, to offer up spiritual sacrifices acceptable to God through Jesus Christ,* being the *chief cornerstone, elect and precious* (1 Pet. 2: 5-6).

In this new heaven and new earth, the Bride *comes down out of heaven from God*, which is the place where the Lord Jesus Christ, in the days of His flesh, told His disciples that He would *go to prepare a place* for them. (John 14:2) But Christ the Husband of the Bride is mystically united to His Bride in an everlasting relationship so that a *loud voice from heaven* says, *Behold, the tabernacle of God is with men...*(v. 3). When the word *men* is used, it is establishing the likeness of the truly resurrected body of individual men who will appear as visible entities that populate the new heaven and the new earth. As a spiritual entity, the individual men are one, united to Christ as His Bride. John's imagery here encompasses all the saints who occupy the city of New Jerusalem. As the Bride of Christ, they enjoy the fulfilment of God promise, foreshadowed in the Old Testament, that God will dwell with them and in them.

He will dwell with them, and they shall be His people. God Himself will be with them and be their God. The uninterrupted communion with His people and with Christ will be continuous and complete in every way because their union with Christ and His people is total. These words are cast in the form of the ancient words of the Covenant with Israel and are invoked in this most perfect relationship with the fully redeemed, adopted and glorified people of the Bride, because the ultimate purpose of the word of Christ in salvation is that *God Himself will be with them and be their God.*

Verse 4 shows us how, in this glorified state, the care of Christ for His Bride will be personal and satisfying. There will be no hurt to cause weeping or even the memory of former trials that might cause sorrow, as God Himself will *wipe away every tear from their eyes*. Death that was always the constant companion in the days of our flesh shall be no more in this place that Christ prepared for His Bride. *Sorrow* and *crying* will be a thing of the past and *there shall be no more pain, for the former things have passed away.*

"IT IS DONE!"

Then, in **verse 5**, Christ who is *the King of kings and the Lord of lords who sat on the throne* is able to say concerning His own work on behalf of the gloriously resurrected order of creation for His Bride, *Behold, I make all things new*. When he says, *all things*, nothing is left undone, everything is complete and not merely renovated but totally *new*.

Then Christ says to His servant John, as he gazes into these extraordinary revelations, *Write, for these words are true and faithful.* John is reassured that this is not some dream of the mind but is true revelation from God that is faithful to all other revelation in Scripture. He is given authority to, *write…these words*, to be included in the corpus of Holy Writ.

Verse 6 continues the conversation between Christ and John. He says, *It is done!* This is to say that everything is now complete and the Covenant of Grace is completely fulfilled, with nothing now left to be done. And with that the Lord Jesus identifies Himself, saying, *I am the Alpha and the Omega, the Beginning and the End.* Using the image of the first and last letters of the Greek alphabet, He uses terms that can be attributed only to God Himself. He is the prime Originator of all things; He the One who supervises all things; all things consist in Him and nothing exists outside Him. He is God alone!

Our Fiancé's encouragements as we wait

Then the Lord Jesus Christ promises wonderful blessings along the way for the people who are reading these words, who belong to the other ages of the Church militant, who are fighting the battles that lead up to this glorious culmination of Christ's final work. There will be those whose eyes are being opened and whose hearts are strangely warmed by the beckoning call of Christ the Saviour, who become thirsty for eternal life, to whom the Lord Jesus promises, *I will give of the fountain of the water of life freely to him who thirsts.* He who asks in his thirst, Jesus will in no wise cast out, but will freely give of the fountain of the water of life.

Verse 7 indicates that there will be others from the former days of the Gospel age who have fought courageously in their earthly battles with the principalities and powers in spiritual places and have overcome as they have looked to the Saviour in faith, according to the will of God the Father. Each one of these is granted a particular promise that *he...shall inherit all things*, as described in chapter 21 of this book of Revelation, with the further promise, *I will be his God and he shall be My son*. That is to say, as the inheritor, each one will be treated as the adopted son who inherits all things that are the Father's.

Verse 8 shows, however, by contrast that some have been given to the perverse works of the flesh and have followed the broad way of the world, who are really, in the end, *cowards*, because they would not make a stand that was unpopular and inconvenient because the Name of Christ was offensive to the world in which they have sojourned. So, they approved and participated as unbelievers did all sorts of abominations. They became angry and filled with murderous thoughts and even committed *murder* through such things as abortion (or at least giving it approval.). They gave in to *sexual immorality* by fornicating before marriage and approving of pornography. Dabbling in false religion and choosing any system of faith that served their own purpose, or even consulting mediums in sheer curiosity, was a casual pastime, and eventually these cowards were given over to worldliness, thus serving the creature rather than Creator in *idolatry*. Misrepresentation, exaggeration and bending the truth in false witness are summed up in the description that such people are *all liars*.

Every thought, word and deed will come under the searchlight of Christ's final judgment. That is graphically and clearly described in these words of the Revelation, particularly *...(they) shall have their part in the lake which burns with fire and brimstone, which is the second death*. The first death is that which we were born into as the sons of Adam, and which could be resolved by trusting in God's promise of the Covenant of Grace in the work of our Saviour Jesus Christ. This first death had its consequences that led to corruption and the departure of the soul from the body that lies in corruption, that is, the estate of death. The second death is a terrifying thing because in the general resurrection, the body of the unbeliever is raised incorruptible and spiritual. Both body and soul, that cannot die, is cast into *the lake which burns with fire and brimstone.*

CHAPTER 17

THE NEW JERUSALEM - REVELATION 21

HERESIES ABOUND!

This passage is extremely difficult to interpret, and a study like this may not reach the depth that this text requires. As one casts one's eyes across the literature associated with the New Jerusalem, the most intricate systems of understanding emerge with the names of Swedenborg, Latter Day Saints (Mormons), Jehovah's Witnesses, Universal Friends, and British Zionism. These are generally described as Restorationist movements. Such movements see the New Jerusalem as a glorious manifestation of a godly order, with the glorified saints dwelling with their Saviour forever in what will be established on a wholly restored earth. In our discussion, and thus far in chapter 21, we have argued for the entire passing away of the finite universe. Any possibility of a restored heaven and earth, which is crowned with a glorious *..New Jerusalem, coming down out of heaven from God*, (v. 2) can lead, and often has led, well-meaning Christian people into error and into trusting in unfounded hope that truncates the real disclosure of Scripture.

Similarly, theologies that have often overwhelmed the Church at this time of history, when secular humanism has been the dominant philosophy. These theologies—such as Emerging Church Theology, Liberation Theology, and Liberal Theology—believe that this world order will evolve into an ideal society and a restored world order. Generally speaking, such theologies can be described as realised eschatologies. Such theologies are a bit like a farmer trusting in the seed of life as an end in itself, rather than trusting in God, who gives life itself and immortality through transformation and resurrection. If the New Jerusalem were simply part of this physical universe, then it would be logical to hide in such a theological construct. We have argued that *the new heavens and a new earth* is of an entirely different order that belongs to heaven itself.

NEW JERUSALEM IS GATHERING IN READINESS FOR THE MARRIAGE OF THE LAMB

We would argue that the New Jerusalem is the gathering in heaven with the Father of the triumphant Church throughout the history of the world. This New Jerusalem is a living city of God made up of the full number of the elect. This entrance into the new heavens and a new earth is the culmination of God's purpose with His Church, but until that time, the Church militant is to testify of a continuing and tireless work of their Saviour on their behalf. The tried and tested Church that is fully sanctified in glorification waits for the adoption of their bodies to be resurrected on the Last Day, waiting in the city of God with the Father, because the Lord Jesus said, *In my Father's house are many mansions...* (John 14:2). This refers to the New Jerusalem, the dwelling place of God with His children. It is right to say that the Church militant is a New Jerusalem due to its connection with Christ in His body, but not glorified and therefore never realised here on earth. The New Jerusalem is entirely of the spiritual order in the same sense that God is spirit, for the true believer, by faith, touches, feels and knows the spiritual reality of God in the New Jerusalem. As the writer to the Hebrews puts it, *These all died in faith, not having received the promises, but having seen afar off were assured of them, embraced them and confessed that they were strangers and pilgrims on the earth…But now they desire a better, that is, a heavenly country. Therefore God is not ashamed to be called their God, for **He has prepared a city** for them* (Heb. 11:13, 16).

The book of Revelation itself intended the reality of the New Jerusalem, both in this world and the next, to be understood spiritually and not in physical or even quasi-physical terms. The Lord says to the Church in Philadelphia, *He who overcomes, I will make him a pillar in the temple of My God, and he shall go out no more. I will write on him the name of My God and the name of the city of My God, the New Jerusalem, which comes down out of heaven from My God. And I will write on him My new name* (3:12). The saints, through their testimony and their faithfulness, will gain through their works of faith, their reward by receiving to themselves the privilege of certain kinds of service within the New Jerusalem. Symbolically, some will be *pillars in the temple of My God* and others may be beams or various other parts within the New Jerusalem. It says specifically that *the twelve tribes* (v. 12) of Israel will be 'twelve gates' with their names inscribed on them.

The physical tabernacle in the wilderness days of the people of Israel was a foreshadowing picture of the true worship of God's people, who today faithfully look to Christ according to the Covenant of Grace. He Himself became the complete sacrifice that brought the true worshiper into communion and union with Christ in the worship of God in spirit and truth (John 4:21-24). The fulfilment of the tabernacle worship was not a physical building but a spiritual practice with the spiritual personalities rendering their role in true worship. The New Jerusalem will not be a physical or even a metaphysical edifice but a living and eternal spirit that is of the same substance and life of God. It is an exact picture of the Bride of Christ herself.

It needs to be said that this picture of the New Jerusalem is a matter of fulfilment rather than an exact allegory. It would be a brave commentator to make hard and fast allegorical constructs of this picture. If we can make some metaphorical connections to the rest of Scripture, we will be doing well.

THE GRAND ENTRY OF THE BRIDE, THE LAMB'S WIFE

Verse 9 describes how *...one of the seven angels...had the seven bowls filled with the seven last plagues...* This spiritual angelic personality, who has apparently seen this disclosure and been a player in the events of *the seven last plagues*, discloses this great event— the grand entry of the bride, the Lamb's wife, to the eternal habitations of Christ and His Church, the very place that the Lord Jesus promised to His disciples when He said, *I go to prepare a place for you...* (John 14: 2).

In **verse 10**, we have a description of how the Apostle John was carried away in *the Spirit to a great and high mountain*, which was a very high vantage point, to see the drama that was to unfold in heavenly places. He was shown *the great city, the holy Jerusalem*. John had seen this event in verse 2, but he had been carried up in the Spirit to this very high mountain so that he could see the events from a panoramic vantage point. From this point, he was able to see many details of this glorified Bride of Christ, that is otherwise described as the New Jerusalem, in her great diversity and her great glory. She *descend[ed] out of heaven from God* for her genesis with her husband Christ, complete in every way with every elect saint, without any spot or wrinkle, the exclusive precious choice of Christ Himself above all other beings. She settles into her eternal abode, never to be assailed by any kind of evil again, in the complete care of her Husband.

THE BRIDE OF CHRIST...HAVING THE GLORY OF GOD.

Verse 11 describes the Bride as *...having the glory of God*. This is the most exalted countenance of any creature in heaven apart from God. No angel or any created thing in heaven or on earth has this description attributed to its personage: *...having the glory of God*. Yet this is precisely how *the bride, the Lamb's wife...the great city, the holy Jerusalem, descending out of heaven from God* (21:9-10) is described. This is not the reflected glory of God (which had to be covered by a veil) that shone from Moses' face after being with God on Mount Sinai, but it is the glory that is attributed to God Himself. She is not God, nor does she become God, for there is only one God the Father, God the Son and God the Holy Spirit who are of the same substance and power. The Bride is not autonomous as God is, for there is only One autonomous Being, the self-existent God who has no beginning and no end. The Bride of the Lamb is subject to her Husband, but she is now of the same substance as her Husband and is one with her Husband in consummated glory.

Her light was like a most precious stone, like a jasper stone, clear as crystal. The light of the New Jerusalem is self-existent light, not reflected light, as she has the purest light of life that is of the substance of God alone, eternal life. This light is *clear as crystal* in pure holiness that is matchless even among the angels. Not only is there no speck or stain of sin or flaw of life; she is separate from any presence that is anything less than royal; she has self-existent pristine holiness that exists only in God Himself.

The perfect Wife!

Verse 12-13 continues, *Also she had a great and high wall with twelve gates and twelve angels at the gates, and names written on them, which are the names of the twelve tribes of the children of Israel.* This *great and high wall* was later measured by an angel to be 144 cubits, which is equal to 65 metres thick, and constructed with the precious stone jasper. The first thing that can be said about the New Jerusalem is that it does include all God's elect from the twelve tribes of Israel and not just those that came into the New Jerusalem in the Gospel era of the New Testament. This includes the whole house of faithful Israel, of both the Old and New Testament eras. Indeed, there are three open gates in each wall that were set in a large quadrangle and each wall was 12,000 furlongs long, which is equal to 2200 km square. The gates face the four points of the compass, *three gates on the east, three gates on the north, three gates on the south, and three gates on the west*. This indicates that the Gospel went out to all the earth, with the free offer of the Gospel to all nations at every point of the compass, and the people freely came into the new Israel. New Jerusalem is inclusive of all elect Jews and Gentiles and none will be lost.

Verse 14 gives more details. *Now the wall of the city had twelve foundations, and on them were the names of the twelve Apostles of the Lamb*. The foundation of the walls of the New Jerusalem is the completed canon of the Scriptures, with which the Apostles were charged. The complete word of Christ, both Old and New Testaments, is the foundation of the city of God. The Lord Jesus Christ personally appointed the twelve Apostles in the days of His flesh. They were witnesses of the resurrected Christ, and by the revelation of God's written, prophetic word, they recorded *in these last days* (of the Old Testament era, i.e., the age of the Apostles) the full Word of Christ, spoken *to us by His Son, whom He has appointed* *heir of all things, through whom also He made the worlds.* (Heb. 1:1-2) The names of the twelve Apostles are inscribed on these foundations, and include the Apostle Paul—as the self-confessed least of the Apostles—but not the Church-appointed Apostle Matthias.

In **verse 15**, we are told, *And he who talked with me...being one of the seven angels who had the seven bowls filled with the seven last plagues* (21:9), *had a gold reed to measure the city, its gates, and its wall.* The righteous standard of the Law of God, which faithfully describes the righteousness of Christ, (which is the royal law, [James 2:8] that is the law of liberty [James 2:12]) is used to measure the New Jerusalem. Its measurements are true and there is no failure of righteousness; its whole construction is perfect in all its proportions and it is perfect in its symmetry and geometry.

Verse 16 tells us further that *the city is laid out as a square; its length is as great as its breadth.* This geometry is unambiguous and straightforward, and its righteousness is absolute, no matter how you measure it. Its righteousness is perfect and complete.

And he measured the city with the reed: twelve thousand furlongs. Its length, breadth, and height are equal. This is an immense structure and its sheer presence is commanding. There is no city of man anywhere on earth that has such proportions of 2200 km square and cubed. And yet when measured in terms of its absolute righteousness, it is exact and symmetrically in proportion. The city of God is perfectly governed by a righteous standard that has no peer, because it is the righteousness of Christ, tested and tried and found perfect.

Verse 17 continues the measuring *Then he measured its wall: one hundred and forty-four cubits, according to the measure of a man, that is, of an angel.* Sometimes the term *an angel* (such as each of the angels of the seven churches 2:1, 8, 12, 18; 3:1, 7, 14) in the book of Revelation refers to the anointed messenger of God, such as the preacher of the Word of God, and this is likely a reference to such an anointed one. One-hundred-and-forty-four is 12 squared, which very probably refers to the preaching of the whole Word of God. This has been achieved by both the angels or the messengers of the Word of God in the Old Testament, and the twelve tribes of Israel and the preachers of the Word of God in the New Testament era, as fully disclosed by the twelve Apostles of the Lamb. Throughout all the ages, to every generation, the ministry of the Word of righteousness has affected the building of a New Jerusalem, and of such ministry of the Gospel of righteousness, the walls of the city of God are in perfect order and perfect proportion.

Verse 18 has a further description. *The construction of its wall was of jasper; and in the city was pure gold, like clear glass.* The whole city of God is made of precious materials. ...*its wall was of jasper... the city was pure gold,* but not any ordinary gold. This gold is so pure that it is like no gold on this earth, *like clear glass*. The Apostle Peter uses a similar reference to gold when he speaks of the labours of the saints in the Gospel: ...*that the genuineness of your faith, being much more precious than gold that perishes, though it is tested by fire, may be found to praise, honour, and glory at the revelation of Jesus Christ...* (1 Pet. 1:7).

Verses 19-20 elaborate further. *The foundations of the wall of the city were adorned with all kinds of precious stones...* We saw earlier that the names on the foundations were the names of the twelve Apostles. It is now further revealed that each of these foundations was made of precious stones. It seems significant that the precious stones mentioned here are the same variety and kind that existed in the breastplate of the Old Testament high priest (there may be some variation, depending on the translation used). The great High Priest, the Lord Jesus Christ, is the foundational basis of access to God and therefore is part of this living city, the New Jerusalem. There is no coming to God, whether it is in the Old Testament or the New Testament, except through Jesus Christ our High Priest who said, *I am the way, the truth, and the life. No one comes to the Father except through Me* (John 14:6).

Verse 21 describes the gates: *The twelve gates were twelve pearls: each individual gate was of one pearl.* The twelve gates were all made of one type of precious jewel, *one pearl.* This was a pearl of such great price and there is nothing on earth with which it can be compared. I would suggest that this is the precious pearl referred to in Jesus's parable: *...who, when he had found one pearl of great price, went and sold all that he had and bought it* (Matt. 13:46). Though there are twelve gates, there is only one Gospel. Any separate Gospel for the Jews that includes the rebuilding of the temple is a blasphemy of the first order and is a direct denial of the Gospel. Such a Gospel has no part in the New Jerusalem.

No temple!

Verse 22 makes the declaration, *But I saw no temple in it, for the Lord God Almighty and the Lamb are its temple.* The symbolism of a temple was obsolete because the substance of the temple is personified in the Lamb of God, who has completed His work. The bride is entirely united to God the Son, and his mediatorial work on her behalf is complete and perfect. Even the Church militant, who awaits her place in the glorified New Jerusalem, worships her Saviour and sustainer in *spirit and truth* (John 4:23, 24) without the *weak and beggarly elements* (Gal. 4:9) of a physical temple. The sum of every individual part of the New Jerusalem is itself the very temple of God for it is in perfect union and communion with her Husband the Lamb of God. *Coming to Him as to a living* *stone, rejected indeed of men, but chosen by God and precious, you also, as living stones, are being built up a spiritual house, a holy priesthood, to offer up spiritual sacrifices acceptable to God through Jesus Christ* (1 Pet. 2:4-5). *Jesus Christ Himself being the chief cornerstone, in whom the whole building, being fitted together, grows into a holy temple in the Lord, in whom you also are being built together for a dwelling place of God in the Spirit* (Eph. 2:20-22). These words are spoken to the Church militant who is not yet glorified, and even to the souls of those who are glorified but who are not yet bodily resurrected (that takes place at the last day) yet part of the New Jerusalem, that holy dwelling place of God's elect saints. Yet in this grand entry of the bride of Christ in her individual glory, composed of her many parts, the New Jerusalem is complete and glorious surpassing any previous estate before the wedding feast and her marriage with the Lamb, her husband.

Verse 23 conveys that glorious truth that *the city had no need of the sun or of the moon to shine in it, for the glory of God illuminated it. The Lamb is its light.* As the Apostle John is gazing on this panoramic spectacle, he may have asked, *Where is the Lamb?* The answer is, "In the glorious light of the New Jerusalem." The light is everywhere in this living city. Even the individual stones are not like earthly stones that block light, but in the New Jerusalem every individual stone, metal or cultured, emits its own self-generating glorious light because *the Lamb is its light*.

These words are further evidence that the New Jerusalem is not some restored physical material of some thoroughly renovated world in this solar system. This city of the New Jerusalem is part of a completely new order of existence that is removed from this finite universe that we have affirmed has *passed away*.

THE NEW JERUSALEM IN THE PAST

Verse 24 gives further information about the City. *And the nations of those who are saved shall walk in its light, and the kings of the earth bring their glory and honour into it.* The New Jerusalem is a historical entity as well as an ever-present eternal reality. In the days of its formation, the Church militant and the Church triumphant waited for its consummation, in this glorious event of *...the holy city, New Jerusalem, coming down out of heaven from God, prepared as a bride adorned for her husband* (21:2). Its illustrious history, which spans the entire history of the Covenant of Grace, sees whole nations, or people groups who are saved and who walk in the life of the New Jerusalem. We also see its kings, who bring their glory and honour into this glorious gathering place of the saints that is otherwise called the New Jerusalem.

Verse 25 gives further encouragement. *Its gates shall not be shut at all by day (there shall be no night there).* During the history of the New Jerusalem, the Gospel has gone out into the four corners of the earth, gathering in the great multitude of the elect and even their nations in fulfilment of the great commission, *Go therefore and make disciples of all the nations...* (Matt. 28:19). The Gospel was freely offered and was not denied to anyone; all who came found the doors of the New Jerusalem opened to them. Every day was the day of salvation and, even in the darkness of some periods of its history, there was no time that was night. There was no time that the people, effectually called, were refused because the gates of the Gospel would never be closed as there was *no night there*.

Verse 26 reveals *And they shall bring the glory and the honour of the nations into it.* This was particularly so in the days of the consummated kingdom of God, during the sustained period where the saints reign with Christ for a thousand years in the millennium.

However, there was the work of God's grace that worked throughout all generations. Believers in every generation were found faithful in their works, so that the Lord Jesus Christ had pre-eminence and, as the humble saint witnessed to Christ, he *inherit[ed] the earth* (Matt. 5:5) and rendered *the glory and the honour of the nations* into the New Jerusalem. Through their good works that were wrought in the Gospel, as they forsook the world of this life and stored up treasures in heaven, the New Jerusalem was further adorned.

Verse 27 serves as a warning: *But there shall by no means enter it anything that defiles, or causes an abomination or a lie, but only those who are written in the Lamb's Book of Life*. There is absolute assurance that, in the New Jerusalem, there will not be a repeat of what happened in the Garden of Eden at the time of the fall of mankind. This is no grand experiment but a society that has been thoroughly tested and tried and knows good from evil. There will by no means enter within the walls of the city anything *that defiles or causes an abomination or a lie*. Here is the very sanctum of God Himself where His very character and personage insure against any malignant spirit that would suggest the possibility of rebellion. This insurance is absolute because the fixed number of those written in *the Lamb's Book of Life* is an unconditional guarantee that nothing will happen or can happen outside the omnipotent, omniscient and omnipresent nature of God Himself. Besides, there is another absolutely secure place: The dry, black, dreary dungeons of perdition, the very lake of fire and brimstone. As the Lord Jesus says to the rich man concerning Lazarus, who had been gathered to his father Abraham, *And besides all this, between us and you there is a great gulf fixed, so that those who want to pass from here to you cannot, nor can those from there pass to us* (Luke 16:26).

CHAPTER 18

THE TREE OF LIFE- REVELATION 22

THE VERY LIFE OF GOD HIMSELF DIRECTLY SUSTAINS HIS NEW JERUSALEM

Verse 1 gives a continuing picture of the New Jerusalem. *And he showed me a pure river of water of life, clear as crystal, proceeding from the throne of God and of the Lamb.* The focus is now on the life of the participating parts or persons of the city of God. There is no disconnect between the inner sanctum of God Himself and the city of God, the New Jerusalem. This is the bride of Christ who makes her grand entry into the place that the Lamb prepares for her (John 14:2), the new heaven and the new earth (21:1).

In Ezekiel's prophecy, there is a flowing river that comes out from under the glorious self-existent temple that has no human origin. It flows into the whole land of God's people, even beyond the vast oceans of the world (Ezek. 47:1-12). This is a picture of the age of the Gospel that commenced with the resurrection of Jesus and concludes on the Last Day before the great white throne of judgment. The Holy Spirit was poured out as the great river of healing and gave satisfying sustenance to all God's elect, both Jew and Gentile. We have maintained that the New Jerusalem exists throughout all generations of Gospel history from the day of the Gospel promise in Genesis 3:15 to the day of her glorious entrance into the specially prepared *new heaven and new earth*. As the New Jerusalem is being perfected with the gathering of the glorified saints in heaven, the same means of life that sustains the New Jerusalem is also at work in the "Church militant" throughout all the ages. There is no temple in the New Jerusalem because it is the very sanctum of God Himself, that is, *My Father's house*, to use the words of Jesus to His disciples (Jn. 14:2).

Now this *...pure river of water of life, clear as crystal, proceeding from the throne of God and of the Lamb* is the very life of God Himself that sustains the holy city of God. This does not make a god of the holy city but does exalt the bride of Christ to the highest in heaven.

Christ the Tree of Life in Time and Eternity, on Earth and in Heaven

Verse 2 gives more details. *In the middle of its street, and on either side of the river, was the tree of life, which bore twelve fruits, each tree yielding its fruit every month...* The river of life courses throughout the New Jerusalem in sumptuous supply and there is no part of the city that has less than another part. In Ezekiel's vision of this river of life, there are *swamps and marshes [that] will not be healed; they will be given over to salt* (Ezek. 47:11) during the ministry of the Church militant. There is no such place in the New Jerusalem. The river is all-embracing. The streets of gold, being as it were the highways of righteousness, are awash with this crystal-clear river, God the Holy Spirit, on both sides. On either side of the river is a variety of tree that exists everywhere throughout the New Jerusalem. This mystical figure, the tree of life, is equally accessible to all parts of the City of God. This is the source of eternal life, the Lord Jesus Christ Himself, the Husband of the bride in His omnipresence.

Indeed, *the tree of life* existed in the knowledge of Adam and Eve, but they did not partake of its fruit. The believer, as he comes to faith in the Lord Jesus Christ, receives eternal life, and thus, as it were, participates in eating all its gracious fruit, which is always sufficient in every circumstance for the believer within the Church militant. However, here in the New Jerusalem, there is a superabundance, for these trees yield fruit monthly and not only annually. This means that the superabundance of eternal life is inexhaustible and, dare we say, this grace is more than sufficient. Indeed, the tree of life *bore twelve fruits*. To interpret such an expression is not easy as we can search the Scriptures and find far more graces in Christ than twelve. The point is that the *tree of life* is unlike any other tree we know because it produces a great variety of fruit that would satisfy any wish or desire. As this tree of Christ is superabundant in His yield, He is also limitless in the diversity of His fruit that sustains the incomprehensible nature of the resurrected body of the New Jerusalem that is in herself incomprehensible to us in her ontological diversity.

The leaves of the tree were for the healing of the nations. The medicinal qualities of the leaves on the tree of life are also incomparable because they can heal the nations. This would indicate that the memory of the nations that exist within the New Jerusalem is real. The days of the Church militant were arduous and filled with suffering, and the trials for that short season were sharp and poignant. Not that the believer will feel that these sufferings were in vain, but all will be able to say with the Apostle Paul, *For I consider that the sufferings of this present time are not worthy to be compared with the glory which shall be revealed in us* (Rom. 8:18). However, in Christ of the New Jerusalem, the tree will serve a medicinal purpose and will heal the wounds of all previous suffering; even their memory will no longer hurt.

The Kingdom of God eternal

Verse 3 reveals that no accusation or curse will be able to be levelled against the New Jerusalem. *And there shall be no more curse, but the throne of God and of the Lamb shall be in it, and His servants shall serve Him.* Christ the Lamb is always the answer to any such petition, and the eternally damned will have absolutely no grounds to file any such suit. The advocate, the Lord Jesus Christ, will be seated upon the throne as God and as the Lamb who has fully paid the price for any sin that may well be in the memories of the damned. The undivided and all-consuming service of all the incalculable heavenly hosts will be to continuously offer worship and undivided service to the Lamb with His bride. The bride, which is the very body of Christ, will be entirely vindicated in her husband the Lamb, who has completed His work on behalf of His wife.

Saints see God's face personally, sealed, sanctified and secured

Verse 4 has still more encouragement. *They shall see His face, and His name shall be on their foreheads.* Among the great heavenly hosts, there will be those who are worthy to gaze upon the countenance of the Most High. In Isaiah's vision of the throne room of God, in Isaiah 6, the seraphim served and worshipped in the glorious presence of God, but they covered their faces and their feet with their wings as they approached the glory of God. Every individual part in the New Jerusalem will have its own glory according to their works and testimony of that part of the body of Christ. However, they shall see the Most High's face and He shall set God's name on each forehead. It is as if they will wear a signet ring bearing the name of the Most High God, the Lamb that gave them full access.

Verse 5 continues the encouragement. *There shall be no night there: They need no lamp nor light of the sun, for the Lord God gives them light. And they shall reign forever and ever.* The New Jerusalem's situation is always, and has always been, in a place other than this world or under these seasons of the solar system. This place in the presence of God is self-existent and not at all dependent upon its context. There is no interdependency and she exists on the basis of God's existence. As we have stated earlier, there is no need for light, for the New Jerusalem is its own light because God in her is light.

Every individual part of the New Jerusalem will rule with differing degrees of authority, but always under the authority and with the authority of God Himself.

CHAPTER 19

A FINAL EXULTATION – MATTER OF URGENCY

INTRODUCTORY NOTES

WHEN DID PREDICTIVE CANONICAL PROPHESY CEASE?

In an unpublished work on the Book of Revelation entitled *The Great Tribulation* we observed the following regarding the "cessation" question: "This prophetic disclosure comes at the end of an introductory age known as the *last days* of the Old Testament (Heb. 1:1). The complete canon of the Old and New Testament Scriptures are about to close and revelational prophecy was now to *cease* (Heb. 1:1-2; 1 Cor. 13:8) as it is now perfect."[108] Jesus Christ is the final prophet spoken of by Moses saying, *I will raise up for them a Prophet like you from among their brethren, and will put My words in His mouth, and He shall speak to them all that I command Him* (Deut. 18:18). The Apostles were directly appointed by

---

[108] Westminster Confession of Faith, Chapter 1:1 puts it this way, *"therefore it pleased the Lord, at sundry times, and in divers manners, to reveal himself, and to declare that his will unto his Church; and afterwards, for the better preserving and propagating of the truth, and for the more sure establishment and comfort of the Church against the corruption of the flesh, and the malice of Satan and of the world, to commit the same wholly unto writing; which maketh the Holy Scripture to be most necessary; those former ways of God's revealing his will unto his people being now ceased."*

the Lord Jesus Christ Himself to inscripturate the word of God that was now fully incarnate in His own person and work. The Apostle John records in his Gospel the words of Jesus: *'These things I have spoken to you while being present with you. But the Helper, the Holy Spirit, whom the Father will send in My name, He will teach you all things, and bring to your remembrance all things that I said to you* (John 14: 25-26). Now the capstone or the final piece of this revelation is being disclosed to "His servants," through the Apostle whom Christ "loved" particularly (Jn. 13:23; 21:7).

This Revelation of Jesus Christ occurred at a time when the Apostle John was incarcerated for his testimony to Christ. He was in a Roman penal settlement on the island of Patmos in the Mediterranean Sea opposite Asia Minor (1:9). There has been a considerable amount of discussion amongst the commentators as to when this revelation was disclosed to John. Most have suggested a later date of A.D. 96 or 110 during the Diocletian persecution. This was a devastating period for the Church, as this persecution was general and brutal. This late-date theory would make the Apostle John an extremely aged man who would not be able to endure the kind of hard labour that was inflicted upon prisoners at Patmos. Also, there is no reference to the momentous apocalyptic event of the age which is described in Jesus's Olivet Discourses as recorded in the synoptic Gospels: the destruction of Jerusalem with her Temple under the Roman general Titus. It seems unbelievable that such a historical event that was pivotal for future history would not be even alluded to in the book of Revelation.[109] The most

---

[109] Of course, those who hold to a partial or full preterist position of the book of Revelation can see all the symbols, characters and themes described in the book of Revelation as applying only to this event. They do this because they are driven by the belief that all prophecy must be fulfilled before the end of the Apostolic Age—see Luke 21:22, which reads: *These are the days of vengeance, in order that all things which are written may be fulfilled.* This text's setting clearly refers to AD 70. The full preterist takes this to mean that *'all*

obvious reason why it is not mentioned as an historical event in the book of Revelation (or for that matter in any other part of the New Testament) is that when the book was given to the Apostle John, this event had not yet happened. The Revelation, therefore, is dated at another time when a very violent but geographically localised persecution by the Romans against the Church in Rome and its region was taking place under the megalomaniac Emperor Nero around A.D 64-68. It would seem that the Apostle John had been caught up in this persecution and exiled to the Isle of Patmos. It was while the Apostle John was imprisoned this first time during the reign of Nero that the book of Revelation was written for circulation around A.D. 66-67.[110] This was after all other inspired Gospels, history and letters had been completed, leaving the book of Revelation to complete the Canon of Scripture. There is historical evidence that the Apostle John ministered in Asia Minor and particularly in Ephesus between the reign of Nero (that ended in A.D. 68) to around the beginning of Emperor Diocletian's brutal reign (that ran from A.D. 81 through to 96).[111]

"THE SOON PROPHECIES"

There is now a change of atmospherics in the remaining part of the book of Revelation as it begins on a concluding sequence

---

of Scripture' finds fulfillment in AD 70. We will discuss the preterist position throughout these notes.

[110] Kenneth L Gentry, *Navigating the Book of Revelation*, Good Birth Ministries, South Carolina, Chapter 2, p. 30, concludes "When we consider all the evidence pro and con regarding Revelation's compositional date we discover that we may make a compelling case for a pre-70 date. In that Revelation is something of an "occasional epistle" ministering to people under dire circumstances (e.g., Revelation 1:9; 6:9-10), we would expect that the internal indicators would betray his date. And as we see, they do. John almost certainly writes Revelation around A.D. 65-66."

[111] See the excellent discussion by Gentry, *ibid.*, Chapter 2, pp. 13- 29.

of exultations *to everyone who hears the words of the prophecy of this book* (22:18). Those that hold to a preterist position on the Olivet discourses of our Lord Jesus particularly and the book of Revelation, have made a wonderful contribution in warding off an attack against the inspiration and authority of the Word of God, and particularly against those on 'the soon prophecies' of our Lord. The German liberal theologian and medical doctor Albert Schweitzer in his book *The Quest for the Historical Jesus*,[112] examined many of the promises of Jesus such as the prediction found in Matthew 26:64, where Jesus said to Caiaphas the high priest at His trial, *It is as you said. Nevertheless, I say to you, hereafter you will see the Son of Man sitting at the right hand of the Power, and coming on the clouds of heaven*. The fulfilment of this prophecy would necessitate Jesus Himself being seen by Caiaphas the high priest in his lifetime, *sitting at the right hand of the Power, and coming on the clouds of heaven*. This could not be referring to some afterlife experience, because it is Jesus that *come[s] on the clouds of heaven*, not Caiaphas coming to Jesus as his Judge on a day of judgment, though that may happen for Caiaphas. Schweitzer, being a Christian theologian, advised Christians that, although Jesus could not fulfil His many promises on this subject immediately, they should follow Him anyway for Jesus was worthy of our trust. This, of course, is an inadequate response, and the atheist Bertrand Russell played havoc with these so-called unfulfilled promises of the Lord Jesus. In his book *Why I Am Not a Christian*, Russell points at every one of these predictions of Christ as failures of fulfilment, leading Russell to discredit Christ and repudiate Christianity.[113]

---

[112] Albert Schweitzer, *The Quest for the Historical Jesus*, (trans., W. Montgomery, A. & C. Black, 1910).

[113] Russell delivered this lecture on March 6, 1927 to the National Secular Society, South London Branch, at Battersea Town Hall. Published in pamphlet form in that same year, the essay subsequently achieved new fame with

On this subject, the preterists present a solid case for the infallibility and authority of Scripture. They address these allegations more than adequately as they deal with the texts relating to the promises made in the Olivet discourses concerning the destruction of Jerusalem and its temple that occurred in A.D. 70, which led to the casting off of the nation of Israel for what has now been a prolonged season. Christ's promises of an imminent return were perfectly fulfilled in this AD70 event and the events leading up to the Roman destruction of Jerusalem. Much Evangelical eschatology would have to be reformed if we were to accept the preterist argument that the entire Olivet discourses of the Lord Jesus were fulfilled in A.D. 70. However, if we are unable to look at Scripture afresh in the light that these preterist theologians have shed on the subject, then people like Schweitzer and Russell have an argument that seriously undermines Scripture, which I find unacceptable and outrageous.

This is not the place to enter into an exhaustive discussion on the Olivet discourse of Jesus, but it does relate to the passage that we are about to deal with in that many preterist theologians maintain that the entire book of the Revelation, except for the passage that we are about to deal with, was also fulfilled in the destruction of Jerusalem and its temple in A.D. 70. In American circles, this is known as "full preterism." The passage we are about to look at is their so-called 'soon prophecies' that look very similar to the 'soon prophecies' of Jesus that were used in the Olivet discourse.

When interpreting the book of Revelation—whether we hold an amillennial, postmillennial, premillennial or even preterist position on the passage—the fact remains that this portion of the

---

Paul Edwards' edition of Russell's book, *Why I Am Not a Christian and Other Essays* (1957).

Apocalypse occurs after everything, and we are all living nearly two thousand years after the events of A.D. 70 and the writing of the book of Revelation. To remain orthodox, whatever position we hold, we have to acknowledge that the general resurrection has not yet occurred. If the General Resurrection has not yet occurred, neither has the Final Judgment and the descending of the New Jerusalem in all her glory. Jesus says, *Behold, I am coming quickly!* (22:7, 12). Then, if we are left in any doubt, in the second-last verse of Scripture, the Lord Jesus emphatically says, *Surely I am coming quickly* (22:20). So even the preterists have great difficulty at this point because we are living two thousand years after John was given this Revelation, and these final very orthodox theological events are still to occur.

I believe that if we see the book of Revelation from a historicist perspective, then we have a more than adequate solution to these 'soon prophecies' of Jesus. With the writing of the final book that closes the Canon of Scripture (written, we believe, sometime before the destruction of Jerusalem in A.D. 70), [114] the predictive requirement of prophecy also ceased. The Lord Jesus has given us a prophetic voice for all generations in the book of Revelation. The Apocalypse is history in a prophetic genre. The book of Revelation is a prophetic word for every generation, and everything in this book has particular application for every believer because his time is short and we cannot afford to miss one day in the scheme of things that this prophecy announces. The battles are intense, the judgments are continuous, and the institutional enemies of the Antichrist are relentless in every generation and every season. However, the New Jerusalem is gathering its fullness and perfecting its glory as each elect saint that is in the Lamb's book of life

---

[114] Kenneth L Gentry, *Before Jerusalem Fell, Dating the Book of Revelation*, American Vision, 1998. Kenneth Gentry presents an excellent case in this very scholarly volume for the authorship of the book of Revelation before A.D. 70.

passes from the Church militant into the Church triumphant. From the standpoint of eternity, our Lord Jesus Christ in His omnipotent, omnipresent and omniscient power is always with every redeemed saint even *in the valley of the shadow of death* (Ps. 23:4). To the saints He says, *Behold I am coming quickly... Surely I am coming quickly* (22:7, 20). We are never alone in the midst of any circumstance. In every situation, in every generation throughout the history of the Church militant, we are encouraged by the promise: *And the Spirit and the bride say, "Come!" And let him who hears say, "Come!" And let him who thirsts come. Whoever desires, let him take the water of life freely* (22:17).

The chart below may help to focus on the "soon prophecies" of the Lord Jesus in a way that is helpful to unravel some of these prophecies.

THE SOON CUES IN PROPHETIC PASSAGES OF SCRIPTURE

The SOON cues in prophetic passages of Scripture can refer to two separate technical terms, i.e., THE LAST DAYS prophecies and THE LAST DAY prophecies.

The term THE LAST DAYS (plural) refers to the last days of the Old Testament dispensation, which concluded formally in A.D. 70 with the destruction of Jerusalem and its temple, casting off Israel for what is now a prolonged season. The apostolic age is a transition that was appointed by God through his twelve Apostles and lasted for a period of some 40 years between the passing away of the Old Testament dispensation and the institution of the New Covenant (Gen. 49:1; Isa. 2:2; Micah 4:1; Acts 2:17; 2 Tim. 3:1; Heb. 1:2; James 5:3; 2 Pet. 3:3).

The term THE LAST DAY (singular) refers to the end of history where the general resurrection and the Final Judgment are instituted after the final satanic rebellion at the conclusion of the millennium (John 6:39, 40, 44, 54; John 11:24; John 12:48).

THE LAST DAYS	THE LAST DAY
Preach to Israel until Christ comes	**When the whole company of saints is "shattered"**
Matthew 10:23; 24:14, 15	Daniel 12:7 (This is at the end of history because it is in the context of the general resurrection)
All the Apostles were still alive at this point, but only "some" would be at the end	**Seal the book—the time is <u>not</u> near** Daniel 12: 4,9
Matthew 16:27, 28; John 21:22	
Not "at the door" now, but will be when they see these things happening	**Heaven & Earth will not pass until** Matthew 5:17, 18 (Jots & Tittles) (End of history prophecy)
Matthew 24:33	
Tribulation will come in this generation some time, so watch for the signs to know when it is near	**General Resurrection–Last Day** (Meaning the end of history) John 6:44
Matthew 24:21-31	
All will be fulfilled Luke 21:22	**The Mystery and Redemption would be consummated in those days** (This is at the end of history because it is in the context of the general resurrection) Daniel 9:24 12:1-13 Ephesians 1:9-14

The powers of the heavens will be shaken	**How long until the end? When the power of the holy people is completely shattered**
Matthew 24:29, 35	Daniel 12:6-9 (During the last great apostasy after the millennium.)
The End of Age coming (Meaning the end of the Old Testament age and casting off of Israel)	**Get out of (Harlot-Beast),** His coming is near
	Revelation 18:4 (This is a pre-millennial prophecy)
Matthew 24:3, 6, 14	22:6, 7, 10, 12, 20
"this generation"	**Tribulation in the Great Apostasy at the end after the Millennium**
Matthew 24:34; Luke 21:32; Mark 13:30	1Thessalonians 4:13-5:11; 2 Thessalonians 1:4-2: 2
Apostasy Will Come	**Do not seal the book—the time is at hand**
False Teachers, Prophets, and Christs	Revelation 22:10
Matthew 24:10-14;	Note: The book of Revelation is a prophetic word for every generation and everything in this book has particular application for every believer because his time is short and we cannot afford to miss one day in the scheme of things that this prophecy announces.
Jude 18, 19; 2 Peter 3:3; etc.	
Redemption will be near at that time	**Heaven & Earth are ready to pass away**
	Hebrews 12:28; 2 Peter 3:13; Revelation 21
Luke 21:31; 19:11-27	
Kingdom will be near when you see these signs taking place	**Last Hour—**
	1 John 2:18
Luke 21:31-32	

They will inherit the kingdom when Christ returns

Matthew 25:34

Apostasy Had Already Begun

1 John 2:18; 2 Thessalonians 2:7

Note: These are prophecies relate to the rise of the Antichrist and his institutional forces of the Harlot, Beast and Babylon the Great along with the false prophet. These forces are prominent throughout the Gospel era but are bound and thrown into the bottomless pit for 1000 years during the millennium. At the conclusion of the millennium, 'Satan will be released from his prison'. The result will be a great apostasy and a great multitude of the citizens of the millennium will be carried away.

Historical Fact: Most of the Apostles except John were dead by AD 70. James had died in AD 44, and several others in AD 63.

Redemption Is Near Now

Romans 8:23

Ephesians 1:14; 4:30

They were seeing all the things happening, He was "at the door" now
James 5:9

Tribulation Now Happening:
Acts 11:19, 14:22; Romans 5:3; 2 Corinthians 1:8-11; 1 Thessalonians 1:6, 3:3; Revelation 1:9; 7:14

Peter refers back to OT prophecies and claims fulfilment of all is near.
1Peter 4:7

The Day is Approaching
Hebrews 10:25

In a very little while
Hebrews 10:37

Time At Hand, Shortly
Revelation 1:1-3, 7-8

End is near
1Peter 4:7,17

Time for judgment
1Peter 4:17

Coming Is At Hand
James 5:8, 9

Continuous prophesies in their season

Isaiah 65:1-66:24 (heaven and earth) (Advancement of the Kingdom of God and its consummation in the millennium)

Times and Epochs: Daniel 2:21 Acts 1:7

Satan and his seed would be crushed: Genesis 3:15; Matthew 23:33; John 8:41-44 (Cross of Christ)

Kingdom was very near, or had arrived. They were receiving the inheritance: Hebrews 12:28; James 2:5; 2 Peter 1:11; Revelation 11:15; 22:10

Satan To Be Crushed Soon! Romans 16:20; 1 Peter 5:1-10; Revelation 22:6, 7

The Mystery and Redemption were now being consummated: Revelation 10:7; 12:10; 21:1-22:21

How long until the martyrs are vindicated? It will only be "a little while:" Revelation 6:10, 11; Luke 18:8

The marriage supper has come: Revelation 19:7-9

The hour to reap has come: Revelation 14:15

This probably raises many questions in the reader's mind and, although it is not directly addressing the text that we are about to look at, there needs to be an adequate response to the questions raised. Right in the middle of all the Olivet discourses, whether it be in the Gospels of Matthew, Mark or Luke, we have a few verses that speak of the coming of the Son of Man, referring to Christ (Matt. 24:29-30; Luke 17:24; 21:25; Mark 13:24-26).

> *29 Immediately after the tribulation of those days the sun will be darkened, and the moon will not give its light; the stars will fall from heaven, and the powers of the heavens will be shaken. 30 Then the sign of the Son of Man will appear in heaven, and then all the tribes of the earth will mourn, and* **they will see the Son of Man coming on the clouds of heaven with power and great glory** *(Matt/ 24:29-30).*

> *And there will be signs in the sun, in the moon, and in the stars; and on the earth distress of nations, with perplexity, the sea and the waves roaring (Luke 21:25).*

> *For as the lightning that flashes out of one part under heaven shines to the other part under heaven,* **so also the Son of Man will be in His day** *(Luke 17:24).*

> *24 But in those days, after that tribulation, the sun will be darkened, and the moon will not give its light; 25 the stars of heaven will fall, and the powers in the heavens will be shaken. 26* **Then they will see the Son of Man coming in the clouds with great power and glory** *(Mark 13:24-26).*

Most of us would automatically want to render these verses in terms of the final coming of our Lord on the Last Day. The context of these verses would militate against such an interpretation on linguistic grounds. However, on theological grounds we want to put these verses at the end of world history because they seem to belong there. To do this, we face several difficulties. In each case, there is a qualifying text after this teaching that maintains that the *generation* that Jesus is speaking to, namely *this generation* of the Apostles, *will by no means pass away till these things take place* (Matt. 24:34-35; Mark 13:30; Luke 21:32-33). And just in case we are tempted to rationalise this away by interpreting *this generation* as the age of the Gospel, our Lord emphatically underscores this soon saying by asserting, *heaven and earth will pass away, but My words will by no means pass away.*

The events surrounding these passages are very localised and would demand a strongly Palestinian application; to skip more than two thousand years ahead is to break all sorts of linguistic contextual rules. In Matthew's Gospel, for example, chapters 23, 24 and 25 have their most natural contextual unity when taken together.

The Old Testament refers to this event in several places in the context of the Babylonian captivity under Nebuchadnezzar in the year 597 B.C. The same apocalyptic language was used at that time by Isaiah, Ezekiel and Daniel. The Babylonian captivity was a great revolution as the people of God were carried into exile from the Promised Land, in covenantal judgment. They witnessed the destruction of the Temple, the stars of heaven and the shaking of the foundations of the earth so that their universe was no longer recognisable.

For the stars of heaven and their constellations
Will not give their light;

The sun will be darkened in its going forth,
And the moon will not cause its light to shine (Isa. 13:10).

All the host of heaven shall be dissolved,
And the heavens shall be rolled up like a scroll;
All their host shall fall down
As the leaf falls from the vine,
And as fruit falling from a fig tree (Isa. 34:4).

When I put out your light,
I will cover the heavens, and make its stars dark;
I will cover the sun with a cloud,
And the moon shall not give her light.
All the bright lights of the heavens I will make dark over you,
And bring darkness upon your land,"
Says the Lord GOD (Ezek. 32:7-8).

In AD 70, an even greater revolution took place such as had never happened in the history of Israel. This was a complete revolution because Israel had become *cast away, broken off* the vine for now a long season, to make way for the Gentile nations to be *grafted in* (Rom. 11). Daniel speaks of this in terms of the Son of Man's coming on this occasion with the Kingdom of God handed to others, so *all peoples, nations, and languages should serve Him* (Dan. 7:14).

I was watching in the night visions,
And behold, One like **the Son of Man,**
Coming with the clouds of heaven!
He came to the Ancient of Days,
And they brought Him near before Him.

Then to Him was given dominion and glory and a kingdom,

That all peoples, nations, and languages should serve Him.
His dominion is an everlasting dominion,
Which shall not pass away,
And His kingdom the one
Which shall not be destroyed (Dan. 7:13-14).

It should be noted that this crucial prophecy is found in the book of Daniel at chapter 7 and not at the end of his sequence of prophecies in chapter 12, which is definitely talking about Last Day events such as the general resurrection. The point is that the very words of our Lord Jesus Christ spoken in the Olivet discourses to His disciples concerning His coming and the *casting off* of His people Israel to include the Gentiles are found in this passage of Daniel. This could not have happened at the end of history – that would have to have occurred when Israel was *cast off*, which is clearly taught by the Apostles during the apostolic years between the ending of the Old Covenant and the institution of the New.

The difficulty we have is that we have a fixed opinion on how the event of the coming of the Son of Man will look. As we have discussed before, many of these prophecies will have a lot of noise surrounding them, but the important issue is that of fulfilment, and when we see it we will know that this prophecy is indeed fulfilled. Many eyewitnesses will see the same prophecy from different vantage points and they will see different things, but all will agree that this is indeed truly a fulfilment. When it says that *the Son of Man is coming on the clouds of heaven* (Matt. 24: 30), what will that look like? Will it mean some fluffy, material substance is going to lower the Lord Jesus Christ onto the ground? Or is it going to be a form of the Shekinah glory that will somehow accompany our Lord's coming? We cannot tell. Indeed, do these prophecies require that Christ come in His glorified flesh on 'terra firma'? There is no evidence in these prophecies that requires such an interpretation. Certainly, when our Lord comes on the Last Day at the Final Judgment it is very explicit that He will *so come in like manner* (Acts 1:11) as He was received into heaven on the day of His ascension, witnessed by a great company of disciples. But in these prophecies of the Olivet discourse and of Daniel's prophecy, there is no such requirement.

Interestingly, there were eyewitnesses at the time of the destruction of Israel and its temple that recorded phenomena that look very much like a fulfilment of the Olivet prophecies of our Lord. The following is a quotation from the Jewish and Roman historian Josephus, who was not a Christian, and not even sympathetic to Christian New Testament prophecy:

Josephus Wars 6:5:3

Angelic Armies in the clouds surrounding Jewish cities "Chariots and troops of soldiers"

(288) Thus were the miserable people persuaded by these deceivers, and such as belied God himself; while they did not attend nor give credit to the signs that were so evident, and did so plainly foretell their future desolation; but, like men infatuated, without either eyes to see or minds to consider, did not regard the denunciations that God made to them. *(289)* **Thus there was a star {d} resembling a sword, which stood over the city, and a comet, that continued a whole year. *(290)*** Thus also, before the Jews' rebellion, and before those commotions which preceded the war, **when the people were come in great crowds to the feast of unleavened**

bread, on the eighth day of the month of Xanthikos *{e}* [Nisan], (Niese: April 25, Capellus: April 8) *and at the ninth hour of the night, so great a light shone around the altar and the holy house, that it appeared to be bright daytime; which lasted for half an hour. (291)* This light seemed to be a good sign to the unskilful, but was so interpreted by the sacred scribes as to portend those events that followed immediately upon it. *(292) At the same festival also, a heifer, as she was led by the high priest to be sacrificed, brought forth a lamb in the midst of the temple. (293)* Moreover, the eastern gate of the inner [court of the] temple, which was of brass, and extremely heavy, and had been with difficulty shut by twenty men, and fastened with iron-bound bars, and had bolts sunk very deep into the firm floor, which was there made of one entire stone, was seen to be *opened of its own accord about the sixth hour of the night. (294)* Now, those who kept watch in the temple, came hereupon running to the captain of the temple, and told him of it; who then came up there, and not without great difficulty was able to shut the gate again. *(295)* This also appeared to the common people to be a very happy prodigy, as if God thereby opened to them the gate of happiness. But the men of learning understood it, that the security of their holy house was dissolved of its own accord, and that the gate was opened for the advantage of their enemies. *(296)* So these publicly declared that the signal predicted the desolation that was coming upon them. Besides these, a few days after that feast, on the twenty-first day of the month of Artemisios [Iyyar], (Niese: June 8, Capellus: May 21) *(297) a certain prodigious and incredible phenomenon appeared: I suppose the account of it would seem to* *be a fable, were it not related by those who saw it, (298) and were not the events that followed it of so considerable a nature as to deserve such signals; for, before sunsetting, chariots and troops of soldiers in their armour were seen (299) running about among the clouds, and surrounding the cities.* Moreover, at that feast which we call Pentecost, as the priests were going by night into the inner *{f}* [court of the] temple, as their custom was, to perform their sacred ministrations, *they said that, in the first place, they felt a quaking, and heard a great noise, (300) and after that they heard a sound as of a great multitude, saying, "We are departing from here."* But, what is still more terrible, there was one Jesus, the son of Ananus, a common man and a husbandman, who, four years before the war began, and at a time when the city was in very great peace and prosperity, came to that feast whereon it is our custom for everyone to make tabernacles to God in the temple, *{g} (301)* began suddenly to cry aloud, *"A voice from the east, a voice from the west, a voice from the four winds, a voice against Jerusalem and the holy house, a voice against the bridegroom and the bride, and a voice against this whole people!" (Jer. 7:34)* This was his cry, as he went about by day and by night, in all the lanes of the city. *(302)* However, certain of the most eminent among the populace had great indignation at this dire cry of his, and took up the man, and gave him a great number of severe stripes; yet he did not either say anything for himself, or anything peculiar to those who chastised him, but still went on with the same words which he cried before. *(303)* Hereupon our rulers supposing, as the case proved to be, that this was a sort of divine fury in the man, brought him to the Roman procurator; *(304)* where he was whipped till his bones were laid bare; yet he did not make any supplication for *(Mt 24:24-26)* himself, nor shed any tears, but turning his voice to the most lamentable tone possible, at every stroke of the whip his answer was, "Woe, woe to Jerusalem!" *(305)* And when Albinus (for he was then our procurator) asked him, "Who he was? and from where he came? and why he uttered such words?" he made no manner of reply to what he said, but still did not stop his melancholy dirge, till Albinus took him to be a madman, and dismissed him. *(306)* Now, during all the time that passed before the war began, this man did not go near any one of the citizens, nor was seen by them while he said so; but he every day uttered these lamentable words, as if it were his premeditated vow, **"Woe, woe to Jerusalem!"** *(307)* Nor did he give ill words to any of those who beat him every day, nor good words to those who gave him food; but this was his reply to all men, and indeed no other than a melancholy presage of what was to come. *(308)* This cry of his was the loudest at the festivals; and he continued this dirge for seven years and five months, without growing fulfilled in our siege, when it ceased; *(309)* for as he was going around upon the wall, he cried out with his utmost force, "Woe, woe to the city again, and to the people, and to the holy house!" And just as he added at the last, "Woe, woe to myself also!" there came a stone out of one of the engines, and smote him, and killed him immediately; and as he was uttering the very same presages he gave up the ghost.

Josephus is a reliable and respected historian both from a Jewish and Roman perspective. Eusebius, the Christian historian who was a contemporary of Josephus during these events, records similar phenomena and recommends that people read Josephus on this account. These are not inspired records and we do not recommend that our case rely upon these records, but the Scriptural arguments are strong and resolve all sorts of questions in terms of the inspiration and reliability of Scripture.

The only other thing that needs to be stated at this point is that when we speak of the coming of Christ, there are many comings of Christ but there is only one final coming of Christ at the Day of Judgment. The character of the final coming outranks any other recorded coming in terms of glory. Our Lord is intensely involved in every providential work throughout history and in every detail in the affairs of this world and man. On this occasion of A.D. 70, Christ came in dreadful judgment. Before this, our Lord personally came to the Apostle Paul *to reveal His Son in me* (Gal. 1:16) to prepare him for the office of Apostle. As a result, the Apostle Paul bore all the marks of a true Apostle, including being a witness to the resurrected Christ and being appointed directly by the Lord Jesus Christ Himself, as the other eleven were. It is said that there have been great baptisms of the Holy Spirit in revival, and witnesses of such revivals are deeply impressed and filled with the fear of God because of the deep presence that is almost physical attributed to the presence of Christ Himself. Jonathan Edwards, the highly respected New England and American spiritual figure, records such phenomena in a book called *Surprising Conversions*.[115] Also in the sacraments there is a real presence of Christ that transforms the believer at worship. These are not conclusive arguments, but it does help us to look a bit wider as we seek answers to the so-called "Second Coming of Christ," which itself is not a Biblical term.

---

[115] Jonathan Edwards, *Jonathan Edwards on Revival, A Narrative of Surprising Conversions,* Banner of Truth, Edinburgh, 1958, pp 7-74.

Notes on the Text

"These words are faithful and true."

Verse 6 gives reassurance to John. *Then he said to me, 'These words are faithful and true." And the Lord God of the holy prophets sent His angel to show His servants the things which must shortly take place.* The Apostle John was reassured that this was not a fantasy or a dream but was sober propositional truth that in itself is the capstone of the Holy Scriptures as a canon complete, both the Old and New Testaments, the 66 books of the Bible.

These particular words of the book of Revelation are a prophetic voice to the churches throughout the history of the Church militant; these words also relate to the Church triumphant. The last book of The Canon of Scripture, the Revelation, had been written by A.D. 70. With the destruction of the City of God, Jerusalem, along with its temple, God's prophetic voice ceased. However, the prophetic deposit of the book of Revelation, which also draws heavily upon the Old Testament prophets, is in itself the continuing prophetic voice of God which describes future events so that the Church militant is not crushed for lack of knowledge. Every part of the book of Revelation makes up the whole, and in every generation, no matter what circumstance or situation may face the believer or the Church militant as a whole, there is a mysterious truth opened up in the book of Revelation that will explain the spiritual forces at work and the historical events that pertain all around them. There is an obvious sequence and order of events that will be successively fulfilled. Therefore, from that point of view, some things are yet to be fulfilled but other things are being fulfilled and still others have been fulfilled.

THIS PROPHECY IS THE FINAL WORD — CHRIST IS ALIVE AND ACTIVE NOW.

Nevertheless, the book of Revelation as a whole is alive and active now, as the words of this prophesy are in no way sealed up, and everything is on the front foot, poised to happen. The battles are intense, the judgments are continuous, and the institutional enemies of the Antichrist are relentless in every generation and every season. However, the New Jerusalem is gathering its fullness and perfecting its glory as each elect saint in the Lamb's Book of Life passes from the Church Militant into the Church Triumphant. Verse 7 gives an urgency to the passage. *Behold, I am coming quickly! Blessed is he who keeps the words of the prophecy of this book*. In light of what has already been said in the Introductory Notes of this section of our discussion, the words, *Behold, I am coming quickly!* are undoubtedly referring to the Mount Olivet discourses of our Lord, when He is predicting the destruction of Jerusalem, with its temple and the *casting off* of ethnic Israel for a prolonged season. In Matthew 24:30, we read of *the Son of Man coming on the clouds of heaven with power and great glory*. This will take place during the lifetime of *...this generation that will by no means pass away till all these things take place* (Matt. 24:34). The Lord Himself intervened on behalf of the Church militant in A.D. 70.

We who live at the end of two millennia are living in a most momentous age, in a world that angrily defies God, and yet the Church of the Lord Jesus Christ is found in a tiny minority in every corner of the earth. She is in the wilderness, hard-pressed on every side. God is powerfully at work revealing His wrath *against all ungodliness and unrighteousness of men, who suppress the truth in unrighteousness* (Rom. 1:18). The true Bible-believing Church is seeing apostates going out from her and has been deeply compromised, and it appears that the days of the Gentiles are fulfilled. The Antichrist in the form of the harlot, the beast and Babylon the Great is very much at centre-stage. The false prophet in Mohammedanism is seizing nation after nation and war is inevitable. The direct intervention of God is needed; but without being specific in our predictions (because there is a lot we do not know) we can confidently say in the words of our Lord, *Behold, I am coming quickly!* As the Lord does intervene, our greatest need is to be clean and focused on one thing; God is at work, we must be found faithful and about our Master's work.

The book of Revelation is not a book about which to speculate. It is those who are spiritually alive and who are conforming to the image of our Saviour Jesus Christ that come into the blessing of the prophecy of this book. Our greatest need is to be better Christians in thought, word and deed. At the end of the Sixth Bowl of God's Wrath amid devastating interventions of God, our Lord announces, *Behold, I am coming as a thief. Blessed is he who watches, and keeps his garments, lest he walk naked and they see his shame* (16:15).

JOHN'S SIN

Verses 8-9 describe the misplaced action of John. *Now I, John, saw and heard these things. And when I heard and saw, I fell down to worship before the feet of the angel who showed me these things.* The Apostle John was so overwhelmed by the glory of what he had seen in these visions, he became unhinged in his disposition and began to worship the greater that had shown him these things and not the Greatest of the Most High. The angel who had been used of God to pour out one of the bowls of the wrath of God corrected John by saying, See *that you do* not *do that. For I am your fellow servant, and of your brethren the prophets, and of those who keep the words of this book. Worship God.* Mere mortals are easily impressed, but there is only one that is worthy of worship—the

Most High God alone. In the end, an angel is but a servant of God, as glorious as he may appear.

THE TIME IS AT HAND

Verse 10 relates this instruction to John: *And he said to me, "Do not seal the words of the prophecy of this book, for the time is at hand."* The prophecies of Daniel—and particularly the last chapter of Daniel—were to be closed because their fulfilment was far off and the sequence of prophetic events was not activated until the coming of the Ancient of Days and the Son of Man. Now He has come, and the words of the prophecy of this book have been written. Although the Canon of Scripture has been closed, and the predictive element of prophecy is no longer required, the words of this book are not to be sealed but to remain open so that the Church militant has a word of prophecy throughout the age of the Gospel even to the end. These prophecies are continually giving the Church a prophetic word concerning the things that *are at hand* throughout all the generations that read the words of this book.

BY THEIR WORKS YOU SHALL KNOW THEM

Verse 11 conveys a solemn warning. *He who is unjust, let him be unjust still; he who is filthy, let him be filthy still; he who is righteous, let him be righteous still; he who is holy, let him be holy still.* Jesus said, *You will know them by their fruits. Do men gather grapes from thornbushes or figs from thistles? Even so, every good tree bears good fruit, but every bad tree bears bad fruit. A good tree cannot bear bad fruit, nor can a bad tree bear good fruit. Every tree that does not bear good fruit is cut down and thrown into the fire. Therefore by their fruits you will know them* (Matt. 7:16-20). This is not to say that those who are unjust cannot be converted, as many who have committed the most hideous crimes have graciously been called into life by the power of the Gospel. The Apostle Paul, for example, was knocked off his horse and transformed by God's grace on the Damascus Road. However, without the sustaining grace of the Holy Spirit, there cannot be a righteousness that will please God. For those that do walk by faith and are exercising the righteousness of God, the exhortation is not to grieve the Spirit but to walk in the graces of righteousness and holiness. Unless the root of the matter is in our hearts, we cannot accomplish the works of faith in the Lord Jesus Christ.

No Time To Speculate

Jesus says, "My reward...is given to everyone according to his work" and quickly!

Verse 12 underlines the issue of imminence. *And behold, I am coming quickly, and My reward is with Me, to give to every one according to his work.* Without going into the "soon" statements again, let us be reminded that every Christian in every generation is in a race, and time is always at a premium. Every Christian has his own purpose and his own path that the Lord Himself is personally directing him to walk. This walk will always be a walk that is according to faith in the Lord Jesus Christ alone, and God never calls His people to do things that He Himself is not enabling them to do. As we walk by faith, we will need the power of God to uphold us in a work that only God can do; this is what we call the works of faith. As we faithfully look to the Lord, the righteous works of faith will be accomplished. Accordingly, the Lord rewards and gives His inheritance according to a person's works and not according to his profession. Our words may speak of our intention, but our works in the Lord Jesus Christ speak of what we are.

This is not a future reward only but also a present blessing that comes from our Lord as we show faithful service in the kingdom of God. When our Lord Jesus was counselling the rich young ruler (who was stumbling at the sin of covetousness, which is idolatry) on how to inherit eternal life, He lovingly said to him, *You still lack one thing. Sell all that you have and distribute to the poor, and you will have treasure in heaven; and come, follow me* (Luke 18:22). The young man *went away very sorrowful, for he was very rich* (Lu. 18:23). Jesus went on to say to His disciples that *it is easier for a camel to go through the eye of a needle than a rich man to enter the kingdom of God* (Lu. 18:25). But the citizens of the kingdom of God have received eternal life because of the work of God that was *impossible with man but possible with God* (Lu. 18:27). He reassured the disciples, *Assuredly, I say to you, there is no one who has left houses or parents or brothers wife or children, for the sake of the kingdom of God,* **who shall not receive many times more in this present time, and in the age to come eternal life.** As Christians, the testimony of the rich rewards that come to us from Christ directly is manifold and glorious. As we glorify God, the children of God are lavished with His blessings. Our greatest difficulty is that these blessings should not become our focus; our true joy should be in the Lord Himself. The immediacy of these blessings is a reminder of the supernatural work of our Saviour and Lord that comes to us regularly and even constantly. *Therefore, since we have this ministry, as we have received mercy, we do not lose heart* (2 Cor. 4:1).

Verse 13 reminds us that the absolute sovereignty of God forms the background of this entire book. *I am the Alpha and the Omega, the Beginning and the End, the First and the Last.* The Lord Jesus Christ is the sum of all things, and in Him all things consist from the beginning of all eternity to the end of all eternity and beyond eternity itself.

Verse 14 contains one of the many beatitudes in this book. *Blessed are those who do His commandments, that they may have the right to the tree of life, and may enter through the gates into the city.* The best expression of righteousness is found in the commandments of God. If we are walking by faith in the Lord Jesus Christ, we will see ever-increasing conformity to the commandments of God. We must know our Saviour and know that in Him there is no unrighteousness. In the work of salvation, He glorifies His Father and God the Holy Spirit because He is *just and the justifier of the one who has faith in Jesus*. Thus He grants His righteousness, which is perfect and complete and is apart from the law, as a free gift credited to the account of every believer. The tree of life, the very person of the Lord Jesus Christ, satisfies the Lord our God on our behalf, which gives us entrance to the delectable fruits of the tree of life, which may also be called the gift of eternal life, the very life of God Himself.

As the believer is made like Christ and refashioned into His image, he learns to die to his sin and live unto the righteousness of our Lord Jesus Christ. He grows in sanctifying grace, which is that growing assurance, and on that day that comes soon in every believer's life, we will boldly go through the pearly gates of the New Jerusalem and be assigned to the place of our eternal abiding residence.

THE THINGS WHICH ARE IMPOSSIBLE WITH MAN ARE POSSIBLE WITH GOD. (LUKE 18:27)

Verse 15 forms a contrast to the previous verse: *But outside are dogs and sorcerers and sexually immoral and murderers and idolaters, and whoever loves and practices a lie*. Without the essential Christ-like inner constitution, wrought by the power of Gospel in Christ Jesus alone, that enables one to walk according to the Spirit and not according to the flesh, there can be no good works in the righteousness of God. On the contrary, we find here every religious substitute known to mankind. Indeed, there will be some that are so self-deluded, that so closely mimic the ministry of the Gospel, that they seek to justify themselves according to this ministry. Their evangelicalism looks so like the real thing that they will come to the Lord on their day of reckoning and say to Jesus, *Lord, Lord.* Notwithstanding this profession of orthodoxy, they shall not enter the kingdom of heaven, as that is reserved for *he who does the will of My Father in heaven.* (Matt. 7:21). God is not mocked! *Many will say to Me in that day, "Lord, Lord, have we not prophesied in Your name, cast out demons in Your name, and done many wonders in Your name?" And then I will declare to them, I never knew you; depart from Me, you who practise lawlessness!"* (Matt. 7:22-23) Such self-deluded people will be counted with the harlot as a child of the harlot and therefore Antichrist.

In reality, they are *wolves in sheep's clothing* posing as *angels of light*. They *are dogs and sorcerers* and more often than not *sexually immoral*, carried away by their lusts for power and pleasure, and paraded everywhere in false religion. The harlot has always been opposed to true religion, which has been defined by fidelity in the Biblical Gospel of Jesus alone in word and deed. Those belonging to the harlot have always in the end been persecutors of "the Bride of Christ" and responsible for murdering tens of thousands, even millions, down through the entire history of the Church militant, and if possible would destroy their souls with all manner of false teaching that is "idolatry." The harlot (Rev. 17) and her beast, with Babylon the Great and the false prophet, with her secret and sometimes not so secret practices, institutionalise the persecuting forces against the true Church. They are master liars who perpetrate sinister deception; organisations such as the Jesuits are legendary for their trail of destruction.[116] All is revealed on the basis of one truth, only the Gospel of the Lord Jesus Christ, but it will be on what is done in the end. Faith in the Lord Jesus Christ *does the will of my Father in heaven* (Matt. 7:21).

---

[116] Edmond Paris, *The Secret History of the Jesuits* obtained via internet.

THE AUTHENTICITY OF THESE REVELATIONS

Verse 16 reveals the intended recipients of this message. *I, Jesus, have sent My angel to testify to you these things in the churches. I am the Root and the Offspring of David, the Bright and Morning Star.* It is as if these words are engraved on our Saviour's signet ring, and they seal the authenticity of these revelations. The revelations have guided the true Church through the prophetic history, turbulent yet all-victorious, of the kingdom *of the King of kings and the Lord of lords*. The personal signet ring of Jesus, the very Son of God, certifies these reassuring words of complete victory to the Churches. He is none other than the King eternal that would sit upon the eternal throne of David in heaven above at the right-hand of the Father as the Sovereign and glorious Potentate, who is also *the Bright and Morning Star*, the one and only Saviour. It was prophesied *...that the Christ would suffer, that He would be the first to rise from the dead, and would proclaim light to the Jewish people and to the Gentiles* (Acts 26:23).

FREELY OFFERED

Verse 17 gives the answer of the Spirit and the Church to the promise. *And the Spirit and the bride say, "Come!" And let him who hears say, "Come!" And let him who thirsts come. Whoever desires, let him take the water of life freely.* The only warrant to this free and open invitation of our Saviour Himself is that one must *hear...thirst...desire*; then, *Come!* says the Saviour. *Let him take the water of life freely,* and of course this water of life is none other than the eternal life that comes from Jesus. There is no precursor of election, names being mentioned in the Lamb's Book of Life, or predestination and reprobation, but if there is a *hearing*, a *thirsting* and a *desiring* then **all** such precursors are *Yes and Amen* in the Lord Jesus Christ.

Solemn Warning

Verse 18 offers further testimony of Christ's authority. *For I testify to everyone who hears the words of the prophecy of this book: If anyone adds to these things, God will add to him the plagues that are written in this book.* The book of Revelation is the cap-stone completing the Canon or Rule of revelation, which is the only rule or standard of true faith and life and is an absolute not to be tampered with or added to or subtracted from. As the Lord Jesus says, *For assuredly, I say to you, till heaven and earth pass away, one jot or one tittle will by no means pass from the law till all is fulfilled* (Matt. 5:18). The inviolate nature of the entire corpus of the word of God itself is in view in this text, even though the specific nature of this particular prophecy in this particular book is referred to here.

The settling of the Canon of Holy Writ has been a matter of ecclesiastical controversy within Church history, but in the minds of the Apostles and the apostolic Church, the marks of canonical books and materials were accepted quickly and with unanimity, which is not a particular subject for our considerations here.[117] The Roman Catholic Church has sought to add the Apocrypha to the Canon of Scripture surreptitiously. This was a subject of considerable controversy during the Protestant Reformation. In modern times, textual critics[118] have sought to add to or subtract from the canonical Scriptures, sometimes for legitimate reasons, but more often than not with unfaithful rather than faithful motives. Within the charismatic movement and modern evangelicalism, there has been an unwitting adding to canonical Scripture by the acceptance

---

[117] Gentry K.L., *Before Jerusalem Fell, Dating the Book of Revelation*, American Vision.

[118] Douglas Kutilek, *Westcott & Hort vs. Textus Receptus: Which is Superior?*

of revelational prophecy. This places revelational prophecy in a position that adds to or reduces the revelation of God, which was completed with Christ's work as *the Prophet* (Deut. 18:15, 18; John. 1:21) and is *now ceased* (Heb. 1:1-2; Westminster Confession of Faith 1:1).[119] All such abuses to the "deposit" of God's Word would come under the sanction of this warning that *God shall take away his part from the Book of Life, from the holy city, and from the things which are written in this book.*

More specifically, the book of Revelation itself has often been misused particularly because of the far-reaching consequences of its symbolic language and imagery. For some it has become an obsession, and others put it into the "too hard" basket and avoid it. The syntax and the Greek in which it was originally penned are straightforward, and adding to this prophecy or subtracting from it will be recognisable. The controversies do not abound in the text of the book of Revelation but in the complex message and imagery of the book. The problem is in its interpretation rather than in its written content. There is divine wisdom in this in that if we had a multitude of technical linguistic difficulties, then it would be very much more difficult. But such is not the case. The text itself is supremely beautiful and straightforward in its linguistic style. The temptation to add to and subtract from the actual text is vastly reduced, but the interpretation is extremely difficult. It is similar to the way in which, in the wisdom of God, the Lord Jesus taught parables, not to make it easier for the foolish to understand, but harder!

> *And the disciples came and said to Him, "Why do You speak to them in parables?" He answered and said to them, "Because it has been given to you to know the*

---

[119] Robert L. Reymond, *What About Continuing Revelations and Miracles in the Presbyterian Church Today?* Presbyterian and Reformed Publishing Company, 1977, pp 20-42.

mysteries of the kingdom of heaven, but to them it has not been given. For whoever has, to him more will be given, and he will have abundance; but whoever does not have, even what he has will be taken away from him. Therefore I speak to them in parables, because seeing they do not see, and hearing they do not hear, nor do they understand" (Matt. 13:10-13).

Spiritual things are spiritually perceived, and without the help of God Himself to open our eyes, the mysteries of the word of God will always be closed to us no matter how intellectually astute we are. Our blindness will not be recovered by earthly wisdom but only by divine and spiritual healing.

Verse 19 contains a solemn warning *...and if anyone takes away from the words of the book of this prophecy, God shall take away his part from the Book of Life, from the Holy City, and from the things which are written in this book.*

The sanction attached to these words is not so much against the foolish who do not already share in the blessings of the salvation in the Lord Jesus, but against a serious act of rebellion that results in the loss of very real and spiritual gain; namely, having his part *taken from the Book of Life, from the Holy City, from the things which are written in this book*.

This act of rebellion is a kind of vandalism to the Word of God. To play "fast and loose" with God's Word is a most serious and dangerous error. What is meant by having his part *taken from the Book of Life*...? This loss is not against the eternal security of the saints. The saints are those *who are called according to His purpose. For whom He foreknew, He also predestined to be conformed to the image of His Son...* (Rom. 8:28-29). Christ *chose us in Him before the foundation of the world that we should be holy and without blame before Him in love, having predestined us to the adoption as sons by Jesus Christ to Himself, according to the good pleasure of His will* (Eph. 1:4-5). Because of this, our names are in the Book of Life. Our election is not a trophy of spiritual achievement, or for that matter a spiritual windfall that we can have as some spiritual jackpot in the lottery of life that has secured our eternal future. This would be treating the doctrine of eternal security presumptuously. However, our assurance of eternal security is demonstrated in the work of God's grace in our spiritual life, because God the Holy Spirit is effecting the grace of sanctification that only God can accomplish as we live by faith in Him. It is therefore more like a spiritual barometer set in our souls that we might grow in confidence and assurance as we walk with Christ. By this we know that our names are in the Book of Life (Phil. 4:3)!

He is a fool indeed who plays "fast and loose" with God's Word and lives in the closest proximity of scriptural teaching, professing Scriptural orthodoxy most ardently, but never finding true obedience in his heart to do the will of God the Father in heavenly places. If we believe, however sincerely yet presumptuously, that our name is written in the Book of Life, what a terrifying epiphany it will be to find to our horror that our name is not there but is, as it were, taken from the Book of Life. No one took Esau's name out of the Book of Life, but a fool may well complain just as Esau did that his birthright was stolen (Gen. 25:23, 33). But if Esau's name were indeed in the Book of Life, he would have treasured the Word of God's promise more than life; and *...worked out [his] own salvation with fear and trembling, for it is God who works in you both to will and to do for His good pleasure* (Phil. 2:12-13).

The writer to the Hebrews describes this spiritual condition: *For it is impossible for those who were once enlightened, and have tasted the heavenly gift, and have become partakers of the Holy Spirit, and have tasted the good word of God and the powers of the age to come, if they fall away, to renew them again to repentance, since they crucify again for themselves the Son of God, and put Him to open shame* (Heb. 6:4-6). *Do not be deceived, God is not mocked; for whatever a man sows, that he will also reap* (Gal. 6:7). The Apostle Judas Iscariot was one such apostate who betrayed the Lord Jesus, who said that it would be better for him if *he had never been born* at all (Mark 14:21). Judas found bitter remorse, but committed suicide for it was impossible to "renew him again to repentance."

THE CONTINUAL NOTE OF URGENCY

Verse 20 conveys the urgency. *He who testifies to these things says, "Surely I am coming quickly." Amen. Even so, come, Lord Jesus!*

As we conclude, probably the most important thing to emphasise is the immediacy of God's work throughout the Gospel era and the dynamic of the new creation (Gal. 6:15; 2 Cor. 5:17) that is declared and demonstrated in the resurrection of Jesus, having redeemed His people upon the cross of Calvary (Rom. 1:3-5). The temple having been *destroyed was raised up in three days* (John 2:19) by the Lord Jesus Christ, and this transformed the way His people the saints worship. He now dwells in a temple of saints who are *living stones* (1 Pet. 2:4) made without hands, who worship God personally with Christ our High Priest and only Mediator (Heb. 8:1-3, 6) who makes intercession on behalf of all the saints with tireless and effectual prayer (Heb. 4:14-16). Now the saints approach God directly, through the Lord Jesus Christ, and *worship God in spirit and in truth* (Jn. 4:24). These are quantum changes to the Old Testament order which has utterly transformed how God is going to work in the Gospel era that has thus far occupied some two millennia.

The risen Lord Jesus Christ commissioned His disciples to declare this Gospel, being the power of God unto salvation (Rom. 1:16), and His kingdom to every nation so that every nation is discipled (Matt. 28:18-20). Jesus ascended on high and is seated at the right hand of the Father (Acts 2:34; Eph. 1:20; Heb. 8:1) as the *King of kings and Lord of lords*, pouring out God the Holy Spirit, (John 1:33) baptising in the Name of the Father, and of the Son and of the Holy Spirit visiting the Church in grace and power (Acts 1:4-8; 2:1-4). We now live in a reconstituted cosmos where the old-world order has passed away. The Lord Jesus Christ has ascended on high and has established the kingdom of God. This kingdom commences as *a stone that was cut without hands* (Dan. 2:34) and is cast upon the nations of the world to crush them and their dominions that rebel against the rule of Christ both in heaven and on earth. The kingdom of God then *grows like a mountain that fills the whole earth* (Dan. 2:44-45). There is a formidable challenge in the rise and rise of the institutions of the antichrist, the harlot and her beast that turns into Babylon the Great, along with the false prophet (1 John 2:18; Rev. 17:5-6). However, in the seasons and purposes of Christ alone, He *must reign till He has put all enemies under His feet*, (1 Cor. 15:25; Rev. 12:7-14) and establishes the kingdom of God within all the nations of the earth (Rev. 11:15). Those who are *the light of the world* and *the salt of the earth* are the very saints of God (Matt. 5:13-16), and are also the citizens of the kingdom of God. They are sanctified, transforming their lives and restoring the world that they live in (Rom. 8:19-22) according to the original Covenant with Adam (Gen. 1:26-3:24) according to His good pleasure in all ages in every day and every moment of the day. *All the ends of the world shall remember and turn to the LORD, and all the families of the nations shall worship before You* (Ps. 22:27).

The citizens of the kingdom may walk along those old paths where many have trod in the past, (as taught in Augustine of Hippo's *The City of God*) along with *so great a cloud of witnesses* (Heb. 12:1), but the path of faith in Christ is something that is personal and individual and there is a sense in which every saint has a unique calling and contribution to make and that nobody else can do such work. As we live by faith in Christ, the work of faith is established as we walk according to the Spirit. Therefore, life is too short for false doctrine, too urgent for worldly pursuits, too rigorous for want of prayer, too profound to give time to the philosophies of this world, too righteous to indulge the flesh, and too holy to fraternise with religion. Each day is a day that has been gifted by God that will never be repeated; to lose that day is to lose it forever. The Christian life is from beginning to end supernatural and can be completed only if *God ...works in you both to will and to do for His good pleasure* (Phil. 2:13; Heb. 13:21). Wherever God's servant is, so too is our Lord.

All appointments are God's appointments because our God foreknows all things and predestines all those that are His (Rom. 8:29-30). In this there is time for everything but the time is short and it is only by faith in Christ that these things can be comprehended and accomplished. In everything, Christ comes in power and grace. He who keeps you, *will not slumber nor sleep*. For the saint says in his heart, *My help comes from the Lord, who made heaven and earth; He will not allow your foot to be moved* (Ps. 121).

Verse 21 is a benediction for all saints: *The grace of our Lord Jesus Christ be with you all. Amen.*

BOOK OF REVELATION - SCOPE AND SEQUENCE IN THE HISTORY OF THE KINGDOM OF GOD

Hosea 6:2	Day one	Day two	Day three	
Daniel 12:7	Time	Time	Half the time	
2 Peter 3:8	Thousand years	Thousand years	Thousand years	
1:1-10	Introduction and Prelude			
1:11-3:22	Churches' testimony in Christ's Word			
4:1-5:14	Heaven and the ascended sovereign Christ			
6:1-11:19	**SEVEN SEALS**			
6:1-2	First Seal - The conqueror			
6:3-4	Second Seal - Conflict on earth			
6:5-6	Third Seal - Scarcity on the earth			
6:7-8	Fourth Seal - Widespread death on earth			
6:9-11	Fifth Seal - The cry of the martyrs			
6:12-17	Sixth Seal - Cosmic disturbances			
7:1-17			The sealed of Israel	
8:1-11:19	**SEVENTH SEAL - SEVEN TRUMPETS**			
8:1-6	Prelude to the Seven Trumpets			
8:7	First Trumpet - Vegetation struck			
8:8-9	Second Trumpet - The seas struck			
8:10-11	Third Trumpet - The waters struck			
	Fourth Trumpet - The heavens struck			
8:12-13	Fifth Trumpet - The locusts from the bottomless pit			
9:1-12	Sixth Trumpet - the Angels from the Euphrates			
9:13-21				
10:1-11		The Mighty Angel with the Little Book		

11: 1-14		The two witnesses, killed and resurrected		
11:15-19			Seventh Trumpet - The Kingdom of God proclaimed	
12: 1-17	**The faithful testimony Christ and her church militant in the wilderness**			
13: 1-18	**The rise of the Antichrist - State opposition to the kingdom of God on earth**			
13: 1-10	The Beast from the Sea - 666	1260		
13: 11-18	1260		The Beast from the Earth	
14: 1-20	**The fruit of the powerful and effectual work of the word of God through the ministers of the Word**			
14: 1-5	The Lamb and the 144,000			
14: 6-13	The proclamation of the three angels			
14: 14-16	**Reaping the Earth's Harvest**			
14: 17-20	**Reaping the Grapes of Wrath**			
15: 1-8		Prelude to the bowls of wrath		
16: 1-19: 21		God's providential intervention in the introduction of the consummated the kingdom of God		
16 :1		The seven bowls of the wrath of God on the Earth		
16 :2		First bowl - Loathsome sores		
16 :3		Second Bowl - The sea turns to blood		
16: 4-7		Third Bowl - The water turns to blood		
16: 8-9		Fourth Bowl- Men are scorched		

16: 10-11		Fifth Bowl - Darkness and pain		
16: 12-16		Sixth Bowl - Euphrates dries up		
16: 17-21		Seventh Bowl - The earth utterly shaken		
17: 1-18	**The Mystery Babylon the Great the Mother of Harlots and the Abominations of the Earth**			
18: 1-24		The fall of Babylon the Great under the final bowls of the wrath of God		
19: 1-21		The King of kings and Lord of lords takes a victory for the kingdom of God on earth as it is in heaven		
20: 1-6			**THE MILLENNIUM**	
20: 7-10				The final Antichrist and the Satanic rebellion crushed
20: 11-15				**COMING OF CHRIST**, General Resurrection and the Final Judgment
21: 1-8				The finite universe passes away and the New Heavens and the New Earth established
21: 9-22: 5				The New Jerusalem and its glory
22: 6-21	**Epilogue and exultation**			

BIBLIOGRAPHY

Books

Adams, Jay E., *Preterism: Orthodox or Unorthodox?* Stanley North Carolina: Timeless Texts, 2003.

Adams, Jay E., *The Time Is At Hand,* n.p., Presbyterian and Reformed, 1966.

Alcasar, (SJ) Luis del, *Vestigatio Arcani Sensus in Apocalpysi*, trans., An Investigation into the Hidden Sense of the Apocalypse, (First Preterist theologian). In the Historical Archives of the Pontifical Gregorian University, 1614.

Alexander, Joseph Addison, *The Prophecies of Isaiah,* Vol. I of II, Edit. Dr John Eadie, Glasgow UK 1865, part of the Zondervan Commentary Series, Zondervan Publishing House, Grand Rapids, Michigan, 49506, Eight printing, 1977, Vol. I, p. 96.

Alford, Henry, *The Greek New Testament,* 4 Vol., Chicago: Moody Press, 1958 (rep. 1849 – 1861).

Allis, Oswald T., *Prophecy And The Church,* Philadelphia, Presbyterian and Reformed, 1945.

Archer, Gleason. L., et al, *The Rapture: Pre-, Mid-, or Post-Tribulational*, Grand Rapids, Michigan: Zondervan, 1984.

Augustine (A Church Father of Hippo), *'Concerning The City of God Against the Pagans,'* Penguin Books, Penguin Classics, trans., n Henry Bettenson, This translation in Penguin Books 1972 London, First published 1467, Eighth printing, 1994.

Baker, Charles F. A., *Dispensational Theology*, Grand Rapids: Grace Bible College, 1971.

Baker, David W, *Looking Into The Future, Evangelical Studies In Eschatology,* Grand Rapids: Baker, 2001.

Baker, William S, and W. Robert Godfrey, eds. *Theonomy, A Reformed Critique,* Grand Rapids: Zondervan, 1990.

Ball, Bryan W. A., *Great Expectation, Eschatological Thought in English Protestantism to 1660,* Leiden, Holland: E, J. Brill, 1975.

Bahnsen, Gregory L., *Victory In Jesus, The Bright Hope In Post-millennialism,* Texarkana, Arkansas: CMP. 1999.

Bass, Clarence B., *Backgrounds To Dispensationalism, It's Historical Genesis and Ecclesiastical Implications,* Grand Rapids, Michigan: Baker, 1960.

Bass, Ralph E Jr., *Back To The Future, A Study In The Book Of Revelation,* Greenville, South Carolina: Living Hope, 2004.

Barnes, Albert, '*Analysis of Revelation 16*,' found in Nigel Lee, *John's Revelation Unveiled,* Lamp Trimmer, The Historicism Research Foundation, El Pasco, 2001, p. 217.

Barnes, Albert., *Notes on the Whole Bible, Bible Commentaries, 110 Vols. – Revelation,* Online Bible Edition, (classic.StudyLight.org/, Rev 19:19).

Bavinck, Herman, *The Last Things, Hope For This World And The Next,* trans., by John Vriend, ed., by John Bolt, Grand Rapids: Baker, 1996.

Bebbington, David W., *Patterns In History, A Christian View,* Downers Grove, Illinois: Inter-Varsity Press 1979.

Beasley-Murray, G.R., *The Book of Revelation,* New Century Bible, ed. RE Clements and Matthew Black, eds. London, Marshall, Morgan and Scott, 1974.

Beeke, Joel R., *Calvin's Evangelism, Microsoft Word– BeekeCalEvangelJournal2004.doc*–Internet Article, 2004, pp1-20, Following. https://s3-us-west-2.amazonaws.com/apuritansmind.com/CalvinsEvangelismJoelBeeke.pdf (14 Apr. 2020)

Berkoff, Louis, *Principles of Biblical Interpretation, Sacred Hermeneutic,* Grand Rapids: Baker Publishing Group, 1977, pp 11-13.

Berkoff, Louis, *The History Of Christian Doctrine,* Edinburgh, Banner of Truth Trust, 1969 (rep. 1937), pp 203-267.

Berkoff, Louis, *Systematic Theology,* The Banner of Truth Trust, 1949 reprint 1974.

Best, Ernest, *A Commentary On The First And Second Epistles to Thessalonians* (Harper's New Testament Commentary), Peabody, Massachusetts: Henriksen, 1964.

Benware, Paul N., *Understanding End Times Prophecy, A Comprehensive Approach,* Chicago: Moody Press, 2006.

Blackstone, William E., *Jesus Is Coming,* old Tappan, N. R., Revell, 1932 (rep. 1898).

Blaising, Craig A. and Darrell L. Bock, *Dispensationalism, Israel And The Church*, Grand Rapids, Michigan: Zondervan, 1992.

Blaising, Craig A. and Darrell L. Bock, *Progressive Dispensationalism, Up-to-Date Handbook of Contemporary Dispensational Thought*, Wheaton, Illinois: Brigepoint, 1993.

Block, Daniel I., *The Book of Ezekiel, Chapters 40 – 48*, Grand Rapids: Eerdmans 1993.

Bloesch, Donald G., *Essentials Of Evangelical Theology, God, Authority, and Salvation*, 2 vols. San Francisco: Harper and Row, 1979.

Bloesch, Donald G., *The Last Things, Resurrection, Judgement, Glory*, Downers Grove, Illinois: Inter-Varsity, 2004.

Blomberg, Craig L. and Sung Wook Chung, eds. *A Case For Historic Premillennialism, An Alternative To "Left Behind" Eschatology*, Grand Rapids: Baker, 2009.

Boettner, Loraine, *Roman Catholicism*, Philadelphia, Pennsylvania: The Presbyterians and Reformed Publishing Company, 1962, rep. 1977.

Boettner, Loraine, *The Millennium*, Philadelphia, Pennsylvania, the Presbyterians and Reformed Publishing Company, .

Bowers, Curtis, *Agenda, Masters of Deceit, I and II*, (Troy, Alabama: Copybook Heading Productions, 2017), DVD, https://www.agendadocumentary.com/.

Brown, David, *Christ's Second Coming, Will It Be Premillennial?* Edmondton, AB: Still Waters Revival, (1882) 1990.

Buswell, J. Oswald., *A Systematic Theology of the Christian Religion*, Vols I -II, Grand Rapids, Michigan: Zondervan Pub. House, 1976, Vol II Part IV.

Chilton, David., *Days of Vengeance, An Exposition of the Book of Revelation,* Ft. Worth, Texas: Dominion Press, 1987.

Chilton, David., *The Great Tribulation,* Ft. Worth, Texas: Dominion Press, 1987.

Chilton, David., *Paradise Restored: A Biblical Theology of Dominion,* Ft. Worth, Texas: Dominion Press, 1987.

Calvin, John, *Commentary On The Book Of The Prophet Isaiah.* Trans. by William Pringle, Grand Rapids: Eerdmans, n.b (rep. 1948).

Calvin, John, *Commentaries On The Prophet Ezekiel And The Prophet Daniel*, vol set 22 vols., originally printed for the Calvin Translation Society, Scotland reprint. Grand Rapids, Michigan: Baker Book House Company, 49506, 1979.

Calvin, John, *Institute Of The Christian Religion,* edited by J.T. McNeill, trans by Ford Lewis Battles, Philadelphia: Westminster Press, 1960.

Calvin, John, *Sermons On The Book of Micah.* Trans. by Benjamin Wirt Farley, Phillipsburg, New Jersey: Presbyterian and reformed, 2003.

Collins, Oral Edmond, *The Final Prophecy of Jesus, An Introduction, Analysis and Commentary on the Book of Revelation,* Wipf and stock publishes Eugene, Oregon, 2007.

Cotton, John, *The Churches Resurrection,* London: Henry Overton 1642.

Cox, William E., *Amillennialism Today,* Phillipsburg, New Jersey: Presbyterian and Reformed 1966.

Cox, William E., *Biblical Studies In Final Things,* Nutley, New Jersey: Presbyterian and Reformed, 1966.

Cox, William E., *An Examination Of Dispensationalism,* Philadelphia, Pennsylvania: Presbyterian and Reformed, 1963.

Clark, David S., *The Message From Patmos, A Post-millennial Commentary On The Book of Revelation,* Grand Rapids: Baker, n.b. (rep. 1989).

Clouse, Robert G., ed *The Meaning Of The Millennium, Four Views,* Downers Grove, Illinois: Inter-Varsity, 1977.

Cunningham, William., *Historical Theology,* A Review Of The Principle Doctrinal Discussions, In The Christian Church Since, The Apostolic Age, Vols I and II, Banner Of Truth Trust, Edinburgh, 1960.

Dallimore, Arnold., *George Whitfield, The Life and Times of the Great Evangelist of the 18th-Century Revival,* 2 Vols Banner of Truth, Edinburgh, Vol. 1, 1970.

Dabney, Robert Lewis, *Lectures In Systematic Theology,* Grand Rapids, Michigan: Zondervan Publishing House, First published in 1870, Third printing 1976.

Davis, John J., *The Victory Of Christ's Kingdom,* Moscow, Idaho: Cannon, 1996 (rep. 1986).

Dawson, Samuel G., *Jesus' Teaching On Hell, A Place Or An Event?* Puyallup, Washington: Gospel Themes, 1997.

Dumbrell, W. J., *Covenant And Creation,* Nashville: Thomas Nielsen, 1984.

Edwards, Jonathan, *History of Redemption,* Collected Works, Vol 1 of 2 Vols, Edinburgh: Banner of Truth, 1976.

Edwards, Jonathan, *Thoughts On The Revival,* Collected Works, Vol 1 of 2 Vols, Edinburgh: Banner of Truth, 1976.

Edwards, Jonathan, *Jonathan Edwards on Revival, A Narrative of Surprising Conversions,* Edinburgh: Banner of Truth, 1958.

Edersheim, Alfred, *Sketches Of Jewish Social Life In The Days Of Christ,* Grand Rapids: Eerdmans [1876] 1970.

End of Days, directed by Peter Hyams (Universal City, California: Universal Pictures, November 24, 1999). DVD

Eusebius, *Proof Of The Gospel,* Ed. And Trans. by W. J. Ferrar, Cincinnati, Ohio: Bethesda Ministers, n.d. (rep. 1920).

Fairbaim, Patrick, *An Exposition of Ezekiel,* Minneapolis: Klock and Klock, 1979 (rep. 1851).

Fairbaim, Patrick, *The Prophetic Prospects Of The Jews, or Fairbaim vs Fairbaim,* Grand Rapids, Michigan: Eerdmans, 1930.

Fairbaim, Patrick, *The Typology Of Scripture,* 2 vols in one, Grand Rapids: Zondervan 1963 (rep. n.d).

Faulkner, Neil, Apocalypse, *The Great Jewish Revolt Against Rome A.D. 66 – 73,* Gloucestershire, England: Tempus, 2002.

Feinberg, Charles Lee, *The Prophecy of Ezekiel, The Glory of the Lord,* Chicago: Moody Press. 1974.

Flavius. Josephus, trans Whiston, William, *The Antiquities Of The Jews,* Wilder Publications, 2009,

Fox, John., *Foxe's Book of the Martyrs,* Angus and Robinson, 2001. (Original title: Actes and Monuments of These Letters and Perilous Days, Touching Matters of the Church, John Day Pub, 1563).

Farrar, Frederic William, *'The Early Days of Christianity,'* London: Cassall Vol 2, 1882.

Gentry, Kenneth L., *He Shall Have Dominion, A Postmillennial Eschatology*, Draper, Virginia: Apologetics Group Media 1997.

Gentry, Kenneth. L., *Before Jerusalem Fell, Dating the Book of Revelation*, Powder Springs, Georgia: American Vision, 1998.

Gentry, Kenneth. L., *The Beast of Revelation*, Powder Springs, Georgia: American Vision, 2002.

Goodwin, Thomas., *Works*, Edinburgh: Miller, 1891 rep., III:28).

Grier, W. J., *The Momentous Event*, London: Banner of Truth Trust 1970 (rep. 1945).

Griffin, Edward G., *The Creature From Jekyll Island, A Second Look At The Federal Reserve*, 5th ed. Westlake Village, California: American media, 2010.

Hall, David. W., *Calvin In The Public Square, Liberal Democracies, Rights, and Civil Liberties*, P & R Publishing, 2009.

Henriksen, William, *More Than Conquerors, An Interpretation of the Book of Revelation*, Inter-Varsity Press, 1973.

Hengstenberg, E. W., *Christology Of The Old Testament*, 2 vols., McLean, Vir., McDonald, n.d. (rep. 1854).

"Hindutva," *Wikipedia,* accessed April 14, 2020, http://en.wikipedia.org/wiki/Hindutva

Hoekema, Anthony A., *The Bible And The Future*, Grand Rapids: Eerdmans, 1979.

Hodge, Archibald Alexander, *Outlines Of Theology*, Enlarged Edition, London: the Banner of Truth Trust, 1879) 1972, Chapter 39, The Second Advent and General Judgement, p. 566.

Hodge, Charles., *Systematic Theology*, Vols. II and III, Grand Rapids, Michigan: Eerdmans publishing company, 1975.

Hodge, Charles, *Commentary On The Epistle Of The Romans*, (First published 1835), First Edition the London: Banner of Truth Trust 1972, pp. 353-82.

Horton, Michael S., *Covenant and Eschatology: The Divine Drama*, Lewisville: Westminster John Knox, 2002.

Hughes, Philip Edgcumbe, *Interpreting Prophecy, Essays in Biblical Perspectives*, Grand Rapids: Erdman's, 1976.

Hulse, Errold, *The Restoration of Israel*, Worthing, Sussex: Henry E Walter, 1968.

Hunt, Dave, *Beyond Seduction: A Return to Biblical Christianity*, Eugene, Oregon: Harvest House, 1987.

Hunt, Dave, *Global Peace and The Rise of Antichrist*, Eugene, Oregon: Harvest House, 1990.

Ice, Thomas. D., "Preface," in H. Wayne House and Thomas D. Ice, *Dominion Theology: Blessing or Curse?* Portland, Oregon: Multnomah Press, 1988.

"Imprecatory Psalms," *Wikipedia,* accessed April 14, 2020, http://en.wikipedia.org/wiki/Imprecatory_Psalms.

"Ignatius of Loyola," *Wikipedia,* accessed April 14, 2020, http://en.wikipedia.org/wiki/Ignatius_of_Loyola.

"Iona Abbey," *Wikipedia,* accessed April 14, 2020, http://en.wikipedia.org/wiki/Iona_Abbey

Johnson, D. E., *Triumph of the Lamb, A Commentary on Revelation*, Phillipsburg: Puritan and Reformed Publication, 2001.

Josephus, Flavius, Trans., William Whiston (1737), Works of Josephus Flavius. *BibleStudyTools.com, accessed April 14, 2020.* https://www.biblestudytools.com/history/flavius-josephus/.

Kendall, E., *Religious Liberty Prayer Bulletin* | RLPB 158 | Wed 09 May 2012 Following.

http://www.ea.org.au/ea-family/Religious-Liberty/HINDU-NATIONALISM-FUELS-VIOLENCE---INJUSTICE-IN-INDIA (14 Apr. 2020)

Kingdon, R.M., *Geneva and the Consolidation of the French Protestant Movement,* Madison: University of Wisconsin Press, 1967.

Kline, Meredith G., *Treaty Of The Great King,* Grand Rapids: Eerdmans, 1963.

Kik, J. Marcellus, *An Eschatology of Victory*, Phillipsburg, New Jersey: Presbyterian and Reformed Publishing Company, 1975.

Kuiper, R. B., *God Centred Evangelism, A Presentation Of The Scriptural Theology Of Evangelism*, Grand Rapids: Baker, 1961.

Kutilek, D., *Westcott & Hort vs. Textus Receptus: Which is Superior?* Accessed April 14, 2020, *http://westcotthort.com/dkutilek/whvstr.html*.

Ladd, George Eldon, *The Blessing Hope*, Grand Rapids: Eerdmans, 1956.

Ladd, George Eldon, *A Commentary On The Revelation Of John,* Grand Rapids: Eerdmans, 1972.

Ladd, George Eldon, *Crucial Questions About The Kingdom Of God,* Grand Rapids: Eerdmans, 1952.

Ladd, George Eldon, *The Gospel Of The Kingdom, Scriptural Studies In The Kingdom Of God*, Grand Rapids: Eerdmans, 1959.

Ladd, George Eldon, *The Last Things, An Eschatology For Lehman*, Grand Rapids: Eerdmans, 1978.

La Haye, T., *Left Behind: A Novel of the Earth's Last Days*, Carol Stream, Illinois: Tyndale Publishing House, 1995.

Lindsey, Hal, *Great Planet Earth*, 1970 followed with *The Terminal Generation*, 1976 and *Countdown to Armageddon*, 1980.

Lindsey, Hal, *The Countdown To Armageddon*, New York: Bantam, 1980.

Lindsey, Hal, *There's A New World Coming*, Santa Ana, California: Vision House, 1973.

Lindsey, Hal, *Planet Earth – 2000, Will Mankind Survive?* Palos Verdes, California: Western Front, 1994.

Lloyd-Jones, D. Martyn, *The Church In The Last Things*, Wheaton, Illinois: Crossway, 1997.

Lee, Frances Nigel, John's *Revelation Unveiled*, Lamp Trimmers, El Paso, Texas: The Historicism Research Foundation, 2000.

Lee, Frances Nigel, *Christians Overcome Papacy and Islam*, Electronic Edition, 2000.

Lee, Frances Nigel, *The Central Significance Of Culture*, Nutley, New Jersey: Presbyterian and Reformed, 1976.

Lee, Frances Nigel, *Communist Eschatology, The Christian Philosophical Analysis of the Views of Marx, Engel, and Lenin*, Nutley, New Jersey: Craig, 1974.

Luther, Martin, *The Babylonian Captivity of the Church*, 1520.

MacArthur, John F. Jr., *The Gospel According To Jesus,* Grand Rapids: Zondervan, 1986.

MacArthur, John F. Jr., *The Second Coming, Signs Of Jesus' Return And The End Of The Age,* Wheaton, Illinois: Crossway, 1999.

Machen, J. Gresham, *Christianity And Liberalism,* New York: MacMillan, 1923.

Marsden, George M., *The Evangelical Mind And The New School Presbyterian Experience: A Case Study Of Thought And Theology In Nineteenth Century America,* New Haven: Yale University Press, 1970.

Marsden, George M., *Fundamentalism and American Culture, The Shaping Of Twenteth-Century Evangelicalism, 1870 – 1925,* New York: Oxford University Press, 1980.

MacPherson, Dave, *The Great Rapture Hoax,* Fletcher, North Carolina: New Puritan Library, 1983.

MacPherson, Dave, *The Rapture Plot,* Simpsonville, South Carolina: Millennium III, 1995.

Mathison, Keith A,. *Dispensationalism, Rightly Dividing The People Of God?* Phillipsburg, New Jersey: Presbyterian and reformed, 1995.

Mathison, Keith A., *Postmillennialism, An Eschatology Of Hope,* Phillipsburg, New Jersey: Presbyterian and Reformed, 1999.

Mathison, Keith A., *When Shall These Things Be? Reformed Response To Hyper- Preterism,* Phillipsburg, New Jersey: Presbyterian and Reformed, 2004.

Mealy, J. Webb, *After The Thousand Years, Resurrection And Judgement In Revelation 20,* Sheffield, England: JOT Press, 1992.

McClain, Alva J., *Daniel's Prophecy Of The 70 weeks*, Grand Rapids: Zondervan, 1940.

McConnell, D.R., *A Different Gospel, Biblical And Historical Insights Into The Word Of Faith Movement*, Peabody, Massachusetts: Hendrickson, 1995.

McDurmon, Joel, *Jesus V Jerusalem, A Commentary On Luke 9:51 – 20:26 Jesus's Lawsuit Against Israel,* Powder Springs, Georgia: American Vision Press, 2011.

McGinn, Bernhard, *Antichrist, Two-Thousand Years Of The Human Fascination With Evil*, San Francisco: Harper San Fransico, 1994.

McGinn, Bernhard, *Visions Of The End, Apocalyptic Traditions In The Middle Ages,* New York: Columbia University Press, 1974.

Morris, Leon, *Acts* (TNT C), Grand Rapids: Eerdmans, 1988.

Morris, Leon, *The Biblical Doctrine Of Judgement,* Grand Rapids: Eerdmans, 1960.

Morris, Leon, *The First And Second Epistles To The Thessalonians,* (NICNT), Grand Rapids: Eerdmans, 1959.

Morris, Leon, *The Revelation Of St John,* Grand Rapids: Eerdmans, 1987.

Murray, John, *The Epistle of Romans,* The International Commentary, In 2 vol, Vol 2, Grand Rapids, Michigan: Eerdmans Publishing Company, pp 65-107.

Murray, John, *Collected Writings Of John Murray*, 4 vols, Edinburgh: Banner Of Truth Trust.

Murray, John, *The Covenant Of Grace*, Phillipsburg, New Jersey: Presbyterian and Reformed, 1988 (rep. 1953).

Murray, Iain, *The Puritan Hope, Revival and the Interpretation of Prophecy,* London: The Banner of Truth, 1971.

North, Gary, *The Dominion Covenant, Genesis,* 2nd ed., Tyler, Texas: Institute Of Christian Economics, 1987.

North, Gary, *Dominion And Common Grace, The Biblical Basis Of Progress,* Tyler, Texas: Institute of Christian Economics, 1987.

North, Gary, *An Introduction To Christian Economics,* Nutley, New Jersey: Craig, 1973.

North, Gary, *Is The World Running Down? Crisis In The Christian Worldview,* Tyler, Texas: Institute of Christian Economics, 1988.

North, Gary, *Marx's Religion Of Revolution, The Doctrine Of Creative Destruction,* Rev. ed., Tyler, Texas: Institute of Christian Economics, 1989 (rep. 1968).

North, Gary, *Millennialism And Social Theory,* Tyler, Texas: Institute of Christian Economics, 1990.

North, Gary, *Moses and Pharaoh, Dominion Religion Versus Power Religion,* Tyler, Texas: Institute of Christian Economics, 1990.

North, Gary, *Rapture Fever, Why Dispensationalism Is Paralysed,* Tyler, Texas: Institute of Christian Economics, 1990.

North, Gary, *The Sinai Strategy, Economics And The Ten Commandments,* Tyler, Texas: Institute of Christian Economics, 1990.

North, Gary, ed., *Theonomy, An Informed Response,* Tyler, Texas: Institute of Christian Economics, 1990.

Owen, John, *The Works Of John Owen,* Ed. by William H Goold, 16 vols, Edinburgh: The Banner Of Truth Trust, 1965.

Packer, James I., *Evangelism And The Sovereignty of God,* Downers Grove, Illinois: Inter-Varsity, 1961.

Paris, Edmond, *The Secret History of the Jesuits,* PDF, obtained via internet, 1975. http://www.easysite.com/SiteData/christ-firstministries-com/Estimates%20Of%20The%20Number%20Killed%20By%20The%20Papacy%20In%20The%20Middle%20Ages%20And%20Later.pdf (14 Apr. 2020)

Paris, Edmond, *The Secret History of the Jesuits,* PDF, obtained via internet, 1975. https://spirituallysmart.com/Paris-The_Secret_History_of_Jesuits_1975.pdf (14 Apr. 2020).

Pate, C, Marvin, ed., *Four Views Of The Book Of Revelation,* Grand Rapids: Zondervan, 1997.

Payne, J. Barton, *Biblical Prophecy For Today,* Grand Rapids: Baker, 1978.

Pentecost, J. Dwight, *The Relation between Living and Resurrected Saints in The Millennium,* Bibliotheca Sacra, vol. 117, Oct. 1960.

Pentecost, J. Dwight, *Things To Come, A Study In Biblical Eschatology,* Grand Rapids: Zondervan, 1958.

Pentecost, J. Dwight, *Thy Kingdom Come,* Winton, Victory, 1990.

Pink, Arthur W., *The Redeemers Return,* Ashland, Kent: Victory Baptist Church, rep. n.d. (1918).

Pink, Arthur W., *Exposition of the Gospel of John* (2:1), Grand Rapids: Zondervan, 1973.

Plaisted, David A., *"Estimates of the Number Killed by the Papacy in the Middle Ages,"* 2006–(A research paper) Following:

"Numbers and Necessities," *World Wide Web Witness, Inc.,* accessed April 14, 2020, http://webwitness.org.au/estimates.html (

"Estimates of the Number killed by the Papacy in the Middle Ages and later," Educacion Libery, accessed April 14, 2020, https://educacionlibreysoberana.files.wordpress.com/2015/03/plaisted-estimates_number_killed_by_the_papacy-2006.pdf

https://fliphtml5.com/bsxh/ofmu/basic/

Ramsay, William, *The Letters to the Seven Churches of Asia and Their Place in the Plan of the Apocalypse,* Minneapolis, James Family Publications Co., 1963 (rep. 1904).

Reymond, Robert L., *What About Continuing Revelations and Miracles in the Presbyterian Church Today?* Presbyterian and Reformed Publishing Company, 1977.

Reymond, Robert L., *A New Systematic Theology Of The Christian Faith,* Thomas Nielsen, 1998.

Renwick AM and Harman AM, *The Story of the Church,* 2nd and enlarged edition, IVP, Leicester, 1993.

Riddlebarger, Kim, *A Case for Amillennialism: Understanding the End Times,* Baker Books, 2003.

Riddlebarger, Kim, *The Man Of Sin, Uncovering The Truth About The Antichrist,* Grand Rapids: Baker, 2006.

Ridderbos, Herman, *The Coming Of The Kingdom,* Philadelphia: Presbyterian and reformed, 1962.

Ridderbos, Herman, *Commentary On Matthew,* Grand Rapids: Zondervan, 1987.

Robertson, A.T., *Word Pictures In The New Testament*, 6 vols. Nashville: Broadman, 1930.

Robertson, O. Palmer, *The Christ of the Covenants*, Grand Rapids, Michigan: Baker Book House, 1980.

Robertson, O. Palmer, *The Final Word, A Biblical Response To The Case For Tougues And Prophecy Today,* Edinburgh: The Banner Of Truth, 1993.

Robertson, O. Palmer, *The Israel Of God, Yesterday, Today, and Tomorrow,* Phillipsburg, New Jersey: Presbyterian And Reformed, 2000.

Rushdoony, Rousas John, *The Biblical Philosophy Of History*, Nutley, New Jersey: Presbyterian and Reformed, 1969.

Rushdoony, Rousas John, *Thy Kingdom Come, Studies in Daniel and Revelation,* Thoburn Press, 1978.

Rushdoony, Rousas John, *God's Plan for Victory, The Meaning of Postmillennialism,* Chalcedon Monograph Series, Vallecito, California: Chalcedon Foundation, 1997.

Rushdoony, Rousas John, *The Institute Of Biblical Law*, Phillipsburg, New Jersey: Craig, 1973.

Rushdoony, Rousas John, *Systematic Theology*, in 2 vols, Vallecito, California: Ross House Books, 1994.

Russell, Burtrum., delivered a lecture on March 6, 1927 to the National Secular Society, South London Branch, at Battersea Town Hall. Published in pamphlet form in that same year, the essay subsequently achieved new fame with Paul Edwards' edition of Russell's book, *Why I Am Not a Christian and Other Essays* (1957).

Sandlin, Andrew, ed., *Creation According To The Scriptures Presupposition Defence Of Literal Six-day Creation,* Vallecito California: Chalcedon, 2001.

Schaeffer, Frances A., *A Christian Manifesto,* Westchester, Illinois: Crossway Books, 1981.

Schaff, Philip, *The Creeds of Christendom, With A History And Critical Notes,* 6th ed. New York: Harper and Bros, 1919, Rep. Grand Rapids: Baker Book House, 1990.

Schaff, Philip, *History Of The Christian Church*, 8 vols, 5th ed. Grand Rapids: Eerdmans, n.d. (rep. 1910).

Schaeffer, Frances A., *The Great Evangelical Disaster,* Westchester, Illinois: Crossway Books, , 1984.

Schweitzer, Albert, *The Quest for the Historical Jesus*, (trans., W. Montgomery, A. & C. Black, 1910).

"Human fatalities in revolutions and wars during the twentieth century," *Source List and Detailed Death Tolls for the Primary Megadeaths of the Twentieth Century,* April 14, 2020, http://necrometrics.com/20c5m.htm#Mao (14 Apr. 2020).

Stuart, Moses, *Several Words Relating To Eternal Punishment,* Philadelphia: Presbyterian Publishing Committee, a.d.

Stuart, Moses, *A Commentary On The Apocalypse*, Andover, Allen, Morhill and Wordwell, New York: M.H. Newman, 1845.

The Omen III: The Final Conflict, directed by Graham Baker (Los Angeles, California: 20th Century, March 20, 1999) DVD. https://tvtropes.org/pmwiki/pmwiki.php/Film/OmenIIITheFinalConflict (15 Apr. 2020)

The Prophecy Film Series, directed by Gregory Widen (London: Dimension Films, September 1, 1995),https://en.wikipedia.org/wiki/The_Prophecy_(film_series) (15 Apr. 2020)

"The X-Files Wiki," 20th Century Fox, accessed April 15, 2020 https://x-files.fandom.com/wiki/20th_Century_Fox.

Thornwell, J.H., *Collected Writings (1871)*, Vol. II of 4, Edinburgh: The Banner of Truth, 1986.

Venema, Cornelius P., *Christ and the Future*, Edinburgh: The Banner of Truth, 2008.

Venema, Cornelius P., *The Promise Of The Future*, Edinburgh: The Banner Of Truth, 2000.

Vos, Geerhardus, *The Pauline Eschatology*, Phillipsburg, New Jersey: Presbyterian and Reformed, 1930 (rep. 1991).

Vos, Geerhardus, *Redemptive History And Biblical Interpretation*, Ed. by Richard B Gaffin, Phillipsburg, New Jersey: Presbyterian and Reformed, 1980.

Vos, Geerhardus, *Biblical Theology, Old And New Testaments*, Grand Rapids, Michigan: Eerdmans Publishing Company, 1948.

Warfield, Benjamin B., *The Saviour of the World*, Edinburgh: The Banner of Truth, 1916. .

Warfield, Benjamin B., *Biblical and Theological Studies*, Philadelphia: Presbyterian and Reformed, 1952.

Warfield, Benjamin B., *Selected Shorter Writings Of Benjamin B Warfield*, John E Meeter, ed., 2 vols. Nutley, New Jersey: Presbyterian and reformed, 1970.

Warfield, Benjamin B., *Studies In Tertullian and Augustinian*, Oxford, University Press, 1930.

Walvoord, John F., *Israel In Prophecy,* Grand Rapids, Michigan: Zondervan Academie, [1962] 1988.

Walvoord, John F., The *Rapture Question, rev. ed.*, Grand Rapids, Michigan: Zondervan, 1979,Ref.

Westminster Confession of Faith, Free Presbyterian Publication, Glasgow G3 6LE, 1985.

Ward, Roland S., *The Bush Still Burns, The Presbyterian and Reformed Faith in Australia 1788 – 1988,* self-published in Melbourne, 1989.

Wells, Thomas, *Christian: Take Heart!* Edinburgh: The Banner of Truth, 1987.

Wileman, William, *John Calvin, His Life, His Teaching, and His Influence,* Gospel Mission Press, 1981.

Witsius, Hermann SP., *Economy of the Covenants (1775),* Vol. III, available as a PDF document on the Internet.

Wilson, Dwight, *Armageddon Now! The Premillennial Response to Russia and Israel Since 1917,* Tyler, Texas: Institute for Christian Economics, [1977] 1991.

Wood, Judy, *Where Did The Towers Go? Evidence Of Directed Free Energy Technology On 9/11. The new investigation,* 2010.

Worth, Roland H. Jr., *Seven Cities Of The Apocalypse and Greco-Asian Culture,* New York: Paulist, 1999.

Wylie, James Aiken, *The History Of Protestantism,* 2 vols. Mourn Missionary Trust, Church Road, Carginagh, Down N. Ireland: Kilkeel Co., 1985.

Young, Edward J., *The Book Of Isaiah, The English Text, how all this – 60 text seems used used With Introduction, Exposition, And*

Notes, Volume III chapters 40 – 66, Grand Rapids, Michigan: Eerdmans Publishing Company, 1972.

Young, Edward J., *The Prophecy Of Daniel*, Grand Rapids: Eerdmans, 1949.

Young, Edward J., *Though Word Is Truth, Some Thoughts On The Biblical Doctrine Of Inspiration*, Grand Rapids: Eerdmans, 1957.

Zins, Robert M., *On The Age Of Apostasy, The Evangelical Romance With Rome*, Huntsville, Alabama: Whitehorse Publications, 1998.

www.ingramcontent.com/pod-product-compliance
Lightning Source LLC
Chambersburg PA
CBHW050132240426
43673CB00043B/1640